Ulrich Gehmann, Martin Reiche (eds.)
Real Virtuality

Ulrich Gehmann, Martin Reiche (eds.)

Real Virtuality

About the Destruction and Multiplication of World

(with a Preface by Gerd Stern)

[transcript]

Bibliographic information published by the Deutsche Nationalbibliothek
The Deutsche Nationalbibliothek lists this publication in the Deutsche Nationalbibliografie; detailed bibliographic data are available in the Internet at http://dnb.d-nb.de

© 2014 transcript Verlag, Bielefeld

Cover layout: Kordula Röckenhaus, Bielefeld
Cover illustration: La Defense, Paris – © Ulrich Gehmann
Printed by Majuskel Medienproduktion GmbH, Wetzlar
Print-ISBN 978-3-8376-2608-7
PDF-ISBN 978-3-8394-2608-1

Table of Contents

Preface

The title of this anthology is an engagement of question and statement, evoking both definitions and suppositions characteristic of our twenty first century's time, binding synthesis of unprecedented contemporary technology with pragmatics of visionary philosophical thought. Hopefully, these following deliberations will lead the way as classical prophetic practice, based in present time extending outward toward positive impacts of future potential.

The binary spatial ontology embedded within the phrase "Real Virtuality" embraces a recognition of the balancing act posed by the essentially spiritual question defined as "yinness" and "yangness" which that dyadic pair eloquently expresses.

Examples of such equations abound. In what I have written, I cite instances of photographic imagery, recalling a paraphrase of Remy de Gourmont's "The idea is merely a worn out image." This might need a little background: during the past century my father was dedicated to his "Leica" while us youngsters relied on the more commonplace box camera. Despite the disparities between equipments they shared the technology of film which required both processing and printing. Decades passed before the advent of "instant" which exposed the conundrum betwixt real time and the virtuality of instantaneous, an ephemeral moment often described as "NOW" but readily understood to exist as an abstraction between the then of past and the then of future.

The realization by Land of Polaroid was viewed as an amazing success although its eventual failure as a commercial enterprise became a lesson on the potentials of corporate mortality. However, the concept and digital possibilities of "instant" experiences now abound at internet services like Instagram, which endows the omnipresence of imagery as available currency to a countless community of users: "Capture and Share the World's Moments." Predicatively, the Portuguese multi-media artist Ernesto de Sousa (1921-1988) wrote, "To achieve in oneself the reality of all the moments in one single extended, profuse complete and distant moment." After which follows a quote of the prophetic poet Paul

Valery about something that accounts more than ever to our new understanding of craftsmanship in the digital, virtual age, and is a key aspect to consider in what we have learnt to call virtual worlds, "Our fine arts were developed in times very different from the present. But the amazing growth of our techniques make it a certainty that profound changes are impending in the ancient craft of the Beautiful."

GERD STERN

Introduction

ULRICH GEHMANN AND MARTIN REICHE

What is a *real* virtuality? According to our common everyday understanding, this is an overt contradiction since things are either real, or virtual – the latter denoting the imagined, the illusioned; which might even look as if it is real but isn't. It is commonly understood that reality is confined to the domain of real physical things, real human relations, to things and events happening in real physical space, although increasingly assisted in the course of the last two decades by 'virtual' means like internet-based communication, the use of QR-coding, geosocial games which make use of both 'real' and 'virtual' settings, devices for new man-machine interfaces, and the like.

Seen from a background of common understanding and technological achievements, what is a real virtuality then? Is it a new kind of the real? Or just an enhancement of a real still existing, that cannot be altered in its essence *despite* those achievements? Frankly speaking, we don't know; or more precise, we don't know yet. This is the reason for making this anthology at all. Because it might be that for the first time in human history, the boundaries between real and virtual become not only blurred but obsolete. Finally (so our thesis), we are not discussing merely some technological achievements to 'enhance' or to 'augment' that which already exists – and which will not be changed in its essence, in its fundamental qualities; irrespective of technological trials to make it more consumable, more intense, or even more real than it already is, devoted to a spirit of the age that has gotten used to hyperlatives. What we discuss is more than that; it is about a new *kind* of the real, one emerging right now, in the midst of our times. And the aim of this anthology is to look at some of its different facets.

Of course, the longing for such a 'new real' did not come out of the blue, and moreover, it isn't even confined to the epoch we commonly label as modernity, although it reached its first unfolding there. To draw a hypothetical line of an overall development, the issue already started in the Renaissance, with the attempt to create real virtual spaces as worlds of their own, for instance in cases like the gardens of Bomarzo, or the parks of a Villa Lante or a Villa d'Este in Italy. An attempt that later on, in the Baroque era, was perfected towards a total landscaping, so to say, the one of the Grand Park. Within those artificial but real 'virtual' worlds, an additional virtualization took place: mini-worlds of an entirely fictitious, i.e. *constructed* nature were made, for instance ideal villages or other sceneries of an "unspoiled" and virtualized "original" nature which stood in a seeming opposition to the park's artificial total scenery.

Figure 1. Virtual world in old reality[1]

The epitome of such attempts in creating imagined worlds and letting them become real was the English Park, by constructing seemingly "natural" sceneries adapted to movement. Whereas the Renaissance and Baroque Park[2] were still essentially static constructions, in the English Park, a typically modern trait was introduced, namely movement. The visitor as *user* of such a spatial arrangement could conceive the 'naturality' of its different perspectives only by wandering

---

1 Villa d' Este, Tivoli, plan of the park, last quarter of 16th century. Sala della Fontana, photography U. Gehmann.

2 Concerning the Grand Park of Versailles as an exemplary case, see Graafland, A. (2012): 84ff.

around, by moving through the arranged sites, not unlike the Scenic Highways to come later, in a motorized modernity. What later turned into a primate of movement and a dynamization of worldly belongings, giving way to the functional worlds as networks laid over an 'original' real had its beginnings here, in the English Park. As regards a *real* virtuality, such arrangements were also called Landscape Gardens. Not only due to their often considerable dimensions (it needs space to move), but first and foremost due to their very intention – to embody extended virtual worlds allowing for the picturesque and the sublime,[3] designed for a natural look of a designed reality: extended, encompassing, and constructed in such a way that it does not look like a construction but *as if* it would be natural. It had to appear as if it would embody a real landscape and not (just) a constructed one.

Figure 2.The construction of imagination: Virtual world of an idealized past[4]

From the Renaissance onwards, all of these arrangements can be labeled programmatic spaces, carefully molded worlds of their own which served certain purposes, or functionalities. Also in cases where the functionality in question

---

3   These aspects are dealt with in Bell, D. (2012): 196f. And in general terms, Cooper, D. E. (2012): 22-30

4   Ideal antique landscape, first quarter of 19th century. Lisbon, Livraria Sa da Costa. Photography U. Gehmann.

consisted in creating an impression of the non-functional – an aspect to return to in the contribution about *Explorable Spaces* – through introducing the picturesque and the sublime in the construction of virtual worlds; an approach that later was both amplified and simplified in the arrangements of Dreamlands.[5] And the thesis is that many of these aspects reoccurred in a technified and formatted shape in a so-called second modernity, an epoch that leads up to our present time.[6]

Although it had become extremely technified after the era of 19th century world exhibitions (another variant of an early virtual real[7]), the construction of imagination still plays an important role in the recent worlds to be looked at here, in this anthology. Next to questions of the human condition and actual as well as possible new forms of the communal which are inevitably linked to technification. What started at the beginning of a new age in the Renaissance was further perfected and in its totality, led to the conception of idealized worlds, or more precisely, in the double meaning of *ideal* as both an optimal state and an inner image, it led to worlds as ideal artifacts, shaped as programmatic spaces. As a hope and an aspiration at the same time, it went so far that even virtual world maps were created, imagining *another kind* of world – which arrived later, with the hybrid space – a 'virtual' one which could supersede, or contrast at least, the real existing world. At the doorway to modernity, at the end of the 18th century, maps of entire utopian terrains were drawn, and they were drawn in such a way that they evoked the impression of embodying real landscapes.[8] The Humboldt-approach treated in this anthology tackles this issue of combining a scientific approach with one of idealization.

To achieve *naturally looking* world-spaces by means of virtualization is just one strain of a real virtuality to follow. Next to others, it can be seen as a mental premise for realizing virtualities as a forerunner for the things to come, first of all in creating spaces that should be entire worlds of their own. Not "just" imagined ones referring to a physically real (see the contribution on Piranesi), but real

---

5   Cf. the *Dreamlands*-exposition in Centre Pompidou, 2010. As well as the contribution about consuming cities as one extremely simplified and functionalized outcome, in this anthology, or the contribution about the zoo. To the origins as programmatic spaces in the Renaissance, see Blum, G. (2011): 176ff.

6   Cf. Carrier, M., and Nordmann, A. (2011).

7   Giedion, S. (2007): 169-193. And to 19th century-world exhibitions where a virtualization of space began at large scale, see the notations on them in Benjamin, W. (1983), mainly in vol. 1: 50ff., on Grandville and the world exhibitions.

8   Yvon, M. (1990): 92f.

virtual spaces designed as *complete* worlds. What began with Piccolomini's *Pienza* in the Renaissance, following a line of development Giedion called the organization of external space,[9] was later perfected (see the contribution on Jefferson). It turned on one hand into its commodified versions[10] like the zoo, the dreamland, or the consuming city, and on the other into worlds consisting of *technogene* spaces which function as real immersive environments,[11] in generating a new kind of the natural; see the contribution on the city of *Abadyl*, and comparable approaches towards a new kind of the real as such. Which means that not only a given, still "objective" and "original" reality is transformed but nevertheless kept; but that a new kind of reality is created.

Figure 3. Apotheosis of the function.[12]

To create a new real as such is the second strain of a real virtuality to follow, and it had its historical forerunners, too. Shaping worlds as programmatic spaces serving a predefined set of functionalities became one of the predominant tasks in the modern age, concentrating upon the construction of extended layers of infrastructural networks, and upon the complete reconstruction of the inherited pre-modern city. In architecture and urban planning in particular, the mythos

---

9 Giedion, S. (2007): 106-125. And Pieper, J. (1990): 95-110, to *Pienza* in particular; also Cooper, D. E. (2012): 22f.

10 See the contributions on the zoo, and the consuming city.

11 See the contributions on immersion and identity in virtual worlds, and on a mixed reality. To the notion of a *technogene space* see Oetzel, G. (2012): 73-75

12 Lisbon, Palace of Justice; detail of the main façade. Photography U. Gehmann.

gained ground that *form follows function*, a sacrosanct and therefore 'true' tale about a world as it should be. The basic procedure was to develop a model of a world *in spe*, a virtual world, and then to impose that model upon an existing reality – which then became a reality "as it was" because it had been transformed entirely by the respective model. In this way, several distinct models, each of them a cosmos of its own serving certain functionalities (as a programmatic space), could be laid over such a reality as it was: street systems, systems of energy and material flows, of drainage, and so on; the idea of a world as network gained ground because *flow* became the decisive structural determinant in shaping those new worlds, not the (classical) static *structure*. The grid turned into the lead artifact and until today, its twin, *the net*, to a leading metaphor. The structures of gridded networks had to ensure flows, not the static prospects of traditional urban places or other sceneries assigned to a "typical" city scape of a premodern age.

Parallel to that, first hybridizations of space appeared, and they did so on a really large scale: the newly created spaces and the kind of spatiality that emerged out of gridded networks had to be camouflaged. As a doorway to an era of functionality, the 19th century had to hide all of its new creations behind the masks of historization, says Giedion, irrespective of the respective domain.[13] Breweries and other production sites were virtual medieval castles, gas tanks were ornamented with gothic-like filigrees, the entrances of metro stations with floral motives from an *art nouveau* (a commoditized back to nature-symbolism), and so forth. As if there was a fear of what really had happened, namely an encompassing functionalization of the world, organized in networks. After the final downfall of a City Beautiful-movement, one gave up camouflage and the attempts to unify the disparate cosmic closures of different networks within the frames of a Unitary City Ideal,[14] turning to the opposite: to adore the function, first and foremost in its dynamic properties. Next to the commodification and functionalization of real physical space[15] according to the emerged frame conditions of a capitalist society, efficiency of flows and performance became prime matters of importance. Efficiency and performance are deeply functionalist issues, and long-termed solidified structures or cast procedures were not very helpful in this. It was the reign of a *creative destruction*, as Schumpeter coined it, with the (better)

---

13 Sigfried Giedion on 19th century-architecture, cited in Benjamin, W. (1983), vol. 1: 513

14 About such attempts see Blau, E., and Platzer, M. (1999)

15 Hetherington, K. (2007)

new replacing the (less good) old in a constant manner, and by that, creating new realities all the time.[16] Reality and its spaces had to be adapted to the rules of accelerated improvement (which efficiency does embody, by its very essence), that is: to acceleration. In different respects, it became one of the dominant perceptions of the real,[17] and alongside with it, the dissolution of former unified spaces, especially city space, and of social bodies[18] into dispersed fragments scattered in space took place, connected via fluid and volatile networks. In case of the city, man the cultural animal's genuine place to live (to cite McLuhan whose saying became proverbial), it meant the emergence of a world-wide phenomenon called Splintering Urbanism, accompanied by the emergence of new kinds of spatiality. The grid, the "most democratic" since equally formatting principle of the urban street network, was superseded by blocked roads for gated communities, and infrastructural islands developed – the former space for all of the cultural animals dissolved into a multitude of spaces, affecting even the Internet as the new "most democratic" of these former democratic networks.[19] With the advent of these new networks, a new way of life came into being, to live basically in a mode of *simultaneity*, to participate in an alternating manner in different, and often disconnected communities and spaces. In sum, these are basic frame conditions within which we live, and the perspectives illuminated in this anthology are a part of it, too those which intend to overcome some of its consequences.

Last but not least because in the wake of such events, the new kind of reality introduced in the beginning has been created, or more precisely, is in the process of being *generated* since we don't know the full impact of its outcomes yet.

For an understanding of this new kind of reality settling upon the developments described so far, the notion of space is central. It is a notion to be re-addressed even though it seems to have been treated exhaustively in academic debate. We cannot understand these developments of world-making and -virtualizing without looking at space, without examining the respective concepts about spatiality which simultaneously underlie, enable and sustain these developments. First of all, it holds true with regard to a so-called mixed reality

---

16 Schumpeter, J. A. (1942): 83

17 From a critical perspective, see Virilio's *dromology* (from Greek *dromos*, run): Virilio, P. (1980)

18 About the social aspect of such a development at the rise of a global capitalism see Breuer, S. (1992). About this aspect at the development's beginning see De Certeau, M. (1984).

19 To these developments see Graham, S., and Marvin, S. (2001): 4f., 97 and 229.

as the latest development, based upon conceptions of hybrid spaces, smart cities, and the like. In terms of Lefebvre, it is about several modes of *producing space*. When we look at modernity and its follower, a so-called second modernity with us as the latter's historical result, first and foremost, it is about abstractions of space and the various formants (in Lefebvre's diction) which led to it,[20] and in their wake, about the new reality and hence, the kinds of spatiality to be looked at in this anthology. The most important of these formants turned into *formats* one day, due to the underlying principle of such abstractions, namely to optimize functionality.[21] What began as a geography-based topological projection of programmatic spaces in the 19th century evolved into a general mode of organization, making functional models of (virtual) worlds become real world(s). Real organizations had to be conceived not as one single network but as layered systems of different networks,[22] with the concomitant belief that reality could be condensed into the terms of an organized functionality.

Figure 4. Production of Space.[23]

---

20 Lefebvre, H. (2007): 285f. About space as an intrinsic part of the human condition see Lussault, M. (2007).

21 Gehmann, U. (2012).

22 Schüttpelz, E. (2007): 33

23 Lisbon, Western main road into the exihibition area. Photography U. Gehmann.

To recur to Lefebvre's saying, our thesis is that all the productions of space examined in this anthology can be comprehended in their social and life world-implications only if the respective understanding of spatiality underlying them is considered. An understanding formulated in different disciplines and hence, perspectives, technical as well as academic and artistic ones. Since the respective conception of the spatial inevitably influences the diverse models (so our thesis) which led to the respective worlds, and to the attempts to shape realities to be examined here.

Aligned, the notion of space was not always the same, and the different notions did not even resemble each other.[24] In the period of time we are regarding here, it too changed as it has become a metaphor for nearly all aspects of science, humanities and arts. In science, it became a common practice to abstract theoretical problems into a spatial representation to make them easier to comprehend. In the humanities, the nature of space has been an extensive subject of research by philosophers and historians,[25] and a major goal of the arts was, and still is, to understand the nature of space from a creative and comprehensive point of view. If space and spatial representations are used in almost all professions, then the knowledge gained by all of these professions can be shared utilizing this common metaphor – which may result in a better understanding of the professions themselves, as well as providing a way to see connections between professions where they have been not visible before.

Summarized, it is about spaces as an embodiment of realities – which worlds were actually generated – as well as about spaces as metaphor: which ideas underly the respective construction, or "production" of space, *idea* to be seen in its direct, etymologically founded meaning as an *eidos*, a vision about reality expressed in images. It does not matter if such a reality already exists and gets expressed via vision, for instance in a comic, exaggerating traits of a 'real' which are seen as constitutive (see the article about *Gotham City*); or if such a reality is a "visionary" one in that it is a real one to be constructed yet. In both cases, the metaphorical spatial perspectives stand for the world it is all about, from rather concrete cases of a city prospect to quite abstract ones like the 'space' of functionalities depicted in a flow chart. Literally, those metaphors as conveyors of

---

24 For an overview, see Schroer, M. (2006): 29-173
25 An anthology of exemplary texts has been collected by Heuner, U., ed. (2008)

ideas[26] show the world as it is – or should be – understood in their basic terms as models shaped in images.[27]

Figure 5. Modern symbolic space.[28]

Taking their double nature of representing realities and of being metaphors, spaces are crucial for understanding realities, in peculiar the hybrid ones emerging today. It refers to space as an embodiment of ideas, and its related symbolic properties: the symbol, as the metaphor, is taken in its literal meaning as "standing for" something. This applies particularly to molded spaces as they are *programmatic*, and thus represent specific symbolic artifacts.[29] Concerning hybrid realities in particular, such constructions rely upon certain pre-understandings of the spatial which become relevant. Since in case of hybrid realities, models of a world are used to create worlds through virtualizing already existing ones.

---

26 From the Greek *meta-pherein*, to transpose something from one domain into another, by using (mental or real) images. Cf. Hoffmeister, J. (1955): 402.

27 For a more comprehensive understanding, see Miller, G. A. (1993): 357ff.

28 Rome, EUR: INPS complex. Photography courtesy of U. Gehmann.

29 In terms of concrete architecture, also in space as *organized* design cf. Gagliardi, P. (1992)

Moreover, since these understandings of space embody a *pre*-understanding, they are often used implicitly, without addressing them as what they are: prejudices in literal terms (pre-conceptions), implicit but nevertheless basic assumptions about what 'space' and hence, 'world' is (or should become), at least in the characteristics constituting what is seen as describing its *relevant* parts.

To question these seemingly self-evident assumptions about relevant worlds and their spaces is one primary goal of our anthology; while as a co-requisite, examples of such spaces will be presented, examples for the historical development sketched in the foregoing. Because taken in their total, those spaces, once realized, make up our world 'as it is'. Our goal is to provide different viewpoints on the notion of space, while having a thematic focus on the historical shift from space as a metaphor *of* the world to space becoming a metaphor *for* the world, in terms of various models becoming the real. Next to these goals, we will pursue the following questions related to them: How do notions of space influence the spaces we live in, and how is the change of space effecting individual experiences of the world? Which effects do these mental representations have on spaces, through human behavior? How does this affect the notion of virtuality? And how did all of this lead to today's worlds of a real virtuality?

Next to considerations of a general nature, the essays in this anthology focus upon selected exemplary cases which are literally symbolical, in revealing the general as it unfolds in the specific, i.e. within the terms of actual realizations. By such a combination, it was tried to gain a sense of what is going on with regard to a virtualization of the real, that tendency of prime relevance today.

THE STRUCTURE

In its total, the anthology is divided into 5 chapters which reflect the overall evolutionary move towards the present state. They start after a *Frame Context* (Ulrich Gehmann) which reflects the general conditions within which that move took place, and is in the process of taking place right now, culminating in the appearance of a new ontology, symbolized by an entity labeled Hybrid Space. The aim is to provide an embracing perspective on the issues to come, in the diverse contributions to follow.

Chapter 1: The Beginnings
The Scientific Image in the Anthropocene, by Sabine Wilke
Taking the exemplary case of Alexander von Humboldt, the principles of reconstructing will be shown, at the beginning of what is now called the "Anthropo-

cene," i.e. a world dominated by our species. How abstraction starts to operate, and how nature – the perceived as well as mythic counterpart of the culture of a rising Anthropocene – is portrayed, just like a paradise already lost and never to be regained (to cite Milton). At the same time, the principles underlying this abstraction will be shown, based on Humboldt's cartography.

Thomas Jefferson's University: An Architectural Masque, by David Bell
Taking again an exemplary case, namely that of Jefferson's design of the University of Virginia, the new world will be shown, molded as a complete artifact trying to incorporate both nature and culture in its concept. It is an attempt to create something like a total piece of art (expressed by the German notion of *Gesamtkunstwerk*), a world as ideal artifact in literal terms. Different spatial tensions are emerging out of this construction, and a dialogue between two classical – and formerly prevailing – conceptions of nature is pointed out, that between a *natura naturans* and a *natura naturata*. The world as a constructed one begins to gain its shape, and by that, it surpasses the attempt of Humboldt.

The Building of a Symbolic Image, by Randolph Langenbach
Based on Piranesi's drawings of a lost world (the Rome of Antiquity) and his use of perspective with multiple vanishing points in his representation of space, the origins of our modern representation in graphic images and photographs will be discussed. Where are the roots of our spatial perceptions, and on the other hand, how has such a "modern" conceptualization of space changed, in the course of time, and what this does mean for our present-day perceptions of places and spaces?

Chapter 2: The Unfoldings
The World as Grid, by Ulrich Gehmann and Martin Reiche
It will be portrayed how the mindset to create a world as artifact took shape, and what this means for our functionalized worlds today. The aim was to create a world as a network of functionalities, and to do so on a large scale after the onset of modernization during the 19th century. Upon the remnants of this world we live today, a historical substrate of our physical life. We will sketch how it developed, and what happened afterwards.

Gotham City, by Martin Cremers
In this example of a distorted and at the same time clarifying perspective upon the world as grid, the comic city in its reference to a "modern reality" will be shown. Also in a historical perspective, since the images of the urban portrayed

here reflect the world as an artifact to live in after the days of Humboldt. It can be seen as an image of the (urban) world as grid: a dystopian second nature of man where the old Aristotelian concept of nature as *physis* begins to unfold; in unprecedented and quite unplanned ways, opposed to the intention of planners of the world as a grid. Like the old *physis* growing out of itself, dark, chaotic and all-encompassing. But as said, it is a mirror, and a characterizing one.

Good Night, Zoo, by Irus Braverman

This essay offers another facet of the "new nature," namely the zoo as an instant event of an artificially preserved version of the natural. Through the exemplary presentation of the natural in children's books, the images of the city, of the natural (exhibited in the zoo), and of the human-nature relationship reveal themselves, together with the spatial worlds that emerge from these images. Children's books, through their socializing effects, interpellate their readers (and listeners, in the case of the bedtime story) into this new nature: how we have to see the world we are living in (epitomized by the city); and what is about nature, the "old" spatiality, in this respect (epitomized by the zoo). In conveying values central to our recent culture, these books adopt the young as prospective adults to the spaces they have to live in later, next to romanticizing nature, that paradise lost. They show the virtualization of real space, taking place yet in a still "physical" world.

Chapter 3: Virtualization Gains Momentum

A Paradise of Decorated Sheds, by Steffen Krämer

Here, an everyday virtual world is presented, that of so-called consuming cities. Settling upon a construction of pseudo-historical urban spaces, a world completely functionalized is the result, serving just one function: to consume. Its virtual urban character serves a real economic need, namely to trigger and to sustain todays' core function of economy, the constant consumption of things needed to sustain its growth. In other words, a very real systemic base is wrapped in its concordant disguise, the consuming city. This is an extreme case of virtualization inside the "old" world of physical space, and at the same time an epitome for our todays' *raison d' etre*: to be consumers, ranging from such cities of consumption to the app in the "new" digital world. Such paradises reveal how our today's life-worlds are functionalized to the bone, and by that, embody virtual worlds which became real ones.

The Man in the Paper-made Folding Boat, by Chris Gerbing
The internationalization of cultural expression is illuminated, an internationalization that at the same time leads to the erasing of cultural differences. Shown by
the case example of artists' movies, it is shown how values and spatial perceptions of an essentially Western culture spread out world-wide, leading to a universal language of "how to see things properly." This effect can be interpreted as
a specific case of how to equalize local cultural differences which formerly existed, and thus, contributing to a destruction of the *cultural* space on a global
scale.

The Community Question, by Manfred Negele
Taking the aspects addressed so far, the question arises what community meanwhile means. The "old" idea of our cultural sphere was that community, by its
essence, is bound to the urban environment, or in other words, that it is the urban
space which is the proper environment to live for man the cultural animal. But
what happens if not only this formerly urban space is fragmented and thereby
destroyed, but also the idea of a *communitas* as such? Which new perspectives
are emerging, perspectives more adapted to our present state of being, namely to
live inside the terms of mixed realities, in fact? More specific, the question arises
if assumptions about a *conditio humana* which were taken for granted up to now
have to be doubted – since they are based on the traditional conception of space
as unity, and hence, of world as unity (see the beginning, on the "frame" context). Is such a traditional concept outdated, and what this could mean for man
the cultural animal?

Real Virtuality, by Gerd Stern
This essay reflects the beginnings of the recent networked society which triggered the phenomena described in the foregoing essay, together with the hopes
and aspirations which accompanied the announced new age of those times. A
new age that should liberate man, heading towards a real democracy of an unlimited and individual communication. It was the time when the metaphor of a
global village came up, and when the essence of the human condition was seen
in communication. Shown by selected artist movements of those days as contemporary witnesses, these hopes and aspirations of a new Renaissance are portrayed in a vivid manner, allowing us to gain a sense of what really happened,
and which of these aspirations are still alive today, irrespective of their different
shape.

The Ambiguous Construction of Place and Space, by Katerina Diamantaki
In this article, the community-question is deepened. With a look at emergent digital technologies, the old issue of man the communal animal located in urban spaces gains a new and additional drive. Since the digital media emerging nowadays remediate our conceptions and practices of space and place, as well as our understanding of proximity, identity, boundedness, continuity and duration. The current situation can be characterized as one of an ambiguous mix of space and place – i.e. these traditional pillars of our very self-understanding as human beings have to be reexamined – and related, of a mix between connectivity and disconnection, concreteness and abstraction. It is about symbolic spaces, place identity and the aligned larger concept of Self. What do these technologies (being more than just technology) and the mixtures triggered by them actually mean for a *conditio humana*? Does there a new understanding of the human condition come up, and in this respect, what is about different digital environments in terms of how they reflect practices of place-making? And first and foremost, what is about their potential to generate new *kinds* of spaces and thus, humans?

The Destruction of Space by Augmentation, by Martin Reiche
This article focuses upon functionalization and hybridization in their manifestations as artifacts and implemented processes nowadays. It will deal with the foundations and implications of augmentation as a technique capable of overriding and redefining the meaning of real world objects in virtual worlds, finally leading to a destruction of the anthropologically relevant space. The described transition marks the next evolutionary stage after the *world as grid* portrayed above, and it settles upon the latest achievements of spatial mixtures. Having the perspective on the chapter to follow, what are the major tendencies of both destruction and simultaneous re-creation today, and how they have unfolded? What this does mean for our traditional understanding of space?

Chapter 4: Facets of Acceleration in Hybrid Spaces

Mixed Reality, by Panagiotis D. Ritsos
To go beyond the world as a grid and to arrive at the worlds described by Diamantaki and Reiche, both a certain mindset and methodology to achieve this are necessary. It is about issues of interactive computer-generated objects which co-exist in space. With the respective techniques, it is like Heidegger's saying about technique: that its nature is more than (just) technical. Since the techniques treated in Ritsos' contribution do not only enable the construction of a mixed reality of new dimensions (compared to the realities treated so far), but are *altering* the

notion of space itself. By their appliance, space transforms from something tangible and concrete into a constructed entity that is something intangible, synthetic but nonetheless existing.

Using Spatial Cognition to Improve Knowledge Construction, by Carl H. Smith and Pierre-Francois Gerard
For a mindset to construct new spaces, knowledge can also be constructed. In other words, it is about new forms of knowing. The question is how knowledge can be organized and engineered, by using space and visualization. The aim is to achieve not just a spatial, but a cognitive enhancement by using virtual architectural structures. Despite the new means and methods applied nowadays, there is some strain of continuity (which makes the issue particularly interesting), since such usage stands in a long occidental tradition of an *ars memoriae*. Now, this tradition is 'enhanced' and augmented, brought about by new technological possibilities expanding the practice of spatial cognition in both virtual and physical environments. In today's context of a technological and visual culture, how do we use this potential of spatial cognition? Can we overcome cognitive limits by combining the ancient pedagogies of an *ars memoriae* with recent technologies? And what this does mean for learning, and for reasoning itself?

Creating and Retrieving Knowledge in 3D Virtual Worlds, by Mikhail Fominykh
In this case example for applying the new kind of space in different domains, the essay explores the utilization of space for conveying understanding, expressing and sharing ideas. Its focus is on the interplay between learning and constructing the learning environment itself. It is a consequent application of a constructivist mindset of how to create worlds, since the environment is no longer a given entity but a self-generated continuum depending on its "users." The contribution relates to Braverman's article, where the connection between learning and socialization has been addressed. But it goes one step further regarding the immersive character of learning and hence, the change of world perception and of actual world-creation.

Identity in Virtual Worlds, by Lyzgeo M. Koshy, Kristoffer Getchell, Marc Conrad, Tim French
Prolonging the line of thought so far, this article will deal with the question of identity in virtual worlds. It will describe means of borrowing, fabricating and inventing identity in these worlds as a result of goal-orientation, bringing the above mentioned mindset of functionalization to its logical end. And it will ex-

amine the perception of the notion of identity and freedom of the user. All this will be exemplified in one milestone of a virtual world, namely Second Life.

Above that, it is about the dynamics of identity imposed, and triggered by virtual worlds after Second Life; and related, questions of behavioral practice since certain behaviors in the virtual world create a positive and negative impact in the former "real," i.e. physical world. More specific, it is about the feedback loops between virtual and real world, how they are understood and exploited in real world activities, and how this impacts and shapes our real world societies.

Beyond the Visible Autonomy, by Erhan Öze
After having discussed the technical possibilities, chances and drawbacks of the ongoing functionalization, this article deals with the aspect of autonomy of these systems, referring to the notion of the cognitive mind. The political nature of this autonomy as well as its implication for spatial perception will be of special interest.

Chapter 5: Beyond Acceleration
"Unheimlich": The Uncanny and Narrative Space in Digital Arts, by Martin Rieser
Another aspect of these kinds of worlds is what Freud called the "uncanny." They may be immersive, by that convincing, multi-faceted and "user friendly," but it seems that always, a quite unfriendly touch remains, related to their lack of actual tangibility. At the same time, narrative spaces are opened which offer the possibility of escaping the now prevailing functionalism of all these worlds, and by that, the possibility of real individual freedom.

Against the Self-evident, by Michael Johansson
With the virtual city of *Abadyl*, new possibilities of real individual expression (besides functionalism) and freedom are further explored. In prolonging Freud, an exploration can take place of what Johansson calls the "unknown unknown." In *Abadyl*, the notions guiding our basic conceptions of both the human condition (*conditio humana*) and of the urban tied to it can be explored in new ways. By that, and by taking into account the above findings, an alternative look upon the future is opened up, a look that could supersede functionalism.

Explorable Spaces, by Martin Reiche and Ulrich Gehmann
To conclude the anthology and to give a contraposition to the ideas in chapter 4, the understanding of the need for explorable spaces shall be established, and

examples of such attempts to create these spaces as virtual worlds are shown. Examining its properties in comparison to traditional functionalized spaces, a generalized model for explorable spaces is presented. Although the idea of explorable spaces had its history too, recent explorable spaces, by being genuinely different kinds of spaces, might serve as a way out of the ongoing functionalization described in this book.

REFERENCES

Bajac, Quentin, and Ottinger, Didier (2010): *Dreamlands. Des parcs d'attractions aux cites du futur*, Paris: Centre Pompidou, catalogue of the exhibition May 5th – August 9th, 2010

Bell, David (2012): "The Panoptic Garden", in: Giesecke, Annette, and Jacobs, Naomi, eds. (2012): *Earth Perfect? Nature, Utopia, and the Garden*, London: Black Dog Publishing: 190-207

Benjamin, Walter (ed. of 1983): *Das Passagenwerk*, 2 vol., Frankfurt/M.: Suhrkamp

Blau, Eva, and Platzer, Monika, eds. (1999): *Shaping the Great City. Modern Architecture in Central Europe 1890-1937*, Munich/London/New York: Prestel

Blum, Gerd (2011): "Naturtheater und Fensterbild. Architektonisch inszenierte Aussichten der frühen Neuzeit" [nature as theatre and the scenic view in early modern age], in: Beyer, Andreas, Burioni, Matteo and Grave, Johannes, eds. (2011): *Das Auge der Architektur* [the eye of architecture], Munich: W. Fink: 176-219

Breuer, Stefan (1992): *Die Gesellschaft des Verschwindens. Von der Selbstzerstörung der technischen Zivilisation* [the society of disappearance: about the self-destruction of technological civilization], Hamburg: Junius

Carrier, Martin, and Nordmann, Alfred (2011): *Science in the Context of Application*, Dordrecht/London/New York: Springer

Cooper, David E. (2012): "Gardens and the Way of Things", in: Giesecke, Annette, and Jacobs, Naomi, eds. (2012): *Earth Perfect? Nature, Utopia, and the Garden*, London: Black Dog Publishing: 20-33

De Certeau, Michel (1984): *The Practice of Everyday Life*, Berkeley: University of California Press

Gagliardi, Pasquale, ed. (1992): *Symbols and Artifacts. Views of the Corporate Landscape*, New York: Aldine de Gruyter

Gehmann, Ulrich (2012): "Formats", Vol. 4, *Journal of New Frontiers in Spatial Concepts*: 13-33

Giedion, Sigfried (ed. of 2007): *Raum, Zeit, Architektur* [space, time, architecture], Basel/Berlin/Boston: Birkhäuser

Graafland, Arie (2012): "The Dance of Versailles: Nature, Circe, and the Garden", in: Giesecke, Annette, and Jacobs, Naomi, eds. (2012): *Earth Perfect? Nature, Utopia, and the Garden*, London: Black Dog Publishing: 84-103

Graham, Steven, and Marvin, Simon (2001): *Splintering Urbanism. Networked infrastructure, technological mobilities and the urban condition*, London/New York: Routledge

Hetherington, Kevin (2007): *Capitalism's Eye: Cultural Spaces of the Commodity*, New York: Routledge

Heuner, Ulf, ed. (2008): *Klassische Texte zum Raum* [classical texts on space], Berlin: Parodos

Hoffmeister, Johannes (1955): *Wörterbuch der philosophischen Begriffe* [dictionary of philosophic terms], Hamburg: F. Meiner

Lefebvre, Henri (ed. of 2007): *The Production of Space* (translated by Donald Nicholson-Smith), Malden, MA, etc.: Blackwell Publishing

Lussault, Michel (2007): *L'Homme Spatial. La construction sociale de l'espace humain* [about social construction of human space], Paris: Editions du Seuil

Miller, George A. (1993): "Images and models, similes and metaphors", in: Ortony, Andrew, ed. (2nd ed. 1993): *Metaphor and Thought*, Cambridge: Cambridge University Press: 357-400

Oetzel, Günther (2012): "Technotope Räume – vom Naturraum zum verbotenen Raum" [about technotopia and its aftermath], in: Gehmann, Ulrich, ed. (2012): *Virtuelle und ideale Welten* [virtual and ideal worlds], Karlsruhe: KIT Scientific Publishing: 65-83

Pieper, Jan (1990): "Die Idealstadt Pienza" [the ideal city of Pienza], in: Himmelein, Volker et al., eds. (1990): *Planstädte der Neuzeit* [planned cities in the modern age], Karlsruhe: Badisches Landesmuseum: 95-110

Schroer, Markus (2006): *Räume, Orte, Grenzen* [spaces, places, boundaries], Frankfurt/M: Suhrkamp

Schüttpelz, Erhard (2007): "Ein absoluter Begriff. Zur Genealogie und Karriere des Netzwerkkonzeptes" [to the genealogy of the idea of the concept of network], in: Kaufman, Stefan, ed. (2007): *Vernetzte Steuerung*, Zurich: Chronos: 25-46

Schumpeter, Joseph A. (1942): *Capitalism, Socialism and Democracy*, New York/London: Harper

Virilio, Paul (ed. of 1980): *Geschwindigkeit und Politik* [acceleration and politics], Berlin: Merve

Yvon, Michel (1990): "Der Zulassungswettbewerb an der Ecole des Ponts et Chaussees im 18. Jahrhundert", in: Himmelein, Volker et al., eds. (1990): *Planstädte der Neuzeit* [planned cities in the modern age], Karlsruhe: Badisches Landesmuseum: 91-94

The Frame Context

ULRICH GEHMANN

Today, we live in a situation the historian Koselleck called a *Sattelzeit*, a period of time where a new perception of the world is emerging, where our relevant ways of conceiving 'world' at all, and what it actually means for us as a whole, is subject to dramatic changes. At first glance, this statement seems to be nothing new, after all what happened in the era that lies behind us, before such a Sattelzeit as our present state of being. It was the era of so-called modernity full of 'dramatic' changes, from an Industrial Revolution to an Internet Age, an era which has been characterized by one of the leading historians of our time, Eric Hobsbawm, as an age of extremes.[1] So, why examine change when we apparently have gotten used to it, what is so dramatic about it any longer? Haven't we gotten used to it for long time, living in the belief that meanwhile, we are able to get it managed, in its overall terms as well as in those of our daily life?

May be, but there is a *But*, a major obstacle to be considered: all those changes presupposed a common ground upon which they could happen at all – the notion of a fixed, i.e. *given world*, and aligned to it, the one of a *given space*. Irrespective of all discussions about an increasing fragmentation of 'world' into many parallel ones, and about the fragmentation or even destruction of space envisaged as major trait of the era of modernity in the prolonged periphery of which we live, one thing seemed secure, despite dramatic changes: that there is one world, in the final, and that there is one space assigned to it, a one labeled as 'real', namely the one we all live in.

---

1   To the notion of a *Sattelzeit*, see Koselleck, R. (1979): 15. As a term, the *Sattelzeit* goes back to Karl Jaspers' notion of an *Achsenzeit*, a term to reflect times when a fundamental change in the general direction of things going on is taking place. Cf. Jaspers, K. (1983): 19f. To Hobsbawm, see his *Age of Extremes*.

This was taken for granted, irrespective of emergent other spaces coined as Cyber Space, Virtual Space, Internet Space, or whatever classification had been adopted to get the existence of parallel spaces next to the one of a 'real world' into our comprehension. Although all those other spaces were perceived as basically differing from a real space, the real space belonging to a real world, and also they were perceived as worlds by their own – with an existence *of* their own and out of that, something other 'real' – they nevertheless were envisaged as virtualizations and enhancements of what already existed, as additions to what is real. And what *remained* real, first and foremost. Despite the mythical aspirations assigned to them right after their start during the 1980ies, to embody worlds capable of truly liberating human kind for the first time in its history, by individualizing it consequently (an aspect to come to), for an everyday understanding, they remained virtual worlds. In the common perception, they were worlds of an *as if*, opposed to a world that really is. Immaterial new spaces opposed to a real of solid, touchable materiality, with real (material) human beings in it and not avatars of a Second Life. Even in cases like the Internet Space where such new worlds intermingled with the old, 'given' one to such a degree that the latters' very existence begun to depend on them, the old ontological distinction was held up: there is one world as the final real, the basic frame of reference, and the others are its enhancements. The old world remained the primus inter pares. And even in the face of attempts to create an Augmented Reality, a reality that is somehow more than just real, we knew one for sure: the real remains real, and the virtual remains virtual. Because you can *augment* something only if this something already exists, and provides the base upon which 'augmentations' can take place. Our basic understanding of reality was not changed; until now, independent from all constructivist or (even) post-constructivist discussions about it, and independent from the rise of new realities in the shape of new immaterial spaces[2] – coining, these realities have been called *virtual*, to distinguish them from "real" reality.[3]

This is going to change. It is about an ontological change, not merely about a certain perspective upon 'reality' in the mode of the constructivist mindset we have gotten acquainted with, while trying to understand our age of extremes. This is not against constructivism, particularly when taking it literally: Modernity, the era in which such a mindset could essentially originate, was characterized

---

2   To the development of these worlds from a broader historical perspective, see Manuel Castells' tripartite opus on a networked society, first published in the 1990ies, the time where these immaterial spaces begun to gain momentum and to spread out.

3   Cf. Grosz, E. (2001).

by a production of various spaces on large scale,[4] leading to their respective worlds, and out of this alone, a constructivist perspective was more than plausible. It is no longer about constructing worlds in mere interpretative terms by literally adopting different world views. These were views upon one and the same thing, since all of these 'constructions' still had one base in common, a real material world really existing as a final frame of reference. And although it became intermingled with these new spaces addressed above, this old reality was not inflicted in its *Being*; since it was not doubted *as such*, irrespective of its manifold interpretations.

With the advent of a so-called Hybrid Space, this is doubted now because the very quality of the old reality shall be changed and hence, the one of the world as it was, in embodying that realities' expression. Whereby 'quality' is to be understood here in its literal terms of origin, as that what makes a world to the world it is, in its essence.[5] With the Hybrid Space, a new kind of reality – and hence, of world – shall be constructed in that the old one is endorsed with additional qualities and through this, adopts in its total another quality, turns into a Being of some other *kind*. It is no longer about a 'reality' that is 'virtual', existing in parallel, and concomitant to the real but about a new *world* with a new quality of the real. In other words, our old frame of reference, valid throughout all of human history so far, is in the process of vanishing, and such an extreme (to cite Hobsbawm) can be seen as a dramatic change, indeed. In using instruments of virtualization of that what existed, it not only blurs the former distinction between real and virtual but fundamentally alters it because such a performance rests upon the idea of creating, and living in what is called a Mixed Reality, a hybrid between virtual (i.e. new) and 'real' (i.e. old) elements constituting in their entanglement the new kind of world to be brought about. Which is more than just a mixture of something still 'real' with something 'virtual'; since such an understanding would presuppose that the real in question would not be altered in its *essence*. The new space makes the real become virtual, and even more important, the virtual becoming real. Which is no playing with words but the attempt to grasp the phenomenon at its basics: a hybridization of that what exists, or to be more precise, of that what had existed, because in a strict sense, the old world doesn't exist anymore since it has been altered. What had started with a

---

4   To illustrate the relevance of the phenomenon of *constructing* spaces, cf. Henri Lefebvre's *Production of Space*, first published 1974 and then repeatedly afterwards, revealing the phenomenon's uncanny presence, also for academic debate.

5   From the Latin *qualitas*, cf. Hoffmeister, J. (1955): 500

hybridization of the postmodern city in its real socio-physical terms[6] continued to unfold in the kind of hybrid we are confronted with now.

The new world is sometimes also named Hybrid Reality, denoting a new real which is more than the mere augmentation of something existing before (referring to the above notion of an Augmented Reality), and is neither the old 'virtual reality', nor the old 'real reality' as we knew it; but as said, another kind of Being. Which still owns recognizable elements from both of these old worlds, but in itself, does embody a new ontological quality. This is the point of relevance in the anthology presented here: to sketch the advent of such a new ontology, in different selected facets.

Figure 1. Hybrid reality[7]

If history can be comprehended in a wider sense as an accumulation of what has grown 'naturally', namely out of its own powers,[8] confined by a 'natural', means real world in its traditional understanding, then human history was a process as natural as biological evolution. This is the old ontology. With the advent of a Hybrid Space, a new ontology gains ground; not just a new one of interpreting what has 'naturally grown', but a new *kind* of ontology in its literal, original terms: an alteration of the Logos of the Being, of the basic comprehension regarding the meaning and description of what 'world' is. By that, everything which formerly existed becomes obsolete. In a way, it is an end of history as we know it, capable of generating a new naturality of historical unfolding, one that could become as natural as the old one has been. To formulate it even more pronounced: what is old, i.e. unaffected by hybridization, resembles a naturality 1.0, an essentially outdated version of history, world and (hence) space which stands

---

6 Cf. Shane, D. G. (2013): 8-11, and the literature cited there.

7 Bamberg/Germany, Dome. Photography by the author.

8 The idea refers to Aristotles' concept of the natural as *physis*, that what grows out of itself, out of its own capabilities and powers, directed by its own processes of unfolding. In recent terms of understanding, a self-organizing, contingent totality; cf. Zimmerli, W. Ch. (1989): 391f.

opposed to a new, advanced and more 'modern' naturality 2.0 of the hybridized space.

In addition, there is one more important aspect related to the individualization of the world mentioned earlier. The new world-space is fluid and multiplied since it became the space of the spectators, or more precisely, the one of *users* defining their relevant spaces with the help of technical means,[9] in puzzling them together out of fragments taken from the old naturality 1.0. The user of the world as it was can seemingly assemble an own world ad libidum, with fragments stemming from the new world, the hybridized one. And all that both enabled and facilitated the recent bloom of hybrid spaces, next to the economic and technological factors to come.

So far the frame conditions of an ontological nature. At this point, some remarks have to be made, concerning frame conditions which come on top of those. First, the overall development sketched here did not appear only in a very recent past. Although it is fully unfolding only quite recently, it has had its historical forerunners; an aspect to come to. Second, the freedom of using world fragments (no matter if from its 1.0 or 2.0 versions) only seems to be one since it always stays tied to strict, and formatted[10] technological conditions; next to a still existing physical substrate also the new space is bound to. Even for a space that is not purely physical in the latters' traditional terms of understanding, you still need physical things, hardware. And it is a remnant of this past that appears in the Hybrid Space: although it became 'immaterial' and fluid, it still depends on these physical things, on concrete entities of a material nature despite all attempts to overcome the traditional materiality. We stay connected to the earth, whether we want to or not.

Moreover, those developments longing for the magic ruse to ban the Being, in constructing a new one – which hybridization is, qua mythic intention – remain finally tied to interests of an economic nature which are as rigidly formatted as are the technological ones; at least in the majority of cases. To keep it down to earth: without economic interests and the respective financial power, there would be no Hybrid Space. Also, seen from this side, the freedom of the user is strictly speaking an illusion. The user may even engage in other activities than those of a primarily economic nature, e.g. in social networks, in creating learning environments or pieces of art, but at the proverbial end of the day, its fi-

---

9 An early stage of such a development has been described by Vilem Flusser (1992): 42, in his journey into the universe of technical images.

10 To the notion of formatization, see Gehmann, U. (2012): 13-33

nal freedom consists in reassembling the pre-assembled, in both a technical and economic direction. Because for these technical and economic formats, the user is an It, not an individual person since the procedures aligned to them (and hence, to the user) are *technical* by their very essence, due to the simple fact that they embody *functions*. So, the user is allowed to use (a), prefabricated, technically formatted fragments in (b), a technically and economically formatted way; for assembling worlds which seemingly "belong" to it (the user), then. So, the freedom of illusion triggers the freedoms of usage. It is about functioning, not about individuality. Apparently, the user is allowed to become used, and gets used to it. We should keep this in mind when speaking about the freedoms these new spaces have to offer.

This might sound rather sobering. And in fact, it is, at least for the majority of cases or "applications" of the technologies enabling these spaces; together with the economic background enabling and triggering both of them. Related to this, the last remark is concerned with normative issues, or formulated in the traditional understanding inherent to a naturality 1.0, with moral questions.[11] As regards their procedures as well as their justification, due to their functional ('technical') nature, technological and economic systems alike are resting in themselves; technically speaking, they are self-referential. A justification *why* such systems are installed the way they are installed – the specific ways in which they actually operate, leading to those and no other results, 'collateral damages' included – cannot be derived *from within* those systems but has to come from the outside, from an "extra-systemic" force, or system. Decisions about the *Why* are value-questions, no functional questions. In traditional terms of understanding, they are moral issues. Because they derive from values believed in, values to provide meaning to human action. Opposed to moral issues, the meaning of economy, if economy is seen in itself and left alone by itself, is only economy, as the one of technology only consists in applying techniques. In traditional terms of understanding, this is the only morality these systems have. Like self-organizing natural systems, both refer to themselves, and their major developmental tendency is to achieve constant optimization.[12] They justify themselves by referring to themselves. Henry Ford is supposed to have said the business of

---

11 The discussion traces back to Immanuel Kant (Uwe Hochmuth, personal communication June 23rd, 2013), as regards the basic modality of how a goal-setting takes place: either in purely *functional* terms, or in terms which consider also "moral judgments" (Kant would have said) settling upon certain *values*.

12 To such a process inherent to any kind of "natural" evolution, see Shane, D. G. (2013): 48

business is business. Related to the spaces examined here, it means that the business of hybridization is more hybridization. In itself, it needs no justification except the one of its bare existence; an existence which then can be optimized; which again means – regarding practical social, mental and psychological consequences – that it can be *intensified* at each moment in time. For directing such processes, it would need frame conditions of a normative, i.e. moral nature, besides those of a purely economic and technological one. Because they are the only "extra-systemic" forces to provide guidance to ongoing optimization.

In recent technological language, it would need a meta-system for enabling ways which are socially accepted, and acceptable. Where do we want to go, and why? Questions like these can only be answered on a moral base; provided by values agreed upon and first and foremost, by values which are actually *lived*. But this would require consensus of what we want. And what "We" really means

in a society driven by diverging interests under the aegis of a certain economy, the so-called neoliberal market – as mentioned, embodying a system resting in itself, and justifying itself solely by its own existence. Like the functional systems do which it nourishes; e.g. the technological ones leading to spaces portrayed in this anthology. So, business became natural, like the technologies assigned to it.

Figure 2. Self-referential system, seen from outside[13]

In addition to those about a new ontology, these frame conditions are not to be neglected. For the time being, they set the stage for recent spatial developments because they embody the final limits for every venture to create new spaces and

---

13 Rome, Via dei Banchi Nuovi. Photography courtesy of the author.

in the latters' wake, also new forms of sociality. For that time being, we are physical, and remain to be so, despite any attempt to overcome this. And we are guided by an economic and technological contextual framework which in fact is freely operating and stays so, despite its various euphemisms, and unimpressed by all critiques or attempts to overcome this. In other words: to better comprehend the things to come, we first have to bring them down to earth.

Nevertheless, the aspects reflected so far are just one side of the entire picture. By its nature, a frame is something rather general and cannot take into account the concrete variety of those individual specifics it actually embraces, and comprises. Which particularly holds true for the mutual relationships of the aspects illuminated in their genesis, and touches another context introduced above as a frame condition of its own rank: the historical perspective, concerned with the question of how and why a naturality 2.0 could emerge. Some of its major outlines shall be sketched now.

The initial and constitutive step to go for such a thing like a second naturality consists in an abstraction of space: to take the given space of a given world not as *given* but to refrain from it, in using its elements by transforming them into another kind of space, and thereby, to create another kind of world. From an architectural perspective, i.e. from the perspective of concrete world-shaping,[14] such a step began with the *grid* as the basic model for town planning and interestingly, was not confined to our cultural sphere, the Occident, but could also be observed elsewhere.[15] In our sphere, we first know it from the plan for Miletus by Hippodamos, and later from the Roman *castrum*, an architectural format that could be placed anywhere inside a given world independent from its geographical or cultural specifics. To pose an abstraction upon the world as it is, independent from its given individualities is the relevant aspect here. And to do so in practical terms, not just in the mind. Such a large scale world-shaping can be seen as specific for our cultural sphere and therefore, appears later again in modernity, on a really large scale (so the thesis). For its performance, it presupposes not only a mindset for doing so, namely the readiness to *transform the world* at all, but in its wake, a basic procedure, too.

Both mindset and concrete procedure are interwoven. It is no question of technique alone, i.e. it does not rely upon entirely on a certain procedure, or technol-

---

14 As a general process, cf. Portoghesi, P. (2000): 93, 137, 161
15 Cf. Delfante, Ch. (1999): 40. And Vercelloni, V. (1994): 5, to Hippodamos; and 11f., to the idea of the complete measurement of a given world in Roman times already.

ogy chosen (here, the grid[16]) – to contradict a beloved misunderstanding of our times with regard to technology in general, and hybrid spaces in peculiar: the technologies are there, ergo are these spaces. For using a technique in a *certain* way, it requires a certain mindset directing in this way. It is no question of technique that we have hybrid spaces, but of a mindset that lends to the techniques appropriate to it, and thus, to a spatiality in accordance with it. The underlying basic procedure is that a model of a world, a virtual world, has to be imposed onto reality, and by that, to create a world in accordance with the model.

Figure 3. World as format[17]

The virtual becomes the real. At first glance, every architectural implementation seems to proceed in this way. But what we are concerned with here is a different case of such a general mode; one specific for our cultural sphere, in particular for one of its phases, the so-called modernity. Because this mode has not been applied just here and there, confined to certain areas or restricted domains of application (as in other cultures), but in general – literally, as a world architecture. This was the mythological intention behind it, and its basic idea was to create a world as ideal artifact, in a double meaning: 'ideal' as a world wanted and deliberately reached for; and as a world conceptualized, *made* according to plan instead of having been merely grown in its 'natural' history.[18] World had to be constructed according to the ideal, not accepted as given and 'naturally' grown.

---

16 Kostof, S. (1991): 95f.

17 Greensboro, North Carolina 1891, http://memory.loc.gov/cgi-bin/query/r?ammem/ gmd:@field%28NUMBER+@band%28g3904g.pm006620%29%29 (Public Domain.)

18 *Ideal* means an "absolute model", and at the same time (as an adjective), stemming from the Latin *idealis*, both the mentally projected and perfected. From Eaton, R. (2001): 11. To the notion of a 'natural' history: see above, on history as natural process.

It had to become architecture in a literal sense, man-made, planned, and ubiquitous. When we look at the above *imago mundi*, we perceive an encompassing artificial network imposed over a given, original world from which only remnants remain visible, and the empty horizon.

The first step towards a Hybrid Space is an artificial space, and here we have it. It resembles a world as an ideal artifact which has been constructed according to strict functionalities; here, of infrastructural needs to cover large spaces in the most efficient, i.e. most economic way, and the economic necessity to parcel the originally given into slots to be sold. And regarding the intention behind it, *all* could look like that, because as already addressed in the foregoing, the spatiality we look at here is strictly functional, having itself as the only frame of reference. Original individualities of a world as it was have been not considered as entities of their own right, but are just kept here and there as picturesque remnants. *In principle*, it is an artificial world, a virtual naturality which became the new real.

The example has been given to reveal the magnitude of transformation that already happened in an early stage of development, and which continues until today. The world it represents is an additional frame context, next to the ones addressed so far, and in its direct impact probably the most relevant of them all. Because the *kind* of world presented in the example turned out to become our relevant world to live in, our life world as it is, an embracing *Lebenswelt* of an artificial nature. As said, it reflects a naturality of own kind which became real but despite that, remains to appear unreal, somehow, in its uncanny dominance of the functional; somehow, it looks like a world that is not real but virtual.

Such a felt Somehow is crucial when discussing about a 'real virtuality' in several respects. Because it applies to the majority of cases treated in this anthology. In modernity, let alone its epoch to follow, we are confronted with spaces that are no longer sensitive in literal terms: they cannot be directly experienced any more, and from that, their anthropological base is missing; which is another frame context of central importance. Even more since every discourse about real virtualities inevitably includes a discussion about the *conditio humana*, too. Either directly in that this condition has to be changed or 'augmented' by the diverse approaches, or indirectly in that it becomes affected by the kind of spatiality we face here; we are confronted with abstract spaces, that is, with non-spaces as regards this anthropological base. What we face is a phenomenon of increasing de-concretization, or as one author has put it, the denigration of the material Being. In the context of the felt Somehow of a 'viewed virtuality' (opposed to a 'real' one), the "[…] real object has been transformed into the epiphenomenal, and instead of communion, there is the unique manifestation of distance."[19] From a historical perspective, it is a process that started in the 19th century on large scale, at the beginning of modern times (see the above world image), and continued since then, and reaches its peak now, with the mentioned naturality 2.0, the natural of a second order. Basically, it consists in a virtualization of the historical, 'naturally' grown object in that the latter becomes annihilated in its physical, i.e. historically grown properties – denigration's core. In a secularized variant of the Christian myth of mind over matter, the process of virtualization equals a denaturalization, and constructs worlds which in their meaning can only be sustained in a projective manner. As it becomes evident by the above image, it happened yet inside the frames of a naturality 1.0 bounded to physical space, before it was intensified in the era of hybrid spaces.

In this context, we have to come back to the anthropological condition. When the nature of architecture consists in constituting an artificial spatiality, the spaces created convey a certain *atmosphere*,[20] or translated into an understanding that belongs to an old naturality 1.0 with its old human beings, their spaces have to be *touchable*, experienced as distinguishable, i.e. *individual* entities which do not look essentially identical and hence, replaceable. This is not the case in the world presented above. In its formatted construction, the only atmosphere it conveys is that of a technical functionality, consisting not of places but of modules. By its essence, it is utopian in a literal sense, namely placeless.[21] What we see here is not just a world as ideal artifact, it is a world as function; a technical format, an *abstracted* space that succeeded to become world, epitome for a placeless modernity and its era to follow.[22] Out of this, such new type of space characteristic for the modern times has been later called, after modern times' unfolding, a Hyper Space, a spatiality that by its very nature is not conform with the perceptional modalities belonging to an inherited (i. e. 'old') human condition still in existence.[23]

Which opens up an additional meaning to the utopian, since modernity: it stands not just for a space which is not real, not here in the world we live in, but also for a space where humans *cannot* live in because it is literally in-human. It is no place for human beings, at least not for their naturality 1.0. The actual denigration and (therefore) destruction of space that was stated so frequently during this time period had its expression in denying space also during post-modernity, and since

---

19 Healey, P. (2012): 67

20 From Beyer, A. and Burioni, M., and Grave, J. (2011): 16f.

21 The Greek origin of the word denotes a utopia as an *ou-topos* (ουτοπος) or non-place.

22 Cf. Augé, M. (1995)

23 Kemp, W. (2009): 163

then: the classical type of modern occidental space, a void Cartesian coordinate system seen as typical (which is synonym to *coining*, literally translated, like a mark on a piece of material) for occidental 'classical' modernity, a type of space coded in a masculine mentality and deliberately produced, following the linear perspective[24] of functional domination, it became superseded by other spatial conceptions which denied its basic homogeneity. To speak with Foucault, it became heterotopian.[25] Like the world and its spaces became structurally functionalized and thereby fragmented and dissolved as unities, the new conceptions of the spatial denied its fundamental cosmic, i.e. solidified properties.

Already before the advent of a Hybrid Space and its aligned Mixed Reality, space became a volatile, fluid and first of all dynamic entity: it became "interstitial", "liquid", even "post-spatial" (suited to the era of a post-modern age), and naturally, suited to those times of hyperlatives, a super- (or hyper-) space.[26]

It was the time where constructivism had its high tide and a new human condition begun to unfold, suited to the capitalism 2.0 of a neoliberal market, the era of humans becoming consequently individualized and by that, to *users* – first and foremost out of the addressed economic reasons – to turn from mere inhabitants of a world as it was to users of a world as it meanwhile became. As a totality, not only actual space became utopian in the above literal sense, but also its users.

Figure 4. Virtual individuals in real community[27]

---

24 Elisabeth Grosz, cited in Kemp, W. (2009): 164

25 To the notion of the heterotopia in urban terms, see Shane, D. G. (2013): 230ff.; and 10, plus 232-236, on Foucault in peculiar.

26 Kemp, W. (2009): 164

27 Selestat/France: window in a shopping mall. Photography by the author.

Despite they had been mobile and dynamic also before that age, they now evolved further on: from beings which were still locally bounded in the frames of their new natural environments depicted in fig. 3 and from that alone, had been still *communal* at least in a formal, so to say merely geographic respect, to beings which had to be no longer locally concentrated in physical terms, in order to be human at all. Being communal in belonging to a community which also has to had its physical expression – namely, the city as man's essential place to live (both in practical and mythological terms) because man was conceived to embody a *zoon politikon*, a communal and hence, 'political' animal – belonged to an old, outdated human condition bound to the frames of a naturality 1.0 although in those times already, this ancient condition begun to erode. [28] Not only physical space, also social space moved in the direction of being dissolved, fragmented, and virtualized, a tendency that has reached its point of culmination today, in recent social media. The new human being, the user, is no longer addicted to pre-given communities it cannot change – like was the space and its world before – it is free to choose the communities it wants, like its (other) objects of consumption. Its former status as a *zoon politikon* became as volatile and liquid as the spaces around it. But first and foremost, it became a matter of *decision*: for the first time in its history, the individual decides to which communities it wants to belong to, to what degree, in which manner, and for how long.

What the old individual of an ancient age of Fordism, mass production and mass society living in worlds of fig. 3 could only decide about its products of consumption now extended into the (former) very core of being human at all, to the community. Like world became a matter of decision in the period beforehand, namely to embody an ideal artifact constructed according to models, so does community now. Also in this respect, the individual became literally utopian.

This for sure was, and still is one strong force which later on led to the idea of hybrid spaces and mixed realities. But nevertheless, the old frames of systemic belongings outlined earlier remained, together with the (still) concrete physical spatiality they generated. Inside the terms of which the liberated individuals still have to live in, because they are still physical. So, the thesis is that an additional force came into play: that much of the efforts to construct Hybrid Spaces on top of such a first functionalized modern, and then hyperized post-modern spatiality are simply

---

28 Individualization with a concomitant formatization has been described as coining for modernity since its first bloom at the last third of a 19th century; see for instance Georg Simmel, in his work about the metropolitan areas and mental life (first published 1903).

due to the anthropological reflex to leave those spaces; to avoid them by constructing other ones, or – if this is not possible – to "enrich" and to "augment" them, in order to make them turn into more *viable* places, in the final.

And to do so again in a strictly individual-based manner – if I, the user, have to live inside the frame context of such a functionalized world, the least I can do is to put its fragments together in my personal mode, for creating a world by my own; and/or to share it with other users (other individuals of the functionalized), to escape from that *what is*, in creating a counter-utopia. That such a mythic longing for another New World got functionalized again by economic systems – the same ones which constructed the old utopia – is the other story, its twin addressed earlier. If we refrain from those frame contexts in their conditioning, the new utopia has no longer to be pursued in the way classical utopias proceeded, namely in pre-planning a community for all as an ideal artifact; but individually based, fluid, and essentially ephemeral since volatile and ever-changing. A recent announcement calling for a new since real 'participatory city' (so the text)[29] gives expression to the hope that "Interactive technologies enable citizens to participate directly", in shaping their urban environments by works of art, that is: to make those environments more viable, after all. Thus, the new citizens "can play an active role in their urban environment instead of being passive consumers." A demand to redefine the notion of participation itself does exist, we read in the accompanying e-mail, i.e. that what made the classical citizen to a citizen has to be re-considered, namely to actively and directly participate in the affairs of his or her city; 'politics' stems from the *zoon politikon*, and the latter derived from the first democratic cities in the Occident, the Greek *poleis*. Now, this is no longer ensured by direct physical participation but will be achieved by technical means, those interactive technologies mentioned. Which are technologies to create a Hybrid Space, finally, the new frame of participation on the level of the communal, too, because it is no longer sufficient to raise awareness but "to look into practices of situated, world-making interventions that redefine reality and can have an impact on everyday life," we read.

What has been introduced in the beginning as embodiment of a new ontology is formulated here as a utopian program. In a literal meaning because it is no longer about *one* city only, the concrete place to live for citizens up to now (also for cities which were "merely virtual" in remaining on the drawing board exclusively), but about many cities in parallel which shall be virtually remolded: the announced project stretches from Aarhus over Sao Paulo to Zagreb. Like the flu-

---

29 http://www.connectingcities.net/node/32, Sept. 2013, and mail from Sept. 12th, 2013

id space, as a Networked Art (so its technical term), it stretches out virtually everywhere, no longer confined to a concrete place although it uses historically ('naturally') grown places as its substrate.[30] It *uses* history for *individual* expression, and this act of renewal shall emerge into something communal, then, since it shall embody a "collective creativity," at the same time (so the text). After the aegis of the Cartesian space of modern dominance with its functionalized worlds and formatted technical and economic belongings, confining the individual to a working and consuming entity, and after the failure of centrally planned utopias in concrete space which were coining for that age of extremes introduced in the beginning, an unprecedented situation occurred: the new citizenship essentially (besides its old remnants) consists in neglecting real concrete circumstances by individually virtualizing them – next to a still ongoing real consume, of course. And this will lead to participative freedom. A citizenship which in its *direct terms of expression* is no longer an issue of concrete humans interacting with each other in a direct way, both physically and anthropologically, but which became a matter of technique. The new citizenship is no longer direct but mediated, technically mediated, and this ensures real human participation; a new hybrid space of the social, taking place in a framework of spaces that are no longer real in an ancient way but which turned into real hybrid ones, by virtualizing the real into an emergent new, that of a real virtuality.

Seen in such a respect, the final fall of a 'modern' age did not happen with the era of post-modernism but is happening right now, with the new ontology of hybrid spaces, and therefore, worlds. Amongst others, one strong reason to examine such ontology more closely. Critics could say that this is utopian mythology; as already said, also in literal terms since it does need no concrete places anymore. Followers could say that only this comes in the near of a true liberation since it refrains from the formerly given consequently. In any case, coming back to the Christian myth of mind over matter, in either version it would embody the latter's teleological fulfillment. Such a connection to history yet exists, despite the attempts to overcome all what has been so far, and up to now. Besides all that and unimpressed by new utopian programs of overcoming the materiality of the so far given, the old real continues to exist as our still concrete, and embracing *Lebenswelt*. Moreover, to keep things down to earth again, in the case of the city as the predominant form of living for human beings as cultural animals (to

---

30 Which demands for a re-definition of the state and of political order, respectively; that fundamental frame condition since Greek days which up to now served as *the* guarantee for public order. To this problem, see the contribution on visible autonomies, in this anthology.

cite McLuhan), it has been enhanced in recent years, although not augmented. Over a period of the last fifteen years or so (depending on the available records), for the first time in its history, the majority of humanity does not live on the countryside any longer – that old bondage to an "old" nature, no matter how deeply the latter became restructured and functionalized – but in cities, with growing proportion. And inside these cities, the majority of their inhabitants live in slums or – euphemistically – "informal cities"; too, with growing proportion.[31] Which too is a frame context of prime importance, hybridized or not. For man the cultural animal living in cities, it also embodies a new ontology in its very literal meaning, next to that of hybrid spaces and 'mixed' realities. The former city – a justified notion because those 'cities' no longer resemble a city in its traditional understanding – turned into its recent form and became *the* natural environment for man the *zoon politikon*, but without offering the coherence and individuality of a man-made cosmos that made the former cities so attractive. This is reality, and in terms of city life, an enhanced one. But a really enhanced one, opposed to its virtualization efforts.

Figure 5. World as abstract artifact[32]

---

31 Dimitris Charitos, personal communication at the Athens conference on Hybrid Cities, May 23rd – 25th, 2013.

32 Rome, Via G. B. Morgagni. Photography by the author.

Parallel to it, there exists a world as network, in prolongation of the mythic wish to create a world as an ideal artifact that concentrates on functionality. Taking its physical bondages addressed earlier as constraints, it is an essentially placeless world, and due to its 'immaterial' nature (since it is about information flows and other 'invisible' things), also a spaceless one. But it exists, worldwide, an essential premise also for hybrid spaces spread out as an immaterial mesh over those new material cities.

Moreover, as regards the old, historically grown cores of today's cities as real physical beings, a deliberate virtualization of them takes place, in a twofold direction: either in copying and reassembling those cores, or in digitally 'augmenting' them, both for strictly individual purposes.

In the first case, a copy of historical architecture is installed to create a pseudo-city where the mentioned atmosphere and authenticity of a 'real historically grown' shall be conveyed, like in some consuming cities or other Las Vegas-architectures.[33] The case of consuming cities is of peculiar interest because it shows how virtualization happens both in real physical space (already), and as a camouflage process, in copying historically grown (and thereby 'real') entities for serving narrowly defined functional purposes, and all that on an individual base. Those pseudo-cities, created *de novo* on an empty space, are fakes of a real in creating it anew; but as a new real serving one individual purpose only, that of the individual enterprise behind it for generating profits. The other individualities involved, namely those who are invited to visit those dreamlands, are not invited to escape into a dream in liberating them from their normal daily circumstances, but to functionalize them for only one purpose again, that of consuming (we recall fig. 2).

As a general process of creating the real anew in borrowing from a historical authenticity, it started with the World Exhibitions in 19th century which represented virtual worlds in real physical space, and mushroomed in the postmodern era with constructions like a Piazza d' Italia in New Orleans. The attempt was to create a new real that rests on using elements of a former old and by that, 'real' real. Its mythic core consisted in constructing an individual world in form of a real virtuality that by its intention, was more real than an original (historically grown) real could ever have been, in concentrating the latter's elements on one spot, and transforming and reassembling them for a world that should look like *as if* it would be authentic. In other words: we, the individual planners and

---

33 For this, see the exhibition catalogue on *Dreamlands*, Centre Pompidou, Paris, May 5th – August 9th, 2010; and the contribution to consuming cities in this anthology.

constructors, create a world by our own that should – qua construction – become 'more' world than an original world could ever be. In historical terms, it was the first attempt to consequently construct worlds as real virtualities, and to do so in real terms, i.e. in physical space. The Piazza d' Italia as one example of such a version of a Hyper Space is of peculiar interest here: inside the existing context of a historically grown city, namely New Orleans, a faked (virtual) historical composition of another grown (and thereby 'real') city became placed, namely Venice; and both these components are intermingled into one space, the one of a faked piazza standing in the midst of a real, i.e. non-faked city.[34]

As a doorway to the new ontology mentioned in the beginning, what happened? A virtual component 'augments' an existing reality and thereby, transforms it into something new, but first and foremost, into something *other*. A hybrid space had been created that *is* something other. What started with the world exhibitions as "spaces of the imaginary" and continued to unfold in Las Vegas-worlds with the attempt to virtualize physical environments for creating complete atmospheric impressions down to their details of a concrete "streetmosphere," for instance in rebuilding Venice by condensing it reassembled,[35] was continued with the Piazza d' Italia as its preliminary peak. The next logical step in this line of development consisted in rebuilding imagined virtual places – that is, places which never existed in this form in history – as historical objects in physical space; like Leon Krier's Atlantis on the island of Teneriffa, the old utopia of the Islands of Bliss that nevertheless was located in concrete physical space (namely the Canary Islands). Or to add newly constructed villages next to (real) old ones, in copying the latter, like in case of Poundbury, England.[36]

Such an 'augmentation' of the existing did already comprise, in itself, a factual annihilation of history in rejecting real, that is, historically grown spatiality by superseding and transforming it. It was the first step towards a Hyper-Reality by creating proto-hyper spaces in the physical domain, although confined to (still) physical means. The next step resembled the second direction mentioned: to transcend these (merely) physical means by digitally hybridizing the physically given and thus, leading to the real hybrid space of a real new ontology mentioned in the beginning. Also here, its starts were laid in the old domain of the physical, with the attempts of the 1960ies to cybernize the historically given by creating the moveable cities of the Situationists, or the instant cities to be reassembled any time like in constructions of Yona Friedman's Paris, Constant's

---

34 Cf. Klotz, H. (1984): 180f.

35 Ory, P. (2010): 73-78. And Hermine Bourgadier to the streetmosphere 152f.

36 Cf. Lampugnani, V. (2011): Vol. II: 829f., to Atlantis anew, and 831f., to Poundbury.

New Babylon or comparable approaches; the politics and cybernetics of freedom, as an author coined it.[37] Free individuals were enabled not only to freely roam inside the frames of an architectonically fixed structure,[38] but to make such a structure become volatile itself, to be changed according to the changing demands of its inhabitants. It was the time where the distinction in hardware and software occurred, and the construction of a first "electronic city." In addition, what was confined formerly to consumer products now had to be applied to architectural constructions: they should have only a very restricted life time, next to their potential to be reassembled any time. The idea of the old functional city and its rigid formats was rejected in favor of a new, individual movability.[39] In anticipation of the recent hybrid space and its *smart city*, the new burgher of the former old city should have the possibility to create his own spaces, a "situative environment" with nearly unlimited possibilities adaptable to the demands and moods of the moment; directed against the prevailing capitalism and its epitome, the functional (old) city. We realize the precursors of the recent movement of a Networked Art portrayed in the foregoing.

The new ideal city, man the *zoon politikon*'s true place to live, should become as volatile as his entire conception of space, and what Baron Haussmann already tried in his remolded 19th century Paris, namely to create a technical yet living organism opened to *all* burghers as *one* space (so his words), was re-tried in those sixties[40], long before the days of a Smart City and a Mixed Reality. It was the idea of a new unity between man and his environment in creating a "living organism," and superseding Haussmann, it culminated in the idea of a symbiosis between man and computer, and that the human being itself can be upgraded.[41] Although a Smart City differs from a Haussmannian Paris, we notice the continuity of a developmental strain, in redefining and dissolving the kind of spatiality belonging to an 'old' naturality 1.0.

---

37 Spiller, N. (2006): 40-53

38 For the rise of modern times, described as "transformations in ideal and reality" see Vidler, A. (2011): 16-127

39 Eaton, R. (2001): 225 and 227, to the new, non-capitalist and freed burgher; 228, to hardware and software; and 231, to the electronic city. And Nerdinger, W., ed. (2012): 290-295

40 Eaton, R. (2001): 229; Baron Haussmann cited in Graham, S., and Marvin, S. (2001): 54f.

41 From Wigley, M. (2011): 119f.

Which leads to the second direction addressed, namely the consequent virtualization of the existing by the new cosmological unity, the individual user. Based upon the idea of a world as network which gained ground yet in those sixties, the net – this ubiquitous frame condition addressed above – was seen as inescapable, and the resulting present frame context has been characterized as follows: "Invisible networks seemingly threaten visible means of defining space, dissolving the walls of buildings [...] Indeed, the idea of space occupied by networks or superimposed by them has been replaced by that of overlapping networks within which physical space only appears as a fragile artifact or effect. Space itself can only be seen when caught in the net. It is as if the modern perforation and lightening up of architecture in the face of speed, industrialized technology, and mass production at the turn of the twentieth century has gone a step farther as buildings dissolve into information flow, to be either discarded as a relic of a previous time or nostalgically preserved as a quaint memento."[42]

The old place of the *zoon politikon* as a nostalgia in which the new user of such environments can place its individual marks, and even more, can reconstruct a history by its own. Either the one of the city it roams through, by transforming it into a hybrid space in which virtual reconstructions of that cities' past are shown (the relics of the relic, so to say); relics which in addition can be commonly shared by a community of users, the new form of participating in public affairs by a virtualized burghership.[43] And which can be *gamified*, in playing with them, either individually, or again in a virtual community. And/or they can be assembled into collages of a history which is strictly individual, in that the single user gets technically enabled to "re"-construct a history by its own, out of historical fragments, for creating a new kind of history, the "subjective city memory" endorsed with the mythological core issues of the new spatiality, in being "immersive, integrative, ubiquitous, omnipresent and interactive."[44]

The last step in this line of development consists in neglecting space altogether, by using it as a virtual domain of reference, in referring to its reality.[45] Which is paradoxical, of course, but this is not the point here. It is the attempt to overcome an old naturality 1.0 through referring to it without needing it any-

---

42 Wigley, M. (2011): 83

43 As an approach to a new reality, presented for instance in Ringas, Dimitrios et al. (2013): 159-166

44 Research project "The Soul of the City", KIT Karlsruhe, department of Building Lifecycle Management, presented July 3rd, 2013.

45 Reiche, M., and Gehmann, U. (2012): 304-307.

more. In fulfillment of the myth of mind over matter, it is the perfect utopia since it embodies a placelessness realized.

But let's come back to earth again. When we recall the actual terms of concrete conditions of living, the two worlds of city and net are the principal ones we are confronted with today. And when we look at the first one as our still existing physical base of being – for the majority of human kind, in the meantime – the demand for augmenting such a reality is at hand. Even if some of these augmentative ventures may be utopian. We are already living in a utopia, so what, one could say, since the initial age of extreme has become even extremer yet. We have nothing to lose but nearly everything to gain; or to regain, depending upon the perspective. So, why not create new realities? The other point is: this is quite dangerous because if doing so with the help of hybridization primarily, we are in a process to lose everything we had, and still have: one world and one space, how chaotic they may ever be. Because as human beings, we are in need of a solid base, and above that, it remains doubtful if volatile and virtualized hybrids are a solution for the problems we face – which are real problems, in a very real world.

REFERENCES

Augé, Marc (1995): *non-places. introduction to an anthropology of supermodernity* (transl. by John Howe), London/New York: Verso

Beyer, Andreas, Burioni, Matteo, and Grave, Johannes (2011): "Zum Erscheinen von Architektur als Bild" [about the appearance of architecture as an image], in: Beyer, A., Burioni, M., Grave, J., eds. (2011): *Das Auge der Architektur* [the eye of architecture], Munich: 10-37

Brunner, Otto, Conze, Werner, Koselleck, Reinhart, eds. (1979): *Geschichtliche Grundbegriffe I* [basic terms of history I], Stuttgart: Klett-Cotta

Castells, Manuel (1996-98): *The Information Age*, Vol. I –III, London/Malden, MA: Blackwell Publishing

Delfante, Charles (1999): *Architekturgeschichte der Stadt* [arch. history of the city], Darmstadt: Primus

Eaton, Ruth (2001): *Die ideale Stadt* [the ideal city], Berlin: nicolai

Flusser, Vilem (ed. of 1992): *Ins Universum der technischen Bilder* [into the universe of technical images], Göttingen: European Photography

Gehmann, Ulrich (2012): "Formats", Vol. 4, *Journal of New Frontiers in Spatial Concepts*: 13-33

Graham, Stephen, and Marvin, Simon (2001): *Splintering Urbanism*, London/New York: Routledge

Grosz, Elizabeth (2001): *Architecture from the Outside: Essays on Virtual and Real Space*, Cambridge, Mass. MIT Press

Healey, Patrick (2012): "The Garden of Earthly Delights", in: Giesecke, Annette, and Jacobs, Naomi, eds. (2012): *Earth Perfect? Nature, Utopia, and the Garden*, London: black dog publishing: 66-83

Hobsbawm, Eric (1994): *Age of Extremes. The Short Twentieth Century 1914-1991*, London: Michael Joseph

Hoffmeister, Johannes (1955): *Wörterbuch der philosophischen Begriffe* [dictionary of philosophic terms], Hamburg: Felix Meiner

Jaspers, Karl (8th ed. 1983): *Vom Ursprung und Ziel der Geschichte* [on the origin and aim of history], Munich/Zürich: R. Piper & Co.

Kemp, Wolfgang (2009): *Architektur analysieren* [analyzing architecture], Munich: Schirmer/Mosel

Klotz, Heinrich, ed. (1984): *Die Revision der Moderne* [revisioning modernity], Munich: Prestel

Kostof, Spiro (1991): *The City Shaped*, New York/Boston/London: Bulfinch Press

Lampugnani, Vittorio (2011): *Die Stadt im 20. Jahrhundert* [the city in twentieth century], 2 Vol., Berlin: Wagenbach

Lefebvre, Henri (1st English ed. 1991, transl. by Donald Nicholson-Smith): *The Production of Space*, Malden, MA/Oxford/Victoria: Blackwell Publishing

Nerdinger, Winfried, ed. (2012): *L'Architecture Engagée*, Munich: Edition Detail. Exhibition catalogue

Ory, Pascal (2010): "Expositions universelles de Paris, espaces de l' imaginaire", in: Seban, Alain et al. (2010): *Dreamlands*, Paris: Centre Pompidou: 73-78. Exhibition catalogue

Portoghesi, Paolo (2000): *Nature and Architecture*, Milan: Skira

Reiche, Martin, and Gehmann, Ulrich (2012): "How Virtual Spaces Re-render the Perception of Reality through Playful Augmentation", in: *Proceedings of the 2012 International Conference on Cyberworlds*, Darmstadt: 304-307

Ringas, Dimitrios et al. (2013): "Infusing Collective Memory Into the City Landscape", in Charitos, Dimitris et al. (2013): *Subtle Revolutions. Proceedings of the 2nd International Hybrid City Conference*, Athens, 23-25 May 2013: 159-166

Shane, David G. (2013): *Recombinant Urbanism. Conceptual Modeling in Architecture, Urban Design, and City Theory*, Chichester: John Wiley & Sons

Simmel, Georg (1903): „Die Großstädte und das Geistesleben" [metropolis and mental life], *in:* von Petermann, Thomas, ed. (1903): *Die Großstadt. Vorträge und Aufsätze zur Städteausstellung. Jahrbuch der Gehe-Stiftung zu Dresden, Vol. IX*, Dresden: Gumbrecht

Spiller, Neil (2006): *Visionary Architecture*, London: Thames & Hudson

Vercelloni, Virilio (1994): *Europäische Stadtutopien* [European utopias of the city], Munich: Diederichs

Vidler, Anthony (2011): *The Scenes of the Street and Other Essays*, New York: The Monacelli Press

Wigley, Mark (2011): "Network Fever", reprinted in Vrachliotis, Georg, ed.: *Netz. Organisationsform & Leitmetapher* [Net. Organizational form & lead metaphor], KIT Karlsruhe: Seminar paper, winter 2011/12

Zimmerli, Walther Ch.: „Technik als Natur des westlichen Geistes" [technique as Western mind's nature], in: Dürr, Hans-Peter, and Zimmerli, Walther Ch., eds. (1989): *Geist und Natur* [Mind and Nature], Berne/Munich/Vienna: Scherz: 389-409

Chapter 1. The Beginnings

The Scientific Image in the Anthropocene

Nature Paintings, Diagrams, and Maps

in Alexander von Humboldt's *Cosmos* and Beyond

SABINE WILKE

Towards the end of his long and adventurous life, Alexander von Humboldt composed his magnum opus, *Cosmos: A Sketch of the Physical Description of the World* (1845), which he prefaces with a motto taken from book seven, chapter one, of Plinius's *Historia naturalis*: "Natura vero rerum vis atque majestas in omnibus momentis fide caret, si quis modo partes ejus ac non totam complectatur animo."[1] To grasp the essence and sublimity of nature, all its parts have to be understood as a whole. The project of *Cosmos*, to sketch a physical description of the world – not a history of the Earth or a history of nature – in his native German language had been hovering in front of Alexander von Humboldt's eyes for decades as he reveals at the beginning of the book: "In the late evening of an active life I offer to the German public a work, whose undefined image has floated before my mind for almost half a century."[2] The particular challenge of such a project consists in the fact that it seeks to treat nature as an entity fueled by inner forces thematically as well as formally which is challenging, as each part of the world that is discussed in a particular section of the book needs to be imagined, visualized, and described in terms of its interconnectivity with all the other parts so that the individual elements of nature are presented in such a way as to emphasize the linkages between other individual spheres thematically as well as aesthetically. Humboldt explains this principle of representation on the example of botany such that: "Descriptive botany, no longer confined to the narrow circle of the determination of genera and species, leads the observer who

---

1 See the original edition of Humboldt, A. (2008).
2 Humboldt, A. (1997): I, 7.

traverses distant lands and lofty mountains to the study of the geographical distribution of plants over the earth's surface, according to distance from the equator and vertical elevation above the sea."[3] The observer on his path to knowledge is led from one class of phenomena to another in pursuit of the mutual dependence and connection that exists between them. And this goal is best accomplished in visualizations such as scientific maps and profiles in addition to the vivid narrative scientific prose that Alexander von Humboldt seeks to compose. This essay locates Humboldt's *Cosmos* and the visual and narrative strategies of representation associated with the project of a physical description of the world at the cross-section between enlightenment science and the full unfolding of modernity that led to industrialization, European colonialism, and the first signs of the age of man that we now capture with the term the "Anthropocene" where humanity and non-human environments are deeply intertwined and where the influence of humanity on the environment has reached the scale of a geological force culminating in the two master tropes of scientific discourse today: accelerated species loss and climate change.[4]

The narratives and scientific images produced in the context of Alexander von Humboldt's *Cosmos* exhibit this principle of interconnectivity in their quest for a visualization of systematic linkages (*Verkettung*) and networks (*Vernetzung*) in an effort to create a proto-anthropocenic worldview of our planet even though they were still composed with a cosmological world view in mind and do not reflect the pure functionalism of modern scientific models. Even though Humboldt's age was not yet sensitive to our current concerns about environmental degradation, both master tropes of the Anthropocene, biodiversity and climate, already play a central role in the scientific prose of *Cosmos*. With the example of two maps from Traugott Bromme's atlas that illustrate these core ideas developed in *Cosmos*, one that deals with climate zones and one that tracks species diversity and the geographic distribution of plants, I discuss the project of *Cosmos* as a form of allegorical visualization of proto-anthropocenic concepts of world creation. Humboldt's idealization of nature puts a world on show that combines dynamism with functionality in an effort to create a holistic model of a virtual reality consisting of networks and hybrid spaces, not unlike the current concept of a "Big History" that "unites natural history and human history in a single, grand, and intelligent narrative" but one that lacks the functionalism of modern scientific narratives and visual representations.[5]

---

3   Humboldt, A. (1997): I, 8.
4   See Crutzen, P., and Stoermer, E. F. (2000): 12.
5   See Christian, D. (2004): 11, and Hinrichsen, D (2011): 15.

THE NARRATIVE PRINCIPLES OF THE NATURE PAINTING

The principles of visualization applied in *Cosmos* amount to nothing less than the core project of what we now call the environmental humanities, i.e., the scholarly effort to restore the dimension of history, ethics, and aesthetics to the scientific knowledge of nature. At the end of his preface in *Cosmos*, Alexander von Humboldt laments that scientific knowledge about natural phenomena, which is based solely on empirical evidence, lacks a historical understanding of data and how these data were produced and aesthetically arranged. Instead, he wishes to emphasize the need for history and aesthetics in the creation of scientific models of a future world that can capture nature in its sublimity and come off as truly transformative: "no one who is animated by a genuine love of nature, and by a sense of the dignity attached to its study, can view with regret anything which promises future additions and a greater degree of perfection to general knowledge. [...] I would, therefore, venture to hope that an attempt to delineate nature in all its vivid animation and exalted grandeur, and to trace the *stable* amid the vascillating, ever-recurring alternation of physical metamorphoses, will not be wholly disregarded even at a future age."[6]

At the core of the project that he pursues in *Cosmos* is the idea of diversity which is the reason why the tropics play such an important role in Humboldt's world view, as they are the place with the greatest amount of diversity on Earth.[7] Thanks to their regularity in climate, abundant fertility, organic richness, and lush diversity of plant and animal life, the tropics also effectively exhibit the causalities and interconnections within nature that have to be visualized by the scientist and presented through animated narrative description and cartographic visualizations. All the scientist needs to do with respect to the tropics is to paint an image of these causalities and interconnections by using words and art.[8] Tropical nature mirrors the planetary and celestial laws and orders on Earth – at least to the extent as that they are perceived by the Western scientist from a temperate climate who is able to recognize them and who constantly wrestles with an adequate form of their representation. Local indigenous knowledge, on the other hand, was not able to appreciate this special status of tropical nature which makes *Cosmos*, i.e., the physical description of the world from a planetary and extra-planetary perspective, a particular concern of Western culture: "In the earliest stages of civilization, the grand and imposing spectacle presented to the minds of the inhabitants of the tropics could only awaken feelings of astonish-

---

6   Humboldt, A. (1997): I, 12.
7   See Humboldt, A. (1997): I, 32-33.
8   See Humboldt, A. (1997): I, 34.

ment and awe. [...] as far as tradition and history guide us, we do not find that any application was made of the advantages presented by these favored regions."[9]

To address the question of representation with respect to natural phenomena whose principles are based on complex linkages and interconnectivities between various spheres, Alexander von Humboldt introduces the concept of the nature painting (*Naturgemälde*) in which processes that cannot be seen with the naked eye can be visualized effectively by drawing lines between individual phenomena or representing them next to each other to invite comparison. The nature painting is a proto-anthropocenic image that looks at Earth and the sky from the standpoint of the universe where the horizon fades into the background and individual phenomena can be understood in their greater context, as if surrounded by a "vapory veil" – an interesting metaphor for a look back at Earth from a planetary perspective. Humboldt describes his nature painting as a "meditative contemplation" that strives to "penetrate the rich luxuriance of living nature, and the mingled web of free and unrestricted natural forces" through "figurative expressions" that "illustrate the point of view from whence [...] individual things blend together in varied groups, and appear as if shrouded in a vapory veil."[10] Such a perspective does not seek empirical evidence in the description of details and also seeks to abstract from human interest in the description of the Earth. Humboldt proceeds from the celestial to the telluric sphere and from there to a cosmic description of the world which includes magnetic and volcanic forces, geognostic formations, the oceans and the atmosphere with its meteorological processes, the geographic distribution of plants and species, and, finally, the stages of human civilizations, but not in terms of a purely functional description, a graph, or a table as was common practice then but in form of a visualization that strives to express how all of these individual phenomena are interlinked dynamically.

This is a particular challenge for scientific prose because of its linear mode of proceeding. Humboldt's prose constantly uses cross-references and comparisons as well as metaphoric language such as the "gaze" onto an object or the "morphological formation" of a natural phenomenon that highlights the visual aspect of his scientific prose, especially when discussing general laws and principles. When he turns to individual examples, Humboldt seeks to discuss them from a variety of perspectives including geographic, paleontological, biological, and historical dimensions. For example, his treatment of the world's plant and

---

9 Humboldt, A. (1997): I, 35. For a critique of this argument from a postcolonial perspective see Wilke, S. (2013): 67-76.

10 Humboldt, A. (1997): I, 79.

animal life combines morphological and physiological descriptions with geognostic and geographic aspects of fossilized data.[11] Humboldt's nature painting of climate is particularly striking, as he seeks to find a narrative representation of phenomena that cannot be detected by the human eye and need to be visualized in scientific discussion.[12] Humboldt's drive to find aesthetic expression for causality and interconnectivity leads him to create certain visualization strategies such as the idea of the line as a connector between certain points of measurement – in the name of achieving greater clarity – that he integrates in his cartographic projects.[13] With his famous introduction of the concept of isothermal lines in the context of comparative climatology Humboldt suggests that "our insight into the *distribution of heat* in the atmosphere has been rendered more clear since the attempt has been made to connect together by lines those places where the mean annual summer and winter temperatures have been ascertained by correct observations."[14] The narrative description of these lines that connect points of average temperatures, sunshine, etc. produces an idealized world in front of the reader's eyes as a proto-anthropocenic model of a world in which all processes interact with and modify each other dynamically. A comparative climatology does not focus on local isolated phenomena but on the consequences of seemingly unrelated causes and events that may have unforeseen consequences somewhere far away as "important changes of weather are not owing to merely local causes [...] but are the consequence of a disturbance in the equilibrium of the aerial currents at a great distance from the surface of the Earth [...]."[15] We may no longer share Humboldt's belief in this equilibrium of natural forces today, but we have to acknowledge his emphasis on the need for narrative visualization of interconnectivity and the aesthetic strategies created for displaying it in the context of his drive to understand and describe a world that is at the brink of feeling the effects of industrialization, population growth, and modern technology. Humboldt's models for interconnectivity are still rooted in a cosmological world view and they transcend modern functional displays but they nevertheless point in the direction of a proto-anthropocenic mode of treating scientific data.

Humboldt calls his visualization strategies "incitements to the study of nature" and he envisions three types: 1) the aesthetic treatment of nature scenes in vivid prose (as in his own essays collected in *Views of Nature*),[16] 2) the modern

---

11 See Humboldt, A. (1997): I, 284-85.

12 See Humboldt, A. (1997): I, 317-28.

13 See Schneider, B. (2012): 181.

14 Humboldt, A. (1997): I, 317.

15 Humboldt, A. (1997): I, 339.

16 See Humboldt, A. (1850).

landscape painting (especially as perfected by painters who traveled to exotic locations and brought back colorful treatments of tropical landscapes), and 3) the
contrastive combination of exotic forms of natural phenomena in panoramic museum displays, zoos, or botanical gardens.[17] With respect to the aesthetic treatment of nature in animate scientific prose, it is important to find a good balance
between the sublimity of the object and the careful choice of rhetorical tropes
and composition techniques, in fact, "the more elevated the subject, the more
carefully should all external adornments of diction be avoided."[18] Landscape
paintings, on the other hand, can illustrate the physiognomic character of a particular landscape in greater detail and intensify in the viewer the "desire for the
prosecution of distant travels, and thus incites men in an equally instructive and
charming manner to a free communication with nature."[19] Parks and exotic plan-
etariums, finally, can provide an animate experience of the biodiversity and
pleasing physical sensations that a traveler from a temperate climate can enjoy in
a tropical context, a notion that rests on the value Humboldt attributes to the
concept of alterity, "one of the most precious fruits of European civilization."[20]
All of these aesthetic strategies mentioned above emphasize the influence of outer nature on the development of human culture, especially on the development of
people's feelings, and they rely heavily on collage elements and emphasize the
hybrid nature of their environments. Moreover, these nature paintings prepare
the reader and spectator for an as yet unexperienced openness toward different
themes, concepts, forms, and experiences of alterity. They are effective tools in
proto-anthropocenic world building given their emphasis on the intensification
of the sensual experience and conceptual openness for diversity that are two important aspects of the truly transformative science that Alexander von Humboldt
is practicing.

Before I discuss cartographic projects that illustrate Alexander von Humboldt's ideas about diversity and climate expressed in *Cosmos,* I want to connect
my preliminary findings with the scholarly discussion on spatiality, topography,
and network theory in cultural studies and with the project of real virtualities
pursued in this essay collection. As opposed to modern functional descriptions of
nature, Alexander von Humboldt's works, not only his *Cosmos,* address an idealized form of nature in the spirit of his time, merging enlightenment science with
Romantic expressions of feelings and paying homage to the contemporary philosophical discussion. Kant and Schelling exchanged ideas about transcendental

17 See Humboldt, A. (1997): II, 19.

18 Humboldt, A. (1997): II, 81.

19 Humboldt, A. (1997): II, 83.

20 Humboldt, A. (1997): II, 105.

idealism, the human perception of the "thing in itself" that can never be known to us, and nature philosophy that seeks to attribute a certain form of subjectivity, if not agency, to nature to counter the force of idealism which had relegated nature into the realm of the object.[21] In his science, especially in his discussions of biodiversity and climate, Humboldt is utilizing strategies of visualization that produce virtual worlds between the imagined spaces indicated by geographic distribution lines, spaces that I interpret to be allegories for a new age of interconnectivity. These allegories function very much like Henri Lefebvre has described modern space in his theory of special architectonics in a real as well as metaphoric sense even though they are still infused with a cosmic vision for a greater whole.[22] Humboldt's nature paintings are allegories of proto-anthropocenic spaces where empirical data is dynamically linked to a variety of interrelated spheres in a spatial and temporal sense giving aesthetic representation to the fact that a locally detectable change in a single natural phenomenon could be caused by a change somewhere else entirely in terms of space and/or time. Humboldt's favorite example for an effective way of displaying an entire ecosystem is the panorama, i.e., a way of displaying virtual worlds in a museum annex in which spectators can adopt a variety of perspectives and still view the entire world from an elevated vantage point.[23] The panorama is a visualization strategy for a world of hidden connections that combines information about that world with a pleasurable sensual experience of it and affords the viewer a liberated gaze that may, at the same time, also function as an instrument of disciplining, effectively serving as the first optical mass media, arguably an important forerunner of the modern cinema.[24] According to Humboldt, these panoramas even create memories by merging sensations from actually observed nature scenes with those that were obtained in the museum context: "Panoramas are more productive of effect than scenic decorations, since the spectator, inclosed, as it were, within a magical circle, and wholly removed from all the disturbing influences of reality, may the more easily fancy that he is actually surrounded by a foreign scene."[25]

Examples such as the nature painting or the panorama link Humboldt's project of a cosmic description of the world to contemporary attempts to rethink agency in a world of interconnectivity such as Bruno Latour's actor-network-theory or human niche construction in the humanities and social sciences. Actor-network-theory looks at the world and the objects therein in terms of social net-

---

21 See Wilke, S. (2008): 1-23.
22 See Lefebvre, H. (1991): 169-71.
23 For literature on the panorama see Sternberger, D. (1981): 15-17.
24 See Oettermann S. (1980): 15-25.
25 Humboldt, A. (1997): II, 98.

works and extends the capacity for actions to humans as well as non-humans, making it possible to conceptualize agency for nature. The most innovative impulse that comes from actor-network theory for an understanding of interconnectivity lies in its capability to conceive of relations in material as well as semiotic terms, thus appealing to research designs deriving from social science contexts such as sociology and anthropology as well as the humanities such as history, philosophy, literature, culture, and the arts.[26] Niche construction theory, on the other hand, seeks to develop a mechanism of endogenous causation and explains natural selection as a function of organism-environment interaction: "NCT provides both a philosophical shift in the way we view and understand evolutionary processes as well as a testable scientific theory."[27] The idea is that both social and physical niches include culturally transmitted knowledge as well as traces of material culture, providing both culturally modified sources of information and culturally modified physical resources in a scheme that seeks to explain individual developmental environments in terms of co-evolution of genes and culture. Alexander von Humboldt's nature paintings are cosmic allegories derived from a similar impulse to map relationality across species and even world spheres in a proto-anthropocenic planetary world view that considers material as well as cultural co-construction of developmental processes. His cosmic description of the world combines an objective scientific concept with an aesthetic model that foregrounds historical, social, and cultural aspects of networked thinking representing a virtual world of dynamic hybrid spaces in the age of man.

VISUALIZATION STRATEGIES OF SCIENTIFIC IMAGES

Cartography and the creation of scientific images such as profiles, diagrams, graphs, tables, and maps plays an equally important role in Alexander von Humboldt's works compared to the challenge of composing vivid scientific prose. The two major visual projects that he completed before turning his attention to *Cosmos* were the picturesque atlas of the Cordilleras, *Vues des Cordillères/Views of the Kordilleras* from 1814, and his geographic and physical atlas of the tropical regions of the New Continent, *Geographischer und Physischer Atlas der Äquinoktial-Gegenden des Neuen Kontinents* from 1834-1838.[28] An early example of Humboldt's interest in cartography is his and Aimée

---

26 See Latour, B. (2005): 35.
27 Kendal, J. et.al. (2011): 785.
28 See Humboldt, A. (1810); also see a recent English translation: Humboldt, A. (2012); and Humboldt A. (2009).

Bonpland's famous plate of the geography of plants in the tropical regions, "Geographie der Pflanzen in den Tropenländern, ein Naturgemälde der Anden, gegründet auf Beobachtungen und Messungen, welche vom 10. Grade nördlicher bis zum 10. Grade südlicher Breite angestellt worden sind, in den Jahren 1799 bis 1803" which accompanied the German edition of his *Ideen zu einer Geographie der Pflanzen nebst einem Naturgemälde der Tropenländer* as frontispiece.[29] The editor of the recent German edition of the geographical and physical Atlas, Ottmar Ette, even calls Humboldt's cartography "something like the hidden psychogram of Alexander von Humboldt."[30] The picturesque atlas *Vues des Cordillères* combines a series of short essays on different natural and cultural phenomena in Humboldt's characteristic vivid scientific prose – true nature paintings – with an image, typically a profile of a mountain range, a black and white landscape, a beautiful colorful etching of an indigenous cultural monument, or an etching of a spectacular nature scene created in Paris according to Humboldt's instructions. This combination of text and image gives visual evidence for the poly-dimensional aspect of Humboldt's thinking. The geographic and physical atlas, on the other hand, was meant to be published together with Humboldt's historical and critical discussion of the historical development of the geographic knowledge of the New World and the progress of nautical astronomy in the fifteenth and sixteenth centuries, *Examen critique*, a project that the new German edition finally realized.[31] Among its thirty-nine plates, it includes a few profiles but is mostly composed of detailed maps of complex river systems and mountainous landscapes applying aesthetic principles that emphasize a cosmic world view.

Birgit Schneider has discussed the significance of the scientific image from an art historical perspective in her work on climate images in which she studies more than two hundred years of visualizations within the climate sciences. She argues that climate and climate change can only be made evident in scientific discussions through visualizations. Climate constitutes itself in models that use certain visualization strategies such as the curve or the line in order to codify an index of normalization.[32] In particular the red curve in contemporary images of

---

29 Humboldt, A., and Bonpland, A.: "Geographie der Pflanzen in den Tropenländern, ein Naturgemälde der Anden, gegründet auf Beobachtungen und Messungen, welche vom 10. Grade nördlicher bis zum 19. Grade südlicher Breite angestellt worden sind, in den Jahren 1799 bis 1803," Staatsbibliothek zu Berlin, Kartenabteilung. This plate first appeared in Humboldt A. (1807), frontispiece.

30 Ette, O. (2009): 230, my translation.

31 See Ette, O. (2009): 231.

32 See Schneider, B. (2010): 81.

climate such as the famous hockey stick graph signals the extent of secure knowledge whereas the grey spectrum around the red curve indicates knowledge that is less secure, an area that tends to shrink as the graph is discussed in policy circles and with the wider public.[33] The point Schneider makes is that these scientific images are not representations of facts or self-evident truths but visualizations of world views that mediate a certain kind of knowledge, in the case of climate images a "modern way of picturing disaster,"[34] leading Schneider to the conclusion that "images picturing climate do not simply represent or illustrate information, but in the process actively *produce* and *shape* knowledge."[35] Alexander von Humboldt's visualization strategies in his nature paintings and in his cartographic work as well as the many contemporary maps, diagrams, and graphs resulting from *Cosmos* must be understood as such images that actively produce and shape knowledge. They have shaped how we depict the results of scientific observation and measurements and turn them into instruments of knowledge production and knowledge communication today.

In the case of Alexander von Humboldt's profiles, for example, the single most important tool in actively producing and shaping knowledge is the line that synthesizes visual thinking and graphical methods to illustrate the idea of *Cosmos* as a holistic ecological system. The line is the tool that depicts networks and turns diagrams into functional graphs, climate zones, for example, or zones of distribution of species.[36] Humboldt's famous snow line is a functional diagram that visualizes a global concept and turns it into a function of elevation and average temperature by combining empirical data with the abstracted laws of nature. These graphically illustrate the science discussed illustrating comparative data and scientific laws and indicating the role of aesthetics in the effort to produce and shape our geographic knowledge of the old and the new world.

The other famous example of a line as the primary tool in the visualization of scientific data is Humboldt's invention of the isothermal line in his "Carte des lignes isotherme" from 1817 that constitutes arguably the beginning of modern climate science where the line transports epistemological knowledge about the shape of global climate zones.[37] The graphic representation of these climate zones is by no means a neutral project; it is an aesthetic project, giving valence to the pleasing curves and the diversity of forms in nature. Schneider concurs that for Humboldt "the question of the reasons for the manifold forms on Earth –

---

33 See Schneider, B. (2011): 197.
34 Schneider, B. (2011): 192.
35 Schneider, B. (2011): 193.
36 See Schneider, B. (2013): 35.
37 See Schneider, B. (2013): 179.

for the different shapes of animals, minerals, plants, and cultures – is eventually an aesthetic one" resting on the physiognomic gaze of his age which valued the synoptic view of a landscape that does not separate (like the view of the botanist) but one that combines and sees individual phenomena in their global context.[38]

This power of actively producing and shaping knowledge attributed to the line can be studied on the example of two maps that were part of Traugott Bromme's *Atlas zu Alexander von Humboldts Kosmos* from 1847, a publication that synthetically illustrates this new semantic principle.[39] As opposed to Heinrich Berghaus's atlas that was co-conceived by Alexander von Humboldt and Heinrich Berghaus,[40] Bromme's atlas has to be considered a separate and independent project resulting from the knowledge produced in Humboldt's *Cosmos* and is further evidence for the wide distribution and reception of the ideas expressed therein. It starts with a map of the world of stars and then turns to the telluric sphere giving graphical shape to geological, volcanic, hydrological, physical, and other features of the world. This atlas covers all continents, oceans, the distribution of plants, animals, and cultures over the Earth and ends with a series of thematic maps about ancient history and exploratory expeditions until 1850 in altogether forty-two maps. The "Map of the Isothermal, Isoclinal, Isogonal, and Isodynamic Lines with the Magnetic Meridians in Stereographic Polar Projection, to Visualize the Connection between Isoclinal and Isothermal Lines" (figure 1) combines four principle categories of averaged data about climate into a representation of the two world hemispheres which are stretched out two-dimensionally with a black and white image of a compass on the upper left-hand side, an image of an *inklinatorium* – an instrument to determine the inclination of the Earth's magnetic lines – on the upper right-hand side, an image of a wind rose – a diagram showing for any given place the relevant frequency or frequency and strength of winds from different directions – in the lower center, a legend for the different lines on the left, a text about magnetic relations on the right, and a graph with a list of the angles of the compass-points with the meridian as reference point on both sides.

This principle of visualization for the connection of two different but related lines that were drawn between different averaged sets of data pays homage to the production of this kind of knowledge with the help of scientific instruments – hence the compass, the inklinatorium, and the wind rose. It also integrates an older form of presenting scientific data – the table – into this new hybrid collage that puts the reader of the image in the vantage point of the surveying perspec-

---

38 Schneider, B. (2013): 190.
39 See Bromme, T. (1854).
40 See Berghaus, H. (2004).

tive using the magnetic poles as the epicenters for the projection. Climate becomes knowledge that is produced and shaped through this projection. The scientific image is a model of a virtual world making where territorial spaces are actively produced and shaped dynamically.[41] These images present world views – in the Heideggerian sense[42] – of imaginary geographies that rest on the principle of comparability between different sets of data and locations in a networked system of ecology.[43]

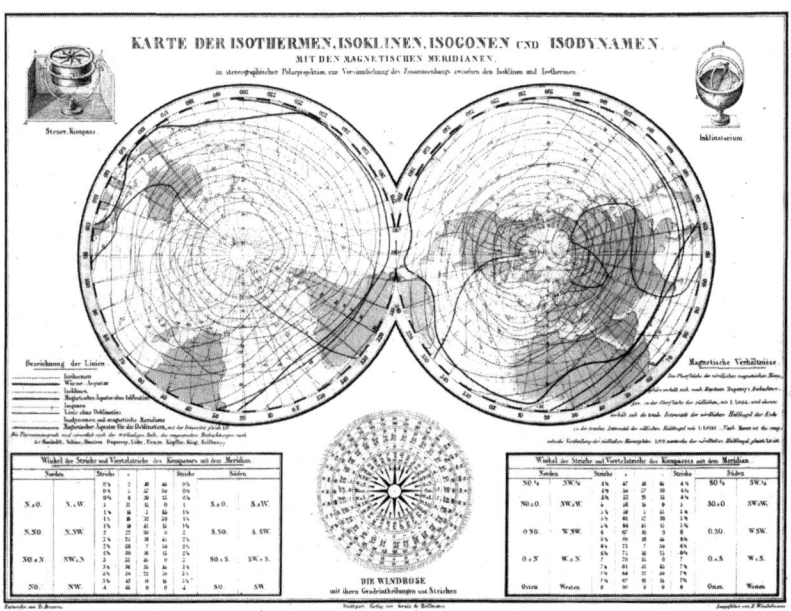

Figure 1. Traugott Bromme, Karte der Isothermen, Isoklinen, Isogonen und Isodynamen mit den magnetischen Meridianen in stereographischer Polarprojektion, zur Versinnlichung des Zusammenhangs zwischen den Isoklinen und Isothermen.[44]

The other example I wish to discuss here is Bromme's map that illustrates a Survey of the Distribution of Plants Horizontally, after A. von Humboldt, J. Schouw and others. It presents an image of a two-dimensional world stretched out flat as if on a table and showing the distribution of plants horizontally with a

---

41 See Günzel, S., and Nowak, L. (2012): 3-4.

42 See Heidegger, M. (1994): 89.

43 See Dipper, C., and Schneider, U. (2006): 15.

44 In: Bromme, T. (1854): Plate 14@Summit Libraries e-book; image in public domain.

table for the twenty-five phyto-geographical spheres established by the Danish botanist Joakim Frederic Schouw and a profile of the world's main mountains and mountain ranges, the Andes, the Pic de Teneriffe, the Himalayas, the Alps, the Pyrenees, and the mountains of Lapland (Finland) showing the distribution of plants vertically.[45]

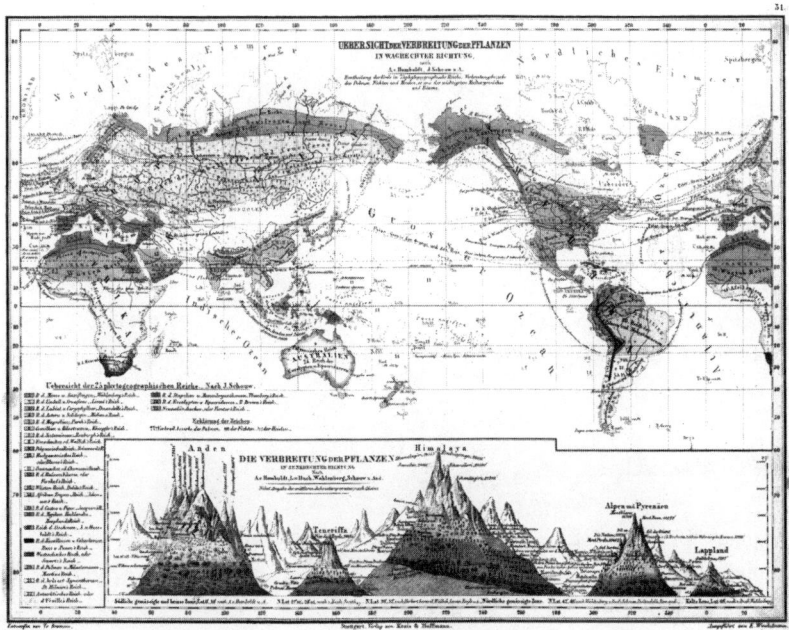

Figure 2. Traugott Bromme, Übersicht der Verbreitung der Pflanzen in wagerechter Richtung nach A. v. Humboldt, J. Schouw u. A.[46]

This image visualizes the active production and dynamic shaping of modern geographical knowledge as a network of data that reaches across the Earth and across the different elevations as dynamic and functionalized hybrid space.

I have called these spaces proto-anthropocenic allegories, as they embody the core concept of radical interconnectivity, i.e., the functionality of modern space as a reflection of the age of the human in which the elements of nature are no longer described in isolation but in terms of their relationship to humanity and its conquest and taming of nature, but also in terms of its enormous and trans-

---

45 For a discussion of a different cartographic project with a similar agenda see Leitner, U. (2003).

46 In: Bromme, T. (1854): Plate 31 @ Summit Libraries e-book, image in public domain.

formative challenge of imagining, visualizing, and creating conditions for life on Earth that embrace the idea of interconnectivity while moving forward sustainably and realizing the transformative potential of a science that is cognizant of society and culture. While Alexander von Humboldt and his contemporaries – even though they inaugurated the age of increased globalization, industrialization, and colonial exploitation – were largely unaware of the limits of growth and the scale of today's exploitation of natural resources, his nature paintings in *Cosmos* and the scientific images produced in the wake of this seminal project put a world on show that as a hybrid space reflects a world view of networks and interconnected spheres of existence that visualizes a virtual reality beyond these images that cannot be seen with the naked eye. Modern topographies are created through these strategies of visualization that produce world views and capture the Earth from a planetary perspective. Alexander von Humboldt's world is a holistic system, a cosmos in the most literal sense of the term.[47] His narrative and cartographic projects are exercises in world construction(s) that project into the future and serve as the bases for imagining a world that is as well as a world that can be. To that extent they are allegories of modern topographies.

REFERENCES

Berghaus, Heinrich (1837-1848): *Physikalischer Atlas*, Gotha: Julius Perthes.

Böhme, Hartmut, ed. (2005): *Topographien der Literatur: Deutsche Literatur im transnationalen Kontext*, Stuttgart: Metzler.

Bromme, Traugott, ed. (1854): *Atlas zu Alexander von Humboldts Kosmos in zweiundvierzig Tafeln mit erläuternden Texten*, Philadelphia: John Weik.

Christian, David (2004): *Maps of Time: An Introduction to Big History*, Berkeley: University of California Press.

Crutzen, Paul J., and Stoermer, Eugene F. (2000): "The Anthropocene," Vol. 41, *International Geosphere-Biosphere Programme Newsletter*, Stockholm: IGBP: 12.

Dipper, Christof, and Schneider, Ute, eds. (2006): *Kartenwelten: Der Raum und seine Repräsentation in der Neuzeit*, Darmstadt: Wissenschaftliche Buchgesellschaft.

Ette, Ottmar (2009): "Zwischen Welten – Alexander von Humboldts Wege zum Weltbewußtsein," in: Humboldt, Alexander von (2009): *Geographischer und Physikalischer Atlas der Äquinoktial-Gegenden des Neuen Kontinents. Un-*

---

47 See Stockhammer, R. (2005): 321, and Böhme, H. (2005): ix.

sichtbarer Atlas aller von Alexander von Humboldt in der "Kritischen Untersuchung" aufgeführten und analysierten Karten, ed. Ette, Ottmar, Frankfurt: Insel: 242-47.

Günzel, Stephan, and Nowak, Lars (2012): "Das Medium Karte zwischen Bild und Diagramm: Zur Einführung," in: Günzel, Stephan, and Nowak, Lars, eds. (2012): *KartenWissen: Territoriale Räume zwischen Bild und Diagramm*, Wiesbaden: Reichert: 1-32.

Heidegger, Martin (1994): "Die Zeit des Weltbildes," in: Heidegger, Martin: *Holzwege*, ed. Herrmann, Friedrich-Wilhelm von, Frankfurt: Klostermann: 75-95.

Hinrichsen, Don (2011): *The Atlas of Coasts and Oceans: Mapping Ecosystems, Threatened Resources, and Marine Conservation*, London: Myriad.

Humboldt, Alexander von (1807): *Ideen zu einer Geographie der Pflanzen nebst einem Naturgemälde der Tropenländer*, Tübingen: Schoell: Frontispiece.

Humboldt, Alexander von (1810): *Vues des Cordillères et Monumens des people indigènes de l'Amérique*, Paris: Schoell.

Humboldt, Alexander von (1834 – 1838): *Examen critique de l'histoire de la géographie du Nouveau Continent*, Paris: Gide.

Humboldt, Alexander von (1850): *Views of Nature*, London: Bohn, http://archive.org/details/viewsnatureorco00bohngoog.

Humboldt, Alexander von (1997): *Cosmos: A Sketch of the Physical Description of the World*, Vol 1, transl. O. C. Oteé, Baltimore: Johns Hopkins University Press.

Humboldt, Alexander von (2008): *Kosmos: Entwurf einer physischen Weltbeschreibung*, 2 Vols., ed. Hanno Beck, Darmstadt: Wissenschaftliche Buchgesellschaft.

Humboldt, Alexander von (2009): *Geographischer und Physikalischer Atlas der Äquinoktial-Gegenden des Neuen Kontinents. Unsichtbarer Atlas aller von Alexander von Humboldt in der "Kritischen Untersuchung" aufgeführten und analysierten Karten*, ed. Ette, Ottmar, Frankfurt: Insel.

Humboldt, Alexander von (2012): *Views of the Cordilleras and Monuments of Indigenous People of America*, ed. and trans. Kutzninski, Vera M., and Ette, Ottmar, Chicago: University of Chicago Press.

Kendal, Jeremy, et.al. (2011): "Human Niche Construction in Interdisciplinary Focus," *Philosophical Transactions of the Royal Society* B, London: Royal Society Publishing: 785.

Latour, Bruno (2005): *Reassembling the Social: An Introduction to Actor-Network Theory*, Oxford: Oxford University Press.

Lefebvre, Henri (1991): *The Production of Space*, Oxford: Blackwell.

Schneider, Birgit (2010): "Ein Darstellungsproblem des klimatischen Wandels? Zur Analyse und Kritik wissenschaftlicher Bilder und ihren Grenzen," Vol. 38, *kritische berichte*, Marburg: Jonas: 81-91.

Schneider, Birgit (2011): "Image Politics: Picturing Uncertainty: The Role of Images in Climatology and Climate Policy," in: Gramelsberger, Gabriele, and Feichter, Johann, eds. (2011): *Climate Change and Policy: The Calculability of Climate Change and the Challenge of Uncertainty*, Berlin: Springer: 191-209.

Schneider, Birgit (2012): "Linien als Reisepfade der Erkenntnis: Alexander von Humboldts Isothermenkarte des Klimas," in: Günzel, Stephan, and Nowak, Lars, eds. (2012): *KartenWissen: Territoriale Räume zwischen Bild und Diagramm*, Wiesbaden: Reichert: 175-199.

Schneider, Birgit (2013): "Berglinien im Vergleich: Bemerkungen zu einem klimageographischen Diagramm Alexander von Humboldts," Vol. 26, *Humboldt im Netz*, Potsdam: Alexander von Humboldt Forschungsstelle: 25-43. www.uni-potsdam.de/u/romanistik/humboldt/hin.

Stephan Oettermann (1980): *Das Panorama: Die Geschichte eines Massenmediums*, Frankfurt: Syndikat.

Sternberger, Dolf (1981): *Panorama oder Ansichten vom 19. Jahrhundert*, Frankfurt: Insel.

Stockhammer, Robert (2005): "Verortung: Die Macht der Kartographie und der Literatur," in: Stockhammer, Robert, ed. (2005): *Topographien der Moderne: Repräsentation und Konstruktion von Räumen*, Munich: Fink: 319-340.

Wilke, Sabine (2008): "From 'natura naturata' to 'natura naturans': 'Naturphilosophie' and the Concept of a Performing Nature," Vol. 4, *Interculture*, New York: Routledge, 1-23.

Wilke, Sabine (2013): "Anthropocenic Poetics: Ethics and Aesthetics for a New Geological Age," Vol. 3, *Rachel Carson Center Perspectives*: Munich: Rachel Carson Center: 67-76. http://www.carsoncenter.uni-muenchen.de/pub lications/perspectives_mainpage/2013_perspectives/index.html

Thomas Jefferson's University

An Architectural Masque

DAVID BELL

THE JEFFERSON ENIGMA

Thomas Jefferson was unquestionably the most enigmatic of America's founding fathers. His imposing intellect, thirst for knowledge, and desire to apply that knowledge in pursuit of his dream for the life, liberty, and happiness of the individual combined with a surprising degree of naiveté and self-deception to create an elusive character that sometimes baffled his friends. His enemies believed his espousal of science, objectivity, and the dispassionate pursuit of knowledge in the cause of human liberty was simply a clever façade to mask his political machinations. The most egregious and inexplicable of the many inconsistencies that pervaded Jefferson's complex personality is that this author of the immortal words "all men are created equal" was a lifelong owner of more than two hundred slaves. The mystery of Jefferson provoked his most reverential and comprehensive biographer Dumas Malone to write of him that "[n]o single term fits one who held in balance a mass of apparent contradictions."[1] Merrill Peterson, another distinguished Jefferson scholar, after more than three decades of study, admitted that "Jefferson remains for me, finally, an impenetrable man."[2] Jefferson's pervasive inconsistency with its attendant contradictions actually constituted his true strength. It was the source of his ability to invent a theory or develop a dream and then detach himself from it. The poet John Keats attributed this quality of pervasive inconsistency to all great men calling it the "Negative Capacity...of being in uncertainties, mysteries, doubts, without any irritable reach-

---

1 Malone, D. (1981): 146
2 Peterson, M. (1970): viii

ing after fact and reason."[3] Perhaps the clearest exposition of the riddle of Jefferson's "Negative Capacity" was in a letter he wrote to Maria Cosway dated October 12, 1785, which he composed as a dialog between his rational side and his emotional side giving full expression to the complex tensions between these two aspects of his character. One side always seemed to act as a mask for the other.

Jefferson's professional training was as an attorney but he had diverse interests and capabilities. He was a scholar of the classics, an amateur philologist and ethnologist, geographer, botanist, farmer, zoologist, astronomer, inventor, political scientist, and moral philosopher – an encyclopedia of talents that perhaps provides some rationale for Malone's "mass of apparent contradictions." It may be most appropriate to describe Jefferson's "Negative Capacity" as eclectic in the way the Enlightenment thinker Denis Diderot defined the term:

»An eclectic is a philosopher who, trampling underfoot prejudice, tradition, antiquity, general agreement, authority – in a word, everything that controls the minds of the common herd – who dares to think for himself, returns to the clearest general principles, examines them, discusses them, admits nothing that is not based on the testimony of his experience and his reason; and from all the philosophies he has analyzed without respect and bias, makes for himself a particular and domestic one which belongs to him.«[4]

Consciously or not, Jefferson concealed his "Negative Capacity" behind a genteel façade of calm, refined, and courtly politesse, which could be both charming and irritating. One of the consequences of his demeanor was that Jefferson considered candor and courtesy as antithetical; to avoid confrontation, he invariably chose the latter over the former. Jefferson's mask of polite and taciturn reserve was often mistaken for arrogance but it also gave the impression that he was deceptive. Charles Francis Adams, the grandson of John Adams, wrote of him:

»He did not always speak exactly as he felt, either towards his friends or his enemies. As a consequence, he has left hanging over a part of his public life a vapor of duplicity, or, to say the least, of indirection, the presence of which is generally felt more than it is seen.«[5]

---

3   Keats, J. (December 21, 1817)

4   This translation of Diderot's definition of the eclectic is by A. A. Long and appears in Dillon, J. M. (1988): 19. Dillon notes that Diderot derived his definition from that given in Jakob Brucker's *Historia critica*.

5   Adams, J., and Adams, C. F. (1856): 616

Like Diderot, Jefferson's thought was deliberately unsystematic, which led him to have a pronounced aversion to and dislike for the entrenched systems of hereditary monarchy and its complicit partner, organized religion. He was also suspicious of philosophical systems and held great contempt for Platonist metaphysics especially with the way he believed it obfuscated the moral clarity and ultimate pragmatism of the life and teachings of Jesus of Nazareth. Regardless of how one might consider Jefferson's many contradictions, he never wavered from his most cherished ideal that challenged the rigidity of systems: the necessity of individual liberty and self-determination, which he believed expansive energetic governments and authoritarian theologies perpetually threatened. He summed this up with succinct profundity in the *Declaration of Independence* stating that every human being has the right to "Life, Liberty, and the pursuit of Happiness," words that are the foundation of the American dream.

Among Jefferson's many interests and capabilities, he was an accomplished if somewhat idiosyncratic architect of numerous buildings. He admired and used exclusively the architectural classicism associated with Rome's Republican period, which he must have seen as simultaneously scientific and lyrical. Of course, classicism is very much a system; it evokes a sense of order and proportional regularity that appealed to Jefferson's sense of harmony. However, its system is quite elastic, adaptable, and open-ended in a pragmatically eclectic way. Given this and Jefferson's "Negative Capacity," when we study closely his largest and most comprehensive work of architecture, the University of Virginia's academical village, we eventually encounter a multitude of interlocking complexities, subliminal subtleties, bewildering array of inconsistencies and, as noted previously, contradictions or paradoxes that are all masked by a seemingly well-mannered serenity, balance, and classical harmony. In every sense, his design and creation of the University is his avatar, a virtual Thomas Jefferson. In order to understand his design, one must consider not only Jefferson's distinctive personality traits but also his philosophy and its sources as all these things are connected in an elaborate network that correlates his architectural tastes with his politics, his educational values, and his views on nature and society.

The Science of Liberty

At Monticello, Jefferson had three portraits prominently displayed of what he called his "trinity of the three greatest men the world had ever produced."[6] Two portraits were prominent leaders of the seventeenth century's scientific revolution, Francis Bacon and Isaac Newton. The third portrait was the legal scholar and philosopher John Locke. Though Locke was not a scientist per se, Jefferson considered him as having delineated scientifically the principles of human liberty and the workings of the human mind. Locke's philosophy may also have been attractive to Jefferson because it was congruent with many of the teachings of Jefferson's three favorite moral philosophers, the materialist Epicurus, the stoic Epictetus, and Jesus of Nazareth.

Although he owed a debt to Descartes' rationalism, Jefferson's Epicurean ideal to be not "pained in body or troubled in mind" suggests that he rejected Descartes mind body duality.[7] This is borne out in Jefferson's attraction to Locke's epistemological premise in *The Essay on Human Understanding* that humans, regardless of circumstances and contrary to Descartes' proposition, are born with no innate ideas, that essentially there is an intimate connection between the senses and knowledge, hence between body and mind. In fact, in a letter Jefferson wrote to John Adams, he simultaneously swerved from and critiqued the intent of Descartes' famous dictum "I think therefore I am;" paraphrasing it he wrote: "I feel: therefore I exist."[8]

Locke's perceptual or empiricist epistemology proposed that all knowledge comes from our reflection on the sensible objects of the outside world – nature takes form in the mind as ideas; knowledge and a vision of the world come through the senses. Locke maintained that this capability allows one's mind to define that person as a unique identity, a self with integrity of consciousness. Although Descartes defined the modern notion of consciousness, Locke's epistemology provided the foundation for modern notions of "the self" and individual identity. Together, Descartes and Locke provided the philosophical basis for the sovereignty of the individual essential to the formation of Jefferson's political views. The *Declaration of Independence* is a manifesto of the individual. Jefferson saw that Locke's fundamental epistemology also had a democratic implication. It meant that knowledge is available to everyone who has the abilities to learn and apply learning, which is essential to his statement

---

6 Jefferson, T. (January 16, 1811)

7 Jefferson, T. (October 31, 1819)

8 Jefferson, T. (August 15, 1820)

that "all men are created equal." Moreover, Locke envisioned a particular kind of social contract for governing civil society that strongly resonated with Jefferson. In order for such government to be effective, it must recognize the natural rights of its citizens and therefore limit the scope of its powers. Locke's theory of the social contract defined in Jefferson's mind the constitution of the American government.

As important as Locke's epistemology was to Jefferson in formulating his ideas about the acquisition of knowledge and its democratic nature, Jefferson's theory of government also had an affinity with the moral philosophy of Francis Hutcheson, a key figure of the Scottish Enlightenment. Hutcheson proposed the quantification of benevolence by developing a simple mathematical formula for morality. To contemporary readers of the *Declaration*, Jefferson's notion of happiness may seem simply to be an expression of generic hopefulness and contentment. However, being an Enlightenment man, Jefferson believed that happiness was scientifically quantifiable, a premise that related directly to Hutcheson's treatment of benevolence and morality. Hutcheson construed a proper social order and the government associated with it as dependent on a *sensus communis* or public sense, which predicates the individual's happiness on a concern for the happiness of others. This would certainly have appealed to Jefferson's Christian belief that each individual has a moral duty to care for others. Despite his advocacy of the sovereignty of the individual, Jefferson was deeply suspicious of unrestrained individualism, particularly in association with what he regarded as the avaricious practices of mercantilist commercialism. In Epicurean fashion, he believed there were limits on the individual as well as on governments. Thus, it would be inappropriate to consider Jefferson's advocacy of limited government as his opposition to government altogether. He understood government as a scientific enterprise that has a mission to engender the improvement of its citizenry as long as those who govern understand that they must be accessible and accountable to the governed. Jefferson accepted that a perpetual and positive tension between the government and its citizens was not only necessary but also beneficial to their ultimate mutual happiness.

Embedded in the Enlightenment's desire to apply the principles of Newtonian science to emergent ideals of social reform was a provocative contradiction. Newtonian science is inherently causally deterministic, which implies the proscription of free will by the forces of nature. Yet, the reformation of society for many Enlightenment thinkers meant a strong advocacy of individual freedom and hence they were champions of free will. Herein lay a troublesome dilemma. One of the most significant of Enlightenment thinkers,

Immanuel Kant, identified this problem as the third antinomy of pure reason and attempted to address this issue by systematically arguing that individual liberty is distinct from the causality that governs the laws of nature. It is a right innate to human beings and exists outside those laws. Jefferson, who appears to have been completely unaware of the philosophy of his older contemporary Kant, was not so systematic in his arguments for the necessity of human freedom. Nevertheless, from the body of his writings, we can ascertain that like Kant Jefferson believed individual freedom derives directly from the laws of nature outside of causality and beyond any humanly devised political system, i.e., freedom is unalienable.[9] Jefferson's acknowledgment of the necessity of such a dialectical relationship is corollary to a larger realization regarding the Enlightenment's principles of individual liberty and self-determination, namely that all perceptions and values are relative, subject to change, and therefore intrinsic to political processes. The values of institutionalized Christianity, hereditary monarchy, and even classical civilization necessarily came into conflict with Enlightenment thought on this point.

THE PASTORAL IDEAL

The New World of the American continent conjured very different images in the minds of its English explorers and colonists. The Puritan settlers of New England perceived that region as a malevolent, inhospitable, and hostile wilderness populated by heathens.[10] In fact, they favored this idea taking it as an article of their faith to civilize it in service to God's will. Alternatively, many of the early explorers and colonists of Virginia considered it an abundant garden inhabited by amicable natives. This portrait of Virginia was rendered in an account written by Thomas Hariot, a crucial member of the Raleigh expedition of the late 16th century. Hariot's reckoning of Virginia as an unspoiled imperturbable Eden-like bountiful garden was simultaneously exotic and reassuring to English readers. Jefferson also had an Edenic view of Virginia but it differed significantly from the one Hariot described. Jefferson believed the destiny of this New World Eden could not be one of invariant harmony between nature and humanity. Certainly, Jefferson appreciated Virginia's primeval qualities but he also realized that as it became settled more densely, some of these qualities would necessarily change

---

9　A lengthier discussion of the relationship between Kant and Jefferson's political philosophies can be found in Creighton, T. A. (2008)

10　See Rasmussen, W. M. S., and Tilton, R. S. (2003)

while others must be preserved. Hence, he wanted to ensure that Virginia's domestication would not compromise its qualities as an unspoiled abundant garden.

The different interpretations of Virginia between Hariot and Jefferson indicate a contrast of two ideals of "garden," one primitive, the other pastoral. The pastoral ideal, especially in literature, extends back to classical antiquity. It is a quasi-utopian notion that extols the virtue and simplicity of rural life. Authors of Roman antiquity such as Virgil and Cicero vigorously cultivated this image and Jefferson knew well and admired their writing. With the revival of classical learning and art in Renaissance Italy, the pastoral ideal that the ancient authors venerated became manifest in the villas and gardens of the nobility and ecclesiastical hierarchy. Gradually this ideal disseminated into the larger European consciousness where England in the eighteenth century embarked on an unprecedented approach to garden design. These new English gardens eschewed the calculated contrast to arbitrary nature of the bounded and static geometric formalities of Italian and French precedents in favor of large-scale landscape gardens where the boundaries between artifice and nature were fundamentally indistinguishable such that the designed garden became virtual nature and reciprocally, perhaps unintentionally, nature became a virtual garden. Although different approaches to this new English landscape garden existed, they all had in common an underlying philosophical basis for their development – John Locke's epistemology.

In *An Essay Concerning Human Understanding*, Locke did not address questions of aesthetics per se. However, he provided a foundation for understanding aesthetic experience by stipulating that the ideas arising in our minds through appropriation by the senses associate with other ideas acquired through other sensations. From this network of associations, we begin to form "sympathies and antipathies" and establish priorities among them.[11] Locke's ideas and the practices they affected regarding nature, landscape, and gardening evolved during the eighteenth century into two unprecedented categories of artistic experience – the picturesque and the sublime – both of which differed significantly from the established orthodoxies and fixedness of classical beauty. They required a greater integration of natural and human, especially psychological, elements in the design of landscape gardens. Joseph Addison, an early eighteenth-century poet and essayist whom Jefferson considered a most eloquent writer, was a particularly important polemicist for a new approach to gardening. One of the reasons Jefferson admired Addison's writing is that like Jefferson, he was an avid disciple both of Locke's empirical philosophy and the pastoral poetics of

11 Locke, J. (1996): 174

Virgil. In the essays Addison wrote for his daily publication, *The Spectator*, he aspired to present philosophical issues such as Locke's empiricism in concrete, everyday terms. In the series "The Pleasures of the Imagination," especially in *The Spectator* no. 414, Addison was critical of the established tradition of English formal gardening and defined a set of principles that inaugurated the naturalistic landscape garden's evolution throughout the remainder of the century.

Addison compared the effects on the imagination of the works of nature to those of art, and found the latter wanting. He argued that works of art have nothing of nature's immensity, which affords

»so great an entertainment to the mind of the beholder [because] in the wide fields of nature the sight wanders up and down without confinement [stimulated by] an infinite variety of images.«

Such "infinite variety" is a factor of nature's "rough careless strokes" and contributes to its superiority over "the nice touches and embellishment of art."[12] Nonetheless, Addison concluded his essay by postulating a kind of aesthetic reciprocity between nature and art. The works of nature become increasingly pleasant the more they resemble works of art, both because of nature's intrinsic agreeableness to the eye and the similitude to nature that art provides. Addison did not equate nature with wilderness believing that the work of art should improve upon nature without reforming it. The same is true for landscape design, which should seek a seamless unity of nature with the garden and allow the eye to wander freely. Addison commingled the forest and the garden and thus connected nature as object of scientific understanding and human intervention with the classical pastoral ideal of nature as a pristine landscape of moral restoration. In other words, the landscape garden is a theater that weaves together nature, art, philosophy, science, and agricultural production. The approach that Addison advocated and was eventually pursued by designers is a hybrid or perhaps rather a conflict between two long established notions of nature, *natura naturans* (nature natured) and *natura naturata* (nature naturing). The first considers nature as active and productive, actively creating reality. The second considers nature as the passive object of empirical inquiry, a decidedly instrumentalist predisposition. Given Locke's empiricism, one might suppose that his approach to nature was more like the latter. However, if, as Locke states, ideas are the impact of the outside world on the senses, then nature must in some way affect the mind and there is an intimate relationship between the two. After

---

12 Addison, J. (1860): 336

all, Locke decrees that human liberty is given by nature. In essence, Addison's Enlightenment interpretation of the pastoral ideal with respect to eighteenth-century English landscape gardening corresponds with a crucial aspect of Jefferson's "Negative Capacity" – the persistent dialectic between Jefferson's own autochthonous proclivities regarding Virginia, where his heart resided, and his cosmopolitan devotion to principles of universal knowledge, reason, and enlightenment, where his mind roamed unimpeded through both time and space. For Jefferson this was a perpetual tension between the real and the virtual.

The new approach to the design of landscape gardens expanded the narrative experience of them to include psychological ramifications in addition to the tradition that their design recounts a myth or tale from classical antiquity. For example, at significant moments in Leasowes gardens, its patron, the poet William Shenstone, had engraved on large stones an accompanying literary reference that alluded to what one should experience while viewing a particular prospect.[13] Jefferson was very much taken with the eighteenth-century English landscape garden, the theories of the picturesque and sublime, and the positive attitude these espoused toward variety, diversity, and nature. His personal library contained an edition of Shenstone's *Works* as well as a number of other treatises on the subject including one on the gardens at Stowe, which he had visited with John and Abigail Adams in spring 1786. In fact, Dumas Malone has observed that Jefferson may have been the first person to include gardening, subsumed under the category of architecture, within a comprehensive system of the branches of knowledge modeled on those of Sir Francis Bacon and Jean le Rond d'Alembert.[14]

Two centuries after Hariot's report on Virginia, Jefferson wrote *Notes on the State of Virginia*, a book that fluctuates in its language between technical description and poetic reverie. In the *Notes*, he described the primeval Virginia landscape in richly sensual, almost tactile, language and explicitly defended the beneficence of rural life. His discussion echoes an Edenic statement Locke made in his *Two Treatises of Government*, a work influential on Jefferson's thoughts as he wrote the *Declaration*: "In the beginning all the world was America."[15] Jefferson's *Notes* reached for accordance between natural systems and the strivings of humanity to attempt a reconciliation between the desire for a return to the lost world of the past with the necessities of science and progress by reformulating and ex-

---

13 Shenstone, W. (1764): 128 and Dodsley, R. (1764): 336-338 and 340
14 Malone, D. (1981): 183
15 Locke, J. (2003): 121

tending the ancient pastoral ideal within the context of his own time and circumstances. Jefferson's pastoral ideal was an affirmation of a political ideal he believed could serve as a guide to social policy. It was the parturition of a new foundational myth, a dream premised on the American continent as the locus of a new world, a new kind of Virgilian pasture that is the site of a successful "Life, Liberty, and the pursuit of Happiness." To do this, Jefferson invented what Leo Marx has called a "middle landscape" for America.[16] The middle landscape is neither wild nor refined; it is the mise en scène for the necessary condition of Enlightenment humanity in the New World. It was a practical conception of humanity's relationship to nature and harbored no delusions that the European settler in America would be metamorphosed into an innocent nature-child after prolonged exposure to its undomesticated beauties. For Jefferson this was an essential part of the "American Dream" and echoes the thought of one of Jefferson's intellectual allies the Welsh moral philosopher Richard Price who wrote of the consequences of the American revolution that it defined "The happiest state of man [as] the middle state between the savage and the refined, or between the wild and the luxurious state."[17] The middle landscape mediates nature and artifice where one is effectively a mask for the other with each perpetually oscillating between being the virtual or the real of the other. For Jefferson, the art of gardening as an aspect of architecture played a large part in realizing this conception.

Jefferson's predicate for happiness in this American middle landscape was its population with a particular type of individual: "the independent, rational, democratic husbandman."[18] He used the term "husbandman" repeatedly in "Query XIX" of his *Notes on the State of Virginia* to describe this archetypal American citizen. Jefferson's husbandman does not struggle alone and unschooled against nature but employs the latest devices and techniques to establish a partnership with it to improve it for his individual needs. However, nature is not to be subdued as an individual or collective entrepreneurial enterprise. Within Jefferson's pastoral vision of life in the middle landscape, there seems to have been a subconscious awareness of a critical point beyond which the husbandman should not impose his anthropocentric purposiveness on nature.[19] Jefferson believed the industrialization and urbanization that were beginning to transmogrify Europe, especially England, unequivocally trans-

---

16 Marx, L. (1964): 126

17 Price, R. (1785): 69

18 Marx, L. (1964): 122

19 Coates, G. (1983) presents an extended discussion of human purposiveness vs natural systems

gressed this limit. This was a particularly acute problem for him because it meant an inevitable confrontation among his principles. On one hand was his love of nature and its role in the fulfillment of his pastoral vision of the United States: life in the middle landscape. On the other hand were the humanistic principles upon which the nation was founded: the sanctity and sovereignty of individual rights and the beneficial aspects of technical progress for all people.[20] Jefferson's rapprochement of this conflict was simple, perhaps simplistic: America should concentrate its efforts on the stewardship and improvement of nature and depend on Europe for manufactured items.[21]

Jefferson believed that agriculture is a primary science, but to adduce Jefferson's pastoral ideal as "agrarian" would place undue emphasis on the economic aspect of life in the middle landscape.[22] It is clear from a passage of "Query XIX" in *Notes on the State of Virginia* that he did not perceive the farm's greatest value in terms of its productive capacities. In mythopoeic language, Jefferson defends his pastoral vision and its major protagonist, the husbandman, on the moral grounds that these two things are essential to assure continued individual freedom:

»Those who labor in the earth [*the husbandmen*] are the chosen people of God [...] whose breasts He had made His peculiar deposit for substantial and genuine virtue [...] Corruption of morals in the mass of cultivators is a phaenomenon of which no age nor nation has furnished an example [...]«[23]

Like the ancient Roman authors he admired, Jefferson saw agricultural activity primarily as a moral force, as a means to preserve the virtues attached to rural life. Because such a life demands intelligent independence and self-reliance, Jefferson believed it would provoke people to remain vigilant in protecting their

---

20 In the English-speaking world of Jefferson's time, men of empirical inclination working outside the traditional academies contributed the most ingenious and useful scientific and technological developments. Together under the inspiration of Dr. William Small, they formed the Lunar Society. Dr. Small, when he resided in colonial Virginia, was Jefferson's beloved teacher and mentor.

21 Jefferson, T. (1853): 176. Twenty years after he wrote the *Notes on the State of Virginia*, during his second term as president and burdened by the disastrous embargo he had ordered, Jefferson relented from the purely rural ideal he expressed in the *Notes*.

22 Marx, L. (1964): 126

23 Jefferson, T. (1853): 176

freedom. America was to be a garden republic tilled scientifically by the hus-bandman. Freedom, in this form alone, would spare the citizenry from the tyranny of interminable repressiveness and consumptive power struggles that plagued Europe.[24] However, Jefferson's pastoral dream for America was neither static nor did it propose an ossified "perfect" society. On the contrary, it was an elastic ideal intended to give shape to the political, social, economic, and physical ephemera that defined the middle landscape. It was a utopian construct, that Jefferson knew would never fully become reality, but rather could guide it. Jefferson's middle landscape was both a garden of liberty and a landscape of virtue. Like all dreams, it postulated a virtual world.

VIRTUE AND VIRTUALITY

In addressing the obsessions of the late twentieth century world, Michel Foucault in "Of Other Spaces: Utopias and Heterotopias" examines the two spaces of his title, each of which presumes to define a direction for humanity's relationship to the world. Foucault argues that the utopia occupies "no place," a space without palpability and propinquity. It is therefore a purely virtual entity; it does not and cannot occupy material space. Alternatively, he considers heterotopia more complex in spatial terms because it is a place but one "that lies outside all places and yet is localizable" and "absolutely *other* with respect to all the arrangements [it] reflect[s]."[25] As such, "[T]he heterotopia is capable of juxtaposing in a single real place several spaces, several sites that are in themselves incompatible."[26] It is a shifting amalgamation of multiple virtualities and materialities; it is both an evanescent plurality and stochastic unity. Foucault cites the mirror as the canonical metaphor for the heterotopia because it reflects the space of the material world whether anyone is there to see into it but it also "has a kind of comeback effect on the place" occupied by the one who gazes into the mirror.[27] Yet, the mirror itself is also a concrete thing occupying real-world space even though the specific nature of its materiality is actually masked by the virtuality of what it reflects. Virtuality is both a means of revealing and concealing.

---

24 Marx, L. (1964): 139
25 Foucault, M. (1997): 352
26 Foucault, M. (1997): 354
27 Foucault, M. (1997): 352

In delineating the various kinds of heterotopias, Foucault discerns that all of them are institutions of some sort and his general thrust in examining them is to consider them primarily as a mechanism of social control, discipline, and exercise of power rather than as a means to enhance or encourage individual virtue. However, it is not difficult to see that some heterotopias, e.g., schools, prisons, and asylums, might presume to stimulate the growth of virtue among their charges as a raison d'etre of their wielding of power. In this latter respect, two kinds of heterotopia are particularly relevant to the present discussion. Although Foucault does not explicitly cite the university as a heterotopia, it is quite clear from his discussion that it is. Alternatively, he is quite specific regarding the garden, which he cites as one of the oldest heterotopias because it attempts to draw the entire world into itself. The visual ambiguity of boundary in the English landscape gardens of the eighteenth century presumed to do precisely this. The pastoral ideal discussed above was both predicated on landscape as garden and a means to a more virtuous life. Moreover, since Jefferson's dream for America lay in its creation as a kind of virtuous garden republic, a new pastoral ideal manifest as the "middle landscape," his University was not only a model for it but presumably would produce graduates who, imbued with those virtues, would preserve it. In essence, just as there is an etymological link between the two words virtue and virtuality, there is also a conceptual and physical link between them that infused Jefferson's intentions for creating the University of Virginia. Obviously virtue and virtuality are not the same thing. Despite their common linguistic root, a vital and variable tension exists between the two. The highest virtue for Jefferson was to live the good life and be free to pursue happiness, the American dream. But it was happiness in the manner described by Epicurus, to live wisely, prudently, and justly. Like all dreams the American dream is a purely virtual thing but eminently real in one's pursuit of it. The highest virtues though understandable are always unattainable; they can only be virtual.

ACADEMICAL VILLAGE AS MASQUE

The plan shown in figure 1 indicates the layout and various buildings of Jefferson's design of the University as finally constructed. The plan has several precedents, all of which arrange all buildings around a single rectangle of space with a principal building at one end and the opposite end open. Jefferson's original plan was like these precedents and required an essentially flat topography. However, because the site he wanted was unavailable, he had to accept one with significant topographical irregularities that precluded using the plan he originally envisioned. He solved this problem by creating a unique variant on the established precedents by considerably reducing the width of the central green space, the Lawn, and adding two outer ranks of buildings to the more irregular east and west slopes of the site's extremities, the east slope being especially pronounced. Conversely, he adapted the two inner ranks to the gentle north to south downward slope of the central part of the site. Jefferson's site design as well as his designs for the buildings have a superficial appearance of harmony and serenity, especially given the patina of time.

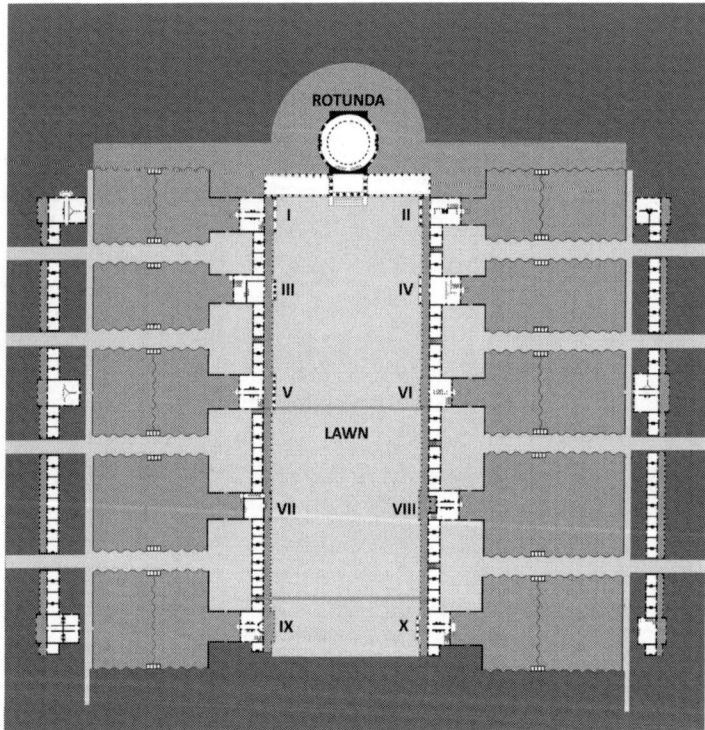

Figure 1. Academical village plan. [28]

However, a closer examination shows that this genteel veneer masks a much more fractious architectural actuality that corresponds with the inherent tensions of Jefferson's "Negative Capacity" and his republican political ideals. It constitutes a

---

28 Figure copyright David Bell & Jillian Crandall.

set of virtual and potentially paradoxical conditions that align well with many of the qualities and characteristics of Foucault's notion of heterotopia. The paradox is particularly evident in the soubriquet Jefferson chose to portray his University as a community of scholars dedicated to liberty – "academic village." However, the University of Virginia cannot be a village in the real sense because it has stringent limits on who can inhabit it. One does not come and go as one pleases. Despite having the formal and spatial characteristics of a well-planned village, it necessarily lacks the programmatic diversity of a typical village. It is a village only in a virtual sense. Jefferson's design is nonetheless an accurate reflection of his view of reality as both an evanescent plurality and stochastic unity composed of a hierarchy of diversities that accepts the occurrence of chance events and change within an ordered framework. Thus, it perhaps corresponds to some of the endemic inconsistencies of the heterotopia that Foucault implies. Tightly woven into Jefferson's design is a socio-political ideal fraught with the pathos and irony of his personal philosophy. Several instances within this spatial fabric of fleeting plurality and aleatory unity suggest a masque-like quality.

The masque may be a suitable metaphor to consider the various subtleties of Jefferson's design because it was a multi-faceted form of performance that used virtuality to provoke reality; i.e., the idea of revealing something by concealing it. The masque was a form of aristocratic entertainment in Europe that probably developed from the ducal courts of Burgundy in the Middle Ages. It involved a variety of different forms of performance such as pantomime, dance, song, and dialog and usually drew its imagery from classical rather than Christian sources. Unquestionably Jefferson knew of the tradition of the masque. Ostensibly, its purpose was the laudatory magnification of the ruler. However, given his anathema toward aristocracy and royalty, it seems unlikely he would consciously have chosen it as a trope for his design of the academical village. Yet, aspects of the masque make it a useful way to describe certain of the qualities as well as the anomalies in Jefferson's design. For example, as the courtly masque evolved through subsequent centuries, it was frequently pastoral and would often illustrate a moral tale or ethical dilemma that invariably had a political or social subtext. Recent scholarship has shown that the masque should "be viewed as a diverse expression of conflicting arenas of interest within court culture" instead of being "primarily a symbolic ceremony vital to the reproduction of monarchical power."[29] It is especially worthwhile to consider the masques created by the seventeenth-century English author John Milton. Jefferson admired Milton's poetry and considered him an important advocate for free speech. Milton's masques have the

---

29 Bevington, D., and Holbrook, P. (1998): 8

teaching of virtue as an important thrust to their allegories; their performance masked an implicit critique of the court and court aesthetics. In particular, Milton's *Comus* has a subtext that repudiated Neoplatonist mystifications, which would have had special appeal to Jefferson.[30]

The paramount importance Jefferson accorded to the individual's natural rights was a declaration of his own inability or unwillingness to give full positive form to the concept of community despite his appreciation of the ideal of *sensus communis*. This dilemma indicates a contrast between two different ways of understanding freedom. One way construes freedom as positive liberty, which is an irrevocable right guaranteed by law, a right that government can stipulate. The "First Amendment" to the *U. S. Constitution* defines such liberty. The other liberty is negative, which is freedom that a person possesses without legal restriction. The "First Amendment" in particular is interesting because it codifies as a positive liberty those freedoms that Jefferson believed were inherently negative liberties, i.e., they are unalienable and given by nature not government. The "Ninth and Tenth Amendments," which address non-enumerated rights, in their concision are even broader with respect to negative liberties, i.e., where community and government may not intrude. Thus, enshrined in Jefferson's design for the University of Virginia is an architectural performance of the great dialectic of democracy – the tension between positive and negative liberties. The necessary freedom of the individual suggested by the unique architectural expression of each of the Lawn's ten Pavilions opposes the rule of law or comprehensive order, which is represented by the uniformity and seeming continuity of the colonnades that bind the Pavilions together (see figure 2a). Each Pavilion is an independent architectural entity that refers back to the whole without capitulating to a rigidly unifying order. This dialectic corresponds closely to what Manfredo Tafuri defines as the great crisis of modern architecture, the tension between the individual building as a discrete, self-sufficient integer, such as the Pavilions, and that building's existence within an urban order, such as a village, in this case an academical village.[31]

---

30 Lewalski, B. (1998): 296-315

31 Tafuri, M. (1976): 16-22

Figure 2. Left: a) colonnade between Pavilions II and IV, right: b) break in continuity at Pavilion V.[32]

Figure 3 (top). Left: a) Pavilion IX, right: b) Pavilion X.[33]
Figure 3 (bottom). Left: c) south entry to Lawn at Pavilion IX, center: d) south entry to Lawn at Pavilion X, right e) oblique view of Pavilion X.[34]

The two Pavilions, IX and X, that terminate the sequence of buildings of the Lawn engender differing, even opposing, impressions depending on how one sees them and therefore both of them embody their own respective virtual images. Seen frontally, each occupies the last terrace of the Lawn as an emphatic termination *á point* to the Lawn's buildings (see figures 3a and b). However, when viewed looking to the north, each combines with the colonnade and single dormitory room to appear as an entry to the Lawn's upward progression to the Rotunda, the University's library and the formal and pedagogical epitome of the entire scheme (see figures 3c and d). When seen obliquely each, especially Pavilion X, appears as a dynamic weaving of the colonnade with the building implying the potential for extension (see figure 3e). This stochastic unity is foiled by the evanescent plurality of the Pavilions taken as a whole. Counter to the similarities of Pavilion IX and Pavilion X as terminations, entries, or implied extension are their respective compositions. The colonnade in front of Pavilion IX obscures its defining architectural order, which supports the arch of its exedral entry. Combined with the building's simple massing, the entry makes the Pavilion appear modest and introspective. Alternatively, the massing of Pavilion X, particularly its recently restored original, rather cumbersome, massing, combines with the assertiveness of its Doric portico to contrast markedly with its opposite on the West Lawn. This dialectical relationship between Pavilions IX and X is a fundamental characteristic of each opposing pair of the Lawn's Pavilions (see figure 4). The spacing between the columns of the portico of Pavilion I is much more relaxed than that of Pavilion II directly across from it. The portico of Pavilion V is a pronounced giant-order hexastyle whereas Pavilion VI has no such portico, the Lawn's Tuscan colonnade is its single-story architectural order. Though they are only a single story high and above the arcade of the first story, the columns of Pavilion VII project from the building mass behind them whereas the columns of its opposite, Pavilion VIII, are giant order and coplanar with their building mass but obscured by the Tuscan colonnade of the continuous portico. Despite the relative similarity of the porticoes of Pavilions III and IV, like Pavilions I and II their respective column spacings differ owing to their distinctive column orders. In fact, each pair of opposing Pavilions has a differing column order. The variety of massing and architectural expression of the ten Pavilions at one time was the object of criticism for not conforming to the unity suggested by Jefferson's overall site plan for the University.[35] However, perceived in a less stagnantly formal way,

---

34 Figure 3c & d copyright David Bell

35 Wilson, R. G. (2009): 57-58

the sequence of oppositions among the Pavilions imparts a consistent east-west dynamic tension across the Lawn space that is most noticeable during seasons when the trees have lost their foliage.

Throughout the entire formal and spatial order of the University, tension such as that between the Lawn's opposing Pavilions is virtually unrelenting and belies one's initial impressions of the serenity of this place. For example, the seeming continuity of the Lawn colonnades becomes quite tentative where major physical changes occur (changes of level and scale, the articulation of ends and beginnings, turns of corners, etc.). At these places, one would expect the architectural statement to be strongest and strident juxtapositions resolved in order to reinforce the unity of the whole, but many of the connections exist only by the propinquity of their respective architectural forms; others are perfunctory and seem somewhat clumsy (see figure 2b). Where the expression of coherence of the whole community of buildings could be most clear and gracious is precisely where it is most ambiguous, indeterminate, and haphazard. This lack of formal resolution may be attributable to Jefferson's amateur status as an architect, but given the depth of his scholarship and knowledge of architecture, it seems unlikely. It may have more to do with his pragmatism, but it could also be due to his proclivity to rebel against the determinism of a too rigorous system of any kind. This is especially the case when we recall the profound influence the thought of Epicurus had on him. Epicurus was an advocate of the controversial atomist view of nature and devised the notion of the *clinamen*, which presumes that large objects form because the indeterminacy of the motion of atoms (*clinamen* means a swerve) necessitates their ultimate entanglement with one another. The ancient Roman philosopher Lucretius, whose work Jefferson also knew and respected, was a disciple of Epicurus' ideas and extended the indeterminacy principle of the *clinamen* to claim it as the thing that differentiates humans from automata.[36] The *clinamen* also has a kind of peripheral relationship to the idea of the *informe* introduced in the 1920s by the French writer and literary critic Georges Bataille. His definition of the *informe* is rather vague but can be described as the tendency inherent in the creation of every form to destabilize or undermine that form's very organizing principle. Bataille's notion of the *informe* had a significant effect on the emergent avant-garde in the 1920s and 30s and eventually on the formulation of various aspects of postmodern thought and architecture in the latter third of the twentieth century.

---

36 The conceptual similarity between Lucretius's ancient atomistic principle of indeterminism and the twentieth-century foundational concept of indeterminism in Heisenberg's uncertainty principle of quantum physics is noteworthy and well known.

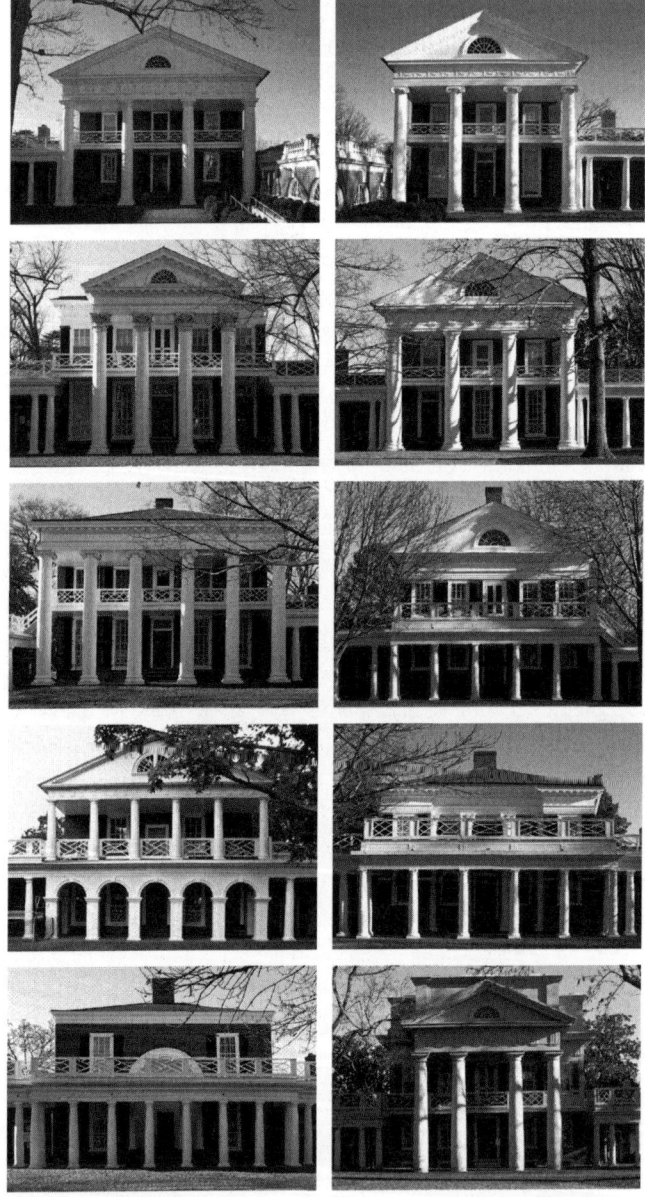

Figure 4. Pavilions in descending order, odd numbered on left, even on right. [37]

---

37 Figure copyright David Bell & Karen Blaha.

Jefferson's University complex manifests yet another distinct aspect of his sense of evanescent plurality. This occurs in the successive lengthening of distance toward the south between the Pavilions on either side of the Lawn. Shown in the plan of figure 1, this lengthening contributes to shifting but meaningful forced perspective illusions. Jefferson did not consciously design in perspective, but the result of his graduating the distances between the Pavilions creates dynamic and contrasting effects of forced perspective illusion that depend on whether one views the Lawn complex from the north or south. The rise of the Lawn's three terraces as they progress northward, reinforce vertically the effect of the illusions. Illusion is inherently a mask; it creates multiple perceptions of the same thing, a flickering plurality of possibilities wherein one of them maintains momentary dominance only to have another supplant it. It is quintessentially virtual but also grounded in a real condition. The relativity of illusion has a dialectical quality that requires the individual observer to make a choice. Because the contrasting perceptions of the Lawn space occur from opposing vantage points rather than the same position, they are not just temporally dependent as optical illusions frequently are. To perceive the different illusions of spatial depth at the Lawn, one must move from its south extremity to the northern one, which introduces to the illusions a factor of spatial as well as temporal displacement. Of course, it is now only possible to get even a remote sense of these illusions during the winter months.

Standing at the southern end of the Lawn on axis with the Rotunda, the forced perspective illusion created by the decreasing distances between Pavilions as the colonnades proceed northward gives the impression that the Rotunda is further away than it actually is. But, the Rotunda is not perceived to be larger than it actually is; it is apperceived to be so and becomes all the more dominant. The Lawn's openness to the distant horizon on the south end is reminiscent of the idea in English landscape gardening to blur the boundary between nature and artifice. The silhouette of the distant mountainous landscape against the sky balances the infinite wonder of nature with the equally infinite possibilities of human aspiration embodied by the Rotunda that dominates its northern end. The forced perspective illusion works in reverse when standing on the Rotunda's terrace facing the Lawn looking southward. In Jefferson's day, the lengthening colonnades between the Pavilions tended to make the distant Ragged Mountains appear closer linking the University more strongly to its natural setting within Albemarle County's rolling landscape. As part of the University's expansion in the early twentieth century, its rector commissioned McKim, Meade, and White to design a complex of three buildings on a site about three hundred yards further south from the Lawn's south end. The centerpiece of this group, Cabell Hall, cuts off this view.

If Jefferson consciously created the Lawn's forced perspective illusions, it demonstrates his "Negative Capacity" to accept the equal validity of conflicting bits of evidence and is no mere perceptual trick. These illusions might subliminally attest to a dilemma that was a constant concern for Jefferson that he alluded to in his *Notes on the State of Virginia*, the tension between the authority of nature as manifested in the distant landscape with the power of human reason embodied in the Rotunda, a tension between *natura naturans* and *natura naturata*. As such, this dilemma implicitly acknowledges a fundamental aspect of the human predicament, which is the nondeterministic nature of ethics as Aristotle defines it in *Nichomachean Ethics*: "that fiber in all people that reveals choice, what sort of thing a person chooses or avoids in circumstances where choice is not obvious."

A curious dichotomy also exists between one's experience of the University along its multiple east-west axes defined by the five pairs of opposing Pavilions versus the views defined by the Lawn's dominant singular north-south axis. Despite the differences in forced perspective views between the northern and southern extremities, views along this axis, tend to reinforce a perception of unity that undermines any consciousness of the formal tensions between the Lawn's east and west opposing Pavilions. Consequently, the space of the Lawn seems continuous, homogeneous, and natural. However, the oppositions between the east and west Pavilions adumbrate the presence of a considerably less homogeneous spatial order that can neither be seen from the Lawn nor all-at-once. It is, in fact, a fractured order, a quasi-virtual order, that has only an inconspicuous linkage among its parts, which are peripherally dispersed throughout the complex. Discovery of this alternate heterogeneous order is difficult because no easily discernible clue exists in any part of it that manifestly suggests a necessary connection to its other parts. The impact of this order is at best subliminal. Its formal expression, the strategic axial placement or non-placement of individual colonnade columns at points of entry to the Lawn from the East and West Ranges, sublimates the tenuously unifying premise of that expression, which is the varying ways one appropriates the space of the Lawn in relation to the irregular topography of the whole complex and its surrounding landscape.

The presence or absence of these individual columns at crucial moments suggests a particular sophistication in Jefferson's design thought at the scale of immediate experience in order to provide a compensatory coherence to the anomalies of the site's topography. Jefferson's final plan of the academical village shows seven approaches and openings to the Lawn from the East and West Ranges via alleys (see figure 5a). Walking along either of the Lawn colonnades and passing by any of these openings one may only be marginally aware of them. Five of these approaches are axially direct; a column of the colonnade framed in the opening of each approach to the Lawn marks the termination of its respective axis. Four of the five approaches with a column on axis occur on the east and only one occurs on the west. The entire East Range is at an elevation considerably below the Lawn. Thus, as one moves up the hill from the East Range to the Lawn, the column in the opening silhouettes against the foliage of the Lawn's trees and is the sole acknowledgment of the capacious presence of the Lawn and its bounding colonnade (see figure 5b). The axial column marks a kind of threshold. Only three entrances to the Lawn come from the West Range where the elevation of the topography in relation to the Lawn varies; it is not nearly as pronounced as that on the east and progresses from slightly lower than the Lawn at the north end of the West Range to slightly higher at the south end. The only approach to the Lawn from the west that has a column terminating its axis, like those on the east, occurs with a slight uphill rise toward the Lawn (see figure 5c). The other two approaches to the Lawn go slightly downhill from the topographical level of the West Range buildings. Each of these two downward approaches eventually opens to the Lawn at a point that corresponds to a change in the level of the Lawn's middle terrace. These two approaches have no axial relationship to a colonnade column so the space of the Lawn itself is never visible until one is actually in the small passageway between buildings that connects the service yard to the Lawn (see figure 5d). Experienced individually without the opportunity to compare the relationship of each to its respective entry to the Lawn and the site topography, the seven approaches, with or without an axial column, seem only to be local irregularities within the larger order. However, in spite of their dispersion and subliminal nature, when understood as a group, the logical consistency yet evanescent plurality and stochastic unity of these lateral entries to the Lawn links the whole of the scheme together in an unexpectedly enigmatic way. Thus, what may appear to be an entirely desultory condition of the relationship of colonnade columns to the points of access to the Lawn from the east and west is actually the vaporous index of the deep order that emerged from the necessity for Jefferson to adapt his original plan to the vicissitudes of the site – a necessity that resulted in a much more sophisticated design than his original plan.

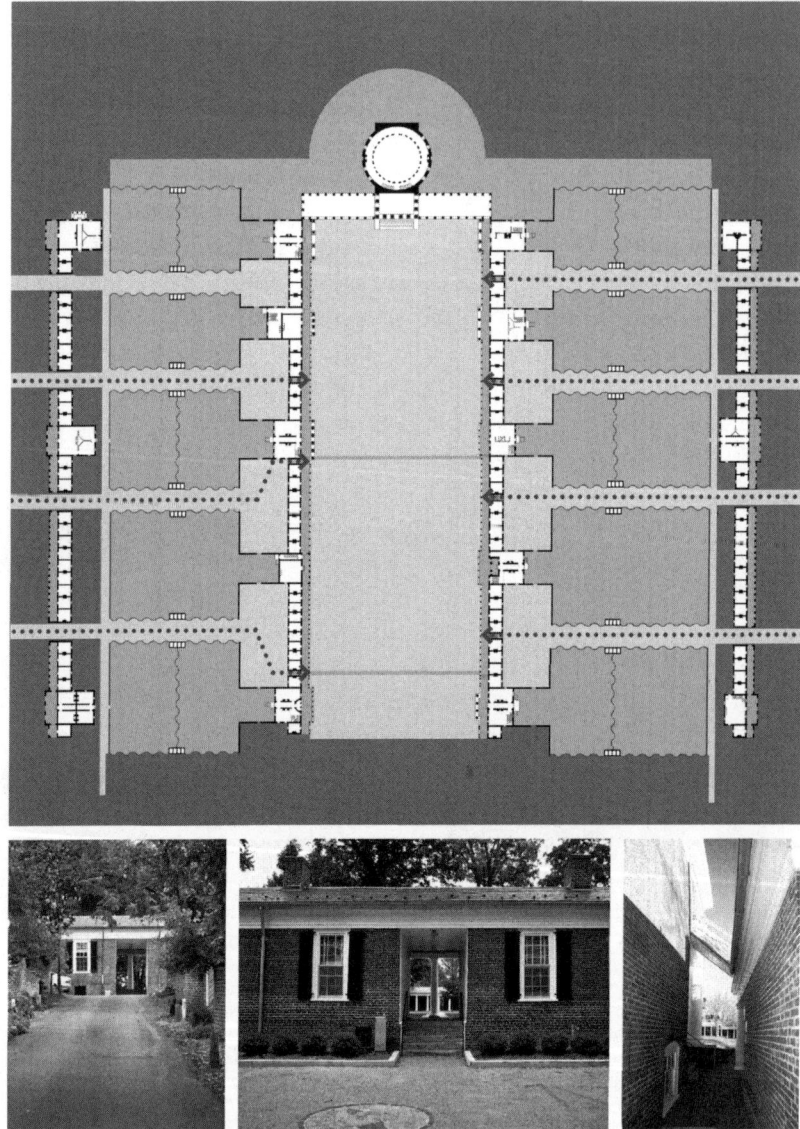

Figure 5. Top:a)Village plan with entries to Lawn from east and west, left: b) approach to Lawn from East Range, center: c) approach to Lawn from West Range, right: d) approach to Lawn from West Range.[38]

38 Figure 5a copyright David Bell & Jillian Crandall, figures 5b, c and d copyright David Bell.

CONCLUSION

The variety of tensions concealed within Jefferson's design are far too subtle to be a polemic that ingrains his philosophy within anyone. In all their rich complexity and inconsistency, they are simply a declaration of Jefferson's beliefs phrased in the penumbral language of space and form rather than the effulgent prose of his *Declaration of Independence*. More importantly, it matters little if Jefferson consciously intended to express these things architecturally. The fact is that they exist because with some effort we can discern them. They are rather like sub-atomic phenomena as considered by quantum physics; they come into existence only in the moment one takes their measure. Before that, they had only a possibility of existing, which is a particularly contemporary way of saying that they inhabit a virtual state.

The philosophy of John Locke also had a profound influence on the eighteenth-century popular author Laurence Sterne whose books were a great favorite of Jefferson because they offered humorous and ironic insights into the human predicament. Jefferson owned at least two Sterne novels, *The Life and Opinions of Tristram Shandy, Gentleman* and its epilogue, *A Sentimental Journey through France and Italy by Mr. Yorick*. Sterne's work is notable for many reasons but importantly for the present discussion because in writing both novels he resorted to virtual authors, Shandy and Yorick respectively. No doubt Yorick's descriptions of his travels in Europe's mainland against the backdrop of the many upheavals occurring there in the mid-eighteenth century captivated Jefferson's imagination because it inaugurated a new way of travel writing that discussed the manners and morals of contemporaneous life in terms of the subjective reflections and individual tastes of its ostensible author. In fact, Mr. Yorick observes that things are not always as they appear to be and ironically conceal themselves in conventions that engender their anomalies – rather like a masque. Yorick's, i.e., Sterne's, words on that matter have several meanings and seem to sum up fittingly Jefferson and his design of the University of Virginia's academical village:

»Hail ye small sweet courtesies of life, for smooth do ye make the road of it! like grace and beauty which beget inclinations to love at first sight; 'tis ye who open this door and let the stranger in.« [39]

---

39 Sterne, L. (2004): 43

REFERENCES

Adams, John and Adams, Charles Francis (1856): *The Works of John Adams, Second President of the United States*, Volume 1, Boston: Little, Brown and Company.

Addison, Joseph (1860): *The Works of Joseph Addison: The Spectator*, Volume VI, George Washington Greene, ed., New York, Derby & Jackson.

Bevington, David, and Holbrook, Peter, eds. (1998): *The Politics of the Stuart Court Masque*, Cambridge: Cambridge University Press.

Coates, Gary J. (1983): "Planning and the Paradox of Conscious Purpose", in *Resettling America: Energy, Ecology and Community*, Andover: Brickhouse.

Creighton, Theresa A. (2008): *Freedom and the Ideal Republican State: Kant, Jefferson, and the Place of Individual Freedom in the Republican Constitutional State*, Office of Graduate Studies, Georgia State University College of Arts and Sciences: http://digitalarchive.gsu.edu/philosophy theses/39.

Dillon, John Myles (1988): *The Question of Eclecticism: Studies in Later Greek Philosophy*, Berkeley: University of California Press.

Dodsley, R. (1982): *A Description of Leasowes*, John Dixon Hunt, ed., New York: Garland.

Foucault, Michel (1997): "Of Other Spaces: Utopias and Heterotopias", in *Rethinking Architecture: A Reader in Cultural Theory*, Neil Leach, ed., London: Routledge.

Jefferson, Thomas (January 16, 1811): *Letter to Dr. Benjamin Rush*, Monticello.

Jefferson, Thomas (October 31, 1819): *Letter to William Short*, Monticello.

Jefferson, Thomas (August 15, 1820): *Letter to John Adams*, Monticello.

Jefferson, Thomas (1853): *Notes on the State of Virginia*, Richmond: J.W. Randolph.

Keats, John (Sunday, December 21, 1817): *Letter to George Keats* (John Keats' brother).

Lewalski, Barbara K. (1998): "Milton's *Comus* and the Politics of Masquing", in *The Politics of the Stuart Court Masque*, David Bevington and Peter Holbrook, eds., Cambridge: Cambridge University Press.

Locke, John (1996): *An Essay Concerning Human Understanding*, Kenneth P. Winkler, ed., Indianapolis: Hackett Publishing Company.

Locke, John (2003): *Two Treatises of Government and a Letter of Toleration*, Ian Shapiro, ed., New Haven: Yale University Press.

Malone, Dumas (1981): *The Sage of Monticello*, Boston: Little, Brown and Company.

Marx, Leo (1964): *The Machine in the Garden*, London: Oxford University Press.

Peterson, Merrill (1970): *Thomas Jefferson and the New Nation: A Biography*, New York: Oxford University Press.

Price, Richard (1785): *Observations on the importance of the American Revolution, and the means of making it a benefit to the world*, Dublin: White et al.

Rasmussen, William M. S., and Tilton, Robert S. (2003): *Old Virginia: The Pursuit of a Pastoral Ideal*, Charlottesville: Howell Press.

Shenstone, William (1982): *Unconnected Thoughts on Gardening*, John Dixon Hunt, ed., New York: Garland.

Sterne, Laurence (2004): *A Sentimental Journey*, Greg Boroson, ed., Mineola: Dover Publications.

Tafuri, Manfredo (1976): *Architecture and Utopia*, Cambridge: MIT Press.

Wilson, Richard Guy (2009): *Thomas Jefferson's Academical Village*, Charlottesville: University of Virginia Press.

The Building of a Symbolic Image

The Juxtaposition of Giambattista Piranesi's *Vedute Di Roma* with Photographs Taken 250 Years Later

RANDOLPH LANGENBACH

Figure 1. Roman Forum from Mayor's office window, 2002, with Piranesi's view from the same vantage point.

INTRODUCTION: THE HISTORY OF A RUIN AS A RUIN

By unique coincidence, I was in Rome for a brief week exactly when the page proofs of this Anthology arrived in my email, forcing me to confront the dialectic between the "real" of being in Rome, with the "virtual" as described in this chapter. It was a rainy week in Rome, and the difference between Piranesi's era and our own was magnified by the experience of looking upon the extraordinarily rich visual scenes of Roman ruins and Renaissance palaces while dodging cars driven at breakneck speed through narrow cobblestone-streets without sidewalks. At one and the same time, the taut urban spaces – real examples of a lost urban design ideal – had been transformed into the urban equivalents of rushing river torrents, leaving the poor pedestrians feeling as vulnerable as if standing on a slippery rock for fear that at any false step may catapult them under the wheels of the passing automobiles.

In the modern day, the Ancient Roman Forum provides an escape from the Roman traffic, but it is a gated park with tourists from afar, crowds of whom are led by flag-waving guides as they traverse the paths between the barricades around the archeological remains.

When undertaking the documentation of the Piranesi *Vedute* 10 years earlier, the temporal scenes of traffic and tourists faded in my consciousness when I retreated to my studio at the top of the Janiculum, where the "real" as documented in my digital photography was slowly transformed into a kind of hybrid space, as I overlaid and merged the photographs into Piranesi's extraordinary images of the same landscapes from a quarter of a millennium ago.

THE HISTORY OF A RUIN AS A RUIN

A visitor arriving today at the site of the ancient Forum in the center of Rome looks out over a ruin that is a veritable symbol of an entire civilization whose origins extend back more than two millennia (Figure 1). What is seen in this and the other archeological sites within Rome is but a tiny fragment of what was actually constructed by the ancient Romans, yet the fragments that are visible in Rome, or likewise in Athens, Cairo or other sites of great ancient cities, form complete visual and cultural artifacts in their own right — in much the same way that the granite cliffs of the Sierra Nevada mountains, eroded by time, form a single image of sublime beauty where they face each other across the Yosemite Valley. One wonders: Could the vandals and lime burners who pillaged the ancient temples of the Forum be said to have inadvertently left behind a singular work of art? Does the Roman Forum's value as a cultural artifact depend on keeping its ruins in as unchanged a state from their current condition as possible?

For centuries the remains of classical Rome were not valued for their cultural or artistic attributes, at least not by those in the position of power to determine their fate. Indeed, they were systematically quarried for lime and building stone over the centuries under permissions and directives granted by the Catholic Popes, who had complete control over the city in that era. Even Bernini's remarkable baldacchino under the dome of St. Peters is said to have been fabricated from the bronze ceiling dismantled from the proanos of the Pantheon and melted down by Pope Urban VIII. Fortunately, in the eighteenth century this pattern of destruction ended, for had it gone on much longer, nothing would have remained as a physical record of classical Rome – a magnificent imperial city of two million residents that was not to be exceeded in size in the West until nineteenth-century London and Paris.

The fact that this pillaging stopped around the time that Giambattista Piranesi's famous Vedute of the ruins of ancient Rome together with the Renaissance city were disseminated throughout Europe was no mere coincidence. While other artists had also illustrated these ruins, it was Piranesi's work that most profoundly elevated these ruins into the consciousness of many Europeans. The wide dissemination of his prints helped launch the "grand tour" to Italy, which then led to the future archeological investigation and conservation of these ruins. As observed by French novelist Marguerite Yourcenar: *"the very circulation of his [Piranesi's] works, counts among the elements which have gradually changed the public's attitude, and finally that of the authorities themselves, and which have led us to the labeled, scrubbed, and replastered ruins of today, object of state solicitude and a national treasure of organized tourism."*[1] In effect, therefore, his illustrations helped transform the views of the ruins in and around Rome into symbolic images – a kind of "virtual reality" – that continue, even today, to influence the way that people look at and see the archeological sites themselves.

In order to fully grasp the cultural meaning of the Roman ruins as artifacts, it is important to acknowledge that the Roman archeological sites have been in ruins for a considerably longer time than they ever existed as intact buildings. It is as ruins that they have become symbols of the classical Roman civilization in contemporary history, literature, and art. For this reason, it is important to recognize their history as ruins. This is a vital aspect of the power of the images created by Piranesi and his contemporaries, and it is part of the reason why the fragmentary remains of the ancient ruins became recognized in the eighteenth century as the icons of a great, but now vanished, civilization. And, it was this very recognition that finally put a stop to their use as quarries and landfill sites after more than a millennium of such abuse.

---

1 Yourcenar, M. (1962): 123

GIAMBATTISTA PIRANESI (1720–1778)
AND THE *VEDUTE DI ROMA*

Giovanni Battista Piranesi was born and raised in Venice, a center of artistic ferment at the end of the Baroque Era. His early work reflects the influence of the theatrical and scenographic imagery for which Venice was famous. Although trained as an architect, Piranesi is known to have designed only one completed building, Santa Maria del Priorato, the Priory Church of the Knights of Malta, constructed in 1765. As an artist, however, Piranesi was extraordinarily prolific, producing approximately 1,200 engravings over the course of his life.[2] Both in his time and since he has been recognized as "one of the greatest artists in the history of etching and the Vedute genre" and as someone who "would permanently alter how people emotionally perceive the ancient world and the city that, in Piranesi's opinion, best represented it – Rome."[3] French novelist Marguerite Yourcenar, in her essay "The Dark Brain of Piranesi," observed:

»The genius of the Baroque has given Piranesi the intuition of that pre-Baroque architecture created by Imperial Rome; it has preserved him from the cold academicism of his successors, with whom he is sometimes confused, and for whom the monuments of Antiquity are no more than scholarly texts. It is to the Baroque that Piranesi, in his *Vedute,* owes these sudden breakdowns of equilibrium, this very deliberate readjustment of perspective, this analysis of mass which is for its period a conquest as considerable as the Impressionists' analysis of light later on.«[4]

Piranesi designed his images to capture a sense of the entirety of complex environments of architectural ruins, so as to represent the experience of the Roman landscape to people who more than likely would not have had a chance to visit Rome in person, not as a vignettes, but iconic views of the monuments in their settings. He aimed to capture the visual and symbolic essence of those artifacts, and to accomplish this goal he frequently, as Marguerite Yourcenar said, adjust-

---

2 Ficacci, L. (2000). This number has been arrived at by taking the number reproduced in this volume and adding approximately 10% to account for others lost or not included. Piranesi used both acid etching and direct engraving in the making of his plates, often with both on the same plate, especially in later states. For the sake of simplicity, the use of the term "engraving" will refer to the final product of either etching or engraving.

3 Ficacci, L. (2000): 11-12.

4 Yourcenar, M. (1962): 97

ed his vanishing points with shifts in the viewpoint and angle of view. At times he also combined views from widely separated viewpoints into a single image as seen for example in figure 7. In terms of the theme of this anthology, Piranesi's *vedute* were, as will be shown below, both remarkably accurate representations of the monuments shown, while at the same time they carried within the flat images a visual power that in certain of his most successful prints has sometimes been seen as more iconic than the real views of monuments portrayed. As described below with a quote from Goethe written shortly after Piranesi's death, a number of the late 18th and 19th century visitors on the grand tour reported disappointment when they arrived at the sites in Rome they were attracted to after seeing Piranesi's prints in their home countries.

Piranesi shared his first and middle names with another famous engraver – Giovanni Battista Nolli (1701-1756) with whom for a time he worked. While Piranesi became the master of the view, Nolli was Rome's greatest cartographer. Even though 20 years Nolli's junior, Piranesi became a colleague of Nolli, reflecting their shared expertise in surveying and topographical detail. Piranesi, the great antiquarian and first generation archaeologist that he became, even took Nolli to task over the placement of the Theater of Pompey in Nolli's *Pianta Grande*. Piranesi was also a contemporary of the other well-known Italian engraver of *Vedute di Roma*, Giuseppe Vasi (1710—1782), but Piranesi's work demonstrated his greater scenographic creativity, producing an extraordinarily large body of work that is more evocative than any of his contemporaries. Piranesi's name has even become an adjective in the English language: "Piranesian" – a reference to the kind of heroic but partially torn and ruined spaces that he both documented and, in other instances, invented.

What makes Piranesi's topographical art so compelling is that he managed in some of his most expressive prints to capture not only the essence of both the buildings and ruins as such, but also included the space that surrounded and enveloped the subjects. No longer are the subjects of his art simply archeological or architectural artifacts on display. The larger visualized spaces have become the subject, inspiring the viewer to seek them out on the ground in order to complete the experience. However, Piranesi was not creating images to serve only as memorabilia. In his writings, Piranesi described a very different and more didactic purpose for his work:

»When I first saw the remains of the ancient buildings of Rome lying as they do in cultivated fields or gardens and wasting away under the ravages of time, or being destroyed by greedy owners who sell them as materials for modern buildings, I determined to preserve them forever by means of my engravings.«[5]

Figure 2. An image from the Piranesi Project showing Piranesi's engraving of the vestibule of the Piccole Terme (Smaller Baths) at Hadrian's Villa, near Tivoli, with the engraving by Piranesi partially dissolved revealing the composite photo of the same space in 2003. This view required ten photographs to cover Piranesi's wide-angle composition, as well as provide exposure compensation for the sunlit and shaded areas.

Piranesi succeeded in his endeavor to a remarkable extent. When his views became famous throughout Europe, they helped to give birth to modern-day tourism to Rome and the rest of the Italian peninsula. As the number of visitors to Rome grew, the systematic pillaging and quarrying of the monuments ceased. The publicity that Piranesi and his contemporaries brought to Rome and its ancient monuments can, therefore, be classified as one of the most successful ex-

---

5   Piranesi, G. (1756)

amples in the history of Europe of preservation activism advanced by the creation and publication of images.

Piranesi's work continues to be influential, but time and change, and, ironically, the influence of photography have tended to separate it from its original subject matter. Tourists are sometimes familiar with his work, but rarely take his images into the field to relate them to the actual sites, and the images only rarely show up in guidebooks. A number of modern-day photographers, notably Herschel Levit and David Brooke, have undertaken to document the sites of his views photographically, but his compositions do not lend themselves to easy replication with a camera.[6] The attempts to capture the Piranesi views with photographs have been frustrated by the inability of a camera – even with the widest of flat-field lenses – to encompass the full scope and breadth of Piranesi's compositions, many of which encompass a horizontal spread of as much as 180°. Thus, rarely have photographic juxtapositions with Piranesi's views succeeded in capturing the engraved scenes in their entirety. More importantly, such photographs also rarely possess the kind of taut energy and dramatic impact that characterize Piranesi's art. This fact may have contributed to the widespread belief that Piranesi somehow radically distorted his views or portrayed the monuments in made-up settings.

Herschel Levit, an American photographer and art professor who undertook a project to photograph the same views engraved by Piranesi that was published in 1976, admitted in his preface that *"it is frequently difficult, and in some cases impossible, to correlate the views. Piranesi used a complete panoramic sweep of 180°. In drawing his sketches, he turned his head to the left and to the right. The camera cannot duplicate this without catastrophic distortions, such as those produced by a fisheye lens."*[7] Steven Brooke, who later undertook a similar project with a view camera with swings and tilts[8] while on a Rome Prize Fellowship at the American Academy in Rome in 1991 also stated that at the outset he *"did not consider fish-eye or ultra-wide panoramic lenses or multiple-image photomontage appropriate for this work...In some cases, no single lens of any kind would encompass what Piranesi included in his image."*[9]

---

6 Herschel, L. (1976) & Brooke, S. (1995)

7 Herschel, L. (1976)

8 Levit used a fixed lens, rather than a zoom lens camera for his images.

9 Brooke, S. (1995)

PHOTOGRAPHY IN THE FOOTSTEPS OF PIRANESI

For a modern-day photographer working in Piranesi's footsteps, the choices are different than they were for Piranesi. Most documentary photographers usually avoid the use of super-wide-angle lenses for the representation of normal subjects, because of the visual distortions that result – distortions that have been used to good effect by Diane Arbus and other art photographers who have deliberately departed from the making of classic topographical images of the kind that Piranesi produced. In addition, standard multi-image photographic panoramas that cover scenes that spread well beyond 90° in width usually look curved or faceted as the camera is revolved around its axis at the station point.[10]

As photographer Steven Brooke correctly determined for his 1991 Rome Prize project, that the use of a fisheye or panoramic lens, or the making of photomontages in the darkroom, would not be as likely to produce images from the same sites with the artistic quality that he could achieve with his view camera, which has the swings and tilts necessary to rectify the images. However, with the invention of digital imagery and computer-based editing software, the technical landscape has changed dramatically, and a different art form has become possible.

During the academic year 2002-03, while on a Rome Prize Fellowship[11] like that received by Steven Brooke 11 years before, I was inspired to follow in the footsteps of both Piranesi and these recent photographers to again photograph the views that Piranesi had etched and engraved on copper in the middle of the eighteenth century. What started as a means to document 250 years of continuity and change in the deeply historic landscapes of Rome also became a voyage of discovery into Piranesi's compositional methods and his use of perspective, all of which had evolved prior to the invention of photography.

My prior work as a photographer during the 1960's and '70's had included extensive experience documenting the landscapes of the Industrial Revolution

---

10 The first known patent for a panoramic camera is 1843, at the dawn of photography itself, and panoramic cameras, particularly the Kodak "Cirkut" Camera, were popular in the turn of the 20th century. Different types of panoramic cameras have been produced in recent decades, but computer software now exists that can merge individual images into panoramas or entire spherical images, such as Apple's Quick Time Virtual Reality (QTVR). (http://www.cirkutpanorama.com/cameras.html, http://www.edb.utexas.edu/teachnet/qtvr/)

11 National Endowment for the Arts Rome Prize in Historic Preservation at the American Academy in Rome.

and the architecture of textile mills and cities in New England, Great Britain and India with a large format view camera, examples of which can be seen at www.conservationtech.com. Just as Piranesi was inspired to draw attention to the value of the ruins of Rome, I undertook the documentary photography of the factory towns as an effort to inspire the preservation of their monumental mills from the wrecking ball. The shift from documentation of early modern industrial archeology to the archeological sites of Classical Rome is not as great a difference as one may think, at least not from a visual and artistic point of view.

I arrived in Rome in 2002 without the equipment for large format photography. Instead, I had 35 mm cameras and lenses, and a new 5 megapixel digital camera with a built-in zoom lens. Despite having purchased a substantial amount of 35mm film for the trip, I found myself shooting digital images, almost exclusively, right from the beginning of the fellowship year in Rome. Unbeknownst to me when I purchased the camera plus the larger computer together with Adobe Photoshop software for the trip, I quickly found that the medium was not just a film-less version of film photography but offered the craft ingredients for a new art form. In the years since this fellowship, I find that I am still exploring the potential of this technology, as both the hardware and software continues to develop to this day. The camera, which was smaller than the 35mm cameras, proved to be flexible and suitable especially because of the restrictions against the use of tripods and professional cameras at the Italian archeological sites.

Another feature that I discovered as the work unfolded was that the moveable screen on the little digital camera proved invaluable in taking photographs from an elevation well above my head, in sites that had been excavated since Piranesi's time. This feature alone made the entire Piranesi Project possible, whereas film cameras lack this feature. Back in the studio, the digital medium – with Adobe Photoshop software – enabled an immediate processing of the images which could then be checked against the 18th century engravings. More importantly, this technology provided the opportunity to "build" the images out of combinations of as many as nine wide-angle photographs that were necessary to overlay in register with digital copies of the work of Piranesi and other 18th and 19th century artists. This is what will be described in more detail below.

The "Piranesi Project" was not a preconceived project, but one that emerged slowly out of the experience of living and working in Rome for the year 2002. In its final form, the slide/video *The Piranesi Project, A Stratigraphy of Views of Rome,* which is now a movie entitled *Rome Was! A Piranesian Vision,* included overlay images not only with Piranesi's 18th century work but the work other 18th and 19th century artists and early photographers. My own decision to abandon the single-point perspective of traditional photography and explore Piranesi's and the other artists' art through the use of digital image montages, which embody varying rules of perspective, was neither a single artistic decision nor intended as an academic art-historical analysis. It emerged when it became clear there was no other way to bring the images separated by a quarter of a millennium into visual register.

TIME AND CHANGE IN THE SYMBOLIC IMAGES

The reason for photographing the *vedute* in Piranesi's footsteps was to explore how a quarter of a millennium had changed what was already a potent landscape of the ruins of a past civilization. As a photographer, the act of taking Piranesi's *Vedute di Roma* to their sites transformed them from disembodied works of art on their own, to pieces that were seamless with the landscapes they illustrate. Suddenly, they extend beyond their frame – both in time and in space. The 250 years of changes, from the massive archeological diggings to the stripping of the vegetation from the standing remains, became a potent part of the story which gave the ruins new meaning as less static artifacts.

Figure 3. (Left) Giambattista Piranesi, Pronao del Tempio della Concordia. (Right) Author's photograph of the same view reformatted to conform to Piranesi's perspective, 2003.

While the usual interpretive information for tourists focuses on the speculative reconstructions of what the archeological sites may have looked like in ancient times, in my experience the viewing of Piranesi's images at their sites had a far more evocative impact. Between Piranesi's time and our own, the ruins of classical Rome have been preserved and at the same time, transformed. No longer is the site of the ancient Forum the *Campo Vaccino* (Cow Pasture) at the edge of the city of Piranesi's time; it is the "Foro Romano" – an archeological site with gates, guards, and regulations for tourist access at the very center of the modern city. Over the course of the 19th century as much as 12 meters (40 feet) of alluvium and debris have been removed to reveal the plinths of the former civic buildings, markets and temples that made up the complex, exposing some of the only remaining marble cladding. The only reason this ancient marble had not been burned for lime was because the river had covered it with alluvial clay during frequent floods at a time when the population of Rome fell from about 2 million to less than 50,000, after the collapse of the Western half of the Roman Empire at the beginning of the era of the Byzantine Empire, centered on Constantinople.

The other change that affected all of the monumental ruins, including the Forum, is the stripping of the vegetative overgrowth. Arriving in Rome as he did at the end of the Baroque era, the manner in which Piranesi captured the sense of time and decay presages the Romantic era. For centuries, except for their use as convenient quarries, the ruins had been largely neglected and allowed to become overgrown. Beginning in the 19th century, this vegetation has been systematically stripped off. The current presentation of archeological remains – denuded of vines, flowers or trees intermingled with the structures – is so accepted today as an inevitable and necessary part of their conservation that many people will be surprised to learn that there was a heated debate over their removal. Indeed, at the time of the first clearing of the vegetation and excavation of the archeological sites, many people shared the view expressed by French novelist Gustave Flaubert (1821-1880), when he wrote in 1846: *"I love above all the sight of vegetation resting upon old ruins. This embrace of nature, coming swiftly to bury the work of man the moment his hand is no longer there to defend it, fills me with deep and ample joy."*[12]

THE PIRANESI PROJECT

As of 2002, digital photography had been widely available for only a few years. It is this more recent invention in the history of the medium that has provided a remarkable opportunity to reverse the rigid optical geometry inherent in photography, and thus take the imagery created by the camera back into the perspective system used by Piranesi before photography was possible. In so doing, it became clear that what some might identify as "mistakes" in the proper use of perspective, were in fact artifices used by Piranesi to accomplish his mission – that of describing his subjects in single flat rectified images with a visual power that

---

12 From a letter to a friend quoted in: Woodward, C. (2001): 72

comes from a breadth of coverage, together with enhanced foreshortening that is impossible to capture in single photographs.

Despite its foundation on optical science, a photograph is as much a two-dimensional abstraction of the original three-dimensional environment as is an artist's handmade image on a copper plate. Ironically, the seeming objectivity of the camera can on occasion be a handicap, as the image produced can lack much of the sense of reality experienced by a person in the particular space. This is especially true when comparing photographs to the work of the most creative and observant artists in their paintings and engravings before the invention of photo-sensitive materials. One only needs to look at color postcards sold at historic sites to witness some of the limits of photography to fully capture the essence of a subject. Joel Snyder in his paper, "Picturing Vision," states:

»Some critics believe the camera image is not only an independent and scientific corroboration of the schemata developed by realistic painters from, say, the time of Giotto onward but is a correction and fulfillment of those schemata...This is quite simply false...To the extent that we believe cameras automatically give natural images, we have lost the sense of what these tools are and have forgotten that they are instruments at all...Cameras do not provide scientific corroboration of the schemata or rules invented by painters to make realistic pictures. On the contrary, cameras represent the incorporation of those schemata into a tool designed and built, with great difficulty and over a long period of time, to aid painters and draughtsmen in the production of certain kinds of pictures.«[13]

Before the age of photography, painters and engravers were called upon to provide realistic views of the built and natural environment. Artists would compose their images so as to best represent their interpretation of the experience and the meaning of the place within the confines of a single picture frame, even if it meant adjusting the perspective of certain parts of the image. While some artists before the advent of photo-sensitive materials used a "camera obscura" to compose their views, even those who are known to have used the device, such as Gaspare Vanvitelli (Gaspar Van Wittel, 1652-1736), did not necessarily feel entirely bound by the results.[14] Consistent with the title of this book, as will be shown below, Piranesi's compositions have been shown in studies to be closer to the real views as experienced and perceived by contemporary individuals, than are photographs taken of the same general scene.

---

13 Snyder, J. (1980): 219-246.
14 Cursi, L. (2002); and Christoph, L. (2005): 315-339

Today, the demand for illustrations of the environment is largely fulfilled by photography. While photography can be very effective at documenting a complex site with a series of images taken from different vantage points, the camera can prove to be limiting when called on to illustrate a place with a single image. Nonetheless, the public has come to believe in the "truth" of photographs when compared to artist's paintings and drawings. This is especially the case where the composition of a painting, particularly in the use of perspective, deviates from that produced by a photographic lens. Yet, as the Piranesi Project progressed, it became clear that departures from single viewpoint linear perspective enabled Piranesi to capture his sweepingly wide-angle views without extreme wide-angle distortion.

Figure 4. The Grandi Terme in Hadrian's Villa with Piranesi's engraving on the left, and the same view in 2003 as a composite photograph by the author on the right. The fragment of the Piranesi image with the people seemingly floating in space shows where the ground plane was in his time prior to the archaeological excavations.

As a first example, I turn to Piranesi's engraving of the *Grandi Terme* (Large Baths) at Hadrian's Villa (Figure 4). This particular image is one of Piranesi's most powerful and compelling images of the archeological ruins, and it was the first image that inspired *The Piranesi Project*. In their wisdom, the curators of the modern-day archeological site at Hadrian's Villa had placed a copy of Piranesi's famous engraving of the ruins of the *Grandi Terme* on an interpretive sign at the site. This was unusual in that more commonly the interpretive signs include reconstruction views showing the sites in the ancient Roman era of Emperor Hadrian. Piranesi's engraving proved that the ruined structure had survived the additional quarter of a millennium from his time essentially in the same state of partial collapse as when he saw it, with the exception that it has been stripped of its picturesque cloak of vines, shrubs, and layers of accumulated debris that had formerly raised the level of the ground well above the original floor.

Taking a digital image on the camera screen of Piranesi's engraving to the very spot where Piranesi would have stood to sketch his view 250 years earlier, it became readily apparent that the view that he documented could not be record-ed in a single photograph – simply because it encompassed a full 180° sweep of vision. Six wide-angle photographs[15] were necessary to capture with photog-raphy the entirety of the *Grandi Terme* that Piranesi captured in his single en-graving. Piranesi had avoided the "catastrophic distortions" that would have re-sulted from a single angle of view linear perspective of this scene by compress-ing the extreme edges of the view so that they would not look stretched and dis-torted, while avoiding the curvature or warping that is characteristic of the usual photographic panorama.

With this compression of the sides, Piranesi was able to make the end of the room that forms the center of the image proportionally larger. Had Piranesi fol-lowed the rules of linear perspective and used a single vanishing point, his image would have looked like it was viewed through the wrong end of a telescope as shown in Figure 6. Even then, the arch that frames the image in the foreground would be missing, as, in reality, it is directly overhead from the only station point that Piranesi could have used because of the wall that is right behind his viewpoint. Piranesi's compression of such a wide field of vision into the frame of his etched image is so subtle and convincing that the viewer is unaware of any more than a modest alteration of the geometric rules of linear perspective when looking at his print. In effect, Piranesi had recomposed this view into a visually undistorted flat image that realistically conveys a visual sense of being in the space, while a modern camera can only cover this view in a single shot with a fisheye lens.

The process of accomplishing the objective of creating a photographic overlay of Piranesi's engraving involved the following steps. First, the six wide-angle digital photos shown in Figure 5 were taken to cover all of what Piranesi included in his image. Second, each of the images had to be "rectified" so that the vertical lines of the subject would be parallel. Third, these six photographs had to be merged into a single image by introducing a similar foreshortening of the sides, just as Piranesi had done to limit the wide-angle distortion (Figure 4).

---

15 A 19 mm lens (35mm equivalent) on a Nikon 5000 digital camera.

Figure 5. The 6 individual photographs taken with a 19 mm lens (35mm equivalent) used to build the composite image of the Grandi Terme.

This photography and the work on the overlays served to expand my perception beyond that gained from years of architectural photography with a large format view camera. For the Piranesi Project, establishing the relative size of elements and setting the angles of perspective recession proved to be more difficult than it would seem at first glance. More than any other experience, this project taught me how different what one sees in the field is from a flat image of the same subject, and how the essence of this art is perceptual, rather than strictly optical.

PERSPECTIVE AND VISUAL PERCEPTION
IN THE CREATION OF FLAT IMAGES

When taking a wide-angle photograph, the visual effect of recession can be very extreme – making most foreground subjects look overly large compared to how they are perceived in space. Interestingly, the limit of the human cone of vision and wide-angle distortion was analyzed in detail as early as 1482 by Piero della Francesca. In his analysis, he noted that *"the eye...can only take in ninety degrees at once,"* demonstrating with geometric diagrams that elements on the side will appear to be stretched horizontally if linear perspective is used for a view that exceeds 90°, but not if the view stays within a 90° cone of vision.[16]

Moreover, in extreme wide-angle photographs, a subject in the middle distance, such as a building or the space between buildings, is very small in relationship to the foreground which may contain less meaningful objects. This problem results from the geometry of the view independent of the use of lenses or cameras, and thus was evident to artists prior to the invention of photography, just as it was to Piranesi when he laid out the composition for the *Grandi Terme*. To offset this effect, Piranesi enhanced the foreshortening of the sides, which served to pull the elements at the center of the image closer so they would appear larger despite the wide coverage of the overall view. (This can be seen by comparing Figure 4 with Figure 6.)

In making these artistic manipulations, Piranesi must have recognized that the creation of non-distorted and realistic views in two-dimensional graphic images of topographical subjects does not rely on rigid adherence to the rules of perspective or the optics of a lens in a *camera obscura*. He had also realized that the relative size of the elements in a two-dimensional composition of a three-dimensional subject can be varied for visual effect without a loss of the sense of realism.

---

16 Elkins, J. (1994): 69. It is interesting to speculate on what method Piero della Francesca used to arrive at 90°. My own findings on these limits comes up with a less geometrically fixed limit, but full binocular coverage is approximately 90°, with the ridge at the top of the nose setting the inside limit of the eye coverage. The outside limit for the two eyes added together is significantly greater than 90°, with each eye covering a cone of about 90°, which overlap in the center with the cone of binocular vision described above. Acute foveal perception, as will be discussed below, is much narrower, being well less than 1°, and the full binocular vision scan of one's eyes side-to-side with the head held fixed in one position is somewhat less than 90°. A good example of the limits to the width of human eyesight perception can be demonstrated by the fact that people usually do not find their vision noticeably confined by spectacles, which allow about a 90° cone of vision.

Rudolf Arnheim describes this as a psychological as well as a visual phenomenon in *Film as Art*:

»Physically, the image thrown onto the retina of the eye by any object in the field of vision diminishes in proportion to the square of the distance[17]... However, we do not in real life get impressions to accord with the images on the retina. If a man is standing three feet away and another equally tall six feet away, the area of the image of the second does not appear to be only a quarter of that of the first...This phenomenon is known as the constancy of size. It is impossible for most people – excepting those accustomed to drawing and painting – that is, artificially trained – to see according to the image on the retina.«[18]

Piranesi overcame this inconsistency between the mechanics of human optics and visual perception by consistently compressing his views to bring the distant subjects forward, as if – had he been using a camera – they were viewed at a distance through a moderate telephoto lens. Unlike photography, however, his perspective shifts were exercised at his discretion, rather than by the application of a single geometric rule as if he had simply moved the station point backward. In other words, it is not possible to see the views with the same perspective and composition that Piranesi used simply by stepping backwards, even where stepping back may be physically possible. While the layouts of his compositions were more consistent with wide-angle views, the perspective applied to the principle elements in the images was consistent with longer focal lengths. Piranesi's creativity is evident in how he managed to make his subjects look realistic and undistorted, even while expanding his horizontal coverage sometimes to 180°.

To test the concept of *"realistic view"* at the psychological level, German psychologist Alf C. Zimmer compared a Piranesi view of the Forum (then the *Campo Vaccino*) with a modern photograph by Herschel Levit from the same vantage point. He found that when tracings of each image were shown to 32 different ordinary tourists in Rome who were asked which *"depicted most correctly*

---

17 Euclid (C. 300 BC) in *Optics,* the earliest surviving work on geometrical optics and perspective, has demonstrated that this statement becomes less accurate the closer that an object is to the viewer, but the truth of his geometric theorem does not refute the psychological point that Arnheim is making. (http://www.cartage.org.lb/en/themes/ BookLibrary/books/rarebooks/Authors/E/Euclid/cc/c2/04.html) (J. B. Calvert, 2000: www.du.edu/~etuttle/classics/nugreek/contents.htm#conts)

18 Arnheim, R. (1957): 13.

the real scenery," 23 selected the tracing from the Piranesi print, while only 2 selected the tracing from the photograph (7 were undecided).[19]

To study this phenomenon, one can analyze how people perceive straight lines in space, and the difference between perfectly vertical and horizontal lines and forms, such as those on buildings. When the human eye traces its way over a scene, it behaves exactly like a lens of a camera, so the convergence of both vertical and horizontal lines is constantly changing as the center of the image seen moves, so one may ask: *Why do paintings, drawings and photographs of exterior or interior architectural subjects usually look less distorted if vertical lines are parallel (unless the view is acutely up or down)?* The image in reality is not rectified by the lens of the eye any more than it would be with a camera lens.

The explanation for this lies in how the human mind interprets the visual data that the physical eye records. This mental interpretation process is different for images than it is for the original three-dimensional environmental space. For the 3D space, the mind automatically "rectifies" the scene. Otherwise people would not be able to look at an object or building located beyond the distance of binocular three-dimension discernment and, for example, interpret the difference in shape between a Roman military fortification, with its battered wall, and a structure with precisely vertical sides. If a photograph is taken of this same scene with the camera pointed upwards, it can be difficult for the viewer of the photograph to distinguish the sloping sides of a battered wall from the converging lines of vertical walls.

Such vertical rectification of the imagery by the artist is, therefore, a manipulation designed to make an optically accurate image look more realistic than it would be if the line of sight were to be placed at the geometric center of the image rather than horizontal. Mathematician Anthony Phillips made the observation: *"Far from being natural, perspective is a calculated illusion, giving the brain false clues so it will construct a virtual reality."*[20] So fundamental is the acceptance of maintaining the verticals as parallel lines in architectural views that few question this, but in fact it is part of the "calculated illusion" that allows the visual construction of a virtual reality. In other words, the works of art demonstrate how artists and photographers have attempted to recreate how the eye/mind combination sees and interprets an image, not just how the eye sees it.

The universal acceptance of rectified images with parallel vertical lines in paintings and drawings since the Renaissance may explain why so soon after the invention of photography, cameras were constructed with a rising front that ena-

19 Zimmer, A. C. (1995)
20 Phillips, A. (2000)

bled the film plane to be precisely vertical while the lens could be shifted upwards to capture the taller subjects. This continues to be the accepted practice for almost all professional architectural photography, but in the present, it has perhaps become less important or influential as the massive proliferation of images has relegated formal architectural photography to architecture journals or advertising. Every mobile phone now has a simple fixed lens camera in it, and converging vertical lines are now seen as "cool." Even now "snapshot" views of familiar Roman monuments divorced from their environs with radically converging vertical lines are painted on the sides of the sides of busses and trains in Rome – a level of abstraction that would have been unacceptable in the art and photography world of the 19th century. Such can be considered to be consistent with the modern perception of the city not as a series of identifiable spaces and architectural forms and enclosures, but as a catalogue of monuments to be seen and ticked off a list – that is of a real virtuality more connected to that of a drive-by experience, than a state of being in an historic place.

PIRANESIAN PERSPECTIVE

Like his colleagues, Piranesi also followed the convention of rectified images, but his work demonstrates that, for the horizontal planes, he departed from the single point perspective that had evolved during the Renaissance. While converging verticals appear to conflict with the human mind's effort to normalize verticals as parallel lines, the introduction of variations in the vanishing points for the horizontal lines do not trigger the same visual confusion. On the other hand, objects at the perimeter of a wide-angle view with a single central vanishing point do appear stretched and distorted, and thus incorrect to the eye. Perhaps from his early experiences growing up in the Venetian tradition of stage scenographic art, Piranesi came to realize that the stretched distortion at the fringes of a wide-angle view is perceived as less realistic than are the subtle shifts in viewing angles combined into the same image.

Working with Piranesi's images by combining them with photographs of the same sites raises many of the crucial issues of recent art historical theory on the "discovery" and use of linear perspective during and since the Renaissance. Intellectual and artistic debates over the correct application of perspective have dominated the discussions of two-dimensional art of Western civilization since the Renaissance. The introduction and proliferation of photography in the 19th and 20th centuries has narrowed that debate by focusing on a new and more limited truth – that of the optical correctness of what the lens can record onto film in a single increasingly short moment in time. This is what has been referred to in scientific and art historical debates as the "snapshot" view. Art historian Sir Ernst Hans Josef Gombrich, (1909-2001), observed that art history *"has been written by critics (ancient, Renaissance, and later) who have accepted the snapshot vision as the norm and who could not but notice how rarely it was adopted in the past. The images of great civilizations such as those of Egypt or of China were never constructed on these principles, and so their essentially different approach was seen as a deviation from a natural norm."[21]*

Gombrich goes on to point out that it is only the center of the eye – the "foveal" area – that records and communicates with the mind at the level of perceptual acuity capable, for example, of reading text. *"Things are not just blurred outside of the foveal area; they are indistinct in a much more elusive way."* Thus, while people see and experience a wide field of view, the mind decodes and interprets that view essentially by scanning it with one's eyes, rather than recording it in its entirety in a single "snapshot" view as a camera does. This is true not just beyond the 90 degree width identified by Piero della Francesca described above, but also across the entire human field of vision, down to the level of a single degree. This means that each and every scene looked at by a person is experienced as a composite image "constructed" from information that contains not one, but many different vanishing points and viewing angles. If one also accepts the active and essential contribution of short-term memory, these composite images will also sometimes include different station points seen in a sequence over time as documented in Figure 7.

This observation is central to the departures from the fixed single viewpoint linear perspective undertaken by Piranesi, as well as by a number of other artists from the same era. Piranesi did his engravings based on what he saw by turning his head in a way that a standard camera cannot record in a single photograph. He thus managed to compose his images in ways that avoided the signature distorted look of most photographic panoramas. Piranesi's compositions are, in effect, a product of his understanding that visual experience is an amalgamation of body and eye movement integrated by a complex cerebral synthesis of the perceived visual information. Cameras utterly lack this synthetic capacity.

---

21 Gombrich, E. H. (1980)

Figure 6. The Grandi Terme photographs used for Figure 4 reformatted to show how the space would look if the view were constructed following the rigorous rules of linear perspective with a single angle of view. The darker image in the center is one frame of the group of six used for this composite image.

For this reason, bringing the modern-day digitally manipulated photographic images together with his eighteenth century views sometimes required as many as nine separate photographs to form a mosaic three images high and wide, and it necessitated an elaborate disassembly and reassembly of the photographic images on the computer. Only then could the resulting single image even begin to cover the breadth of Piranesi's view without "catastrophic" wide-angle distortion or panoramic curvature. In these multi-photograph assemblies, the images on the sides have a different vanishing point from the others, resulting in a perspective recession that is slightly splayed. At the same time, the side elements are foreshortened more than they would be had a single viewpoint and direction of view been used (see figure 4 and figure 6). If undertaken in a subtle way, these manipulations of the image data are not usually perceived by the viewer as distortions. The objective is to produce a realistic two-dimensional image of a three-dimensional space.

Figure 7. The Augustinian Firewall, by Piranesi, together with the three individual photographs taken with a 19 mm lens (35mm equivalent) and the composite image constructed from them by the author. The photo on the left is taken approximately 100 meters from the one in the center, which is 30 meters from the one on the right. The width of the street was the same in Piranesi's time as it is now.

Piranesi also used other important compositional techniques. In his view of the firewall of the Forum of Augustus, for example, (see figure 7) there are multiple station points, yet the resulting image appears remarkably realistic. This is true, even though most likely the entire length of the firewall has never been visible from a single viewpoint since Roman times, simply because buildings on sites occupied during and since ancient times block the view of the wall along the narrow lane where it jogs around a corner. Even though one cannot actually see this wall in a single view, individual photographs of it fail to capture the sense of grandeur that it has when one walks along it from one end to the other. This provides a good illustration of another aspect of human perception of importance to artists such as Piranesi – the element of *time*. At the site, the wall in all of its magnitude can only be perceived as a sequence of vignettes while walking along it, whereas Piranesi has collapsed this into a single flat image.

In my own experience, it took a visit to the site with Piranesi's image in hand to realize that his image could not be photographed from a single station point, regardless of the angle of view. This was true despite my prior familiarity with the wall. My experience of viewing the wall by walking along its length in the narrow lane had coalesced in my mind into an image of the wall as a single artifact consistent with Piranesi's illustration which convincingly shows the magnitude and extent of the wall, in a way that no single photograph can convey.

One of the important reasons why a composite image can look more realistic than a simple unmanipulated photograph of the same site is that the three-dimensionality of the actual subject space can only, in fact, be experienced on site by moving one's eyes and turning one's head, even if it does not require walking from one viewpoint to another. This simple phenomenon – the fact that we must move our eyes and turn our heads to see the world in front of us – may be the one most important reason why Piranesi's seeming violations of the fixed geometric rules of linear perspective often have resulted in images that, as A. C. Zimmer demonstrated, appear to people to be more "realistic" than unaltered photographs of the same scenes.[22]

THE MEANING OF "TRUTH" IN ART AND PHOTOGRAPHY

These observations about the making of photographs that are edited to match Piranesi's compositions with different perspective systems in the same image raise the question: Are these composite photographs false? Answering such a question, of course, raises the equally troubling inquiry as to what constitutes "truth" in representational art? In fact, when it comes to Piranesi's art, this is not a new question. Over the past two centuries, as the work and fame of Piranesi spread throughout Europe, some of the people who came to Rome sometimes expressed disappointment when encountering the ruins they first had seen in his images. Johann Wolfgang von Goethe (1749-1832), said in his Italian Journey (1788), *"The actual appearance of the ruined baths of...Caracalla, of which Piranesi has given us so many a rich imaginary impression, could hardly satisfy even our*

---

22 Piranesi was not always fully successful in avoiding visual distortion in his views, as a few of his engravings do look visibly distorted, but these were avoided when I was making the choices for the photographic overlays.

artistically trained eye."[23] Of course, one can only speculate as to which elements of Piranesi's images made his views more powerful than the real-life experience for this author.

With the advent of photography, what is accepted as truth has shifted primarily because the lens of a camera imprints the three-dimensional scene onto film according to rigid rules of optical geometry. However, this type of objectivity rarely was the primary objective of the pictorial or topographical artist. A more important goal for the pre-photographic era artist when documenting a real landscape or architectural subject is capturing the spirit of the place in a single iconic view. Piranesi touched upon this phenomenon when he wrote:

»These ruins have filled my spirit with images that accurate [architectural] drawings...could never have succeeded in conveying. ...Therefore, having the idea of presenting to the world some of these images, but having little hope that an architect of these times could effectively execute some of them...there seems to be no recourse than for me...to explain [my] ideas through [my] drawings and so to take away from sculpture and painting the advantage...they now have over architecture.«[24]

The experience of working with the multiple photographs to "build" single images itself raises the question of whether the resulting images that are constructed to approximate Piranesi's views of the same scene are themselves "false" because they no longer conform to the unretouched reality of what was originally exposed through the camera. In response to this question, one must recognize that a camera's rendition of the three-dimensional scene into a two-dimensional photograph is no less a transformation of the actual scene than are the results of the further transformations done on the computer to convert them to the pre-photographic perspective system of Piranesi's era, and bring them into register with the best of Piranesi's compositions.

Digital photography and computer-based editing software has made it possible to manipulate photographic images in ways that are difficult to detect – placing people together who actually have never been introduced, for example, but the topographical imagery that I was creating out of the photographs of Roman ruins were not intended to combine scenes to create fantasy views. These composite images were intended to reproduce real and familiar spaces in ways that would still look familiar. The editing changes made were done only with the

---

23 Goethe, J. W. v. (1989): 363
24 Piranesi, G. (1743)

elements already in the photographs taken at the site, but the perspective, fore-shortening, station points, and boundaries of the images had been changed.

It was not until the first showing of the Piranesi Project in Rome that I had the chance to validate the difference between literal and perceived truth of the images. This and subsequent showings in Italy did not lead, as I had feared, to questions and criticisms on the veracity of the photographic images. On the contrary, most were startled by how "realistic" the photographs were. In fact, the composite photographs actually served to rehabilitate Piranesi's reputation in the minds of some Roman scholars as to the accuracy of his views. Historians, archeologists, and architects at the American Academy and in Rome, as well as the city planners of the City of Rome repeatedly commented that, until they saw the show, they had believed that Piranesi had manufactured a great deal of what he had drawn in his *Vedute di Roma* series, but that the photographic overlays dissuaded them from that belief for the first time. In other words, the creation of the photo-mosaic from the multiple sets of images in the field did *not* make the resulting images unrealistic. Just as A. C. Zimmer demonstrated, looking "accurate" is as much a subjective as an objective process, and that perception is conditioned by how we perceive three-dimensional space by scanning the view with our eyes rather than remembering it as a "snapshot" view. Joel Snyder commented on the phenomenon of visual memory and interpretation when he said:

»Since the Renaissance, artists have had the ability to move ahead of the viewer, to make fresh discoveries about what we really see. This is not an unconditional freedom, but its very possibility implies a paradox. The artist can depict what we see because what we see is pictorial. And yet, in his paintings, the artist can achieve fidelity to his own vision based upon his knowledge of vision and depiction, and we will accept the picture as credible and warranted even though we may insist at the same time that we never quite saw things that way before.«[25]

Art historian James Elkins made a similar observation when he commented: *"Any perspectival picture that has more than a single object will suffer from internal inconsistencies because every painter assembles parts that don't belong together. That is true even of careful, analytically minded paintings."*[26] What I came to realize while undertaking this project is that the manner in which Piranesi turned his head and incorporated the shifted perspective into his views comes closer to the reality of how all people perceive a view, than does an image

25 Snyder, J. (1980): 234
26 Elkins, J. (1998)

constructed from a single vanishing point. As we scan a view with our eyes, our sense of the perspective is constantly shifting in the same way that it does when we turn a camera to face in a different direction. The mind merges all of this information into a rational image of the scene – not with a single perspective geometry, but a composite one. Thus the composite photographs in the Piranesi Project looked even less distorted than did many of the unedited photographs before they were assembled into a single image. As E. H. Gombrich observed: *"Perspective cannot and need not claim to represent the world as we see it."*[27]

CONCLUSION

The act of "building" the composite photographic images based on Piranesi's compositions offered an opportunity to take documentary still photography in a direction I had never explored before – well beyond the realm of visibly overlapping snapshots, such as those done by David Hockney, or the curved or faceted panorama views that now can be executed automatically with software on a computer and even now on many digital cameras. In the course of this work, I found that when buildings and landscapes are pictorially portrayed on the flat plane of a painting or print, there is no single rule or mathematical formula that can be used to fully explain how they can be most realistically perceived, especially after the artist has made his contribution to the nature of that perception.

Working with the Piranesi images provided the opportunity to document more than a quarter of a millennium of changes to an iconic human landscape. It also offered the chance to learn a great deal about the relationship between the imagery of a space and the space itself. Thus, while photography provides us with a documentary tool, the science of what makes both drawings and photographs of landscapes and cityscapes expressive and meaningful representations of the artifacts of human history and culture is a window into how the human eye sees and interprets space, rather than simply how the camera lens dispassionately directs light to form an image on film or an electronic chip. This exploration of imagery across a quarter of a millennium of time also provides an opportunity to experience a connection to the city of Rome that transcends the modern-day sense of fragmentation discussed in the opening paragraph – that is, it provides an escape from the sense of collision between the monuments and coherent urban spaces of the past and a modern urban world most often characterized by fragmented scenes and the sights and sounds of continuous movement.

---

27 Gombrich, E. H.(1980): 209-10.

Piranesi's gift was his ability to make the subtle adjustments of perspective necessary to gain an all-encompassing view of his subjects in his images without apparent wide-angle distortion. These then became the symbolic images that brought the existence of these disappearing cultural artifacts into the consciousness of all of Europe, and helped to save those artifacts for posterity. The experience of working on this project has made me realize that the same subtle adjustments can be integrated into photographs, not only of Rome, but also of other places around the world with the aid of the digital medium.

As a documentary tool, the ability to make such creative manipulations may, in fact, be a powerful gift, as it has the potential to expand documentary photography beyond its previous confines to show sweeping views of a subject that can then, not only inform, but also stimulate the viewing public to grasp – perhaps for the first time – the full magic of the powerful and deeply historic buildings they see and the urban landscapes they traverse.

REFERENCES

Arnheim, Rudolf (1957): *Film as Art*, Berkeley & Los Angeles: University of California Press.

Brooke, Steven (1995): *Views of Rome,* New York: Rizzoli.

Cursi, Lia Viviani, ed. (2002): *Gaspare Vanvitelli e le origini del vedutismo*, Rome: Viviani Arte.

Elkins, James (1994): *The Poetics of Perspective*, Ithaca: Cornell University Press.

Elkins, James (1998): "Precision, Misprecision, Misprision," *Critical Inquiry*, Volume 25, Number 1, Fall 1998.

Ficacci, Luigi (2000): Giovanni Battista Piranesi, The Complete Etchings, Köln: Taschen.

Goethe, Johann Wolfgang von (1989): *Italian Journey (1786–1788),* trans. Heitner, New York: Suhrkamp.

Gombrich, E. H.: Standards of Truth: The Arrested Image and the Moving Eye. In W. J. T. Mitchell, ed. (1980): *The Language of Images.* Chicago: The University of Chicago Press.

Hillard, George Stillman (1853): *Six Months in Italy*, Boston: Ticknor, Reed and Fields.

Levit, Herschel, (1976): *Views of Rome Then and Now,* New York: Dover.

Lüthy, Christoph (2005): "Hockney's Secret Knowledge, Vanvitelli's Camera Obscura," *Early Science and Medicine*, Volume 10, Number 2.

Phillips, Anthony (2000): review of J. V. Field, *The Invention of Infinity: Mathematics and Art in the Renaissance* (Oxford: Oxford Univ. Press, 1997), *Notices, Journal of the American Mathematical Society,* January 2000, Volume 47, Number 1, Washington DC: American Mathematical Society.

Piranesi, Giambattista (1756): *Le Antichità Romane*, Rome.

Piranesi, Giambattista (1743): *Prima Parte, Prima Parte di Architetture e Prospettive* [First Part of Architecture and Prospect Views] Rome: Fratelli Pagliari.

Snyder, Joel (1980): "Picturing Vision," *Critical Inquiry 6* (1980), republished in W.J.T. Mitchell, ed., *The Language of Images*, Chicago : University of Chicago Press.

Yourcenar, Marguerite (Richard Howard, transl.) (1962): *The Dark Brain of Piranesi and other Essays,* New York: Farrar Straus Giroux, 1980 translation of French first published.

Woodward, Christopher (2001): *In Ruins*, New York: Pantheon.

Zimmer, A. C.: "Multistability – More than just a Freak Phenomenon," in: Kruse, P., and Stadler, M. (1995): *Ambiguity in Mind and Nature*, Berlin: Springer.

ACKNOWLEDGEMENTS

The author thanks the American Academy in Rome for support for this work, and specifically Professors Claudio Varagnoli and Allan Ceen in Rome for contributions to this article.

Chapter 2. The Unfoldings

The World as Grid

ULRICH GEHMANN AND MARTIN REICHE

The following is about grids and networks. We want to present them as the realized outcome of an idea to express world, the entirety of that which is, in functional terms and related, to create a world as function. Both aspects belong together and in their combined impact, led to the world as we know it; so our thesis. Referring to the anthologies' general theme of a *real* virtuality, that idea embodies the latters' underlying procedure: to abstract a world which was given in its original terms into something functionally constructed and through that, to turn an 'artificial' world into becoming a real one. No matter what these original terms had been, in their respective cases – a primordial nature, a historically grown city, even entire landscapes – the procedure consists in abstracting from these individual peculiarities by 'virtualizing' them and afterwards, to transform them into spaces of abstraction. Spaces which follow only certain rules of functionality and by that, turned into other beings than they have been before. For instance, when an original forest is virtualized by expressing its trees as certain icons (tree type a, type b, and so on), and its concrete geography by abstract lines which stand for the different levels of altitude that forest covers in its actual terrain, it turned into an abstraction. By that, it has lost its individuality because *all* forests can be expressed in such a way, irrespective of their concrete (individual) 'original' reality.

What can be done with worlds already existing can too be performed for ones which shall exist, being composed of modeled spaces destined to become real. Opposed to the forest example where a real already existing is transformed into its virtualized version, here, the process is reversed: a virtual version of a world is transformed into a reality. For a better understanding, we have to examine what 'virtual' means. On one hand, it can denote something thst is not real, opposed to that what really is – our common notion of the virtual; e.g. when we speak about the 'virtual worlds' presented in fantasy films, comics, in the background worlds of digital games, utopian city prospects, or baroque ceiling frescoes. Despite their refinement and detail needed to be recognized as *world* – for which the presented segment is standing for, showing such a world's *nature* – we nevertheless know that we are confronted with worlds of imagination, of fantasy. They look *as if* they were real worlds but we know that they aren't since we realize at the proverbial first glance that a world like this can never be real. To be perceived as worlds, they need not only refinement but our imagination. Because we have to complete their actually presented segments in our mind, to gain the overall impression that we are looking at a part of an entire world and not merely at some picture.

Figure 1. Common virtual world[1]

On the other hand, a 'virtual world' (again, represented by its spaces) can also denote one which is not real in physical reality but which *could* be since it owns both the capacity and the potential to become real.[2] Which in other words is ca-

---

1   Detail from a ceiling fresco, cloister Rot an der Rot/Germany. Photography by U. Gehmann.

2   To both meanings of the *virtual* as an As If and as a potential see Hoffmeister, J. (1955): 481, 648

pable of changing its ontological status from an As If into an It Is – provided the proper conditions are met and we, its constructors, want it to become real. Such a kind of virtuality is the one we are concerned with in this contribution, and it requires imagination, too; albeit a different one than the one described. Here, spaces are conceptualized which are destined to turn into reality. A model of a world as it shall be is imagined and then imposed upon a given reality, in order to change the latter. The model of a world – the virtual – shall become the world, the real; a new real to be created, by constructing it in accordance with its model. Expressed through its imagined spaces, a model of the world shall become world – in all its relevant parts. Since real worlds are complex issues due to their richness in variety, like the case of the above-mentioned forest such a model must be abstract in a literal meaning, has to refrain from the individual concrete appearances but is forced to summarize, to lay out the future relevant world only in its constituting elements and relations. The picture on the opposite shows Hippodamos' plan for the city of Miletus, 479 B.C., able to "ensure homogeneity and an immediate conception of the spaces"[3] which make up the relevant world in question.

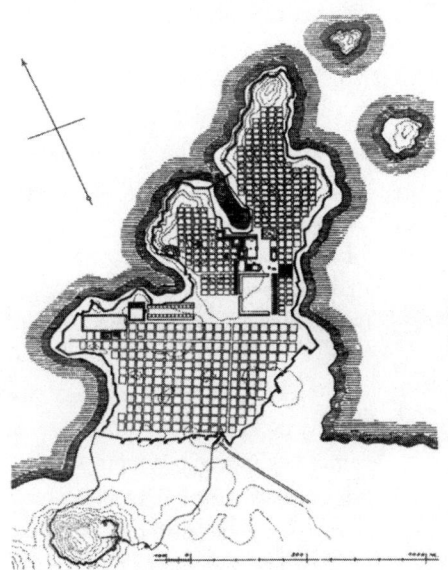

Figure 2. Abstract virtual world[4]

In this model of reality to come into existence, we see the relevant world condensed into its own abstraction. The coastline is indicated by its grey shape, the terrain by lines of altitude (like in case of the forest), the city by its rectangular grid, intersected by scattered areas of prime importance. In order to understand that world, there is nothing missing, at least nothing of relevance. For the prospective citizens of Miletus at least, their relevant world got schematized here, showing it as it has to appear in its total, brought down to its essential issues.

---

3   Delfante, Ch. (1999): 40f.

4   http://upload.wikimedia.org/wikipedia/commons/f/ff/Miletos_stadsplan_400.jpg

Nevertheless, there is something missing. This world is essentially dead because it is only a model for what shall be. For making it alive, we have to employ a third kind of imagination, next to the other two described so far. We have to translate this model from its abstract terms of being into those belonging to a real world, one inhabited by humans, plants, and animals, one of real buildings, noises, smells, movement, light and shadow. As it appears here, it is no vivid entity but only a plan, an abstract figure. A functional diagram of what life should be, but not life. When looking at such a world, we understand its *principal terms of being* but not how it should really operate in its concrete terms of being alive, i.e. in being a *real world*. The major problem consists exactly in this contradiction, namely that spaces like those had been designed for real life entities. Spaces which were not only based upon functional abstractions, but moreover, had the function of formatting those entities according to their principles. In the next picture, such a world is portrayed. Starting in the 19th century, such a kind of world

had been installed on grand scale, in the wake of Industrialization and emerging mass societies, and in its total, it embodies the physical substrate upon which we still live today, further developed from that era onwards.

Brought down to its core, the underlying idea was to create a world as function, or more specifically, a network of functions which should serve the different purposes of handling masses. In distributing and allocating these masses to the places where they had to function again, as workers, consumers, in- and outputs of material, and so forth.

Figure 3. Real virtual world[5]

---

5   Mosch Center, Karlsruhe/Germany. What looks like an abstract functional object in this vertical grid is the balcony front of the inhabitants, i.e. an intended *living* space. Photography by U. Gehmann.

Functional systems for distribution and allocation were needed, ranging from the handling of physical masses to those of an 'immaterial' nature, like the flow of information and capital required to handle the physical ones.[6] Summarized, it was about the domination of masses through managing them, in constructing an encompassing network of different functional flows and deposits, of "nodes" or "hubs," and "lines", as it was called later. It was a world that turned into the Logistic Landscapes of today,[7] a virtual world of pure and abstract functionality becoming a real world of the functional.

Moreover, in the frame context of a capitalist economy, these flows had to be accelerated (time is money) and economized, i.e. to be performed efficiently to avoid unnecessary slacks and hence, costs. All in all, the things of this world had to be moved in order to let them work, and aligned to it, directing, controlling and optimizing the associated flows became a matter of prime importance. The world and its cities in peculiar became an infrastructural network, a domineering tendency of "how to make worlds" until today, focusing on the construction of spaces for mobility and flow.[8] And what began in physical space was continued within other domains of life. Next to its physical substrate of a so-called functional city stemming from those days, and following the ideal of a city as machine, this world of masses embodies the other heritage of ours. Still today, long after the days of a Fordian society organized according to the requirements of mass production, mass consume, mass direction and -housing, we are confronted with the problem of how to handle masses. Despite the fact that the spatial arrangements constructed in those days are in the process of becoming slowly eroded (wherefore they are an *inherited* substrate only), replaced by phenomena of a "splintering" urbanism and a more amorphous, mutative city,[9] and although the ways of handling masses changed over time, the problem itself remains; peculiarly since the days of so-called globalization which

---

6 About these phenomena, see for instance Vance, J. E. (1990): 283ff., on the rise and unfolding of modern cities. And to capitalist industrialization and the new city, see Bayly, Chr. A. (2006): 212ff.

7 Cf. Waldheim, Ch., and Berger, A. (2012): 76-83.

8 Graham, S., and Marvin, S. (2001): 11. In historical perspective, it was the time of the so-called Cine Citta (from Greek *kinesis*, movement, and Italian *citta* for city) devoted to the organization of (primarily) physical flows. Cf. ISOCARP 2001.

9 To the aspect of mutation, see Shane, D. G. (2013): 6f. This kind of city, our prevalent city form today, is also called "informational", "networked", or Tele Citta (59, 61f., 72) and as a *Gestalt*, is essentially amorphous.

aggravated this problem into an unprecedented dimension.[10] That we are still confronted with managing masses, despite all measures to flexibilize and virtualize them, is a simple and mostly overseen fact, also after the days of a Fordian society. And the best since most effective way to handle masses is formatization, to proceed them according to strict algorithmic rules in a "technical" way, that is, in refraining from their individuality and to treat them like abstract entities. In other words, to virtualize their real being through abstracting it into technical, functionalized parameters. This too hasn't changed since the days of Fordism and mass society, and irrespective of the promises of recent social media to deliver unrestricted freedom to the individual by technical (i.e. formatted) means.

In this respect, it is important to note that it were not certain techniques which were primarily responsible for certain cultural and socioeconomic outcomes. But a certain mindset, leading to the application of certain technical means, and hence, to certain outcomes of them, a mindset of how to form world at all, and in which ways.[11]

For doing so, some means are more suited than others; in our case, it was the functional network, first realized by the grid. As an instrument, the grid is best suited for an equal distribution of land, parcelling real estate, to keep under watch a restless population and most important for the aspects regarded here, it has the potential to virtually grow ad infinitum. Historically, it had two main purposes: to facilitate colonization of formerly 'original' terrain , from Greek time onwards; and to be used as an instrument of modernization, for replacing an unorderly since naturally grown old (the original) by an orderly since planned new, from Roman time onwards.[12] That is, to transform a given real through creating a new one, by imposing an abstraction of a virtual real upon a real 'as it is' (the original) and thereby, to generate a new real, namely the one of a realized abstraction: the old Miletus becomes the new, by imposing the grid upon the former. In undertaking such a transformation of the real, the mentioned mindset comes into play since it is the mindset, not the instrument in itself which determines the *degree* of such an operation – how far it should reach, how many

---

10 To a new global economy and its mass requirements in its beginning, cf. Castells. M. (2003): Vol. I, 83ff. To recent periodical mass migrations, see Shane, D. G. (2013): 310f. Not to speak of the masses of other entities required, like information, material, and the like.

11 Exemplified in case of cities, see Shane, D. G. (2013): 29-33.

12 Cf. Kostof, S. (2007): 95 and 101f.

domains of a given real-life world shall be embraced by it. If it is confined to certain areas and domains of use, e.g. serving only as a military or town planning device as domains of use which in addition, are restricted to certain geographical areas only, leaving the "rest of the world" untouched; or if it shall embrace virtually everything, making full use of the instrument's inherent potential (see above, on the 'virtual') to grow ad infinitum. In other words, the degree of application primarily depends neither on the instrument's inherent potential, nor on given practical needs, but on its *intended* use. Which is a matter of mindset, first and foremost, and its underlying basic assumptions and cultural codes.

We can validate this hypothesis by looking at the historical record. As a mere *instrument*, the grid has been used in other cultures also[13] and moreover, it has been used for a very long time: one of the first known consequently performed grids, epitome for a rational mindset of planning, stems from Egypt in the 14th century B.C.,[14] ages before Hippodamos' Miletus. In fact, it is the commonest device for planned cities in history, by far superior to the later romantisized "organic pattern" of human settlement which, after the onset of modernity, became culturally coded as the opposite of a straight forward-rationalism with its aligned functionalistic attitude.[15] Inside our own cultural sphere, the grid was already applied in Miletus and other Greek cities of that era, since the very start of an occidental urban culture.[16] And although the instrument to form reality was the very same, and although its underlying purpose consisted in a functionalization of the real, too, its mindset differed significantly from that of a modern era when the grid became applied on broad scale. It became the "comprehensive plan" of how to transform reality, in peculiar urban reality, to reach an objectified infrastructure for "the demands of technology, speed, flow control and scale increases".[17] Not only caused by the sheer necessity of managing growing masses but as said, first of all by a certain mindset of how to transform the whole world according to principles of functionality – those masses of people, material, capital, products, built structures, information, energy and waste were then the result of.

---

13 Delfante, Ch. (1999): 40

14 Vercelloni, V. (1994): 2

15 Kostof, S. (2007): 95, to the grid; and 43f., to the organic pattern.

16 Benevolo, L. (2000): 143

17 D' Hooghe, A. (2010): 78. With regard to cities, it began to gain ground since the 1970ies, with the rise of a more flexible, 'systemic' capitalism; cf. Fujita, M. et al. (2000): 181-205

This *all* is important because it is not a consequence of the grid as such. To understand the importance of mindsets in applying instruments, we have to juxtapose such a preliminary end point of development with its beginning: the idea in those Greek days was to hold a unity of man and nature, *despite* using grids for city planning; it was the idea of *synoecism*, of a co-habitation of town- and country sites in mutual harmony.[18] Since modernity, it became a paradise forever lost but as an idea, it reappeared frequently, in various shapes, and it accounted for much of the romanticism mentioned. Ranging from garden cities (mainly gridded) to constructions of living in an encompassing park, to relieve their inhabitants' industrialized existence inside the frames and terms of functionalized networks. One has just to consult the respective city plans of that era, from Le Corbusier's *piloti*-constructions allowing to stroll through a park landscape that reaches even underneath the sites of habitation (which means that it is real encompassing), to the *Hansa Viertel* in Berlin, or modern suburban hab- itats. Which were designed as privatized garden regions based on the ideal of Frank Lloyd Wright's *Broadacre City* as the home of democratic, dispersed and thus, truly modern individuals who no longer live (or have to live) in the close communities of the past.[19] Translated into the language of the mythological, base for every mindset, it meant that the old conflict between *cultura* and *natura*, between man and an 'original' since 'natural' state of being had to be resolved in this way. After a true synoecism became impossible, nature had to be incorporated again in man's genuine living space as a cultural animal – to cite McLuhan, protagonist of a later world as network – namely the city. By their essence, artificial ('virtual') worlds were laid as networks over an originally given. During the course of modernity, this became man's new 'natural' environment.[20] And with regard to cultural-specific mindsets, no wonder that the first city plan completely standardized appeared at the doorway to modernity. Developed 1594, it consisted of identical houses posed alongside straight

---

18 Vance, J. E. (1990): 73, 77

19 Cf. Wright, F. L. (1950). He says (p. 13): "The value of earth as man's heritage is gone far from him in cities centralization has built." Instead, in the forerun of the things to come and culminating in The Cloud, he propagates (p.17) the nomad as the "prototype of the democrat." To Broadacre Cities' explicit considerations unifying man with na- ture, and to its influences for developments to follow see Shane, D. G. (2013): 49; and Eaton, R. (2001): 209-212, to that city itself, which had (coining) no urban center an- ymore.

20 To the development in its general terms, see Whatmore, S. (2002)

running rectangular streets and watercourses, made of formatted and (probably) even prefabricated building blocks, long before Industrial Revolution.[21]

But the principle can be applied also elsewhere and related, it does not have to stay rectangular, or even physical. Because next to its potential of being virtually infinite, the equal parcelling and hence, standardization and unification of a given real is its other one. Thus, it can be extended to all of a given world, for instance through maps.

In occidental history, maps have been the first attempts to really cover *wholes*, by their very intention. And to do so not just in a symbolic or pictorial way (as most of other cultures did), but as formats. It is not the point that other cultures too had maps; again, it is a point of the mindset in question of how to make maps, i.e. according to which principles, and how to use them. Fundamental to mapmaking as we know it inside the terms of our own cultural sphere is the grid, it accounts for the accuracy in depicting the relationships between maps and the real world. Like Hippodamos' Miletus, the first clearly identifiable gridded map stems from a relatively early period of our history, namely from Ptolemy, and shows the world as a encompassingly rastered one. Individualities do not count since every detail, i.e. every concrete entity can be identified by its coordinates of latitude and longitude, and all those entities – no matter their individual being – can be plotted (a), relative to each other, and (b), relative to the whole earth, represented by a globe, means: by an *abstract totality*.[22] Whereas in other cultures, maps had mostly a symbolic value, showing a symbolical cosmos as "the world as it is" in its cosmic (metaphysical) properties, here, it is about *relations*, not about absolute entities or cosmic forces, and these relations can be *measured*. Such a appealingly modern mindset reappeared in the Renaissance again, that doorway to the later 'modern' times. Leonardo da Vinci's map of Imola looks like a modern one, showing only the relevant, and abstract, pattern of things.

Important are not its details but its overall shape, its *Gestalt*. It reveals a completely abstracted view upon a real world, a so-called aerial view (beloved in modernity then) directly from above; so far from above that the concrete things in their plasticity – which makes up a world *in concreto* – are not visible. Because this is unimportant; instead, the principle counts: to show a general,

---

21 The ideal city of Simon Stevin, cit. in Feuerstein, G. (2008): 49f.

22 Short, J. R. (2003): 20, to the grid; and 53, to Ptolemy. To using of maps to show cosmological properties: 19, 44f. One exception is the Islam, but in gridding the world, it never went thus far as the Occident (70).

abstracted perspective upon a concrete lifeworld. Just like in the cases examined earlier, it needs imagination to conceive it as an Imola really existing, and not just as some abstract virtuality.

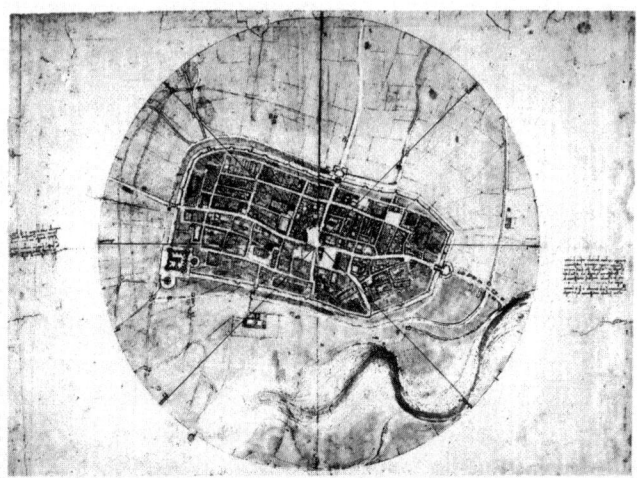

Figure 4. Aerial view of Imola, ca. 1502[23]

Maps have always had a symbolic importance, giving meaning and direction to life by "centering" people. And in representing the respective world(s) for orientation, all maps are distortions of a given and 'true' real they project.[24] It is not just a matter of scale but of implicit judgements what the world, and in particular, the world of relevance does embody, resting upon assumptions which led to the respective perspectives on a 'real' world the counterpart of which was then projected in the map.[25]

What began with a real world's geographic properties – to format them according to the functionalities they had to serve for – could also be extended to worlds not yet in existence: 'virtual' worlds purely functional could be imagined, worlds which had no real forerunners in geographical and physical terms (unlike Imola, and also unlike Miletus), but which could be invented and then posed upon a 'world as it is' – since the 19th century, also systems of flow which then become the relevant functional worlds, each of them a cosmic structure of its

---

23 http://commons.wikimedia.org/wiki/File:Leonardo_da_vinci,_Town_plan_of_Imola.jpg

24 Short, J. R. (2003): 9, to the symbolic character, and 13f., to distortion and orientation.

25 Short, J. R. (2003): 15, to implicit judgements.

own but despite its fixed structures, devoted to depict a *system* of relevant *processes*.

In a literal meaning of the symbolic, they *stood for* certain functionalities, and even genuine human belongings could be expressed, and more important, moulded by them. For instance, in terms of traffic- or communication flows, or

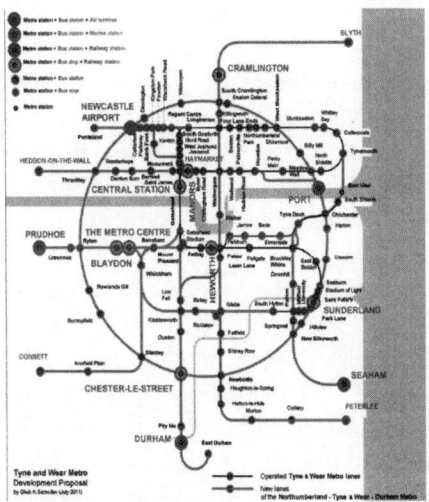 in terms of distributions as *result* of flows: how many minorities are distributed in a city, for instance, and what were their moves in a certain time interval from one city area to another; and so forth. The common point was to show systems of flows crucial for a larger system's viability (e.g., a city, a society, certain worldwide economic functions) as *structures* inside which peculiar *dynamics* happened, expressed as functionalized processual moves.

Figure 5. Cosmos of the functional[26]

It was about movement, dynamics, and the structures as its images were those dynamics' symbolic representations. So, it became possible to define a set of functionalities serving certain purposes, and then – via their structuring as patterns of process flows – to control them. Such worlds of functional networks became the relevant worlds of modernity. The above picture shows an example of such a relevant world. The tangible spatiality the plan has imposed upon an original world is omitted. There is no topography, not even a coastline (as opposed to the already abstract scheme of Miletus). The sea, not a relevant part of the world in question, is an uniform and empty grey area (the rim of the cosmos depicted), and the relevant world is not a pattern of concrete places but a diagram of process lines leading to hubs of different sizes. That's it; more is not

---

26 Northumberland Metro System, 2011. Drawing by Gleb K. Samoilov. http://commons. wikimedia.org/wiki/File:The_Integrated_System_of_Internal_and_Extenal_Public_ Transport_of_Tyne_and_Wear_Conurbation,_formed_by_NORTHUMBERLAND_- _TYNE_and_WEAR_-_DURHAM_METRO.jpg?uselang=de

necessary to understand, and first and foremost, to operate and to control this world.

In such ways, the original utopia – the non-place of the respective structured world as a virtual pattern of flows – could become a real one, by being imposed upon an original 'world as it is', or better, was. Starting in the 19th century on large scale, it can be understood as the first move towards a widespread, and most importantly, life-relevant real virtuality. Because the technical and functional networks it creates develop their own geographies which remain independent from originally given ones and by that, generate their own spatialities. Those infrastructural networks (as they are called, by their technical term) create worlds by their own.[27] In this respect, for the first time, literally 'utopian' since essentially placeless ventures had the chance to become reality; plans like the one above could be posed everywhere, and utopia was no longer a synonym for the impossible. The format of the functional could become a real virtuality, and although its operative principle is total visibility like in Jeremy Bentham's Panopticon, it itself is never concrete in classical terms of physical world perception,[28] cannot be grasped as a total (as a *Gestalt*) by our senses and by that alone, is 'placeless' – nobody can actually *see* the metro system depicted above – it is an abstractum that moulds realities as for the city's inhabitants it has become an important point of reference for navigation in the city.

What began with the gridded ideal for all, a Unitary City Ideal and a City Beautiful-movement which were formatted but nevertheless still visible, directly experiencable and hence, *comprehendeable* constructions, now ended up in functionalized – and at the same time functionalizing – abstracta determining the shape of real belongings. The ideal of a city as machine, a comprehensive place for all structured according to overall valid principles,[29] now gave way to a city as network, and with it, to its dissolution in disparate albeit globally connected centers of activity, driven by peculiar groups of 'actors'. And in terms of a broader cultural frame context, it is of little wonder that it was in those days that the Actor-Network-Theory (ANT) came up, relating the world's issues to

---

27 To such effects, see Graham, S., and Marvin, S. (2001): 189
28 To that, and to Foucault's metaphor in its actual development after the advent of a "digitalized age", see Bell, D. (2012): 205f.; and Bingham, N. (1996), to the general historical context.
29 To the city as machine according to its functional paradigm as regulated by CIAM, see Shane, D. G. (2013): 47; and 51, to its underlying world view.

different groups of users and leading to a virtualization of worldly belongings, alongside with their actual truncation through abstraction and functionalization.[30] With the advent of a "network society" and a neoliberal capitalism to free new masses, that old mass building of a unitary city has had its days; a so-called splintering urbanism came into existence, unbundling the formerly unified networks for the needs of different, and varying, 'customer groups' of users, generating new spaces, and urban places. The *civis*, former burgher and inhabitant of a city as a communal entity, had turned into an individualized *user* concentrated upon certain demands,[31] using the city not as a primarily *communal* place but as consume product for his personal needs. The formerly defining domains of human life, namely the temporality and spatiality of the Euclidean space as the so far overall frame of reference, also for a unitary city ideal, dissolved into the various and ever-changing flows of discontinuity and fragmentation.[32] The city, whose physical form became almost irrelevant already in the 1970ies,[33] had turned into an assemblage of actor group-enclaves globally connected in their networked functionalities, an entropic landscape. Well in line with the metaphoric used in recent chaos theories, these enclaves were the interconnected islands of order in a sea of chaos – a sea of the functional relations and life circumstances of all those not belonging to our respective individual network. Or formulated in an even more pronounced manner, we are faced with "relational ecologies of fragments and enclaves."[34] As regards the remaining total, that sea of chaos as the physical substrate for all those individualized groups of actors, the aerial view first presented in Imola became the general view of how to shape things: a so-called Landscape Urbanism developed, "larger systems" were planned as a network of patterns, cultural and natural. And the city, located within such a patterned relational net and once home of the *civis*, became a "generic city," a "place of continuous creation" (to cite Rem Koolhaas), and city design turned into "situational architecture"[35] resting upon the historical layers of its archeological remnant, and upon those of the different networks.

---

30 To the ANT, see Schüttpelz, E. (2007): 37f.

31 To its major causes see Graham, S. and Marvin, S. (2001): 385f., and to the new spatialities created: 184, 211. To the new *civis*: Shane, D. G. (2013): 29f.

32 To its beginning, see Emberley, P. (1989).

33 Shane, D. G. (2013): 59

34 Shane, D. G. (2013): 306

35 Shane, D. G. (2013): 69, 75f. to Landscape Urbanism; and 70, to Koolhaas.

What started in Ebenezer Howard's design for a garden city at the end of 19th century as a cosmos of functional networks and locations soon spread out into the infinite. Howard's pattern of a functional network was a still closed cosmos, centered around the metropolis of those days. But like each functional network, its inherent format allows for being cloned virtually ad infinitum, already starting with his construction: if a certain threshold of overall growth was reached, it could be duplicated elsewhere. Nevertheless, his construction was still a closed cosmos, settled upon the idea of a real physical communal existence, trying to unify man, culture, and nature.[36] Later on, such an attempt was kept, but in patterns of the virtually endless: constructions like Le Corbusier's *Ville contemporaine* and Hilberseimer's *Hochstadt* redefined man's place to live on rational grounds, towards the above-mentioned pattern of a Landscape Urbanism. Hilberseimer can serve as a pars pro toto, his basis was "[...] the individual rectilinear spatial cell, reproduced *ad infinitum* to encompass everything from an individual room to the city and eventually the landscape."[37]

As in case of maps, this new geography of man the cultural animal was really embracing; but unlike the situational architecture, still unified. One of the last attempts in this direction was Doxiadis' *Ecumenopolis* developed in the 1960ies. It was a world-encompassing network of nodes and lines between which protected natural areas should remain, i.e. an intended perfect unity of man and nature, leading to a global garden superimposed on the worldwide mesh of *Ecumenopolis*.[38] Due to its uniform pattern and global coverage it is an essentially placeless and by that, literally 'utopian' space for human kind. There are two main aspects of interest here: on one hand, the above-mentioned attempt of a unified solution, a utopian but nevertheless closed cosmos; and on the other, a beginning immaterialization of relevant human frames of reference, first of all of space; opening the door for the issues of hybridization dealt with in this anthology. Outlined in the Delos conferences held with Doxiadis, McLuhan and Buckminster Fuller (from the sixties until the early seventies), "space itself can only be seen when caught in the net. It is as if the modern perforation and lightening up of architecture in the face of speed, industrialized technology and mass production at the turn of the twentieth century has gone a step farther as buildings dissolve into information flow."[39]

---

36 Eaton, R. (2001): 148-150

37 Bell, D. (2012): 204

38 Doxiadis, C. A. (1967)

39 Wigley, M. (2011): 83

It was the same era when the classical, i.e. still physical city became moveable and a situationist assemblage of places for the now fully individualized and thus, fully freed former *civis*.[40] Within the classical terms of a still physical frame, what began with Frank Lloyd Wright's *Broadacre City* found its end point here. But not its logical end point of development; this was done in the *Ecistics*-conceptions at Delos. The aim was to represent "[...] the evolution of cities with sequences of "electromagnetic maps" and computerized "cartographatrons" showing shifting patterns and hidden force fields through time [...] What counts is a city's trajectory rather than its form [...] Growth becomes movement [...] Buildings are but "shells" for movement patterns that reach out far beyond them. Whereas buildings house function, networks are pure function, function without shell."[41]

Based on world views like this one, the developments sketched in chapters three and four of this anthology become more evident. It all moved towards the hybrid city to come later, allowing for "masses of individuals meeting each other in unprecedented numbers" in volatile and mostly virtual, self-organized groups.[42] With this, a new kind of naturality emerged (so the thesis), through creating those groups own 'natural' environments of a dispersed, and essentially immaterial participation. To recur to the beginning, during a visit of the Delos-group to the remnants of Miletus it was announced that these were "[...] the birth place of western philosophy, the place where the first rational myth was born, the myth which gave wings to man's mind and power to his hands to conquer and transform the world."[43]

With this historical background we can even argue if the (relatively current) emerge of the smart city[44] stems from the need to be able to handle the city in its whole again. The ever-increasing complexity of the functionalized infrastructure makes it harder for the human to use the city in the way he may intend to, be it

---

40 Cf. Eaton, R. (2001): 218-222. It is about the attempts of Yona Friedman, Constant and others to flexibilize the urban physical net for individual and changing demands.

41 Doxiadis cited in Wigley, M. (2011): 87f.

42 Shane, D. C. (2013): 310f.; literal quotation: 310

43 E. Papanoutsos, quoted in Wigley, M. (2011): 116; from *Ecistics*, October 16th, 1963

44 While Caragliu, A., Del Bo, C., and Nijkamp, P. (2009) argues that the concept of the smart city is still fuzzy and common definitions have focused too much on the role of communication infrastructure, it offers a more narrow definition: a city can be called a smart city if "investments in human and social capital and traditional (transport) and modern (ICT) communication infrastructure fuel sustainable economic growth and a high quality of life [...]".

for leisure, work or any other activity. And this problem obviously gets even worse when the city is unknown to the person. All in all, it seems obvious that if a city infrastructure has been optimized based on evaluable criteria, such as connectibility, minimum transportation time of goods, and so on, this technical optimization has its direct partner in the technological means of handling this artificially created environment: the inhabitants understand that their functionalized city is hard to understand and thus create technological artifacts to handle the city. An artificial environment has been technologically created and in order to rule this new environment, technology is created again. To give an example, understanding metro systems can be a hard task even for inhabitants, thus metro planning software has been created to ease the selection of the shortest route from A to B inside of the city. A system whose complexity might have already been at its limit of the human capability to understand is now usable again – and that with ease. What naturally follows is that this system can now increase in complexity: more metro lines added, shorter train intervals until the complexity limits given the current technological means are hit again. The next iteration step would be to create more technological artefacts to handle the new infrastructure system again. And yet, this process is not taking place only in transportation infrastructure like the metro system, but in all infrastructural systems.

The thesis here is that the process of virtualization of reality by creating models and applying them in order to create new models later (which was explained earlier) creates the need for new and also virtual artifacts in order to make the human being capable of using the virtualized space again. This gets very close to the idea of the forbidden space[45] (a special version of the technotopic space[46]), which is a space that is – without technological means – no longer accesible for the human being. A striking example for such a space is the 'forbidden zone'[47] around the Chernobyl nuclear power plant in Ukraine: the catastrophe resulted in contaminating space which is now only accessible to humans if appropriate radiation protection suits are worn, which themselves are technological artifacts. This shows the endpoint of this development: anthropological space gets transformed into virtual space (which itself still has physical properties, it is still there) which is not accessible (even if through an accident as the case with the Chernobyl disaster) and as a result no longer

---

45 Cf. Oetzel, G. (2011)

46 Cf. Ropohl, G. (2009)

47 Officially the Chernobyl Nuclear Power Plant Exclusion Zone, covering an area of around 2,600 square kilometers.

experiencable for the human being that is not equipped with the necessary technological artefacts in order to bear the hazards (or complexity) that this new virtual space inevitably embodies. This space is virtual even in the same sense as the metro system is virtual: I am fully aware of the complexity or the hazards of the space, which means I am aware of the existence of the space, but I can not experience the space in an unmediated way (the metro system cannot be seen in its whole as well as I cannot take off my radiation protection without facing serious health damage afterwards). Both virtual worlds are created by technology itself: they are the result of the application of a model of the world. And this world can of course be handled as long as the technological artifacts still work. If they don't, we face a serious problem, as the space has already been created, i.e. it is existing in a physical sense, while our technological artifacts (protheses in their very sense) are only based on the assumptions that our models of reality (which is our thoughts about these worlds) hold and at the same time the technological preconditions are given (a computer system needs power in order to run, radiation protection equipment has to be created first, and so on). We have run into a technological dependence. We have changed the physical substrate of our world to overcome (e.g. complexity) limits and therefore created a dependence on the artficats that help us handle the new and more complex ('more advanced') systems.

The question at this point is, of course, if this process can be stopped or reverted in any way. As mentioned earlier, it is grounded in a certain understanding of the world, a certain world view, a myth: the myth that technological progress is important.[48] This myth drives the acceleration of the aforementioned process: technology makes it possible for us to use space more efficiently, but only if we commit ourselves to using technological artifacts for that exact purpose. These artifacts push the limits of what the space is capable to offer again, until these boundaries are hit again and the process starts over. In terms of general functionalization terminology, the physical space is the world, and the artifacts are the model. In fact, if you take the example of the metro system again, the artifact is the map or the computer-based itinerary system. That the map is a model is quite obvious, and even for the computer-based system it gets obvious if you understand that the system itself will use models to calculate the itineraries internally. Technology creates artifacts to overcome its own boundaries over and over again – and at that time, the physical, the real gets

---

48 For 'modern' myths related to that, see Gehmann, U. (2003): 108-110, and 115f. To the related capitalist cosmos and its myth of progress, see Gehmann, U. (2012): 104f.

changed to fulfill the needs of the abstract models that are needed in order to accelerate its own acceleration.

REFERENCES

Bayly, Christopher A. (2006): *Die Geburt der modernen Welt* [The Birth of the Modern World, 2004], Frankfurt/New York: Campus

Bell, David (2012): "The Panoptic Garden", in: Giesecke, Annette, and Jacobs, Naomi, eds. (2012): *Earth Perfect? Nature, Utopia, and the Garden,* London: Black Dog Publishing: 190-207

Benevolo, Leonardo (ed. of 2000): *Die Geschichte der Stadt* [the history of the city], Frankfurt: Campus

Bingham, Nick (1996): "Object-ions: from technological determinism towards geographies of relations", *Environment and Planning D: Society and Space,* 14: 635-657

Caragliu, Andrea, Del Bo, Chiara F., and Nijkamp, Peter (2009): "Smart cities in Europe", in: *Serie Research Memoranda 0048,* VU University Amsterdam, Faculty of Economics, Business Administration and Econometrics

Castells, Manuel (ed. of 2003): Vol. I, *Der Aufstieg der Netzwerksgesellschaft* [the rise of the network society], Opladen: Leske + Budrich

Delfante, Charles (1999): *Architekturgeschichte der Stadt* [architectural history of the city], Darmstadt: Primus

D' Hooghe, Alexander (2010): "The Objectification of Infrastructure: The Cultural Project of Suburban Infrastructure Design", in: Stoll, Katrina, and Lloyd, Scott, eds. (2010): *Infrastructure as Architecture: Designing Composite Networks,* Berlin: Jovis: 78-84.

Doxiadis, Constantinos A. (1967): "The coming era of ecumenopolis", *Saturday Review,* March 18, 1967: 11-14

Eaton, Ruth (2001): *Die ideale Stadt* [the ideal city], Berlin: nicolai

Emberley, Peter (1989): "Places and Stories: the challenge of technology", *Social Research,* 56: 741-785

Feuerstein, Günter (2008): *Urban Fiction,* Stuttgart/London: Menges

Fujita, Masahisa et al. (2000): *The Spatial Economy: Cities, Regions and International Trade,* Cambridge, MA: MIT Press

Gehmann, Ulrich (2003): "Modern Myths", Vol. 9, No. 2, *Culture and Organization,* June 2003, Durham: Routledge: 105-119

Gehmann, Ulrich (2012): "Der kapitalistische Kosmos als mythisches Bestreben. Die Virtualität des Realen" [the mythic longing of a capitalist cosmos: about the virtuality of the real], in: Gehmann, Ulrich, ed. (2012): *Virtuelle und ideale Welten* [virtual and ideal worlds], Karlsruhe: KIT Scientific Publishing: 85-105

Graham, Stephen, and Marvin, Simon (2001): *Splintering Urbanism*, London/New York: Routledge

Hoffmeister, Johannes (1955): *Wörterbuch der philosophischen Begriffe* [dictionary of philosophic terms], Hamburg: Felix Meiner

ISOCARP (International Society of City and Regional Planners) 2001 Congress, Utrecht: „Planning in the Information Age", http://www.isocarp.org/index.php?id=133#c412

Kostof, Spiro (ed. of 2007): *The City Shaped*, New York/Boston/London: Bulfinch Press

Oetzel, Guenther (2011): "Technotope Räume – vom Naturraum zum verbotenen Raum" [technotopic spaces – from natural space to forbidden space], in: Gehmann, Ulrich, ed. (2012): *Virtuelle und Ideale Welten* [virtual and ideal worlds], Karlsruhe: KIT Scientific Publishing: 65-83

Ropohl, Guenther (ed. of 2009): Allgemeine Technologie. Eine Systemtheorie der Technik. [General technology. A system theory of technology], Karlsruhe: KIT Scientific Publishing

Schüttpelz, Erhard (2007): "Ein absoluter Begriff. Zur Genealogie und Karriere des Netzwerkkonzeptes" [to the genealogy of the idea of the concept of network], in: Kaufman, Stefan, ed. (2007): *Vernetzte Steuerung*, Zurich: Chronos: 25-46

Shane, David G. (2013): *Recombinant Urbanism. Conceptual Modeling in Architecture, Urban Design, and City Theory*, Chichester: John Wiley & Sons

Short, John R. (2003): *The World Through Maps. A History of Cartography*, Toronto: Firefly Books Ltd.

Vance, James E., Jr. (1990): *The Continuing City*, Baltimore/London: John Hopkins Univ. Press

Vercelloni, Virgilio (1994): *Europäische Stadtutopien* [European utopias of the city], Munich: Diederichs

Waldheim, Charles, and Berger, Alan (2012): "Logistiklandschaften" [logistic landscapes], no. 205, *arch plus*, March 2012: 76-83

Whatmore, Sarah (2002): *Hybrid Geographies: Natures, Cultures, Spaces*, London: Sage

Wigley, Mark (2011): "Network fever", reprinted in Vrachliotis, Georg, ed.: *Netz. Organisationsform & Leitmetapher* [Net. Organizational Form & lead metaphor], KIT Karlsruhe: Seminar paper, winter 2011/12

Wright, Frank L. (ed. of 1950): *When Democracy builds*, Chicago: Univ. of Chicago Press

Gotham City

A Dystopian Comic Book World as an Arena of Modern Myths

MARTIN CREMERS

THE MANY FACES OF A CITY

We have different images in mind when we think of Gotham City. At present, many may think of Batman navigating heavily armored vehicles through urban canyons in his nighttime fight against outlaws and madmen as seen in Christopher Nolan's blockbuster movies *Batman begins* (2005), *The Dark Knight* (2008) and *The Dark Knight Rises* (2012). Some remember over-sized balloons among the city's rooftops at the Joker's grotesque street parade in Tim Burton's *Batman: The movie* (1989) or the march of remotely controlled emperor penguins through snow-covered alleys prepared to launch their attached cruise missiles in *Batman returns* (1992). Others can't avoid to think of the loud colored movies *Batman forever* (1995) and *Batman & Robin* (1997) by director Joel Schumacher, where city walls are soaked in black light graffiti and neon advertisements. Some may have pictures in their minds of a dark manlike silhouette wearing a waving cape in front of an infernal red metropolitan skyline as seen in the opening sequence of each episode of *Batman: The Animated Series* starting in 1992. Some still see Batman and Robin in their funny-fashioned outfits climbing up the city's brick-lined facades in the *Batman* TV-series of the 1960s. Others remember themselves gliding over virtual street lines controlling Batman in the acclaimed video game *Arkham City* (2011). And then, of course, many have some of the countless panels in mind showing a dark urban background, narrowing tower buildings and the yellow outlined image of a bat projected onto the city's night sky as pictured in thousands of *Batman* comic book releases since the year 1939. Most of us though may not just think of one of the above when Gotham City comes to mind, but imagine a mixture of pictures, combining different elements.

In any case one can say that Gotham City has become one of the most famous virtual worlds of our days. Each month there is a binary number of new comic book releases which have Gotham City as its setting. It is an inherent part of several Hollywood blockbuster movies, breaking the records of box-office takings consistently. It also is the virtual environment of some of the most popular video games. Gotham City is lived by fans who visit comic conventions dressed as their favorite Batman villains. It is getting real in the children's rooms due to several toy lines from action figures to Lego Batman. By now *Batman* has become a similar phenomenon as *Star Wars*, present in many parts of the world.

In the following, the reasons for The Dark Knight's popularity shall be analyzed. Emanated from the presumption that Batman's whole appearance depends on the dark environment of Gotham City, this particular dystopia itself shall be the matter of interest. A depiction of its reference to our world and to other comic book cities as Superman's Metropolis and Walt Disney's Duckburg shall expose Gotham City's outstanding significance. Prospects of the steadily increased attention to details picturing Gotham as well as its relationship to some of its most important inhabitants shall pave the way for the further pursuit of the question, to what extent Gotham City can be understood as a place generating modern myths.

LOCALIZING GOTHAM

When comic artist Bob Kane and writer Bill Finger created Batman in the late 1930s they were inspired by contemporary fiction as well as by newspaper headlines. According to Bob Kane the two most influential movies have been *The Mark of Zorro* (1920) about "a wealthy landowner who maintained both an alter ego as a masked and caped crime fighter and a secret cave-hideout beneath his mansion"[1] and *The Bat Whispers* (1930), "in which the villain wore a bat-like costume [...]."[2] Apart from this Bill Finger's inspiration derived from Sir Arthur Conan Doyle's *Sherlock Holmes* stories and contemporary pulp magazines. Real-time events like the emerging conflict in Europe, which has led to World War II, and moreover the exploits of Chicago's criminals Al Capone and the recently killed John Dillinger had a grave effect on Finger's storytelling.

Even over seventy years later the characterization of many of Batman's foes still reminds of gangster bosses and mobsters from the 1930s. Chicago's

---

1   Boichel, B. (1991): 6
2   Kane in Steranko, J. (1970): 44

atmosphere of these days is still noticeable in today's story telling. For this reason, comic book artists such as Neil Adams compare Gotham City to Chicago. Director Christopher Nolan, who apparently shares this opinion, decided to film the first two Batman movies in Chicago.[3]

However, DC is a New York publishing house and both Bob Kane and Bill Finger lived in New York when they worked on the first Batman stories. Consequently, the setting of their hero's adventures had to be Manhattan. It took almost two years until the release of *Detective Comics* #48 on February 1st, 1941, when the name Gotham City appeared for the first time. About the decision to move Batman's place of work to Gotham, Bill Finger said: "We didn't call it New York because we wanted anybody in any city to identify with it. Of course, Gotham is another name for New York." (Steranko (1970), p. 45) Bill Finger here refers to "Gotham" as an old nickname for New York, which can be traced back to Washington Irving. In February 13th, 1807, he wrote in one of the first issues of *Salmagundi*, a satirical magazine created by Irving himself:

»One of the most tickling, dear, mischievous pleasures of this life is to laugh in one's sleeve – to sit snug in the corner, unnoticed and unknown, and bear the wise men of Gotham, who are profound judges of horse-flesh, pronounce, from the style of our work, who are the authors.«[4]

Washington Irving in turn refers to the small town Gotham in England's Nottinghamshire, whose inhabitants shall proverbial have been well-known for their "foolish ingenuity."

A year before Batman entered the scene, in the year 1938 publisher DC already introduced Superman, the world's first superhero. Superman was the American answer to the "Übermensch" ideals contended by the Nazis. Apart from a few similarities, Batman and Superman couldn't be more different. Batman is human and driven by an enormous will power to prevent that kind of crime he had to experience as a small boy when his parents were shot dead in front of his eyes. He has become a creature of the night, hiding in the shadows, striking in secrecy, to use the fear of the unknown as his most powerful weapon. Superman in contrast is an alien from the planet Krypton with extraordinary physical abilities on earth. He is quasi-invulnerable, flies faster than a speeding bullet and has nearly unlimited strength. In a bright-colored outfit he operates at day, visible to anyone, bringing hope to the righteous.

---

3   According to Urrichio, W. (2010): 122
4   Irving, W. (1807): 39

Even though there are these differences, Batman's Gotham City and Superman's Metropolis are both based on the city of New York. In the DC universe both places are located to the American east coast, approximately to the area of New Jersey. And like Manhattan, at least one city part is divided from the mainland by rivers: New Troy in Metropolis and with Uptown, Midtown and Downtown almost all of Gotham City. In spite of these common geographically similarities to New York, the two cities considerably differ from another, which reflects the differences between Batman and Superman.

To underline Gotham's gothic and crooked character, some particular characteristics of New York are used far more often in portraying Gotham rather than Metropolis. Most of Gotham City is not modernized and reminds of the edged New Yorker architecture from the late 19th and early 20th century, such as the Brooklyn Bridge (completed in 1883), the Park Row Building (1899), the Woolworth Building (1913) or the Manhattan Municipal Building (1915). Façades consist of raw brick walls, stone-made gargoyles decorate the upper levels and rooftops are topped by the typical large wooden water tanks which take care of an adequate water pressure in the whole building. The police use of zeppelins (in *Batman: The Animated Series* and several comic book stories) enforces the image of Gotham City being old New York but placed to our present time.

As a contrast, Metropolis is often called "the city of tomorrow." Its orientation towards the future not the past is illustrated by a higher quantity of modern buildings. Metropolis' façades are smooth, clean and consist in large parts of glass. New Yorker counterparts for example would be Trump Tower (completed in 1983) or the World Financial Center (1988). Some constructions, especially Lexcorp Building, technically are on such a high level that Superman stories obviously exceed the border to science fiction, even without the arrival of further extraterrestrial visitors in Metropolis.

Former Batman editor Dennis O'Neil characterizes Gotham City and Metropolis considering different aspects of New York with the following two sentences:

»Gotham is Manhattan below Fourteenth Street at 3 a.m., November 28 in a cold year. Metropolis is Manhattan between Fourteenth and One Hundred and Tenth Streets on the brightest, sunniest July day of the year.«[5]

---

5   Cited after Boichel, B. (1991): 9

Figure 1. Switched Worlds: Batman in Metropolis and Superman in Gotham City.[6]

---

6   Taken from Superman/Batman #53, New York, DC Comics 2008. Written by Michael
    Green and Mike Johnson; Artwork by Rags Morales, John Dell, Nei Ruffino and Rob
    Leigh. © DC Comics.

Or as Frank Miller, writer of the acclaimed Batman comic book *The Dark Knight Returns*, puts it: "Metropolis is New York in the daytime; Gotham City is New York at night."

Beyond the assignment of different New Yorker vibes, some of New York's most famous places are reflected in either Gotham City or Metropolis: Gotham's Blackgate Island is a reference to New York's prison on Rikers Island and the Statue of Liberty sometimes is placed in the harbor of Metropolis (for example see *Action Comics* #143 (April 1950) or the movie *Superman IV: The Quest for Peace* (1987)). The coexistence of both cities, Metropolis and Gotham, in the same fictive world raised some serious problems of continuity. According to most comic books Metropolis is located in the state of New York, Gotham City in contrast is placed in the state of New Jersey. But depending on the respective writer the distance between both cities varies. These issues become more evident whenever New York itself appears as a separate (third) city in DC comic books. For example the headquarter of the Teen Titans, a team of young superheroes lead by Batman's first Robin Dick Grayson, is located to New York in 1980. These problems of continuity concerning Gotham City are part of the next section.

Moreover, the city of Gotham was significantly shaped over the years. Wayne Manor and its Batcave, Crime Alley, where Bruce Wayne's parents have been murdered, and the Gotham City police department aren't any longer the only few constant places of action. Over the years it has been enriched by permanently new scenes such as the clock tower, where the former Batgirl Barbara Gordon supports her allies with information from the world wide web since the Joker paralyzed her – to give just one example. Beyond this, every corner of every district seems to have its own proper name by now. They often are named after comic book writers who crucially shaped today's Gotham such as The Robert Kane Memorial Bridge, Finger River, Grant Park, Miller Harbor or Dixon Dock. Gotham City has slowly turned from the background (as the basic setting of the first Batman stories) to the foreground and has become an irreplaceable element, shaping the stories as fundamentally as their main characters.

Along to Gotham's proceeding environmental specification the first city maps came up. In the *No Man's Land* storyline of 1999, which for several months extended to all Batman related comic book titles, a detailed map of Gotham City prefixed all issues. For fans it is now well traceable how long a ride with the Batmobile may take until the caped crusader arrives at Arkham Asylum for example.

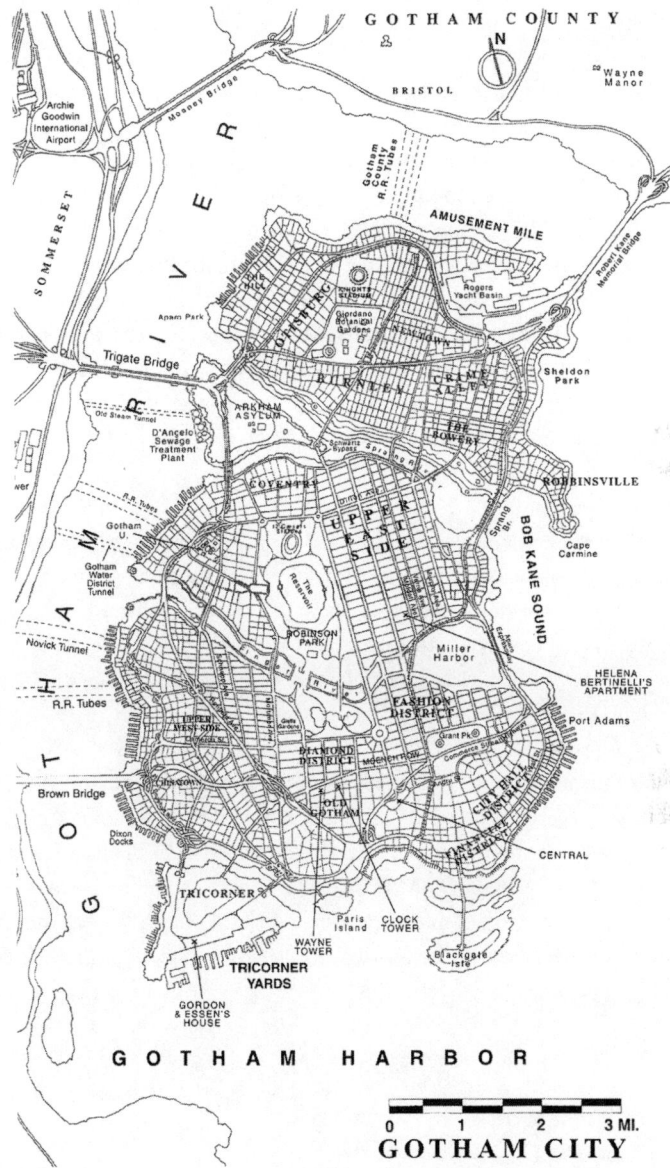

Figure 2. Gotham City street map as published in No Man's Land, New York, DC Comics 1999.[7]

7 © DC Comics. Taken from http://batmangothamcity.net/wp-content/uploads/2012/04/-
gotham-city1.jpg

The increased precision in presenting Gotham's ground plan, of course, is an indication for the generally grown interest in Batman's dystopian working environment: the more details revealed, the more realistic and familiar the world. On the other hand, this precision comes along with a certain loss of the reader's personal contribution to the story. The more of Gotham's parameters are fixed over the years, the less freedom is left for own imagination. The more alleys of the city are lighted, the less darkness is left for own interpretation.

It is important to mention that the urge for finalization hasn't affected all artificial comic book worlds yet. Walt Disney's Duckburg for example is largely safe from being locally (and temporally) determined. There also is no official city map[8] of Duckburg and no definite position of Scrooge McDuck's money bin. Duckburg today still is as shapeable as in the late 1940s when writer and artist Carl Barks started his much vaunted work on Walt Disney's Donald Duck ten-pagers.

»Barks [...] just drew what he needed for his plots. If he wanted to tell a sea adventure [...] Duckburg lies on the shore. If he liked to tell a winter story he let snow fall in the streets where normally palms would grow. Or he had Duckburg situated at the foot of a mountain chain – that Duckburg that we can see [on the last panel of page 8 of the story *Statuesque Spendthrifts*, first released in *Walt Disney's Comics and Stories* #138], lying in the plains, surrounded by nothing more than farmland.«[9]

Back in the '40s no more characteristics were attributed to Gotham City than to Duckburg. But in contrast to Donald Duck's hometown, Gotham's city limits were narrowed down more and more. It's a phenomenon of the last decades that some virtual worlds such as Gotham City claim to be more precise and less apparitional. This development may be understood as a counterpart to our reality, which these days appears in such a high degree of complexity, that the framework seems to get lost.

---

8   The attempt of the German Donald Duck scholars Jürgen Wollina and Christian Pfeiler to trace an accurate map of Duckburg took Wollina 13 years of research. (see Bröker, J. (2008): 41) Though every single location can be proved by an adequate panel, it is impossible that any artist working for Disney could have had that kind of map in their minds.

9   Platthaus, A. (2010): 259

GOTHAM AND CONTINUITY

As seen at the example of Gotham City's map, present authors of superhero stories have to fit their ideas to a predetermined scheme with just a little space of tolerance. Back in the first two eras of comic book history, the Golden Age (from the late 1930s to the mid-50s) and the following Silver Age (until approximately 1970), creativity was far less limited.[10] Former editor Dennis O'Neil, who was responsible for writers meeting the publisher's guidelines in the early 1990s, compares this freedom with a storyteller's work of today using the following words:

»Julie Schwartz did a Batman in *Batman* and *Detective* and Murray Boltinoff did a Batman in the *Brave and Bold* and apart from the costume they bore very little resemblance to each other. Julie and Murray did not coordinate their efforts, did not pretend to, did not want to, were not asked to. Continuity was not important in those days. Now it has become very important, which is decidedly a mixed blessing. [...] Comics are not read on a hit or miss basis anymore. They are read by fewer people than they were in the '40s but the current fans read a great deal more intently and with a great deal of care.«[11]

Dennis O'Neal here refers to the former impossibility for comic book readers to get every issue of each title – one important reason for the avoidance of continuity in the first decades of comic book publishing. Every comic book's story had to be told as if standing alone until the early 1970s. Then the direct market was born, an institution that enabled comic book specialized shops to order certain

---

10 It has to be mentioned that comic book stories in the '50s already were exposed to some awkward controls. In his best-selling analysis *Seduction of the Innocent* the psychiatrist Fredric Wertham pointed out the assumed coherence between superhero comic books and the adolescent misdirection of his time. For example, his critique in Batman comics is focused on the suspicion of a homosexual attitude between the two main characters Batman and Robin as well as Alfred the butler. To go against Werthams prejudices and in fear of decreasing sales figures the Comics Code was drafted, a label decorating each issue's front page guaranteeing the childproof content of the inside. During the funny and bright-sided Silver Age, the Batcave was therefore enriched by Kathy Kane (Batwoman) and her niece Betty (Batgirl). Alfred was replaced by Aunt Harriet. And Ace the Bat-Hound completed the new bat-family. Nevertheless, apart from the compliance with the new Comics Code, authors still have been quite independent of editorial instructions.

11 Pearson, R. E., and Uricchio, W. (1991a): 23

quantities of certain titles for the first time. Readers from then on could be sure to obtain every issue of their favorite series. And writers used this opportunity to expand their stories beyond the last page of a single issue. The complexity of storytelling and therefore developments in character relationships and continuity of time and space increased rapidly.

The beginning of comic book history's Bronze Age (or Dark Age, as writer Grant Morrison calls it[12]) is dated to the time around 1970 and focuses on a more realistic, less funny storytelling. The fundament of what DC Comics are today is built in these days. Batman is lead back to his "dark and violent pulp roots,"[13] Robin outgrows his boy wonder pants and a discord between both partners lets Batman and Robin tread separate paths. During the following decades heroes die and even Bruce Wayne was temporarily replaced as Batman (*Batman: Knightfall* [1993-94]).

Continuity slowly raises the importance of Gotham City. As a "Punctum Archimedis," a spatiotemporal constant in Batman comics, it becomes an indispensable element, accompanying the stories' dark atmosphere. Gotham City appears as a self-contained microcosm, cut loose from the residual DC Universe with all its superpower heroes and space invasions. In a way Gotham City itself becomes an intervening character, when most of its districts get destroyed during an earthquake (*Cataclysm* and *Aftershock*, both 1998). The impossibility to appease the looting and rioting population leads the government to the desperate measure to destroy all bridges and separate Gotham City from the mainland (*No Man's Land*, 1999). In this story the allegory of Gotham City as a microcosm becomes more appreciable than ever before.

Nevertheless, crossover stories between different super heroes of the DC macrocosm have dramatic consequences on Batman's world, too. Supernatural events in storylines as *Crisis on Infinite Earths* (1985-86) or *Zero Hour: Crisis in Time* (1994) may cosmetically correct mistakes in the continuity or change a character's origin. Today the DC Universe is a place of countless parallel existing worlds, all separated and yet with large effect on each other. Readers as well as writers and editors can't keep track of the storyline anymore. The more events take place and the more crowded the universe gets, the more confusing this world appears to us as their visitors. Superhero comics in this reading become a mirror of our own world: They show us the inapprehensible and the obscure. With conflicts in continuity and a "multiverse" almost no one is able to over-

---

12 Morrison, G. (2012): 146
13 Morrison, G. (2012): 146

look, they remind us of the complexity of our reality, where economical, ecological or demographic issues overburden our comprehension.

The opening scene in the beginning of Tim Burton's first *Batman* movie carves out this point. It shows a small family, father, mother and their young son, roaming through Gotham City's streets. As the son fights with a map trying to help winning orientation in this hopeless situation, his father tells him: "Put that away. We'll look like tourists."

CONSULTING GOTHAM'S REGISTRATION OFFICE

An obvious way to define Gotham is to have a closer look at its inhabitants. No city can be described without considering its population living in it. Of all the main characters appearing in Batman comic books the only ordinary people seem to be Bruce Wayne's butler Alfred Pennyworth, commissioner James Gordon and some of his colleagues at the Gotham City Police Department. Most of the other figures are mixtures of criminal masterminds, madmen and athletic vigilant crime-fighters. A closer characterization of the three villains Joker, Poison Ivy and Ra's al Ghul shall provide an insight into what makes Gotham a dystopia.

The Joker

Alfred's characterization in Nolan's second movie *The Dark Knight* expresses all what the Joker is about in a few sentences: "Some men aren't looking for anything logical like money. They can't be bought, bullied, reasoned or negotiated with. Some men just want to watch the world burn."

When the Joker first appeared in the first issue of Batman's independent ongoing series in 1940, their creators must have sensed the potential of this character for further comic books. For this reason the Joker didn't end up dead when the last page was reached, a fate often met by villains of former Batman stories. Over the years the Joker consistently has established himself as the most dangerous Batman villain. He gets the credits for several disturbing traumata hitting the good guys of Gotham City: He shot and paralyzed Gordon's daughter Barbara (Batgirl) in *Batman: The Killing Joke* (1988), he battered the second Robin Jason Todd to death in *A Death in the Family* (1988/89) and killed Gordon's second wife Sarah Essen in *Detective Comics* #741 (2000) during the *No Man's Land* storyline. In Tim Burton's first Batman movie he is also responsible for the death of Thomas and Martha Wayne and therefore for their son Bruce becoming Batman.

The Joker's true nature is hard to define. Different comic book writers focus on different degrees of his lunacy. Even the Joker's real name and origin aren't settled at all. In his cinematic realization Christopher Nolan responds to this fact when at two different occasions the Joker tells two incompatible stories about his background.

To the rational Batman the Joker is his chaotic counterpart. When Batman is predictable, calculating and serious, the Joker is irrational, capricious and contrary. He is a social dropout with just one single ambition: to show the rest of Gotham that their system is a failure and that there is no superior concept leading us through life. There is only chaos. The Joker terrorizes Gotham just to verify this mindset over and over again. On the showdown pages with the caped crusader in the much acclaimed Joker story *The Killing Joke* the Clown Prince of Crime explains himself with the words: "It's all a joke! Everything anybody ever valued or struggled for... It's all a monstrous, demented gag! So why can't you see the funny side? Why aren't you laughing?" And Batman answers to him: "Because I've heard it before ...and it wasn't funny the first time."[14]

Poison Ivy

Dr. Pamela Lillian Isley studies botany and biochemistry as she gets poisoned by ancient herbs. The effect doesn't kill her, but alters "her biochemistry in a way that renders her body immune to all toxins, her kiss toxic to others, and her mood subject to violent swings."[15] Often described to be more plant than human Poison Ivy is anxious for helping flora regaining its biotope.

In a microcosm like Gotham City, which lacks avenues and where park areas are suppressed as far as possible, Poison Ivy tries to realize Jean-Jacques Rousseau's ideas and find a way back to nature. She breeds resistant climbing plants and man-eating carnivores to destroy civilization and give nature back its habitat. Her fight against Batman (natura versus cultura) bares one crucial attribute characterizing Gotham City: its grown urbanity comes along with the total expulsion of all natural.

---

14 Bolland, B., and Moore, A. (1988): 39-40.
15 Langley, T. (2012): 127.

Ra's al Ghul

The man whose name is translated with "The Demon's Head" is actually no inhabitant of Gotham City, he's not even American at all. Nevertheless his focus of interest constantly lies on Gotham.

Born several centuries ago the Lazarus Pit – some kind of fountain of youth in the DC Universe – preserves Ra's al Ghul from dying, or rather enables his resurrection periodically. During his long life he becomes witness of numerous changes in human history. He outlasts dozens of generations of people, sees mankind spreading all over the world and finally arrives at the conclusion that the ruthless human domination of planet earth must be stopped.

In the story arcs *Contagion* and *Legacy* (both 1996) Batman and his allies see themselves confronted with the deadly Ebola virus unleashed by Ra's al Ghul. In Nolan's *Batman begins* he argues: "When a forest grows too wild, a purging fire is inevitable and natural." Gotham City is not chosen randomly as Ra's al Ghul's first target for decimating mankind. The great number of insane freaks and cold-blooded killers, corruptive mayors and bribable police officers, junkies, drug dealers, panderers and other low-lifes make Gotham City our time's hotbed of sin.

Some comic books of our days are sophisticated in a way that the reader's sympathies may even switch from the "good" but often grim and unsociable Batman to his "bad" but very emotional antagonist. Mr. Freeze, who in many stories commits crime to help his ill wife Nora in cryostasis, is one example. A character named Anarky introduced in 1989, who fights against irresponsible enterprises and governmental institutions to stop worldwide social inequalities, may be another. In those stories the limits of Batman's scope of action are revealed. He fights crime with methods the police will never be able to apply, but he never questions the constitutional law itself, even if moral laws sometimes may dissent.

Batman in this spirit *is* Gotham City, a microcosmic mirror of our world. He fights the renegades of our society, who with their twisted convictions advocate an alternative to our capitalistic and pseudo-free system. In this reading not the colorful dressed Clown Prince of Crime or the eco-terrorizing plant-woman make Gotham the dark and uninviting place it is, but Batman does.

Gotham City as an Arena of Modern Myths

»Batman and Robin are the postindustrial equivalent of folk figures. Because these characters have been around for 50 years [75 by now], everybody in the country knows about
them. They have some of the effect on people that mythology used to and if you get into
that you can't avoid the question of religion.«[16]

The relation between figures of ancient myths and today's comic book superheroes is distinctive. Some comic books intend even to be the direct sequel to
Homer's *Iliad* or to continue the Norse mythology.

Amazon queen Hippolyta, famous for her girdle which had to be obtained
by Hercules during his ninth labour, is in DC Comics the mother of Diana, prin-
cess of Themyscira. As Wonder Woman (created by the American academic
William Moulton Marston) Diana represents her people in our present world of
mortals. In the monthly comic book series *Wonder Woman* the Olympian gods
and other figures of the Greek mythology, such as the evil sorceress Circe, are
frequently appearing characters.

The Norse gods of Asgard in contrast find their way into Marvel Comics by
the series *Thor*. To teach his presumptuous son a lesson in humility, Odin exiles
Thor to earth. Increasingly protective of humanity, in particular of the nurse Jane
Foster, Thor decided to defend earth against evil, among other things by co-
founding the super hero team The Avengers. His arch nemesis is Loki, known
from Norse mythology as well.

Countless further examples of comic book characters inspired by ancient
myths could be cited. The Flash refers to the Greek messenger of the gods, Hermes. In DC Comics The Flash is called "the fastest man alive" and his headgear
is decorated by two little wings (as Hermes' ankles are). Green Lantern is inspired by *One Thousand and One Nights* as protagonist Alan Scott (modified
Aladdin) finds a railroad lamp with the power to bring imagination into being.
Green Lantern was "the first superhero influenced by the esoteric culture of the
East: His wish-fulfilling gem recalled the language of *The Tibetan Book of the
Dead*, while the Lantern was Arabic, Islamic, and exotic."[17] And with Namor the
Sub-Mariner and Aquaman both publishers Marvel *and* DC Comics have their
own undersea comic book hero surfaced from the sunken city of Atlantis.

Batman's mythological influences don't seem to be this obvious. As expli-
cated above, Batman's character refers to contemporary movies and pulp maga-

---

16 Pearson, R. E., and Uricchio, W. (1991a): 23
17 Morrison, G. (2012): 29

zines. However, Gotham City as our time's hotbed of sin provides a direct association to mythological originals. The two cities Sodom and Gomorrah mentioned amongst others in the *Book of Genesis* were destroyed by God due to the fact that no ten righteous men could be found. This image is transferrable to many Batman comics, whose pages are crowded with dodgers, tricksters, villains and worse. The biblical Babylon as an origin of sin and human hubris would adjust the perception of Gotham to a similar focus. However, the titles *Batman* and *Detective Comics* still are comic book series intended for teenagers. Sexual content or explicit violence are found on rare occasions. A comic book world where the presence of the mentioned archetypal hotbeds of sin may be more perceptible is Basin City from Frank Miller's series *Sin City*. With stories basically located to strip clubs, red-light districts and run-down quarters where criminality dominates, *Sin City* contains considerably more brutality and sexual perversion. Gotham City can be merely seen as a primary stage in comic book history to a "Neo-Gomorrah" as Sin City.

Maybe the underworld of ancient Greek mythology is a more convenient reference, when trying to find Gotham City's roots in the history of ideas. Like Hades, Gotham City appears to be a place that is cut from the outside: a microcosm on its own, with its own rules and yet with a set of sagas significant for our world above. As already mentioned, this picture is actually drawn in the story arc of *No Man's Land*, when all bridges above the encircling rivers are destroyed and no ferryman is allowed to cross over to the other side.

Hades and Gotham are both places of darkness, but nonetheless occupied by heroes who defy the shadows. According to Albert Camus, Sisyphus is the most notable hero in Hades and his similarities to Batman may be notable as well. Though the motives for the gods to expose Sisyphus to his eternal agony differ, the torments of his punishment are well known. In Tartaros, the deepest and darkest region of Hades, he is compelled to roll a rock to the top of a mountain. Whenever he is about to reach his destination, the stone falls back into the valley. Sisyphus has to descend to start again. Camus sees in this very moment the analogy to every man's tragedy, when he gets conscious and aware of the absurd:

»I see that man going back down with a heavy yet measured step towards the torment of which he will never know the end. That hour like a breathing-space which returns as surely as his suffering, that is the hour of consciousness. At each of those moments when he leaves the heights and gradually sinks towards the lairs of the gods, he is superior to his fate. He is stronger than his rock.«[18]

Batman is today's Sisyphus. Determined by the moment his parents were killed Batman fights the same fight every night. His codex denies him to kill. So he knows that every exhausting defeat of an enemy is not about to last. Every criminal Batman locks up in Blackgate Prison, every madman he commits to the psychiatrists of Arkham Asylum eventually will return and has to be fought again. Conscious about this destiny, as someone "who knows that the night has no end, he is still on the go."[19] Camus here refers to Sisyphus – but these words characterize Batman as well.

Myths can be told in many different ways. Numerous writers and artists, movie makers and video game developers constantly enrich Batman's dystopian world by new points of view. The narrative form may vary from subtle to entertaining, from serious to funny, from drawn to filmed, but the mythological essence persists. If one admits it, it is the same essence one can find in their ancient predecessors.

REFERENCES

Boichel, Bill (1991): *Batman: Commodity as Myth*, in: Pearson, Roberta E. and Uricchio, William, eds. (1991): *The many lives of the Batman. Critical Approaches to a Superhero and his Media*, New York: Routledge: 4-17

Bolland, Brian, and Moore, Alan (1988): *Batman: The Killing Joke*, New York: DC Comics.

Bröker, Jürgen (2008): *Dem Erpel auf der Spur*, in: *Die Zeit* Nr. 49, Hamburg: Zeitverlag Gerd Bucerius: 40-41.

Camus, Albert (2005): *The Myth of Sisyphus*, London: Penguin Books.

Irving, Washington (1807): *Fashions*, in: Irving, Washington; Irving, William; Paulding, James (1807): *Salmagundi*; Chicago/New York: Belford, Clarke & Company.

Langley, Travis (2012): *Batman and Psychology. A Dark and Stormy Knight*, Hoboken: John Wiley & Sons: 2012.

Morrison, Grant (2012): *Supergods*, New York: Random House.

---

18 Camus, A. (2005): 117
19 Camus, A. (2005): 119

Pearson, Roberta E., and Uricchio, William (1991a): *Notes from the Batcave: An Interview with Dennis O'Neil*, in: Pearson, Roberta E., and Uricchio, William, eds. (1991): *The many lives of the Batman. Critical Approaches to a Superhero and his Media*, New York: Routledge: 18-32.

Platthaus, Andreas (2010): *Calisota or Bust: Duckburg vs. Entenhausen in the Comics of Carl Barks*, in: Ahrens, Jörn, and Meteling, Arno (2010): *Comics and the City. Urban Space in Print, Picture and Sequence*, New York: Continuum International Publishing Group: 247–264.

Steranko, James (1970): *History of Comics – Volume One*, Reading/Pennsylvania: Supergraphics.

Urrichio, William (2010): *The Batman's Gotham City. Story, Ideology, Performance*, in: Ahrens, Jörn, and Meteling, Arno (2010): *Comics and the City. Urban Space in Print, Picture and Sequence*, New York: Continuum International Publishing Group: 119–132.

Good Night, Zoo

A Children's Guide to Humanimal Spaces

IRUS BRAVERMAN

> Becomings-animal are neither dreams nor
> phantasies. They are perfectly real.[1]

The first page of *Good Night, Gorilla*, a children's book by Peggy Rathmann,[2] is vibrant and splashy. "Good night, Gorilla," says the zookeeper, turning away from the cages, not seeing the young and smiling gorilla stealing the brightly colored key ring from his belt. In the cage, we see a tire, a bicycle, a small stuffed toy in the shape of a gorilla, and what looks like a children's book on whales with its pages wide open. The gorilla climbs out of his pen, and along with a mouse, who courageously carries a banana bigger than himself on a string, follows the zookeeper through the zoo. At each cage, the zookeeper – nametagged "Joe" – says good night to the elephant, the lion, the hyena, the giraffe, and the armadillo (a range of exotic zoo animals, notably all mammals). In the space between one page and the next, the gorilla has freed another animal to follow along after the keeper. Every animal, save the lion and the armadillo, are kept company in their cages by small, stuffed, simulacra of themselves (the lion is licking on bones and the armadillo has a Sesame Street Elmo toy).

The keeper leaves the zoo to go to his home, which is situated just across a lawn from the tall pink gate of the zoo, and the animals all follow him into the house, standard expectations of physical dimensions notwithstanding. Inside, the zookeeper's wife is already asleep, and does not open her eyes as her husband and the gorilla climb into bed with her. "Good night, dear," she says, switching off the lights, and a chorus of "Good night" responds, although none apparently

---

1 Deleuze, G., and Guattari, F. (1980): 238.
2 Rathmann, P. (1994)

come from Joe himself. The woman switches the light on to see the gorilla grinning at her from the side of the bed. Flipping the page, we see the woman leading the animals back into the zoo, then returning home with a, "Good night, zoo," failing to see the gorilla and the mouse once again following her back to her domicile. The gorilla turns to the reader and presses a finger to his lips, signaling our complicity in this arrangement. "Good night, dear," says the woman, and the zookeeper finally responds "Good night," as the gorilla and the mouse crawl back into bed in between the couple, the banana eaten, this interspecies grouping asleep at last. On the nightstand the family photo that was vague in the previous pages is finally focused: it features the family of the zookeeper, his wife, and... an infant gorilla.

Like many other children books, *Good Night, Gorilla* is a bedtime story. As such, its narrative depicts the twilight zone between day and night and between awake and dream states. Alongside this liminal temporal dimension, the book also explicates and challenges the boundaries between captivity and freedom, living and nonliving things, feminine and masculine and, most importantly perhaps, between city and wilderness, home and zoo, and human and nonhuman animality. *Good Night, Gorilla* illustrates such bounded spaces, but then, gently, almost unnoticeably, questions these boundaries. To borrow Donna Haraway's title, this book considers what happens *When Species Meet*, creating a hybrid space where the real becomes virtual and the virtual becomes real.

THE ZOO IN THE CITY:
WILD ANIMALS INVADING THE HUMAN BEDROOM

»Utopias and dystopias seem to be the only scenarios possible, and yet the future is likely to lie in between: complex, messy and contested.«[3]

It is no coincidence that most zoos are situated in the city: it is precisely at the heart of human civilization that nonhuman animals must be displayed, acting as spectacles for human dominance over nature.[4] Since the zoo is the site where wild animals are brought into the city and yet not allowed to be wild, they represent a "variably constructed and opposed nature ... [which] inscribe[s] a cultural sense of distance from that loosely defined realm."[5] Zoos, then, are the "urban

---

3   Redford, K. et al. (2013)

4   Acampora, R. (2005): 75, Berger, J. (1980): 26, Braverman, I. (2012): 71-91, Wolch, J. (1998): 129

5   Anderson, K. (1998): 28

simulacra" which mediate human experience of animal life and cause "real live animals . . . [to] actually come to be seen as less than authentic since the terms of authenticity have been so thoroughly redefined."[6] "Zoos tell us, something, then, about the construction of metropolitan cultures and identities, of what it was, and is, to be a modern city dweller."[7] Moreover, if the city is a human zoo, the zoo is a reproduction of the modern city.[8] Desmond Morris argues that North American zoos are a product and symbol of the alienation of urban life: overcrowding, anxiety, aggression, and nervous disorders characterize both.[9]

Zoo critics such as Jennifer Wolch and Christopher Philo argue for a new sense of geography and urban space that can adequately account for the presence of nonhuman animals in city life. Wolch, in particular, has argued for "zoöpolis," a model that "asks for a future in which animals and nature would no longer be incarcerated beyond the reach of our everyday lives, leaving us with only cartoons to heal the wounds of their absence."[10] *Good Night, Gorilla* may be just such a cartoon, and yet the interactions between human and nonhuman animals modeled in this speculative projection go beyond the generic cityscape of Wolch's critique, envisioning a space of interspecies coexistence.

HUMANIMAL ESCAPES

Alongside their subjection to civilization's power, wild animals are also objects of romantic admiration. They are our exotic others, hinting at our boundaries, at our limitation as humans. They are also our only way out of our human selves and hence, "zoos increasingly provide an escape for their visitors by transplanting them from the urban space in which they live into a completely different geographical space that is natural and wild."[11] This is an interesting goal as zoos are usually perceived to be places of non-Nature, or places of virtual naturality. Thus, the boundaries of city and wilderness, home and zoo, and human and nonhuman animality begin to collapse.

To manage our complex psychological relationship toward wild animals, humans erect and regulate spatial and classificatory boundaries. Although situated within the city's borders, the zoo is its own separate zone, encircled by physi-

---

6   Wolch, J. (1998): 128

7   Braverman, I. (2012): 28

8   Baratay, E., and Hardouin-Fugier, E. (2003): 224

9   Quoted in Braverman, I. (2012): 28

10 Wolch, J. (1998): 135

11 Braverman, J. (2012): 7

cal walls (pink in this story) and a less physical, perhaps, but no less important, wall of rules that regulate the unfortunate occurrence of an animal escape from the zoo into the city. Clearly, the boundary between the zoo and its surrounding city represents an extremely fragile space that must be constantly surveilled. With this need for regulation and surveillance, it may come as no surprise, then, that this border between zoo and city resembles the surveillance boundaries of Foucault's "panopticon."[12] The boundary between the zoo and its surrounding city in *Good Night, Gorilla* adds the institution of the zoo to the list of hierarchical structures, like the army, schools, hospitals, and factories, that Foucault argues have evolved through history into manifestations of the panopticon.

Yet alongside the fear, there is always an immense temptation: What might actually happen when wild animals and humans cross the spatial, legal, and taxonomic divides? What would take place when species meet? Such "meetings" have occasionally occurred despite the provisions – and were mostly fatal. That is, they either resulted in the death of the human involved, such as the incident of the child who was killed by a pack of African wild dogs when he fell into the enclosure at the Pittsburgh Zoo,[13] or in the death of the nonhuman animal, as in the tiger escape at the San Francisco Zoo in 2007.[14]

Many zoos prepare for natural disasters by organizing plans for recapturing escaped animals, as in the cases of the Tama and Ueno Zoos in Japan, which regularly stage drills whereby employees dress up as animals and "escape."[15] However, in the case of Nikica the hippo, who escaped her pen at a private zoo in Montenegro when the pen flooded, and in the case of the Lake Superior Zoo in Duluth, Minnesota, where a polar bear and a seal escaped during a flood, the animals either moved to high ground (the polar bear stood on top of his enclosure), or simply relocated to other human spaces. According to the *Guardian*, Nikica the hippo was in fact "being fed at the swimming pool of a restaurant owned by Pejovic [the zoo owner] and his brother" during the flood.[16]

In March 2012, a silverback gorilla named Koga escaped its enclosure at the Buffalo Zoo into the keepers' space, biting a keeper in the process. "A veterinarian used a handheld blowpipe to sedate Koga through a porthole," writes a reporter, while a SWAT team cleared the area.[17] "That was the scariest thing I've

---

12 Foucault, M. (1995): 197

13 Begos, K. (2012)

14 Fagan, K. et al. (2007)

15 BBC 2010 (2012)

16 The Guardian (2010), Mother Nature Network (2012)

17 Gulley, N. (2013)

ever done in my career," said the SWAT team's Captain to the news crew.[18] Koga is a zoo-born gorilla. He has never set eyes on an African savannah and, for that matter, he had never before left his cage. "What drove Koga to try to escape its enclosure?" I asked the zoo's director shortly after this event. "Curiosity," she responded, explaining that once the wild animals manage to get out, this curiosity quickly replaces itself with a strong desire to get right back into the familiarity of their cages.

Good Night, Gorilla centers on both the human desire toward – and the human fear of – animals that cross the lines, yet presents a totally different scenario for what happens when they do. When the animals in this story escape from their zoo enclosures, they simply walk through the zoo gate and across the small green lawn straight into the bedroom of their human zookeeper and his wife. The zookeeper's wife seems to be the only one aware of, and disturbed by, this transgression. This role of the zookeeper's wife is in conflict with Donna Haraway's feminist metaphor of the "cyborg," which troubles the traditional limits of female identity politics. Haraway's cyborg questions any separation of the "human" from, for instance, the "animal" or the "machine," as the cyborg is part human and part machine.[19] So, whereas the cyborg "does not dream of community on the model of the organic family [...and] would not recognize the Garden of Eden," the zookeeper's wife seeks to keep the Oedipal family unit in tact.[20] Using her husband's flashlight, she takes the gorilla by the hand (with all the other animals following closely behind) back across the lawn and into the zoo (figure 1). "Good night, zoo," she exclaims, seemingly relieved to reestablish the spatial divide that will allow her to rest for the night. But the gorilla is not so easily constrained. He somehow manages to get out and follows the woman back across the lawn and into her bedroom. I will return to the role of the gorilla in this story later.

Another key characteristic of the book that blurs the human/nonhuman divide is its minimal use of human language. In the entire book, the only words uttered are "Good Night," in various combinations: "Good Night" to each of the animals, "Good night, dear," "Good night, zoo," and "Good night, gorilla." In fact, most of the book's pages contain no words at all, again producing a virtual space whereby animals and humans interact differently than in the conventional, species-limited and speech dominated space of modern city life. As Haraway notes, many biologists of the twentieth century followed the Enlightenment discourse of reason in their determination that "human biology was the prerequisite

---

18 Gulley, N. (2013)
19 Haraway, D. (1991): 150
20 Haraway, D. (1991): 151

of a development of an elaborate way of life, for which the differentiations separating humans and apes were bipedalism, tool use, and speech."[21]

Figure 1. Zookeeper's wife leading gorilla by the hand across the lawn from home back to zoo, with the other animals following closely behind.[22]

Speech, or *logos*, has been the dominant marker of nonhuman difference since Aristotle; this was also the reason why Jeremy Bentham's prioritization of suffering over reason was so revolutionary. "Logocentrism is first of all a thesis regarding the animal, the animal deprived of the *logos*," writes Jacques Derrida of the previously dominant strain of discourse on the animal, "this is the thesis, position, or presupposition maintained from Aristotle to Heidegger, from Descartes to Kant, Levinas, and Lacan."[23] Between the minimal use of human language and the spread of that use across species boundaries, *Good Night, Gorilla* takes advantage of the virtual space of the children's book to provide human and nonhuman animals with vehicles for interspecies communication. With such minimal use of human language in the book, other modes and means of communication open up and become more important. In fact, the aesthetics of the children's book communicates with the reader in ways that elide traditional, logocentric logic. The vibrant images and colors and the liminal setting between daytime and nighttime that constitute the dreamspace of the book rely on mood to affect the reader. The children's book, thereby, becomes a vehicle for interspecies communication that goes beyond traditional human language.

---

21 Haraway, D. (1989): 214

22 Used by permission of G.P. Putnam's Sons, a division of Penguin Group (USA) LLC.

23 Derrida, J. (2008): 27

INSIDE THE ZOO

Good Night, Gorilla resides in three distinct yet interconnected spaces: the zoo, the house, and the lawn. Despite their clear demarcation, the images and colors that constitute these three spaces blur and fuse. *Good Night, Gorilla* is vibrant and cheerful in its three spaces. The zoo and the cages are immersed in a deep lush green that continues in the space outside of the zoo, which is similarly lush; the inside of the gorilla cage is green, and so is the zookeeper's uniform; the indoor living room through which the animals enter into the bedroom is painted in green, and a pink balloon flies from the mouse up to the sky in the first scene and reappears almost in every page of the book, weaving together the book's three spaces into one interspecies interface.

If the space of the zoo represents the wild and other within the city, and the houses and humans represent the social and the artificial, the lawn is the liminal space in between: it is, conceivably, both natural and artificial, domestic and industrial, private and public, and city and country. Moreover, the lawn is probably the quintessential American landscape. Indeed, "fifty-eight million Americans enthusiastically plant, weed, water, spray, and mow an estimated twenty million acres of lawn."[24] Given the domesticizing role of the lawn as an extension of the American house, it is hardly coincidental that Rathmann chose the lawn to figure in between animal/zoo and human/city spaces.

Figure 2. Caged gorilla stealing zookeeper's keys; mouse with pink balloon in center.[25]

The book's depiction of the zoo also draws on the actual design of the urban zoo as it was and as the author likely knew it at the time she wrote the book (the

---

24 Bormann, H., Balmori, D., and Geballe, G. T. (2001)

25 Used by permission of G.P. Putnam's Sons, a division of Penguin Group (USA) LLC.

book was published in 1994, concluding ten years of work). Essentially, Rathmann's zoo consists of a set of relatively small cages containing individual animals, each cage painted in a distinct vibrant color. Inside the cages, most of the animals have human artifacts and toys to keep them company (see, e.g., figure 2). This was indeed what most urban zoos in North America looked like, albeit not as cheerful, at the time of the book's writing. In zoos during the nineteenth and twentieth centuries, "bars and cages encoded a bold sense of separation between the penultimate categories of keeper and kept."[26]

Immersion design, currently the *bon ton* of zoo design, was not commonly used in zoo design back then. In immersion, the cages are typically hidden so that the zoogoer may feel immersed in the animal's habitat. Contemporary zoo design, according to prominent zoo designer Jon Coe, is a place of "stunning realism and authenticity," with naturalistic scenes to immerse the zoogoer and realistic functions to enrich the animal.[27] A bicycle at a gorilla exhibit – as this book has it – would probably be considered a gross violation of the principles of naturalistic immersion design, as well as a problematic anthropomorphizing of the animal, and so would the animal's miniature stuffed simulacrum.

Figure 3. Humans watching gorillas, gorillas watching humans at the Louisville Zoo's gorilla exhibit.[28]

Take a "real" gorilla exhibit as an example. The award-winning Gorilla Forest exhibit at the Louisville Zoo (figure 3) was designed to immerse zoogoers in an experience of the Congo rainforest. Unique design features use illusion to bridge the audio and tactile barriers between human and animal. For instance, the goril-

---

26 Anderson, K. (1998): 41
27 Braverman, I. (2012): 35
28 Courtesy of the Louisville Zoo.

las may choose to press a button to broadcast their own sounds into the atrium.[29] "The big idea," zoo designer John Coe told me, "is to try to make the gorilla areas and the public areas indistinguishable from each other, all one family."[30] Whereas at the Louisville Zoo, the one family narrative is promoted through erasing the cage within the space of the zoo, in *Good Night, Gorilla* the mingling happens at the human home, and cages continue to exist at the zoo. In this sense, the book freezes in time the spatial design of zoos before the stronghold of immersion design.

Whereas today's daytime public exhibit in North American and European zoos looks quite different from their portrayal in *Good Night, Gorilla*, their nighttime spaces are altogether different. Most zoo animals, and the larger ones in particular, reside within what is referred to in zoo terminology "holding areas," and not in their outdoors exhibit as *Good Night, Gorilla* implies. This practice, zoo professionals have told me, is intended to protect zoo animals from both the city's wild animals and its humans.[31] Holding areas are typically situated inside buildings. And because they are inaccessible to the public, they do not include naturalistic elements and are typically not green. For example, the gorilla holding area at the Buffalo Zoo contains a television and a fish tank to keep the gorillas entertained (figure 4).

Figure 4. Television and aquarium, gorilla holding area, August 2009.[32]

---

29 Braverman, I. (2012): 7
30 Braverman, I. (2012): 7
31 Braverman, I. (2012): 81
32 Courtesy of Cyndi Griffin / Buffalo Zoo.

PRIMATE VISIONS

The role of transgressing the lines is assigned in this story to the gorilla for a reason. In *Good Night, Gorilla*, the gorilla is not domesticated, but it seems that he is domestic – or at least, under the purview of the domestic. In *Primate Visions*, Donna Haraway explores the intimate relations and fascination of humans with apes, suggesting that this taxon is "a taxonomic and *therefore* political order that works by the negotiation of boundaries achieved through ordering difference."[33] While early instances of primatology, predicated as they were on their contemporary cultural ideologies, privileged a "self-making dialectic of culture and body" in which differences between human and ape were absolute, more recent narratives in primatology "privilege continuities and patterns of dynamic relationships."[34] These changing origin stories muddle the bio-social divide between human and animal. Physically and symbolically, the gorilla is thus part of the human family. Here, it features in the zookeeper's family pictures, which in an earlier page depict the gorilla held in a nursing position by the woman during his infancy.

Indeed, scientific studies suggest that over 99 percent of the most critical DNA sites in humans and chimps are identical,[35] suggesting that humans and higher primates belong to the same species. John Locke already documented stories of forbidden couplings, such as women who "have conceived" by apes or baboons, with certain slave protagonists utilizing these stories to dehumanize African women ("sometimes [orangutans] endeavor to surprise and carry off Negroe women into their woody retreats... an oran-outang husband [would be no] dishonor to an Hottentot female"[36]).

"Focusing for a moment on the bedroom scene," writes Susan McHugh about documentary projects surrounding domestic spaces shared by humans and nonhuman animals, "indicates how the different agents populating stereotypically human scenes of sexual intimacy complicate notions of agency in the lives of companion species."[37] While a gorilla is not a traditional "companion animal," it might qualify as a "companion species," what Donna Haraway identifies as nonhuman animal species that determine and are determined by "a story of cohabitation, co-evolution, and embodied cross-species sociality."[38] These stories

---

33 Haraway, D. (1989): 10

34 Haraway, D. (1989): 215, 336

35 Ferreira, A. (2008): 224; quoting from Hecht.

36 Quoted in Dayan, C. (2011): 118

37 McHugh, S. (2011): 124

38 Haraway, D. (2003): 4

are necessary, McHugh argues, because "amid the de/sexing regulative norms that increasingly define human-animal cohabitation, these everyday struggles of narrative and visualization are … necessarily ongoing, in order to foster any meaningful dialogues about (let alone deliberation of) sex across species."[39]

Figure 5. Final page of Good Night, Gorilla: the interspecies bed, with flashlight directing attention to family photo with gorilla.[40]

DEBUNKING BOUNDARIES, MAKING LIFE

»The very concept of species is deeply fraught, the most recent scientific consensus being that there is no one authoritative definition of species.«[41]

»The proximity between humans and animals is sometimes tenuous. Boundaries are permeable, and taxonomies are necessary to ensure the order of things. But when the pressure is on… categories and terminologies get muddled. The hierarchies no longer hold.«[42]

Although this might be a stretch to the original intentions of the book – likely: that the picture on the nightstand can just as easily be that of a human "fostering" an animal, a perfectly ordinary experience for zookeepers, at least with small mammals – I would like to offer my own creative interpretation. I shall do so by asking the following, provocative, question: So what happens in the page after last of *Good Night, Gorilla*, namely, after the animal and the human sleep in the same bed? Perhaps a human-gorilla hybrid, or an interspecies chimera? Such a taboo fantasy that humanizes the animal and bestializes the human has often

---

39 McHugh, S. (2011): 125
40 Used by permission of G.P. Putnam's Sons, a division of Penguin Group (USA) LLC.
41 Ferreira, A. (2008): 223
42 Dayan, C. (2011): 116

found fictional and filmic expression.[43] Although hybrids and chimeras share similar metaphoric meanings – that of genetic mixture – the processes through which the two come about are quite different. Whereas a hybrid is the product of breeding two different species such that "each cell in the hybrid body has a mixture of genes from both of the parents," a chimera "consists of a combination between two different species" such that "the genes of the two species do not combine as with a hybrid."[44] Carrie Friese notes:

»The hybrid has long been viewed as problematic to the notion of species because these animals represent sexual reproduction between two different kinds of animals, resulting in a genetic mixture at the nuclear level. Chimeras are similarly troubling as genetic mixtures, but the mode by which these mixtures occur furthers the difficulty of classifying these biological organisms.«[45]

Friese's identification of critical and metaphorical potential of the genetic chimera or the hybrid follows in the tradition of Donna Haraway's cyborg, a certain instance of the animal-machine hybrid. Chimeras, like hybrids, embody interspecies genetic mixture; however, unlike hybrids, chimeras are "cells and bodies containing DNA from different organisms or species through processes that differ from sexual reproduction."[46]

Hybrids and chimeras have existed for a long time. In Greek mythology, the chimera was a fire-breathing female monster with a lion's head, a goat's body, and a serpent's tail. The first human-made chimera was a mouse born in 1961 – perhaps accounting for the presence of the mouse alongside the gorilla in the interspecies bed of *Good Night, Gorilla*. Myra Hird discusses the extent to which chimerism presents "challenges to western heteronormative notions of kinship" by extending the "notion of kinship to include non-human animals as well."[47] She notes that, "Of all the cells in a human body, 10 percent are eukaryotic (derived from bacteria) and 90 percent are bacteria."[48] Sagan states along the same lines that "the human body... is an architectonic compilation of millions of agencies of chimerical cells."[49] "We are all chimeras," exclaims Haraway.[50]

---

43 Ferreira, A. (2008): 223
44 Seyfer, T. (2008)
45 Friese, C. (2010): 146
46 Friese, C. (2010): 146
47 Quoted in Ferreira, A. (2008): 224
48 Hird, M. J. (2009): 83
49 Sagan, D. (1992): 368
50 Haraway, D. (1991): 150

In the world of species conservation and captive breeding programs, such distinctions between species and subspecies are often hotly contested. Chimeras are mixtures at the level of mitochondrial DNA. "These biological organisms," writes Friese, "call into question the very notion of 'species' itself," since the genetic mixture of the chimera only shows itself in certain individuals of the species.[51] The genetic division of chimerical individuals has created a parallel division between conservationists, who contest the importance of genetic difference when it occurs in mitochondrial DNA. Friese marks this as a five-way split, where conservationists differ based on their relative responses to the issues of hybridization, the male-female split in inheritance of mitochondrial DNA, and the importance of mitochondrial DNA itself in determining species difference.[52]

De-extinction projects aim to "reconstitute the genomes of vanished species in living form," essentially bringing back these species from extinction through a combination of "back-breeding," cloning from cryopreserved tissue, and genetic hybridization using existing species.[53] Reproductive technologies such as IVF and stem cell research as well as the emerging field of synthetic biology are all "producing life" – either from another life form or from nonlife. The field of *transbiology* – a biology that is "not only born and bred, or born and made, but *made and born* – is indeed today more the norm than the exception."[54]

EPILOGUE

While *Good Night, Gorilla* takes place in a zoo, not a lab, the acts of movement across the supposedly uncontaminated border between the zoo and the home, here typified by the lawn, demonstrate that the interface between "animal space" and "human space" is not only possible but also inevitable: when the human family can encompass nonhuman animals, it becomes impossible to exclude them from the human home. In this way, the slipperiness of the distinction between human and animal, and domesticated and wild animals reveals itself as an object of surveillance and regulation. As I have argued in *Zooland*, "The wildness of these animals, along with the presentation of their captivity at the heart of the modern city, is the zoo's main appeal."[55] The zoo's institutional survival thus depends on the survival of both captivity and wildness, and of city and wilder-

---

51 Friese, C. (2010): 147

52 Friese, C. (2010): 153

53 Long Now (2013)

54 Franklin, S. (2006): 170-71

55 Braverman, I. (2012): 61

ness, as bifurcated ideals. Captivity and wildness are codependent: if not for freedom, incarceration would make no sense (and vice versa).[56] City and wilderness are similarly interlocked in a binary existence: if not for wilderness, the city would make no sense and vice versa. Accordingly, in the book's last page, where the framed photograph finally becomes clear, we see the family portrait of Joe the zookeeper, his wife, and the gorilla. This is a fantasy of interspecies pregnancy painted in primary colors.

Yet this family unit does not include a machine of reproductive technology. In this sense, it is unlike the parable of technoscientific hybridity in Charis Thompson's "Confessions of a Bioterrorist," which Aline Ferreira describes as "providing speculative visions of alternative family configurations as well as interrogating the ethical consequences of this dance of technology and species identity."[57] Also unlike the vexed and ethically fraught circumstances of the interspecies chimeras in the foci of Ferreira's examples, *Good Night, Gorilla* presents these possibilities within the dreamspace of a children's book, where the presence of the gorilla in the family photos does not threaten or invalidate preconceptions of order but is portrayed, rather, as a perfectly natural occurrence. After all, children around the globe go to bed with an animal every night.

The position of the gorilla (and the mouse) in the bedroom and in the family photographs in *Good Night, Gorilla* is not that of lover; rather, its placement as child still implies a cross-species narrative of intimacy. We are thus forced to ask: if the gorilla is in the family photos, why is he led back to his cage at the zoo?

ACKNOWLEDGMENTS

I would like to express my gratitude to my wonderful research assistant Eleanor Gold for her ideas and enthusiasm. This contribution is dedicated to my daughters Ariel and Tamar, who have patiently endured my numerous readings of this book and the endless questions that accompanied these readings. To them, who have been my greatest teachers on the futility of animal-human divide and on the richness of interspecies connections. The research for this article was assisted by the American Council of Learned Societies' Charles A. Ryskamp Research Fellowship and by the Baldy Center for Law & Social Policy.

---

56 Braverman; I. (2012): 61

57 Ferreira, A. (2008), 231.

REFERENCES

Acampora, Ralph R. (2005): "Zoos and Eyes: Contesting Captivity and Seeking Successor Practices." *Society & Animals* 13.1: 69-88

Anderson, Kay (1998): "Animals, Science, and Spectacle in the City.", in: *Animal Geographies: Place, Politics, and Identity in the Nature-Culture Borderlands*. Edited by Jennifer Wolch and Jody Emel, 27-50. London: Verso

Baratay, Eric, and Hardouin-Fugier, Elisabeth (2003): *Zoo: A History of Zoological Gardens in the West*. Reaktion Books

BBC (2010): "Japanese zoo trains staff to catch a runaway 'tiger'." February 10, 2013, http://news.bbc.co.uk/2/hi/asia-pacific/8508623.stm

BBC (2013): "Japanese zoo carries out drill to recapture loose animals." February 1, http://www.bbc.co.uk/news/world-asia-pacific-21291094

Begos, Kevin (2012): "Pittsburgh Zoo: Boy Dies After Falling Into Exhibit With African Painted Dogs." *The Huffington Post*, November 4, http://www.huffingtonpost.com/2012/11/04/pittsburgh-zoo-boy-dies-a_n_2073268.html.

Berger, John (1980): *About Looking*. New York: Pantheon Books

Bormann, Herbert, Balmori, Diana, and Geballe, Gordon T. (2001): *Redesigning the American Lawn: A Search for Environmental Harmony*, New Haven: Yale University Press

Braverman, Irus (2012): *Zooland: The Institution of Captivity*, Stanford: Stanford University Press

Dayan, Colin (2011): *The Law is a White Dog: How Legal Rituals Make and Unmake Persons*, Princeton & Oxford: Princeton University Press

Deleuze, Gilles, and Guattari, Felix (1980): *A Thousand Plateaus: Capitalism and Schizophrenia*, Minneapolis: The University of Minnesota Press

Derrida, Jacques (2008): *The Animal That Therefore I Am*, translated by David Wills, edited by Marie-Louise Mallet, New York: Fordham University Press

Fagan, Kevin, VanDerbeken, Jaxon, Koopman, John, and Lagos, Marisa (2007): "Investigation continues into fatal tiger attack at S.F. zoo." *SFGate*, December 27, http://www.sfgate.com/news/article/Investigation-continues-into-fatal-tiger-attack-3299013.php

Ferreira, Aline (2008): "Primate Tales: Interspecies Pregnancy and Chimerical Beings." *Science Fiction Studies* 35.2: 223-237

Friese, Carrie (2010): "Classification conundrums: categorizing chimeras and encacting species preservation." *Theory and Society* 39.2: 145-172

Foucault, Michel (1995): *Discipline and Punish*, translated by Alan Sheridan, New York: Vintage Books

Franklin, Sarah (2006): "The Cyborg Embryo: Our Path to Transbiology." *Theory Culture Society* 23: 167-187

Gulley, Neale (2012): "400-pound gorilla escapes, bites zookeeper at Buffalo Zoo." *Reuters*, March 19, http://www.reuters.com/article/2012/03/19/us-gorilla-idUSBRE82I13720120319

Haraway, Donna (1989): *Primate Visions: Gender, Race, and Nature in the World of Modern Science*, New York: Routledge

Haraway, Donna (1991): "A Cyborg Manifesto: Science, Technology, and Socialist-Feminism in the Late Twentieth Century.", in: *Simians, Cyborgs, and Women: The Reinvention of Nature*, London: Free Association:149-81

Haraway, Donna (2003): *The Companion Species Manifesto: Dogs, People, and Significant Otherness*, Chicago: Prickly Paradigm Press

Haraway, Donna (2008): *When Species Meet: Gender, Race, and Nature in the World of Modern Science,* Minneapolis: University of Minnesota Press

Hird, Myra J. (2009): *The Origins of Sociable Life: Evolution After Science Studies*, Houndmills, Basingstoke: Palgrave Press

Long Now Foundation (2013): *Revive and Restore Extinct Species Back to Life*, http://longnow.org/revive/

McHugh, Susan (2011): *Animal Stories: Narrating Across Species Lines*, Minneapolis: University of Minnesota Press

The Guardian (2010): "Nikica the hippo enjoys taste of freedom after floods in Montenegro." January 13, http://www.guardian.co.uk/world/2010/jan/13/montenegro-escaped-hippo-floods

Mother Nature Network (2012): "Polar bear, seals escape after U.S. zoo flooded." June 21, http://www.mnn.com/earth-matters/animals/stories/polar-bear-seals-escape-after-us-zoo-flooded

Rathmann, Peggy (1994): *Good Night, Gorilla*, New York: Putnam

Redford, Kent et al. (2013): "How will synthetic biology and conservation shape the future of nature?" Framing Paper (Clare College, Cambridge, UK, 9-11 April, 2013)

Sagan, Dorion (1992): "Metametazoa: Biology and Multiplicity." In: *Incorporations: Fragments for a History of the Human Body*, Crary, Jonathan, and Kwinter, Sanford, eds., Zone: 362-385

Seyfer, Tara (2004): "What Are Chimeras and Hybrids?" *Ethics and Medics* 29.7

Thompson, Charis (1999): "Confessions of a Bioterrorist: Subject Position and Reproductive Technologies." In *Playing Dolly: Technocultural Formations, Fantasies, and Fictions of Assisted Reproduction*, Kaplan, E. Ann, and Squier, Susan, eds., New Brunswick, NJ: Rutgers University Press: 189-219

Wolch, Jennifer (1998): "Zoöpolis", in: *Animal Geographies: Place, Politics, and Identity in the Nature-Culture Borderlands*, Wolch, Jennifer, and Emel, Jody, eds, London: Verso: 119-138

Chapter 3. Virtualization Gains Momentum

A Paradise of Decorated Sheds

Consuming Cities, Virtuality and Postmodernism

STEFFEN KRÄMER

The department store building type became the official construction task of the 2nd half of the 19th century. The contemporaries regarded the famous *Grand Magasins* of Paris, such as the in the years 1868-1887 constructed Bon Marché, as perfect examples of architectural splendor and uniqueness. Founded upon a perfectly calculated sales strategy, the layout conception was supposed to evoke the public's attention. The impression of elegance and an exotic flair was imparted with the help of modern skeleton construction methods. Émile Zola called the Belle Époque department store "The Ladies' Paradise" in his eponymous novel, first published in 1883.

At the dawn of the 21st century these architecturally linked sales strategies are experiencing a renaissance, only this time implemented in the context of new and sophisticated urban planning concepts, so-called "consuming cities." At the outset of this urban development are American shopping malls, such as the Horton Plaza in downtown San Diego, planned in 1977 by Jon Jerde and carried out between 1982 and 1985.[1] Instead of building a fully air-conditioned and roofed-over shopping center, the architect transformed an in the 1970's utterly neglected downtown area of San Diego into an urban landscape containing plazas, streets and colorful facades, behind which the typical consumer offer of stores and fast-food restaurants was to be found. This shopping mall is a six city-block sized public space, incurring a sales volume of 5 billion dollars and counting 9 million visitors annually.[2]

---

1 Steiner, D. (2003); Herwig, O. and Holzherr, F. (2006): 34-36; http://en.wikipedia.org/wiki/Jon_Jerde; http://en.wikipedia.org/wiki/Westfield_Horton_Plaza

2 Guratzsch, D. (2011)

This exceptionally successful concept was continued with the planning of so-called "consuming cities," at first in North America and subsequently also in Europe. Here a frequently chosen form of operation is the "Factory-Outlet-Center," FOC for short, within which well-known producers offer their brand-name products at reduced prices.[3] By 1995 324 FOCs were built in the U.S.A. alone, by 2009 160 in Europe. These stupendous numbers do not only point to a recent boom in urban planning and construction, they also substantiate the economic efficiency of consuming cities.

Within architectural-historical research the phenomenon of consuming cities has received little attention and hence the scientific consensus is accordingly disparate. "Potempkin Village" or "brutally indifferent architecture" has been heard, as well as "dream worlds" and "paradise of consumption."[4] On the other hand, consuming cities are comprehensively discussed within the cultural and social sciences.[5] Notwithstanding that their fast-paced urban development is well recognized, criticism of consumer-oriented pragmatism within planning prevails. This pragmatism of course causing privatisation and commercialization of public space. Consuming cities are often interpreted as "non-places" (Non-Lieux), in the sense of the word coined by Marc Augé, referring to places not holding enough significance, such as amusement parks and shopping malls.[6] And last but not least consuming cities represent the urban nadir of postmodernism's continuity after the turn of the millennium, while their architectural stock often is a part of those "constructions with postmodern frills" which Ingeborg Flagge and Romana Schneider did not include in their well-known exhibition catalogue "Revision der Postmoderne" due to mediocrity and banality.[7] Regardless of one considering consuming cities a "fascinating trend" or damning them as a "Disneyland of shopping": no survey meeting formal criteria exists evaluating this urban phenomenon of town construction forms and architectural structuring.[8]

Three consuming cities in the specific operational form of a Factory-Outlet-Center are the focal point of the following analyzes: the Palmanova Outlet Village in North-Italian Palmanova in the vicinity of Udine, the Ingolstadt Village in Upper Bavaria and the Wertheim Village in Franconian Wertheim west of

---

3   http://en.wikipedia.org/wiki/Factory-Outlet-Center

4   Borrmann, N. (2009): 182-83; Herwig, O. and Holzherr, F. (2006): 150

5   Miles, S., and Miles, M. (2004); Gerbing, C. (2012)

6   Augé, M. (1994): 94

7   Flagge, I., and Schneider, R. (2004): 7; Wefing, H. (2004)

8   Miles, S., and Miles, M. (2004): 128; Gerbing, C. (2012): 107

Wuerzburg.[9] Having total areas ranging from close to 10,000 up to 24,000 square meters, the size of these consuming cities is quite typical for a factory outlet center. These cities have had several million visitors since their openings between 2003 and 2008 in the urban peripheral area.

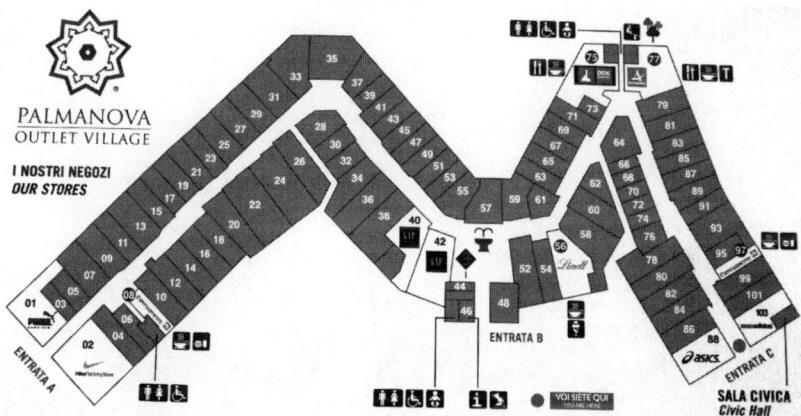

Figure 1. Palmanova, Palmanova Outlet Village, overall plan.

All three cases are a matter of a site similar to a village consisting of a main street as a central axis with access to the middle section and to both narrow sides (figure 1). The configuration of the streets is not based upon an orthogonal grid, but rather shows multiple curves and indentations, letting small open places emerge. The individual buildings surround the street configuration densely, but the facades are offset unequally. Not letting the whole appearance of the consuming city give the impression of being newly planned was carefully looked after. The axial configuration is reminiscent of old city centers in Europe, whereas the staggering of the fronts evokes the impression of being built at different times. The diagrammatic plan of the consuming city should imply a development over a longer period of time – somewhat like the buildings showing a kind of organic growth – so as to compensate the shortcoming of being built as a whole on neutral ground in next to no time.

The main entrances, closed after business hours, show that the analogy to an historic town or city layout is based on the adoption of formal design principles (figure 2). No people live in the consuming city. There are no private dwellings, no communal buildings that could host public events. Almost all buildings

9 http://en.wikipedia.org/wiki/Factory-Outlet-Center;   http://www.promosbrescia.it/en/
   palmanova-outlet-village.html

contain businesses and the daily masses consist of sellers and buyers. The urbanity of these commercialized enclaves bordering city centers is merely virtual. After shop closing time the consuming city is hermetically locked-up and reopens with the beginning of shopping hours. Reminding us of the – since the 1970's – increasing phenomena of gated communities, the operating procedure of a consuming city is concentrated on consumption alone, a rather rigid type of ghettoization.[10]

Figure 2. Wertheim, Wertheim Village, main entrance.

Every building receives a noticeably different front; material, color and form are distinctly different (figure 3). In Ingolstadt and Wertheim glass wall membranes alternate with crenellated plaster facades, also with curved and tiled gables. This creates the illusion of buildings dating from different architectural eras. Templates from the Middle Ages up to modern times were used to create an architectural potpourri with varied references to different styles. On the other hand Palmanova orientates itself on old central city streets in Italy with their two-story palaces and their arcaded sidewalks (figure 4). The appearance of variety is attained here by the change of architectural motifs, such as columns, arches and

10 Erben, D. (2012)

gables. Intense and bright coloring contributes to the overall impression of opulence in all three consuming cities.

Figure 3. Ingolstadt, Ingolstadt Village, main street.

Figure 4. Palmanova, Palmanova Outlet Village, main street.

Every commercial building gets an individual character and also shows a historicizing design vocabulary, thus inaugurating an exchange with architectural history, in order to cancel out an obvious absence of any kind of past. The planning does not bear reference to a specific architectural heritage as it would if being comparable to older buildings in the aged city centers, such as the later gothic style found in Ingolstadt. The planning is not really connected with local building traditions; it just has to seem compliant with the accepted historiography of the region. Towers reminiscent of the Middle Ages define the remote view of Wertheim, whereas Italianesque Palazzi dominate Palmanova. The point is not to build in a largely authentic manner in relation to a local context, but to create a historic illusion for the visitors strolling through the consuming city by using these facades. As soon as a shop is entered, this illusory world ends abruptly, since behind the facade hard-to-change standardized sales areas are to be found. The purism of these interiors is hardly mitigated by their décor, but now it is all about the consumer and the most important thing is buying high-quality brand-name products at a reduced price.

The American architecture theorist and critic Charles Jencks would certainly have declared these consuming cities paradigms of postmodern design had they been built during the last quarter of the 20th century. After all, Jencks did – as a world-renowned leading figure of this movement in architecture theory – demand a postmodern radical eclecticism.[11] Simultaneously, the appearance of these three consuming cities represents the principle of double or multiple coding which – according to Jencks – is a core value of increased communication in architectural postmodernism.[12] Architecture as a phenomenon analogue to language must reach a level of increased communication through "coding," as Jencks typifies the languages of architecture. Double-coding – building around two languages – is a fractual formula and can hence be supplanted by multiple-coding. Through the constant change of taste and culture, the language of architecture must submit to transformation by short-lived codes and therefore a postmodern architect must use a severalfold-coding in order to convey a message.

Behind Jencks' approach to defining postmodern architecture we find a simple principle of combination which can easily be applied because it is so readily understood. The dazzling historical array seen in the three consuming cities is based upon the intent of reaching different target audiences with distinct codes. In order to encourage consumption, the architectural designs must show high variability in expression, only by doing this can they remain able to deliver their message. This is achieved by the use of a multitude of stylistic elements and forms.

---

11 Jencks, C. (1988): 92-94
12 Krämer, S. (2010)

DECORATED SHED

Figure 5. "decorated shed"[13]

Inevitably the design of the facades takes center stage because of the primary importance of the outer appearance of the stores. At the same time, the stores' interiors are chosen rather indifferently and are of a simple standard type. The contrast between the utilitarian neutral inside and the flamboyant portentous outside is another dictum of postmodern building, just as first theoretically expressed by the doyen of American postmodernism, Robert Venturi. In 1972, Venturi, Denise Scott Brown and Steven Izenour published the famous manifesto "Learning from Las Vegas."[14] The main subject of the research project was the optical impact of the Las Vegas Strip – with its multitude of enormous billboards using bright colorful neon lights to give notice to the cities' casinos, hotels and restaurants. As signal bearers these were more important than the buildings themselves, which were often somewhat set back from the main street and unaspiring utility constructions. The split of the signal bearer and the building itself was the most important insight gained by Venturi through the exceptional symbolism of Las Vegas' architecture. The result of his research was the so-called "decorated shed" which clearly demonstrated this breach (figure 5). Basically, Venturi expresses the fact that the "show-side" of a building can carry a

---

13 Venturi, Robert, Brown, Denise Scott and Izenour, Steven: Lernen von Las Vegas. Zur Ikonographie und Architektursymbolik der Geschäftsstadt, Braunschweig 1979 (First Publ. Cambridge/Mass. 1972), 107

14 Venturi, R., Brown, D. S., and Izenour, S. (1979)

message, while the construction itself needs no special attention. It is difficult to describe the design principle of the buildings in the three consuming cities in a more suitable manner than with Venturi's theoretical ideas. They are all decorated sheds and they are all hiding the indifference of their standardized interiors behind mock historic facades.

The close relationship between a building's facade and the street area which dominates the basic structure of a consuming city also assumed an important role during the consolidation stage of postmodern architecture. In 1980, the First International Exhibition of Architecture took place with Paolo Portoghesi as President of the architectural section of the Venice Biennale, and the theme chosen was "La Presenza del Passato" – The Presence of the Past.[15] The centerpiece of the Biennale was the so-called "Strada Novissima," an imaginary main street with facades done by 20 world-renowned architects, which visitors could stroll past. The architecture of the interiors behind the facades was irrelevant and so no attempt was made to give them a specific architectural design. The majority of the facades should pertain to architectural history, as the official theme of the exhibition required. The magnificence of colors and shapes shown by the mock historic facades of the Strada Novissima made up – using Venturi's expression – a closely spaced series of "decorated sheds." His postulate of a division between an unpretentious utilitarian interior stated in 1972 and a message-bearing show-side was thus fulfilled during the first exhibition – with international participation. Even today's consuming cities are nothing more than imaginary main streets with the visitors strolling past postmodern facades. Just as the Strada Novissima in the Biennale of Venice assisted postmodernism's breakthrough, we can well observe the repercussions today in consumption-oriented city-planning, even in rural areas of northern Italy, in Franconia and in Upper Bavaria.

One last reference to postmodern architecture theory shall be shown. In the year 1965, Charles Moore – next to Venturi one of the most important American postmodern architects – published an essay with the strange title "You have to pay for the public life."[16] Moore researched the then existing urban architecture of the American west coast in regard to the question if it in any manner evoked public life. He found out that public space and public life had no role in urban planning concepts – with one exception – Disneyland, built in the vicinity of Los Angeles in 1955. Moore didn't care about the amusement park's glittery illusions. What exited him were open public spaces in Disneyland, the streets, the

---

15 Pirovano, C. (1980)

16 Moore, C. (1965)

plazas and the star-shaped rondels: exactly those urban qualities he missed in the contemporary urban architecture of the west coast. To be able to enjoy high-quality public life back in the 1960's, you had to visit an amusement park. This wasn't for free and isn't for free today: "You have to pay for the public life."

In the three consuming cities, rondels and small plazas bring the streets to life. Frequent seating accommodations along the street ensure the opportunity of a short rest for consumers, whereas trees and rather limited flowerbeds green up the exterior. Even on busy days the impression of a well-tended traffic-free environment is given. The whole area is litter-free, no bums sit on street corners, because an ample security staff and numerous street cleaners are employed. Basically, we see here a clean, safe and commercially attractive traffic-free zone, just as it is a reality in major city cores, since many municipalities have extended and broadened their maintenance and care of urban centers.[17] Besides this, the visitors flocking to the consuming cities and wandering down the main street demonstrate a typical urban behavior of anonymity and discrete distance while shopping. Ultimately almost all of them are consumers, busy spending their money. So we can reinterpret Moore's 1960's slogan as: "You have to consume for the public life," because being in a consuming city has a very commercial nature.

In spite of the fact that research repeatedly deals with the appearance of consuming cities, one vital question remains: what are the exact characteristic traits and particular architectural mechanisms?[18] Furthermore, a detectable undercurrent of critical sentiment is expressed, often just like the undertheorized scathing critique heard in the early 1990's, when postmodernism was declared dead.[19] The claim that consuming cities are "postmodern illusory worlds" or "shopping Disneylands" is an assertion with next to no value, based upon an already well-known line of argument found in social, culture and architecture theories.[20] Umberto Eco already referred to Disneyland as the "quintessence of consumerism" in 1977, and one year later Jean Baudrillard called it "a perfect model of the intricacies of simulacra."[21] In 1978 Rem Koolhaas labeled the phenomenon Lunapark "a large cardboard reality."[22] As these examples demonstrate, targeting at a perfectly calculated consumer ideology while using illusory reality

---

17 Wiegandt, C. C. (2011)

18 Bormann, R. (1998): 33; Bittner, R. (2001): 16, 226

19 Krämer, S. (1995): 105

20 Bormann, R. (1998): 33; Gerbing, C. (2012): 107

21 Eco, U. (1987): 82; Baudrillard, J. (1978): 24

22 Koolhaas, R. (1994): 42

and mirages as arguments does have a kind of tradition. The fundamental question – with which architectural methods the sales strategy is accomplished – remains unanswered.

The design maxims of the 1960's and 1970's postmodern architecture, such as Charles Jencks' double and multiple coding, Robert Venturi's decorated sheds and Charles Moore's demand for the revitalization of public space are as a whole still valid in the 21st century as far as consuming cities are concerned. This new urban phenomenon attracts little attention within the "Revision der Postmoderne" because it does not seem to show "a positive effect of pluralism and complexity" in the present.[23] But in this case one of the present concepts of international urban planning is not heeded, within which the so often heralded "death of postmodernism" just didn't happen. The consuming city is a paradigm of the continued existence of postmodern architecture in the new millennium.

The reasons for using this type of architecture for planning consuming cities are obvious: The impression of an organically grown traffic-free town center is supposed to help gain the visitors' trust, and he is supposed to feel comfortable strolling down a traditional street area, because it seems to be familiar. The variety of the shapes and forms used in designing the facades not only demonstrates the multifariousness of the products for sale but also lets every brand-name store have a special appearance. The colorful mixture of architectural forms and styles from different epochs is expected to draw the visitor's attention towards the individual storefronts. He is supposed to be encouraged to enter the salesroom so that – at last – the prime function of the consuming city can be fulfilled, namely selling. The focal point of the detailed sales strategy of a consuming city is the direct addressing of the customer. A high degree of transmitting information is wanted, exactly as offered by postmodern architecture, since it has been interpreted – from the beginning – as analogue to language and allows a very high degree of communication.

Since the 1990's, a style of "New Abstraction" dominates the international vanguard of architecture, but simultaneously does not permit this method of communication.[24] Based upon the abstract and non-representational language of classic modernism, it is classified as a kind of "Second Modernism."[25] Contemporary trends such as textual or sculptural architecture deliver new meanings, but do not fit in a scheme of pre-planning a perfected sales strategy.[26] The use of a

---

23 Flagge, I., and Schneider, R. (2004): 7

24 Klotz, H. (1994): 153-61

25 Klotz, H. (1994): 153-61; Klotz, H. (1999)

26 Pahl, J. (1999)

postmodern form language in the conceptual design of a consuming city is no great surprise because of the easy transmission of the planned and desired content.

The criticism of the consuming city phenomena by cultural and social sciences is no doubt justifiable. This is because simulated urbanity serves the sole purpose of commerce. Urban life is broken apart and reduced to fragments, but these still have an enormous impact as they remain an important part of today's "consumer culture."[27] Moreover, a consuming city is not only an urban-style illusory world but is developing towards an increasingly dominant parallel reality.[28] The large number of intensely discussed and/or already approved plans for new FOCs in Germany during the past few years is proof enough.[29] These developments explain many fears municipalities have concerning the desolation of the inner parts of towns and cities. For this sole reason, criticism of a consuming city is sensible and meaningful but scientific research must also deal with this design phenomena because the high attraction of a consuming city rests upon its form language and thus upon formal criteria.

On the other hand, consuming cities do exert a strange fascination, international corporations let these ideal consumer-oriented miniature cities pop up one after another without worrying a bit and not caring about scientific objections of any kind. It seems like a kind of a gold rush in international urban development with astounding dynamics in spite of its downsides. It looks as if the dictum of the English historian Ruth Eaton will be consistently implemented – that in the future, the planners of ideal cities will have to operate locally.[30] In the beginning of the 21st century, the legacy of the ideal city has turned into urban worlds of illusion, the "promised land of consumerism."[31] In spite of the pragmatism of pure commerce, the consumer city is seen as a Foucault-type heterotopia with its urbanity as an exactly planned and orchestrated illusion; or as Umberto Eco said, "the reality of commerce playing with fiction."[32]

If we regard the rising number of publications dealing with "amusement architecture," we find urban virtuality and simulation booming.[33] Despite of all the

---

27 Bormann, R. (1998): 43

28 Bormann, R. (1998): 33

29 http://en.wikipedia.org/wiki/Factory-Outlet-Center

30 Eaton, R., (2001): 241

31 Miles, S., and Miles, M. (2004): 23

32 Guratzsch, D. (2011): 25; Eco, U. (1987): 80

33 Herwig, O., and Holzherr, F. (2006); Bittner, R. (2001); Quentin, B., and Ottinger, D. (2010)

criticism, many authors hope for new impulses concerning urban planning when they research the vital mechanisms of theme- and amusement parks or event- and consuming cities. By doing this, they are perpetuating a tradition within architecture theory, the beginnings of which are Venturi's and Moore's appraisals of Las Vegas and Disneyland. "Learning from Las Vegas" must now be taken seriously again, even if the researched objects are today more complex than in the Sixties and Seventies.

The commercial success of consuming cities justifies its important role and at least in Europe, no end is in sight. Consuming cities can teach us valuable facts if we refrain from viewing them as pure illusions of urban virtuality. The results are impartial and unprejudiced and can be either of a positive or negative nature. A department store, or as Émile Zola called it – The Ladies' Paradise – is comparable to a consumer city since the architectural concept is in both cases determined by the sales strategy. The exotic and exclusive interior of the department store had the role the exterior of the consuming city – with its colorful facades – has now. There seems to be no more fitting description of the consuming city than Venturi's terminology: a Paradise of decorated sheds.

REFERENCES

Augé, Marc (1994): *Orte und Nicht-Orte. Vorüberlegungen zu einer Ethnologie der Einsamkeit*, Frankfurt/M.: S. Fischer

Bajac, Quentin, and Ottinger, Didier, ed. (2010): *Dreamlands. Des parcs d'attractions aux cités du futur*, Exhibtion Cat., Centre Pompidou Paris, Paris: Edition Centre Pompidou

Baudrillard, Jean (1978): *Agonie des Realen*, Berlin: Merve

Bittner, Regina, ed. (2001): *Urbane Paradiese. Zur Kulturgeschichte modernen Vergnügens*, Frankfurt/M.: Campus

Bormann, Regina (1998): "Spass ohne Grenzen. Kulturtheoretische Reflexionen über einen europäischen Themenpark", in: *Sociologia Internationalis, Internationale Zeitschrift für Soziologie, Kommunikations- und Kulturforschung*, Vol. 36/1, 1998: 33-59

Borrmann, Norbert (2009): *"Kultur-Bolschewismus" oder "Ewige Ordnung". Architektur und Ideologie im 20. Jahrhundert*, Graz: Ares

Eaton, Ruth (2001): *Die ideale Stadt. Von der Antike bis zur Gegenwart*, Berlin: Nicolai

Eco, Umberto (1987): "Die Stadt der Automaten", in: Eco, Umberto (1987): *Über Gott und die Welt. Essays und Glossen*, Munich, dtv: 78-88

Erben, Dietrich (2012): "Architektur des Frivolen – über Gated Communities", in: Gehmann, Ulrich, ed. (2012): *Virtuelle und ideale Welten*, Karlsruhe: KIT Scientific Publishing: 127-139

Flagge, Ingeborg, and Schneider, Romana, eds. (2004): *Die Revision der Postmoderne*, Exhibition Cat., Deutsches Architektur Museum Frankfurt/M., Hamburg: Junius

Gerbing, Chris (2012): "Meet me at the Totem Pole – Shopping Malls des 21. Jahrhunderts oder die Realität virtueller Welten", in: Gehmann, Ulrich, ed. (2012): *Virtuelle und ideale Welten*, Karlsruhe: KIT Scientific Publishing: 107-126

Guratzsch, Dankwart (2011): "Architektur der Lust. Shopping Malls reichen nicht mehr. Nun baut uns der Handel reine Kaufstädte", in: Die Welt, 8. June 2011, 25

Herwig, Oliver, and Holzherr, Florian (2006): *Dream Worlds. Architecture and Entertainment*, Munich etc.: Prestel

Jencks, Charles (1988): "Postskriptum für einen radikalen Eklektizismus", in: Welsch, Wolfgang, ed. (1988): *Wege aus der Moderne. Schlüsseltexte der Postmoderne-Diskussion*, Weinheim: VCH: 92-94

Klotz, Heinrich (1999): *Architektur der Zweiten Moderne. Ein Essay zur Ankündigung des Neuen*, Stuttgart: dva

Klotz, Heinrich (1994): *Kunst im 20. Jahrhundert. Moderne – Postmoderne – Zweite Moderne*, Munich: C. H. Beck

Koolhaas, Rem (1994, first publ. 1978): *Delirious New York. A Retroactive Manifesto for Manhattan*, Rotterdam: 010 Publishers

Krämer, Steffen (1995): "Der entwürdigende Durst nach einer frevelhaften Stimulanz", in: *Architectura, Zeitschrift für Geschichte der Baukunst*, Vol. 25/1, 1995: 105-119

Krämer, Steffen (2010): "Charles Jencks und das Prinzip der Doppel-, Mehr- und Überkodierung. Kommunikation und Interpretation der postmodernen Architektur", in: *Kunstgeschichte. Open Peer Reviewed Journal*, Bd. 10. Internetpublikation: http://www.kunstgeschichte-ejournal.net/archiv/2010/kraemer/

Miles, Steven, and Miles, Malcolm (2004): *Consuming Cities*, New York: Palgrave Macmillan

Moore, Charles (1965): "You have to pay for the public life", in: *Perspecta*, Vol. 9/10, 1965: 57-87

Pahl, Jürgen (1999): *Architekturtheorie des 20. Jahrhunderts. Zeit – Räume*, Munich/London/New York: Prestel

Pirovano, Carlo, ed. (1980): *The Presence of the Past*. First International Exhibition of Architecture, Exhibition Cat., Venice 1980: Edizioni La Biennale di Venezia

Steiner, Dietmar (2003): "Der völlig normale Mensch. John Jerde, Prophet des neuen öffentlichen Raumes", in: *DU*, Vol. 742: Utopisches Bauen. Volles Risiko. Architektur als Abenteuer, December 2003: 28-31

Venturi, Robert, Brown, Denise Scott, and Izenour, Steven (ed. of 1979): *Lernen von Las Vegas. Zur Ikonographie und Architektursymbolik der Geschäftsstadt*, Braunschweig: F. Vieweg & Sohn

Wefing, Heinrich (2004): "Ohne Säule fehlt mir was. Anmerkungen zur Fortwirkung der Postmoderne in der amerikanischen Alltagsarchitektur", in: Flagge, Ingeborg, and Schneider, Romana, ed. (2004): *Die Revision der Postmoderne*, Exhibition Cat., Deutsches Architektur Museum Frankfurt/M. Hamburg: Junius: 86-91

Wiegandt, Claus-C., ed. (2011): *Öffentliche Räume – öffentliche Träume. Zur Kontroverse über die Stadt und die Gesellschaft*, Münster: LIT

The Man in the Paper-made Folding Boat

Artist's Movies as Virtual Worlds

CHRIS GERBING

Movies[1] are virtual worlds par excellence: Well prepared, they offer a fictional world where the spectator is able to immerse himself into another setting, due to well-known parameters from his real surroundings. This is not remarkable in itself, as we are talking about a reflection of what happens in the real world. But it applies in particular for artist's movies, which experienced rapid growth over the past years. Because, "combined with sound, music or spoken dialogue and text, the medium opened up new aesthetic ground for exploring time, motion, sound, and image relationships in a broad range of contents," starting as early as in the late 1960s, and continued until today.[2] Two exhibitions which had been on display more or less simultaneously at the beginning of 2013 at the Center for Art and Media (ZKM) Karlsruhe show this development significantly and are thus predestined for the underlying thesis of the growing of a global pictorial memory. Furthermore, these exhibitions – "One Sixth of the Earth. Ecologies of Image" (November 2012-April 2013) and "Move on Asia. Video Art in Asia 2002-2012" (February-August 2013) – have one significant and interesting char-

---

1 The term "movie" is used in reference to Wulf Herzogenrath's definition of the video film: "I understand 'video art' as all early activities … in the beginnings produced mostly on 16 mm-film but aimed on TV, on the television picture, on a new, another, an artistic medial approach towards TV." Herzogenrath (2006): "Videokunst und die Institutionen: Die ersten 15 Jahre", in: *Exhibition catalogue Düsseldorf/München/Leipzig/Karlsruhe 2006*: 20; translation by the author). Proceeding from this assumption, the data carrier – regardless of 16 mm-film, VHS-cassette, or DVD – is irrelevant as the presentation on a TV set is paramount. Cf. *Exhibition catalogue Karlsruhe/Aachen et al. 2009/10*.

2 Lovejoy, M. (2004): 95.

acteristic in common: No visitor knows the name of any presented artist within these exhibitions, as the movies were produced in the countries of the Former Soviet Union and in Asia, and the global art market still focuses mostly on the Western industrial nations. This is inasmuch remarkable as the idea of a unidirectional cultural transfer from the West to the East falls short of the mark. In particular the countries of the former Eastern Bloc, especially Hungary and Poland, "held an outstanding artistic position as early as in the 1970's."[3]

Even though, and this is quite surprising, these movies talk in such a universal language that they are understandable even in Western Culture as they present pictures and subjects with which we are also familiar. Thus we are talking about an internationalization of art. But, to be more specific, it is a western understanding of art and spaces with which artists work. If the (moving) picture should contain a real statement about today's world, it even more is a reflection of the real surroundings. For all that, intermediation is more necessary than ever as the world lost its tangibility. Even though it is nothing new that art reflects ideal worlds a significant change took place: We realize that next to its (seemingly) facilitation our world got much more complex. To that extend, selected movies offer themselves as basis for the examination of the question for the parameters that are necessary to create such universally understandable virtual worlds. We can furthermore ask for the mechanisms artists are bound within a globalized world, and what brings this loss of tangibility for the local culture. And at the same time, what does this mean for an artist and his creativity today.

THE FORMATION OF UNIVERSAL VIRTUAL (MOVIE-)WORLDS

"Architecture evokes human moods. It is thus the duty of the architect to refine the mood. The room has to be cozy; the house has to look livable. The court has to look like a threatening gesture towards the secret vice. The banking house has to tell people via its architecture: your money is secure and well preserved with honest people."[4] According to the precedent quote by Adolf Loos, said in 1910,

---

3 Eckstein, B. (1996): „Aktuelle Videokunst aus Zagreb", in: *Exhibition Catalogue Stuttgart/Bonn 1996*: 6.

4 "Die architektur erweckt stimmungen im menschen. Die aufgabe des architekten ist es daher, diese stimmung zu präzisieren. Das zimmer muss gemütlich, das haus wohnlich aussehen. Das justizgebäude muss dem heimlichen laster wie eine drohende gebärde erscheinen. Das bankhaus muss sagen: hier ist dein geld bei ehrlichen leuten fest und gut verwahrt." Loos, A. (1910): 102 f. (translation by the author).

provisions from the atmosphere of a building can be derived when mood and atmosphere can be equated. Atmosphere is created by architecture, meaning that it can be experienced in three dimensions. Therefore it is the architects' task to create atmospheric spaces with the aid of architecture.

If we understand filmmakers as architects of a virtual world we can adopt the words of Adolf Loos for movies. As early as in the 1990s, they were recognized as "ideal media" for self-awareness and "for the experience of space and time."[5] By that, new perspectives evolved through contact with art for artists and viewer at the same time, because the used materials and the media play a role in everyday life of the viewer. Therefore art and daily life can be compared with each other; the daily life can be aligned by using art. Nam June Paik, one of the pioneers of video art, said as early as in 1976: "Video art replicates nature, not in its appearance or in its material but by imitating its inner 'time design.'"[6] From today's perspective, another aspect has to be added: The consumer goods industry, the architecture, even the televised journalistic formats become aligned; brands, signs, symbols are already universally comprehendible. Worldwide, the logo of Mercedes Benz is recognized, Frank Ghery is building museums as bizarre mega-sculptures regardless of the precise location. In New York, Berlin or Tokyo we wear H&M, GAP or Benetton, drink coffee at Starbucks and eat French fries at McDonald's.

The universality of the actual artistic movie (that left long ago its experimental stage) therefore seems to have a certain logic: If everyday images are already universally understandable, if there is a growing approximation between North and South, East and West, it seems that a further approximation via omnipresent pictures and globally discussed topics – in short: via art – is a logical consequence. In particular, if the "digitalization represents a new role model, the transition from simulacrum to simulation, from copying to modeling."[7] Seen from this point of view, the arts and the movies become a reflection of our view of the world, a "Brave New World," like Aldous Huxley's dystrophic society novel.

---

5   Decker, E. (1990): 3.

6   Nam June Paik, quoted in: *Exhibition catalogue Köln/Hamburg/Karlsruhe et al. 1982/83*, jacket text.

7   Andrew Menard, quoted in: Lovejoy, M. (2004): 152.

THE ECOLOGICAL SYSTEM: WORLDWIDE ENDANGERED?!

But is it really a brave new world, the world outside, the movie world? Ghenadie Popescu's artist movie *Navigable Bîc* (2008)[8] invites us to interpret the "Brave New World" ironically: The artist himself – clad in a suit made out of that kind of plaid low-cost synthetic material we immediately associate with the bags which symbolize the hard-discount "Russian" flea markets – he pulls a little ship through the reed of the river Bîc which flows across the Moldavian capital Chişinău where Popescu lives and works. The oversized paper-made folding boat is made out of the same synthetic material, and looks child-like and pathetic at the same time because of its design and the used material. The river is a dirty runlet, the man within that dreariness through which he pulls the little boat is characterized as bizarre nomad, and his monologue a feature that indicates that there is a great divergence between pretence and reality in Moldavia (like in a lot of other places as well), as he recites from the environmental laws adopted by the Moldavian government thus offering an obvious contrast to the actual condition of the river Bîc which is a dreary, dirty swill that seems to be smelling strongly – even by watching the movie.

On the one hand, Popescu asks ironically and with underlying humor for the condition of the post-communist state which seems to be stranded with the inherited waste of the old communist system in the new capitalistic one. On the other, the movie looks beyond the question of the ideological systems and its own location: By paralleling recitative and reality, the spectator realizes that environmental pollution is a global theme, that the reality of the hard-discount "Russian" flea markets takes place on the steps of our doors, and that the globalized networks of consume take part in the destruction or pollution of rivers – of nature in general, regardless of its concrete location. The plastic bag, the childish-naivety of the "paper-made folding boat" and the pictures of destroyed nature make the frame for a universal comprehensibility; which we nearly automatically associate with the pictures of the devastating tanker accident of the *Exxon Valdez* (1989) and the *Tasman Spirit* (2003), as well as the damaged oil platform *Deepwater Horizon* (2010).

---

8   Ghenadie Popescu, *Navigable Bîc*, Single-Channel-Video, color, sound, 17:40 min. © Ghenadie Popescu 2008.

Figure 1. Ghenadie Popescu, Navigable Bîc, Single-Channel-Video, color, sound, 17:40 min.[9]

But: If Popescu's movie is a plea for the preservation of our nature, an appeal for ecological activism, or an ironic view on a small country in the Northeastern parts of Europe, is a question for the spectator himself. What applies in this regard is comparable to Judith Butler's remarks on the pictures of the torture scandal of Abu Ghraib,[10] which applies to photography in general, and to film (especially documentations and, in a certain way, for artist's movies as well) to a certain extend: The production of pictures and the visible perspective is related with a series of open and hidden general conditions. It depends on the pictures the photograph is able to see what he wants to see and what he seems worthy of presentation; if the photograph reaches the "circuit of pictures". But on the same time, it depends on which pictures are authorized and come into circulation.[11] Taking the pictures, which drones, surveillance cameras and video observance systems produce by themselves, control over pictures is not as easy to define as it had been in former days. But even though the assumption of Barbara Basting is correct who classifies the American renouncement to publish photographs of

---

9 © Ghenadie Popescu 2008

10 Butler, J. (2010): 73.

11 Basting, B. (2012): "Die Macht der Bilder ist die Macht der Filter", in: *Exhibition catalogue Frankfurt 2012*: 183.

the dead Osama Bin Laden as "a quantum leap in the attempt of the USA to get a grip on the media pictures."[12] Regardless of press photo, documentary or artistic interpretation of a subject – whether we understand the implied intention of a picture quite significantly depends on the obvious fact that we need to be familiar with the implemented message because the image content is greatly influenced by it. Therefore the "retrospect of selection" is gaining in importance in the light of the explosively increasing pictures, therefore we register all the more decelerated pictures[13] – whether we are talking about photorealistic pictures by Gerhard Richter or photographic images by Thomas Demand, or about slowly moving images of an artistic action like Popescu's happening doesn't matter that much any longer in light of the daily flood of images published in print, on TV, or in the internet. Thus I agree with Barbara Basting on the half-life period of the iconic image: "Considering the short half-life period of present-day media images they profit from the art context as ideal space for reflection because they can be linked up with a tradition of production and a reflection of historic images."[14] Within the artists' movie, this statement can be expanded towards the moving image which is comparable with photography concerning its medial duration. And, again comparable with photography, movies create strong, universal pictures if we already have real pictures (distributed by mass media) in mind which we can match with the art.

CAMOUFLAGE WITHIN THE WAR OF IMAGES

Another "brave new world" offers the Korean artist Yong-baek Lee: birds twitter, a gorgeous sea of flowers, reminiscent of the colorful opulence of Asian temple feasts, masquerade at first glance a perfect world. But soldiers with rifles in position creep through the gigantic video "picture" *Angel Soldier*. Initially,

---

12 Basting, B. (2012): "Die Macht der Bilder ist die Macht der Filter", in: *Exhibition catalogue Frankfurt 2012*: 185.

13 Cf. *Exhibition catalogue Wolfsburg 2011/12*.

14 Basting, B. (2012): "Die Macht der Bilder ist die Macht der Filter", in: *Exhibition catalogue Frankfurt 2012*: 192. For further information see: Stocker, G. (2012): "The Big Picture. Weltbilder für die Zukunft", in: Leopoldseder, H., Stocker, G., and Schöpf, C., eds. (2012): 16–19, and Ullrich, W. (2013): "Das Brausen, von welchem ich sprach", in: *Exhibition catalogue Herford 2013*: 119–129.

they are almost imperceptible as everything happens in slow motion.[15] As Lee works with the latest three-dimensional technology, the recognition of the soldiers changes the images' vista immediately into a frightful one, thus creating an indissoluble contradiction between the formerly intact appearance (created only by the first naïve and chaste view) and the "real" image of the soldier symbolizing imminent peril. The art work had been Lee's contribution to the 2011 Biennale di Venezia representing Korea. His website informs about the piece that it would bluntly reveal the social conditions of our generation in showing the drastic contrast between angel and soldier.[16] And in fact it seems to be an indissoluble antagonism between the wonderful, atmospheric, peaceful ambiance and the cruelties that the soldiers obviously intend to accomplish. Whoever creeps through the picture, the gun in outlined line of fire, intends nothing good. According to the name tags personifying the soldiers, the spectator sees Lee's artistic paragons: Nam June Paik, John Cage, Joseph Beuys and Marcel Duchamp move slowly through the sea of flowers attired in their uniforms with flower patterns (which have a similar disguising effect like "normal" uniforms due to the scenery). Attached on their jackets are further logos like the Internet Explorer. Lee characterized his work as a "counterpoint" against the Biennale aggression, against the concurrence of the picture and against the financial resources deployed. For while the Americans spent 2.7 Mio Euro for a tipped over tank for their pavilion Lee decided to "move in the opposite direction ... To make clothes out of soldierly uniforms symbolizes halt and peace and is a sign for a non-warlike posture for freedom."[17] Obviously, the current political situation of Ko-

---

15 Yong-Baek Lee, *Angel Soldier* (2011), One-Channel-Video, color, sound, 23 min. © the artist/gallery Hakgojae. Additionally, Lee provides uniforms with flower imprint and film stills for the installation version. During the film festival DMZ which took place for the 4th time in the demilitarized zone of Korea in 2012, he extended his art work by implementing a tank parade "Angel Soldier and Flower Tank" in Paju. Real tanks decorated with flowers on the occasion became a symbol for the hoped for peace. Additionally, Lee designed the official poster for the festival. For further information on the 4th DMZ Docs in Paju/South Korea see www.dmzdocs.com [access date 19.9.2013]

16 Cf. www.korean-pavilion.or.kr/11pavilion/INTRODUCTION_eng.html [access date 18.9.2013].

17 Yongbaek Lee in an interview with Mi-seok Koh: "Die Schwere der Wahrheit hinter der Pracht der Oberfläche". Lee Yongbaek 2011 Biennale di Venezia, in: *Koreana*. A Quarterly on Korean Culture & Arts. Herbst 2011, online see www.koreana.or.kr [access date 19.9.2013].

rea, the separation and the latent feeling of fear and tension have to be taken into account, as well as showing a counterpoint for the goings-on of the Biennale. It is thus comparable with Walter Benjamin's text "On the Concept of History" which had been inspired by the drawing *Angelus Novus* by Paul Klee. Benjamin says there: "But from paradise there blows a storm which catches its wings, so strongly that the angel can no longer close them. This storm pushes it ceaselessly towards future, to which it turns its back, while up to heaven, ruins accumulate. This storm is what we call progress."[18] Symbols for this "storm of progress" are the logos on the soldiers' uniform jackets and the submachine guns – they can be used for destruction but contain medial pictures of progress and danger as well. Lee reverses the self-imposed artistic taboo of beauty and uses it for his own purposes.[19] In fact, at first the spectators' attention is attracted by the underlying beauty; inevitably he will be overcome by the strange sensation after detecting the soldiers clad in their flower-patterned uniforms. This is related to the fact that "Perspective and photography have taught us to expect virtual spatial relations to be precisely metric (and film and television shows us that time is also metric – ›real time‹, slow motion, fast forward), but, such representations aside, virtual space is intrinsically endlessly flexible..." Therefore they "apparently describe spatial and temporal relations."[20] With these considerations we forge a relationship with the virtual reality that is even more able to frighten because it feigns real images and simulated realities.[21]

Obviously, both videos – *Navigable Bîc* by Popescu and *Angel Soldier* by Lee – imitate time, and not any longer the world: Maurizio Lazzarato developed the thesis that the new media in general broach the issue of time in their effort to compress and expand it.[22] Indeed Popescu's video seems to have fallen out of time and Lees *Angel Soldier* dawn only gradually into awareness. With that, both follow the tendency of slow down that becomes visible within the actual image production.[23] It seems to belong to our current experiences that an increasing ac-

---

18 Benjamin, W. (1940), Thesis IX.

19 Yongbaek Lee in an interview with Mi-seok Koh: "Die Schwere der Wahrheit hinter der Pracht der Oberfläche". Lee Yongbaek 2011 Biennale di Venezia, in: *Koreana*. A Quarterly on Korean Culture & Arts. Herbst 2011, online see www.koreana.or.kr [access date 19.9.2013].

20 Summers, D. (2003): 432.

21 This is the title of an exhibition catalogue as well: *Exhibition catalogue Oldenburg 2006*.

22 Lazzarato, M. (2002).

23 For further information see: *Exhibition catalogue Wolfsburg 2011/12*.

celeration can result in a complete stop, as well as progress is not accomplished only by rapidity. Cultural theorists already proclaim the "art of deceleration" as a "resource for a sustainable future" and a "new shape of intelligence" to oppose the breathlessness of accelerated events in politics, economy and media with a cultural-critical counterpoint.[24] But Yong-baek Lee's video emphasizes that even in a peaceful slow motion and the seemingly beautiful film still the horror might lie dormant. It can be seen in the succession of Robert Wilson's *Video Portraits,* where slow motion pictures give at first the impression of a film still where the very slow movements captivate hypnotically the viewer.[25]

Figure 2. Yong-Baek Lee, Angel Soldier (2011), One-Channel-Video, color, sound, 23 min.[26]

WHAT IS REAL?

In his 2012 article "How Do World Pictures Take Shape?" Thomas Macho asks if each era creates its own conception of the world and how these conceptions come into existence.[27] It is typically German to distinguish between universally

---

24 Böhme, H.: "Wollen wir in einem posthumanen Zeitalter leben? Geschwindigkeit und Verlangsamung in unserer Kultur", in: *Exhibition catalogue Wolfsburg 2011/12*: 8.

25 Cf. *Exhibition catalogue Karlsruhe 2011.*

26 © the artist / gallery Hakgojae.

27 Macho, T. (2012): "How Do World Pictures Take Shape?", in: Leopoldseder, H., Stocker, G., and Schöpf, C., eds. (2012): 22–31.

readable images and the conception of the word. If, following Heidegger,[28] the world is an image because the vast distances have been eliminated due to technical inventions and achievements like airplanes and mass media, it does not have to mean reverse that at every place worldwide images are understood similarly and have the same meaning. But if the world moves together due to the advance of globalization and increasing networking, it is relatively likely that this occurrence will take place. And Meiro Koizumi's video *My Voice Would Reach You* is a good example for that.[29] Koizumi, Japanese by birth, documents within this video the loneliness of the modern human being in an exuberant, vibrant, loud, even crowded city. Here, it is Tokyo, but likewise it could be Paris, New York, London, Shanghai or Delhi. It therefore is a city that seems to be an allegory on the "era of the capitalist turbo principle" as it radiates a permanent pulsation, and does not seem to have limits for space, time or motion any more.[30] Koizumi's protagonist is a role model for typical street behavior in European cities (taking place a little later then in the USA and in China): he telephones. But by that he produces one tragicomic even embarrassing situation after another as he wants to invite his mother to spend a weekend together – because in fact, he is not at all talking to his mother but with call center staff of Japanese companies. In doing so, he called more than 200 different hotlines, designing a colorful picture of the upcoming weekend, approving his "mother" sometimes, dissenting other aspects of the call, of what she says. Thus he is communicating with service employees of a call center he himself is portrayed as a lonesome man without roots, without family backing. Furthermore, the "mother" he wants to get invited has passed away recently.

---

28 Heidegger, Martin (1950): "Die Zeit des Weltbildes", in: same author (2012): *Holzwege*. Frankfurt/Main: Klostermann: 81 f.

29 Meiro Koizumi, *My Voice Would Reach You* (2009), Single-Channel-Video, color, sound, 16 min. © Museum of Modern Art New York.

30 Cf. Reheis, F. (2011): "Befreiung vom Turboprinzip. Die Diktatur des Geldes und die Perspektive einer Ökologie der Zeit", in: *Exhibition catalogue Wolfsburg 2011/12*: 12–17.

Figure 3. Meiro Koizumi, My Voice Would Reach You (2009), Single-Channel-Video, color, sound, 16 min.[31]

In his video, the artist undertakes emotional manipulations to demonstrate the isolation of the individual within the skyscraper jungle of the metropolis and at the same time drawing our attention on the public release of the private which is an inevitable consequence of phoning in public spaces. – Marshall McLuhan calls him a personality that since Kopernikus had been "downgraded to the position of a margin particle."[32] At the same time Koizumi subtly questions the value of the video recording: As Walter Grasskamp points out, the "quality of a highlight" (and as such he describes video recordings in general as they result out of the worthiness of the object to be recorded) is assessed not only by counting the number of spectators but as well by taking the "usage of media" into account as "a measurement of their value. What is considered worthy to be photographed or even recorded is deemed completely different for ordinary consumers if the 'media theater' is left out."[33] Koizumi is questioning decidedly this statement by showing an obviously embarrassing situation – at the same time, it is another conception of time underlying the video by showing the simultaneity of the non-

---

31 © Museum of Modern Art New York

32 McLuhan, M. (1995): 310.

33 Grasskamp, W. (2009): "Video in Kunst und Leben, Teil 1: Betrachtungen vor gut 30 Jahren…"/"Teil 2: … und die Fortschreibung heute, nach 30 Jahren", in: *Exhibition catalogue Karlsruhe/Aachen et al. 2009/10*: 60–71.

simultanous,[34] satirizing it as we are confronted by images that cannot be as they are not real: The protagonist is not able to call his mother because she is dead. Anyway, communication takes place but even though it is a real phone call it is surreal because he talks with a call center and not with the true recipient, because being surrounded by crowds of real people (possible counterparts for his fruitless communication), he tries to communicate with the one person where a communication is not possible. While the person on the other side of the line – trained for the service and maintenance of one special product – tries desperately to make sense of the provided information. The typical Japanese politeness does not allow a termination of the call, thus providing another tragicomically aspect for the video. On the other hand, we recognize that Koizumi creates an island of enforced tranquility within the hectic of the city due to the perpetual conversation which can be paralleled with the plea for an "ecology of time" by Fritz Reheis.[35]

Koizumi himself said about the video he "forcibly inserted an extremely personal sense of 'honne' (true feeling), into the mental mechanism of 'tatemae' (facade) in which a connection with the other is avoided. It was an attempt at a departure from a creative process that involved being holed up in a studio and filming in a way that can be perceived an 'otaku' (nerd) mentality, of avoiding any contact with the outside world."[36]

Especially by exploring the boundaries between private and public sphere Koizumi deals intensively with his own cultural and social roots: the private is a domain of specific importance within Japanese culture. Without going into details, it should be noted that there exists a cultural interlacing of private and public in Japan but no clear line of separation.[37] The political system in particular "captures almost all areas of society, and additionally the mutual interference of public and private dimension have occurred by supporting a rapid economic development."[38] In this respect (and I add this restrictively), the public behavior of

---

34 Cf. Foucault, M. (1967): "Von anderen Orten", in: Dünne, J., and Günzel, S., eds. (2006): 317 ff.

35 Reheis, F. (2003).

36 Meiro Koizumi about his video *My Voice Would Reach You*, online accessible under www.annetgelink.com/artists/22-Meiro-Koizumi/works/video/12201/ [access date 20.9.2013].

37 Cf. Mae, M. (2002), online accessible under www.dijtokyo.org/doc/dij-jb14-Mae.pdf [access date 26.9.13].

38 Mae, M. (2002): 242, online accessible under www.dijtokyo.org/doc/dij-jb14-Mae.pdf [access date 26.9.13].

the young man might appear more absurd, comical and strange on a western viewer but on someone with far-eastern background. By communicating his thoughts and emotions, Koizumi's video transports the cross-reference of cultures (which is typical for post-war Japan anyway)[39] because communicating such personal information is more a western "accessory" and thus, a conscious fraction with the rules of Japanese society.

Putting it in the way of Stefan Münkler and Alexander Roesler who point out that "our society is a media society, and our world is medialized in all its facets" whereas they conclude that "media is omnipresent; the term 'media' as well."[40] Following Harro Segeberg, these are only "specifications what media should be or could be in way that could mean everything and nothing," asking therefore "Who else than the media scientist who copes with the Universal in a universal manner should have the responsibility to deal with these questions?"[41] In light of the artists' videos this article refers to, the answer to this question could be: the artist. For exactly such a work of art like Koizumi's touches the uncomfortable narrow ridge that lies between cruelty and comedy and presents us with the universal of this singular example. The simultaneity of the private within the public, as well as the parallelism of reality seems to result in images in the media age. Therefore we can alter the Latin quote to "in imago ergo sum."[42] Additionally, we are entitled to add "In velocis imago ergo sum," as the velocity of images developed proportionally to the rapidity of mobility: Even remakes of science fiction movies like *2001 – Space Odyssee* (1968), or the TV classic *Space Patrol Orion* (1966) have been edited with more speed to adapt them on today's cut speed.[43] Needless to point out that even most of the fans did not register the alteration, as we are used to faster speed – but even though, it appears quite strange in the light of longer life expectancies and a far greater number of leisure time in comparison with people in former times.

Therefore Koizumi's video becomes a parabola on our time as well: we rush from one appointment, from one activity to the next, we can get as much amusement as we want, but at the same time the social fabric gets increasingly

---

39 For further information see for example: Lenz, I., and Mae, M. eds. (1997).

40 Münker, S., and Roesler, A. (2008a): "Preface", in: same authors (2008): 7 and 11.

41 Segeberg, H. (2012a): Antimimetische Mimesis. "Zur Medialität und Digitalität des Kinofilms", in: Segeberg, H., ed. (2012): 13.

42 Quoted in: Beckmann, A.-M. et al.: "Making History", in: *Exhibition catalogue Frankfurt 2012*: 10.

43 Cf. Klein, S. (2011): "Im Tsunami der Reize. Von der Droge 'Geschwindigkeit'", in: *Exhibition catalogue Wolfsburg 2011/12*: 30.

fragile, and every own people is searching for help with hotlines instead of friends – but they themselves went into the internet, are part of facebook and social media, have been plunged in virtuality as well.

ARCHITECTURE AS A VISION

The global ecological system: in acute danger to be destroyed as much that it endangers mankind as well. Military conflicts: trickery, subterfuge and deceptionist. Human bonds: in the process of being dissolved, in transition to a real online society. Considering the amount of ignorance and neglectance towards real necessities and social constraints – all impediments to be overcome in a globally interconnected world – it is not surprising that even architecture is facing up literally, within Dimitrij Gutov's video *From Flat to Flat* (2002).[44] It enables the viewer changing perspectives and insights in the Moscow street called Rubljovka, or "Street towards Felicity." While the video's title derives from a real experience Gutov gained amidst moving house in his home town sitting in a box van covered with canvas tarpaulin,[45] the utopian name of the street appears in strange contrast to the visible reality: The post-war architecture with its utopian visionaries perverted into faceless urban areas due to the incredible amount of rather clone-like monotonous blocks, the real theme of the video. In particular because of the headstand of the images, the dreariness caused by the architectural clone gets into focus – that does not want to fit to the promising street name.

Gutov made his video by driving along Rubljovka, holding two video cameras out of the window. But he held them upside down which results on the revolved image. The images thus make a headstand comparable to a camera obscura. But in difference to the 17th century attraction, the "real" camera obscura, in Gutov's art work, the mirror is missing that turns the image upright therefore keeping it 180° rotated. For Ekaterina Degot, this evokes the provocative question whether it would be exaggerated to "interpret the mirror as a symbol for reflection, and the gesture of the artist as a humble renouncement of it, on the capi-

---

44 Dmitrij Gutov, *From Flat to Flat* (2002), Two-Channel-Video-Installation, © Dmitrij Gutov und Guelman Gallery, Moscow.

45 See: Degot, E. (2005): "The Cinema of Painting/Film der Malerei." Fragment of a manuscript, taken from: Groys, B., von der Heiden, A., and Weibel, P., eds. (2005), online accessible under www.gutov.ru/texti/degot_de.htm [access date 26.9.13].

talistic position of the viewer?"[46] This term is understood as inquiry of progress "with the methods of technical progress and its dispersive effects on the world and subjectivity." In this respect, media art in general has the task not only to question the 'technologically new' but as well its preconditions. As Anke Hoffmann and Yvonne Volkart, two Zurich based curators, say, the "medialization of the world is not only a technical improvement of resources and media. Moreover, we are talking about specifically economic interests within the new world order of global capitalism which manifests itself in the interaction of resources and media."[47]

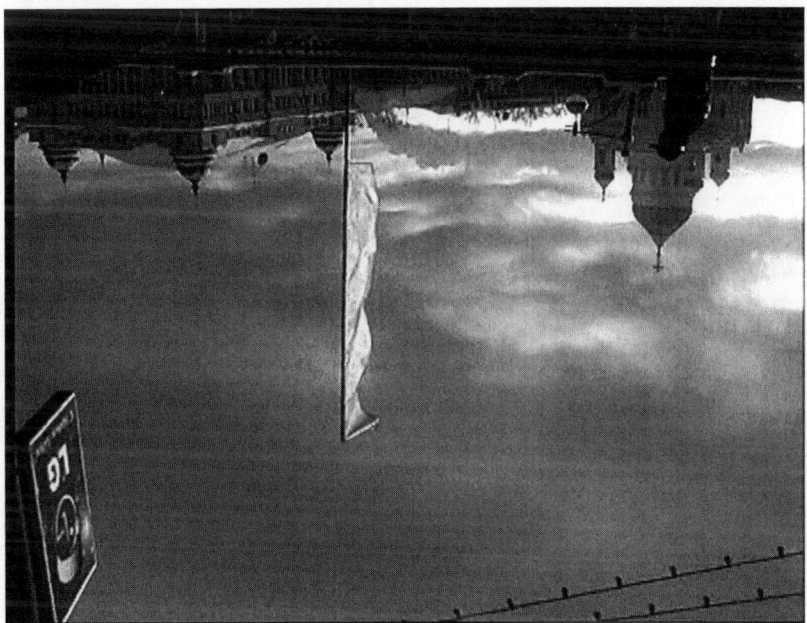

Figure 4. Dmitrij Gutov, From Flat to Flat (2002), Two-Channel-Video-Installation.[48]

---

46 Degot, E. (2005): "The Cinema of Painting/Film der Malerei." Fragment of a manuscript, taken from: Groys, B., von der Heiden, A., and Weibel, P., eds. (2005), online accessible under www.gutov.ru/texti/degot_de.htm [access date 26.9.13].

47 Hoffmann, A., and Volkart, Y. (2011): "Connect. Kunst zwischen Medien und Wirklichkeit", in: *Exhibition catalogue Zurich 2011*: 29.

48 © Dmitrij Gutov und Guelman Gallery, Moscow.

Gutov himself takes a critical approach towards western modernism and contemporary art. This ambivalence can be associated with the film music: It is the romance *Amid the din of the ball,* composed by Tchaikowsky on the text written by Lew Tolstoj. The romance elevates the splendor and misery of the neo-capitalistic metropolis after the end of the Cold War and the fall of the Eastern Bloc which Gutov portrays in "human resignation" (as he himself points out), by omitting the mirror and thus leaving out the reflection presenting the images with relentless candor.[49]

Looking from that perspective, it does not seem to be a wonder that after the 1990's, a certain "infatuation with ruins" especially in artist videos is recognizable. In any case, on *Flat to Flat* applies what the British critic Brian Dillon published in the *Frieze Magazine* 2010, stating generally: "The variously thoroughgoing or superficial archeology of architectural and artistic Modernism that has exercised so many artists in the last decade is patently, on one level, a discourse on ruins in a Romantic mode."[50] It is possible that this way of romantic looking backwards, always combined with this "infatuation with ruins," might be a counter reaction on the ideology which influenced Russia for the last 100 years. Therefore, Gutov's video might be read as reference on Karl Marx' and Friedrich Engels' *Deutsche Ideologie* which refers explicitly on the idea of a Camera obscura: "If within the whole ideology mankind and their conditions seem to be upside down, this phenomenon results as well from their historical process of living as the rotation of items on the retina results from their physical process."[51] Matthias Bohlender points out that ideology has the intrinsic characteristic to reverse ideas that are based on the living conditions of the people, that depend on the "material way of life of people and finds its adequate determination in form and content."[52] With his video, Dimitrij Gutov makes us aware of reality in a way that Timothy Druckery defines as a result from images; whereas

---

49 Dmitrij Gutov, quoted in: Degot, E. (2005): "The Cinema of Painting/Film der Malerei." Fragment of a manuscript, taken from: Groys, B., von der Heiden, A., and Weibel, P., eds. (2005), online accessible under www.gutov.ru/texti/degot_de.htm [access date 26.9.13]. For further information on his artistic background see: Gutov, D. (2005).

50 Cf. Dillon, B. (2010), online accessible under www.frieze.com/issue/print_article/ decline_and_fall/ [access date 26.9.13].

51 Marx, K., and Engels, F.: "Deutsche Ideologie (1845/46)", in: same authors (1969): 26 [translation by the author).

52 Cf. Bohlender, M. (2010): "Die Herrschaft der Gedanken. Über Funktionsweise, Effekt und die Produktionsbedingungen von Ideologie", in: Blum, H., ed. (2010): 46.

"it was simply never the case that the 'image' was much more than the staging of 'realities', whose 'presence' or meaning oscillated between credulity and incredulity, 'real' and rendered, record and simulation. In short, our representations never endured as reliable signifiers but rather as ciphers."[53] Generally speaking, we can ask ourselves how real the images (of cities) are which we carry within us. A question that gets particularly interesting if we compare them with global images. Does the viewer perceive the video in China like the one in Mexico, in Japan as well as in America, in Paris likewise as in New Delhi? In the face of the rapid growth of internet and social media we might answer yes.[54] But we have to take into account all advantages and disadvantages of "performative democracy" which have been caused by new technologies,[55] because all advantages of active participation, of interconnectedness and mobility have an equal drawback. Not only by leaving data traces, it is getting increasingly easy to draw reliable conclusions on the people behind. But on the other hand, real and virtual, genuine and fictive are mixed up – weather it is a video, a movie or within a shopping mall seems to be irrelevant in creating brave new worlds. Gutov presents the viewer his version of the contemporaneousness of the non-contemporaneous in his parable-like video: in Russia, new wealth and new poverty stand side by side more or less abruptly. Is it an upside down world? Or is it our ideas that are totally out of place facing this discrepancy? Considering the establishment of internet as a new cultural area which "asks even more for new answers on the question of 'material' reality than science," the "unspecific universality," Fabrizio Plessi is still talking about in the 1980's transformed into a universal space of experience where the metaphor of journeys to fictitious places seems to be appropriate.[56] At the same time, the distinctions between real and fictitious become blurred; what reality means to one person someone else calls virtuality.

---

53 Druckery, T. (2006): "Palimseste oder déjà vu. Alles nochmal von vorn…", in: *Exhibition catalogue Oldenburg 2006*: 22.

54 Between 2005 and 2010, the amount of internet user doubled and exceeded the two billion mark in the meanwhile. Pingdom, a Swedish monitoring company, predicted another rapid increase for 2011 to 2013. Cf. Whitney, L. and Beiersmann, S.: Studie: Weltweit nutzen 2,1 Milliarden Menschen das Internet, in: *ZDnet*, 19.1.2012, online accessible www.zdnet.de/41559492/studie-weltweit-nutzen-2-1-milliarden-menschen-das-internet/ [access date 27.9.13].

55 Peter Weibel in an interview with Peter Unfried: "Die Bürger möchten das Monopol einer parteipolitischen Kaste brechen", in: *taz*, 29.1.2011, online accessible www.taz.de [access date 27.9.13].

56 Cf. Haustein, L. (2003): esp. 36.

A VIDEO ALWAYS FITS BETWEEN REALITY AND VIRTUALITY

"Like photography and possibly more than traditional fields of the arts video is a media with which artists can respond rapidly and spontaneously to actual social and political developments."[57] It is therefore not surprising that video art increased notably during the last decades, as well within the arts. It also comes as no surprise that never before "so many and complex shapes of 'moving images' have been developed" as during the last 30 years.[58] In particular the connection to the truth and reality of images had been (and is still) an important aspect of artistic video production. Due to the time context which is imminent to video, the "emphasize on time based structures of video and sound transpired as a main category of artistic production of the 21st century."[59] It is used worldwide, worldwide the production of (artistic) images takes place, which are understandable globally (with some extend) because (or especially when) the underlying subjects are global ones. However, as Marshall McLuhan emphasizes in his 1962 publication *The Gutenberg Galaxy*, the general alphabetization is the fundamental basis for a global understanding of images and symbols. This fact stresses Wolfgang Coy in his introduction to the German edition in 1995 as well: "The symbolic space which is placed behind the visual space takes over fundamental characteristics of the visual space like continuity, uniformity, or local correlation." Whereby the "general alphabetization ... marks the beginning of the long dominance of the sense of sight" because "even within the transformation of the spoken word, alphabetic visualization is implemented... The ability to write and to read marks the change of the spoken and the heard into a spacial, visual sphere."[60] To that effect McLuhan distinguishes between the alphabetized, western public and the "African spectator" who has an intrinsic inclination to participation which is lost to us because of alphabetization: "The emphatic contribution which is by nature appropriate for an oral society and similarly for the auditory-tactile human being, is destroyed by the phonetic alphabet which breaks up the visual components from the complex."[61]

---

57 Eckstein, B. (1996): "Aktuelle Videokunst aus Zagreb", in: *Exhibition Catalogue Stuttgart/Bonn 1996*: 7.

58 Schmidt, S. M. (2009): "Am richtigen Ort zur richtigen Zeit? Kurzer Bericht zur aktuellen Videokunst", in: *Exhibition Catalogue Karlsruhe/Aachen 2009/10*: 36.

59 Schmidt, S. M. (2009): "Am richtigen Ort zur richtigen Zeit? Kurzer Bericht zur aktuellen Videokunst", in: *Exhibition Catalogue Karlsruhe/Aachen 2009/10*: 38.

60 Coy, W. (1995): "Introduction", in: McLuhan, M. (1995): IX.

61 McLuhan, M. (1995): 49.

However, it seems that there exists another perspective which again is related only to industrialized nations: the view of the artist. And by stating this, we have to acknowledge the gap between the global comprehensibility of the art works and the international noticeability of the artist who produces them: Ekaterina Degot explains that the question about the integration of artists from post-Soviet countries in the international art world is very difficult because "the post-Soviet artists lost their interest in it." Following Degot, this can probably be explained with their socialization which took place within a system where "certain words (i.e. 'economy', 'career', 'money') effectively did not exist, and other ones (i.e. 'happiness', 'work', 'art' or 'artist') meant completely other things then today."[62] On the one hand, this statement can be extended to all the former Eastern bloc Asian countries. On the other hand, the decidedly interest in these regions and in the artists from countries of the former USSR and Asia which becomes obvious in such exhibitions like at ZKM results obviously from a change taking place at the moment. The art market tails the images which already accomplished the start into a globalized world. The presented artists work in a way that can be subsumed under the "documentary approach" which "always wanted to reflect a political self-conception." Even though it had actually been considered to be obsolete in the 1980's, today it answers on the changed global situation, on global problems and subjects, which artists reflect in their own way.[63]

On the basis of Koizumi's and Gutov's video working as role models it had been possible to demonstrate that the boundaries between virtual and real places become indistinct. It is thus appropriate to adopt the definition of virtual worlds by the American art historian David Summers: "Virtual spaces may be made to describe and record actual places and times, or they may simply seem to do so, projecting and elaborating imaginary ones. In all cases the space itself is credible, occupiable and traversable only in imagination; it can also never adequately represent a real space, or correspond to one."[64] But even if their representation and equivalent have only a virtual truthfulness, the places get real by contemplating them. This is a result of the worldwide convergence (not at least because of the globalization of architecture!) causing the possibility to understand the places to a certain degree even if not feeling at home there.

---

62 Degot, E. (2005a): "Der Tod der Kunst und die Geburt des kreativen Schaffens. Die dialektische Moderne in der UdSSR und in Russland", in: Groys, B., von der Heiden, A., and Weibel, P., eds. (2005): 539.

63 Cf. Pickshaus, P. M. (2006): "Video als Fach – und wer denkt dabei was", in: *Exhibition catalogue Düsseldorf/München/Leipzig/Karlsruhe 2006*: 86.

64 Summers, D. (2003): 44.

"The artist" may cover the small local myths but regarded from a superior perspective, we can detect a globalization of the arts comparable to the globalization of economics and interpersonal relationships. This is the reason why the arts are able to create a universal picture language by requesting something from the viewer particularly industrialized societies have least of all to spare: time. Even more impressive in terms of experience are video installations because they "oscillate between illusionary spaces and attachment within the factual space," thus combining the idea of museums with the one of movies resulting in a "heterotopic place."[65] I do not want to go any further into the real experiences resulting of these virtual images because the chosen videos out of the two exhibitions that had been on display at ZKM had been discernible "only" as video not as an installation.[66] Following Marshall McLuhan, "the human being exteriorized parts of his nature by using material technology [in this case especially mass media, annotation of the author], then his entire ratio defers."[67] If, upon reversion, the modern human being has access to education and is alphabetized, we can adhere that his imagination is conformized as much by mass media that he is without any problems able to understand global images – something which is even recognizable with children visiting a museum.

REFERENCES

Basting, Barbara (2012): "Die Macht der Bilder ist die Macht der Filter", in: *Exhibition catalogue Frankfurt 2012*: 183–192

Beckmann, Anne-Marie et al. (2012): "Making History", in: *Exhibition catalogue Frankfurt 2012*: 10–19

Benjamin, Walter (1940): "Über den Begriff der Geschichte.", in: same author: *Werke und Nachlass – Kritische Gesamtausgabe*, vol. 19. Ed. by Gérard Raulet (2010). Berlin: Suhrkamp

Blum, Harald, ed. (2010): *Karl Marx/Friedrich Engels. Die deutsche Ideologie.* Berlin: Dietz

---

65 Frohne, U. (2010): "Passagen: Projektionsräume im Museum", in: *Exhibition catalogue Köln 2010*: 123. For further information cf.: Holert, T. (2010).

66 Cf. Meiro Koizumi about his video *My Voice Would Reach You*, online accessible under www.annetgelink.com/artists/22-Meiro-Koizumi/works/video/12201/ [access date 28.9.2013].

67 McLuhan, M. (1995): 327.

Böhme, Hartmut: "Wollen wir in einem posthumanen Zeitalter leben? Geschwindigkeit und Verlangsamung in unserer Kultur", in: *Exhibition catalogue Wolfsburg 2011/12*: 2–8

Bohlender, Matthias: "Die Herrschaft der Gedanken. Über Funktionsweise, Effekt und die Produktionsbedingungen von Ideologie", in: Blum, Harald, ed. (2010): 41–58

Butler, Judith (2010): *Frames of War*. New York: Campus

Coy, Wolfgang (1995): "Introduction", in: McLuhan, Marshall (1995): VII–XVIII

Decker, Edith (1990): "Von der Aktions- zur Videokunst. Die Ausweitung des Werkbegriffs", in: *Funkkolleg Moderne Kunst*. Saarländischer Rundfunk, Hauptabteilung Kulturelles Wort. broadcast 14.5.-20.5.1990

Degot, Ekaterina (2005): "The Cinema of Painting/Film der Malerei." Fragment of a manuscript, taken from: Groys, Boris, and von der Heiden, Anne, and Weibel, Peter, eds. (2005), online accessible under www.gutov.ru/texti/degot_de.htm

Degot, Ekaterina (2005a): "Der Tod der Kunst und die Geburt des kreativen Schaffens. Die dialektische Moderne in der UdSSR und in Russland", in: Groys, Boris, von der Heiden, Anne, and Weibel, Peter, eds. (2005): 539-567

Dillon, Brian (2010): "Decline and Fall. Tracing the history of ruins in art, from 18th-century painting to 21st-century film", in: *Frieze Magazine*, April 2010, online accessible under www.frieze.com/issue/print_article/decline_and_fall/

Druckery, Timothy (2006): "Palimseste oder déjà vu. Alles nochmal von vorn...", in: *Exhibition catalogue Oldenburg 2006*: 20-25

Eckstein, Beate (1996): "Aktuelle Videokunst aus Zagreb", in: *Exhibition Catalogue Stuttgart/Bonn 1996*: 4-10

Exhibition catalogue Düsseldorf/München/Leipzig/Karlsruhe 2006. Frieling, Rudolf, and Herzogenrath, Wulf, eds. (2006): *40jahrevideokunst.de – Teil 1. Digitales Erbe: Videokunst in Deutschland von 1963 bis heute*. Ostfildern: Verlag Hatje Cantz

Exhibition catalogue Frankfurt 2012. RAY Fotografieprojekte Frankfurt, RheinMain, Horvay, Andrea, ed. (2012): *Making History*. Ostfildern: Hatje Cantz

Exhibition catalogue Herford 2013. Marta Herford gGmbH, ed.: *Atmosphären der Veränderung/Visions. Atmospheres of Change*. Ostfildern: Hatje Cantz

Exhibition catalogue Karlsruhe 2011. Weibel, Peter, Falckenberg, Harald, and Shattuck, Mattew, ed.: *Robert Wilson Video Portraits*. Köln: König

Exhibition catalogue Karlsruhe/Aachen et al. 2009/10. Blase, Christoph, and Weibel, Peter, eds. (2010): *record > again! 40jahrevideokunst.de – Teil 2.* Ostfildern: Hatje Cantz

Exhibition catalogue Köln 2010. Engelbach, Barbara, ed. (2010): *Bilder in Bewegung. Künstler & Video/Film.* Köln: König

Exhibition catalogue Köln/Hamburg/Karlsruhe et al. 1982/83. Herzogenrath, Wulf, ed. (1982): *Videokunst in Deutschland. 1963–1982.* Stuttgart: Hatje

Exhibition catalogue Oldenburg 2006. Himmelsbach, Sabine, ed. (2006): *Playback_Simulierte Wirklichkeiten.* Heidelberg: Kehrer

Exhibition catalogue Stuttgart/Bonn 1996. Eckstein, Beate, and Lenz, Iris, and Winkler, Monika, eds. (1996): *Real Life! Aktuelle Videokunst aus Zagreb.* Stuttgart/Bonn: Ifa-Galerie

Exhibition catalogue Wolfsburg 2011/12. Brüderlin, Markus, ed. (2011): *Die Kunst der Entschleunigung.* Ostfildern: Hatje Cantz

Exhibition catalogue Zurich 2011. Bundesamt für Kultur Bern, Hoffmann, Anke, Volkart, Yvonne, eds. (2011): *Connect. Kunst zwischen Medien und Wirklichkeit.* Nürnberg: Verlag für Moderne Kunst

Foucault, Michel (1967): "Von anderen Orten", in: Dünne, Jörg, and Günzel, Stephan, eds. (2006): *Raumtheorie. Grundlagentexte aus Philosophie und Naturwissenschaften.* Frankfurt/Main: Suhrkamp: 317-329

Frohne, Ursula (2010): "Passagen: Projektionsräume im Museum", in: *Exhibition catalogue Köln 2010*: 121-128

Grasskamp, Walter (2009): "Video in Kunst und Leben, Teil 1: Betrachtungen vor gut 30 Jahren…"/ "Teil 2: … und die Fortschreibung heute, nach 30 Jahren", in: *Exhibition catalogue Karlsruhe/Aachen et al. 2009/10*: 60-71

Groys, Boris, and von der Heiden, Anne, and Weibel, Peter, eds. (2005): *Zurück aus der Zukunft. Osteuropäische Kulturen im Zeitalter des Postkommunismus.* Frankfurt/Main: Suhrkamp

Gutov, Dmitrij (2005): "Die marxistisch-leninistische Ästhetik in der postkommunistischen Epoche. Michail Lifšic", in: Groys, Boris, and von der Heiden, Anne, and Weibel, Peter, eds. (2005): 709-737

Haustein, Lydia (2003): *Videokunst.* München: Beck

Heidegger, Martin (1950): "Die Zeit des Weltbildes", in: same author (2012): *Holzwege.* Frankfurt/Main: Klostermann : 69-104

Herzogenrath, Wulf (2006): "Videokunst und die Institutionen: Die ersten 15 Jahre", in: *Exhibition catalogue Düsseldorf/München/Leipzig/Karlsruhe 2006*: 20-33

Hoffmann, Anke, and Volkart, Yvonne: "Connect. Kunst zwischen Medien und Wirklichkeit", in: *Exhibition catalogue Zurich 2011*: 28-38

Holert, Tom (2010): "Im Zweifel mit den Bildern. Dokumentarische Strategien zwischen Repräsentationskritik und Gedächtnistheater", in: *Exhibition catalogue Köln 2010*: 217-224

Klein, Stefan (2011): "Im Tsunami der Reize. Von der Droge »Geschwindigkeit«", in: *Exhibition catalogue Wolfsburg 2011/12*: 30-34

Lazzarato, Maurizio (2002): *Videophilosophie. Zeitwahrnehmung im Postfordismus*. Berlin: b_books (original Italian edition Rome 1997)

Lenz, Ilse, and Mae, Michiko, eds. (1997): *Getrennte Welten, gemeinsame Moderne? Geschlechterverhältnisse in Japan*. Opladen: Leske und Budrich (= publication series *Geschlecht und Gesellschaft*, vol. 4)

Leopoldseder, Hannes, Stocker, Gerfried, and Schöpf, Christine, eds. (2012): *Ars Electronica 2012*. Ostfildern: Hatje Cantz

Loos, Adolf: "Architektur" (1910), in: Opel, Alfred, ed. (1982): *Trotzdem. 1900–1930* (unaltered reprint of the first edition). Wien: Prachner: 102 f.

Lovejoy, Margot (2004): *digital currents: art in the electronic age*. New York/London: Routledge, Taylor & Francis Group

Macho, Thomas: "How Do World Pictures Take Shape?", in: Leopoldseder, H., Stocker, G., and Schöpf, C., eds. (2012): 22-31

Mae, Michiko (2002): Öffentlichkeit und Privatheit im japanischen Modernisierungsprozess, in: *Japanstudien. Jahrbuch des Deutschen Instituts für Japanstudien der Philipp-Franz-von-Siebold-Stiftung*, issue 14/2002, pp. 237-266, online accessible under www.dijtokyo.org/doc/dij-jb14-Mae.pdf

Marx, Karl, and Engels, Friedrich (1845/46): "Deutsche Ideologie", in: same authors (1969): Werke, vol. 3. Berlin (Ost): Dietz: 8-530

McLuhan, Marshall (1995): *Die Gutenberg-Galaxis: Das Ende des Buchzeitalters*. Bonn/Paris et al.: Addison-Wesley (first edition 1962: Toronto: University of Toronto Press)

Münker, Stefan, and Roesler, Alexander, eds. (2008): *Was ist ein Medium?* Frankfurt/Main: Surkamp

Münker, Stefan, and Roesler, Alexander (2008a): "Preface" to: same authors (2008): 7-12

Pickshaus, Peter Moritz (2006): "Video als Fach – und wer denkt dabei was", in: *Exhibition catalogue Düsseldorf/München/Leipzig/Karlsruhe 2006*: 79-91

Reheis, Fritz (2003): *Entschleunigung: Abschied vom Turbokapitalismus*. München: Riemann

Reheis, Fritz (2011): "Befreiung vom Turboprinzip. Die Diktatur des Geldes und die Perspektive einer Ökologie der Zeit", in: *Exhibition catalogue Wolfsburg 2011/12*: 12-17

Schmidt, Sabine Maria (2009/2010): "Am richtigen Ort zur richtigen Zeit? Kurzer Bericht zur aktuellen Videokunst", in: *Exhibition catalogue Karlsruhe/Aachen et al. 2009/10*: 34-39

Segeberg, Harro, ed. (2012): *Film im Zeitalter Neuer Medien II. Digitalität und Kino*. Paderborn: Fink (= *Mediengeschichte des Films*, vol. 8)

Segeberg, Harro (2012a): "Antimimetische Mimesis. Zur Medialität und Digitalität des Kinofilms", in: same author, ed. (2012): 9-25

Stocker, Gerfried: „The Big Picture. Weltbilder für die Zukunft", in: Leopoldseder, H., Stocker, G., and Schöpf, C. (2012): 16-19

Summers, David (2003): *Real Spaces. World Art History and the Rise of Western modernism*. New York: Phaidon

Peter Weibel in an interview with Peter Unfried: "Die Bürger möchten das Monopol einer parteipolitischen Kaste brechen", in: *taz,* 29.1.2011, online accessible under www.taz.de

Ullrich, Wolfgang (2013): "Das Brausen, von welchem ich sprach", in: *Exhibition catalogue Herford 2013*: 119-129

Whitney, Lance, and Beiersmann, Stefan: "Studie: Weltweit nutzen 2,1 Milliarden Menschen das Internet", in: *ZDnet,* 19.1.2012, online accessible under www.zdnet.de/41559492/studie-weltweit-nutzen-2-1-milliarden-menschen-das-internet/

Yongbaek Lee in an interview with Mi-seok Koh: "Die Schwere der Wahrheit hinter der Pracht der Oberfläche". Lee Yongbaek 2011 Biennale di Venezia, in: *Koreana*. A Quarterly on Korean Culture & Arts. autumn 2011, online see www.koreana.or.kr

All photographs published with the kind permission of ZKM I Center for Art and Media (Media Museum and Museum of Contemporary Art) Karlsruhe and the artists.

The Community Question

MANFRED NEGELE

INTRODUCTION – OBSERVATIONS OF CONTEMPORARY FORMS OF ENCOUNTER

Due to enormous progress in technology and with the expansion of the WWW the life of people (not only in the western world) has changed. A direction or an end to this development is not in sight. The internet has created unforeseen possibilities for information flows, communication and the economic market. Access to the internet via the radio network and smart phones has given it another new dimension. Every single user can, from almost everywhere in the world, access the network and, on the other hand, also be contactable all the time and everywhere. With this, the opportunities for communication have become tremendously varied.

The connection with others is therefore possible at any time; the willingness to make contact with others seems unlimited. This arguably expresses the desire to not be alone, to be taken seriously by others and to have their attention. It is an expression of the search for community. In the process, many close themselves off from their immediate surroundings by concentrating on their device, sometimes also with headphones.

The contacts that are maintained in this way are only in part via spoken language. Many are realized via the platform of Facebook, on chat forums, in online games etc. The question of whether communities come about in this way, ones which may only ever remain virtual communities, has been discussed regularly in research over the past decades. In this, on the one hand, certain basic patterns appear that outlast the technological progress. On the other, the technology and its users are often far ahead of the contemplation of the changes.

This article aims to consider some fundamental aspects of the new communication forms, and to ask the question of whether it can still be considered as a "community," or whether community is threatened by decay.

WHAT DOES "COMMUNITY" MEAN?

Initially the question arises about the nature of community. Where do we find community? Can the human manage without community? Does it belong to his nature? Has the nature of community changed in the age of modern communication? Is it at threat of being lost? Or are new forms of community created?

When we look at the German term for community, "Gemeinschaft," the etymology of the word offers a first access. Essential features are already named here.

»Etymologically the term 'community', which goes back to the Latin term *communitas* and refers to the common unit *(comm-unitas)*, first of all designates that which is not individual, and this traditional meaning is in contrast to particularism or isolation. At the same time *communitas* contains the word *munus*, which refers to a social quality in the sense of an obligatory barter of gifts. In both these dimensions it also refers back to the Greek *koinos*, which in the form of the common is set against the own *(idios)*.

The German adjective *gemein* (common) has, through the word stem *munus* (German main), the same origin as *communitas*. The framework of signification of *communitas* and *koinos*, as well as *Gemeines* and the *Gemeinschaft*, are extensive. Only in the course of modernity and modern times have demarcations of content developed and the terms become systematised.«[1]

A return to the Latin term *communitas* shows what is decisive: Community is a unit of individuals. Who are these individuals? They are humans, individuals, and people. This type of gathering is crucial to our context. (Naturally, there are also other forms of community: There are communities of interest, working communities, communities of commercial enterprises, of countries etc. Some live in a community with their pets. In this context it is, however, not a matter of these communities.)

If we look at the German term "Gemeinschaft," then according to Juliane Spitta there is a special feature.

»It is due to the specifics of the political-historical development and the features of German community thinking that the term can ultimately not be translated into other languages. This affects the depth dimension of political identity which connects community and nature as well as the contrast to society. In French, for example, it is absurd to set

---

1   Spitta, J. (2013): 16

communauté against *société* and the same applies to English, Italian, Dutch, Spanish or Icelandic.«[2]

Since Ferdinand Tönnies published his fundamental work "Community and Society" (Gemeinschaft und Gesellschaft) in 1887, which for some represents the start of modern sociology, we have been accustomed in German to differentiating these two terms from one another.[3] The shortest summary is offered by the dictionary:

»According to F. TÖNNIES, who in 1887 introduced the term C[ommunity] as a fundamental term in sociology, C. is a naturally growing, inner drive for C.-building (the "essence of desire"), in comparison to "society" which is defined as a rationally constructed association of purpose for common interests. Prime examples of C. are, according to TÖNNIES, groups such as family, clans, tribes, spatial units such as the village or the former town, intellectually intimate groups such as the master and his disciple, and friendships.«[4]

Whether this differentiation is justified or whether the terms should not be separated is still discussed by sociologists today. This debate will not be entered into here as I am not a sociologist.

If we look back to the beginnings of contemplation about community/society, then with Aristotle we find the well-known sentence that the man is a *zoon politikon physei*, a creature that is by nature political and social.[5] According to Aristotle the human cannot live as an individual; he is dependent on others and must live together with them as part of an orderly whole and in a defined territory. Community and society here appear to represent a synonym. We find something similar in Plato's ideal "state," which however, in contrast to Aristotle, knows no family unit.[6]

---

2   Spitta, J. (2013): 18
3   A good summary and critical representation of Tönnies is found in Opielka, M. (2006): 23-40. Tönnies is cited or at least mentioned in all articles or publications on the topic of "community."
4   21st Brockhaus Encyclopedia (2006): Book 10, 401
5   cf. Aristotle, Politics 1253a. Höffe, O. (1999): 248-256 compares Aristotle's position and its critique in modern times.
6   It should be noted that Plato does not conceptualize the state for the desires of the state, but rather because it should offer the best possible general conditions within which the individuals can perfect their souls.

What community and society have in common – insofar as one wants to separate them – is the connection (a term that Tönnies also uses in this context) of individuals. This connection must be structured. This applies to the connection between two people just as it does for the connection between many.

Now two approaches to the topic of "community" can be found. Either one sees the order structure as the same and tries to conceptually grasp its essence. Or one goes on the level of experience and asks where and how community and society is experienced. Both from the conceptual side and from the side of the experience it is appropriate to differentiate community from society. Under society can be understood the ordered structure of many people living together, who are defined by conventions. Community doesn't have a completely different meaning to this. There is an order underlying it, too. But it is aiming at the experience of the unit with other people, be it few or many. In the research question given here I plead that community and society should be conceptually separated. Even if this isn't common in other languages, a differentiation can help to analyze the phenomenon.[7]

Philosophically, each term that we use and that means something specific poses the question which Socrates often asked: "What is it?" What is community? An initial answer is offered by a dictionary:

»*gen.*: A broad term that refers to the mutual relationship between people that are connected on the basis of historical relations, religious ideology, political ideology, ideals or a narrowly limited functionality: A people, nation, country, church, (religious or political) municipality, marriage, family, friendship, interest groups, associations et. al.«[8]

This definition brings some important aspects. But as is often the case in such definitions, the further explanations of what "mutual" and "connected" actually mean are missing. Therefore the question is posed: What connects people mutually? In my opinion the most important aspects are as follows:

- In the first place, it should be understood that community lives in the mutual recognition by the participants. If it should truly become a community then the participants must consider it to be one.
- Connected with this is the attention that each individual in a community should give to the others.

---

7   Tönnies saw the community as natural, the society as something that was arbitrarily created. This differentiation was the source of much criticism, but doesn't lack certain plausibility.

8   21st Brockhaus Encyclopedia (2006): Book 10, 400f.

- Commitment: One must be able to rely on the community partners. Community conveys security. But the members of the community must all contribute to this security.
- Community demands a certain durability. From this comes reliability.
- Community gives everyone *their* (spiritual) space and at the same time offers a *communal* living space.
- Community needs a physical or virtual location or a space in which it can be realized.
- Affiliation or feeling of affiliation. All people seem to want to be affiliated with one or more groups.
- The prerequisite is a common goal or interest. This can be for a specific purpose or based on freedom.
- Togetherness without dependency would be the ideal.
- Community not only connects, it also excludes. This occurs as a matter of principle. It can also occur that there is a conscious expulsion from the community when its existence is otherwise endangered.
- Community creates identity.

If we ask about the basic module of community (as with society), then we find the individual humans. We have the conception of ourselves as individuals. We describe this individuality as a person. Theoretically this person – Tönnies describes it as a fiction[9] – cannot be grasped. But we can discover what underlies this representative. According to Martin Buber we discover this in the encounters with other people. In this, for Buber, we have the experience of community.

MARTIN BUBER – ENCOUNTER

"All true life is encounters." This is a central idea of Martin Buber.[10] What does this mean? The answer can be very different depending on what one views as constructive for encounters. We also encounter other people with the help of modern means of communication. The question is whether this is an encounter in the full and true sense. In which manner do I need to encounter someone in order to "truly" have encountered him or her?

For Buber an encounter is discussion or dialogue that is carried out from person to person in a real togetherness, face to face. Personal presence is only

---

9   Tönnies, F. (1972): 174

10 Buber, M. (1973): 15

one prerequisite. So that a true discussion comes about it also requires the acceptance of the other and unreserved openness. "The sphere of the interpersonal is facing one another; it's development if what we call dialogic."[11] What occurs in the minds of the dialogue partners is secondary for Buber. The psychological is "only the secret accompaniment to the discussion itself, a phonetic event loaded with meaning, whose meaning cannot be found either in one of the two partners nor in both together, but rather in their living interaction, in their intermediate."[12]

In this one presents to the other must not only be a (possibly even fictitious) self-image (this would be simply a "pseudo"), but rather it must be as far as possible reveal his "being." The goal is thus to not hide oneself behind a mask but rather to discard the mask even if this is only possible in the presence of the other and for the encounter with them. Then there are more results than the discussion participants could consciously be aware of.

There seems to be differences in presence. If someone is standing in front of me then the exchange is considerably more comprehensive than if I can hide myself behind a piece of paper or a medium (imaging or not), or need to use it. Facial expressions or gestures work alongside the spoken word as forms of communication. The person as an individual appears in their entirety and the other. This is the classic form of an encounter. It makes it possible for two or more people to meet and create a community. In coming together, in mutual revealing of oneself the possibility arises of overcoming the boundaries of the individual person and in this way experiencing a unity with the other. Buber calls this encounter an "I-you-relationship."[13] He interprets this as "talking to (someone)." It often moves to the "I-it-relationship," the "talking about (someone)." With this slide, community in its true sense is lost. More drastically Buber pushes this in view of the "current" times (1953; however it still applies 60 years later) in the following passage:

»By far the majority of everything that is today called conversation amongst people should more accurately, in a precise sense, be called chitchat. In general people don't truly talk to one another, but rather although each is facing the other they are in fact talking to a fictitious instance whose presence is exhausted by listening to him.«[14]

---

11 Buber, M. (1973): 276
12 Buber, M. (1973): 276
13 For a full account: Buber, M.: "Ich und Du (I and you)", in: Buber, M. (1973): 5-136
14 Buber, M. (1973): 282

The openness that is demanded by Buber, which is indispensable for a true encounter, can only occur in a private sphere. A "false sense of openness" prevents a true conversation:

»In our time, in which the understanding of the nature of true conversation has become rare, its conditions from the false sense of openness have been so thoroughly misjudged that one supposes that such a conversation can be organised in front of an audience of interested listeners with fitting journalistic assistance. But an open debate of such a high »level« can be neither spontaneous nor completely unreserved; an interview performed for a sound bite is completely divorced from a true conversation.«[15]

Speaking is not the only possibility of letting community be created. However, in order to find community we need a medium that is in a position to connect various individuals. "Medium" has a twofold meaning: For one a system of signs and also a carrier for these signs. Communication (even in here is *comm-unitas,* a unity of many) and thereby community is not possible without a common "language," whether it be spoken or articulated in non-verbal symbols. What is created when community comes into being is however more than just the sum of the connected parts.

TOOLS OR MEDIUM FOR THE ENCOUNTER

Not only since the invention of telecommunications, the radio and the television etc. has the human helped themselves to a wide variety of tools in order to engage with others, to inform them of something. Every external sign, that has an addressee and certain permanence, can be used here. A highly developed form of this is e.g. a letter. With the development of technology in the 20th century new possibilities of communication arose and at the same time new experiential spaces. What is the farthest away is suddenly close. We follow events which we would never have known about without these tools.

The technical medium, however, has the disadvantage that it makes everything equally available. Distances are brought onto the same level. This prompted Martin Heidegger, as early as the 40s of the 20th century, to call attention to the danger in the (then) modern technology that the human can no longer experience proximity and distance due to television, radio and telephone.[16] Everything

---

15 Buber, M. (1973): 297
16 Heidegger, M. (1994): 3-77

is equally close and far away, and therefore to a certain extent equal. With this, everything threatens to become exchangeable. This affects the products of modern technology in general and it affects the messages that these modern mediums supply. The human is surrounded by this uniformity. And he is permeated by it. It pulls the human into himself. The human is therefore himself threatened with becoming something interchangeable. He is in danger of becoming a template, of losing his individuality. With this he would lose his sense of being human.

True encounters according to Buber imply precisely this personality or individuality. It lives from the tension of diversity, which in real conversations between people lifts in order to make space for the experience of a supra-personal unity.

One should not take this warning as a condemnation of modern technology. It is an identification of a danger. As this identification it should be taken seriously.

Do the new technologies and technological possibilities for communication also offer an opportunity along with the danger? Are the new media bringing out new forms of encounter, of community?

IN CYBERSPACE AS IN REAL LIFE – VIRTUAL COMMUNITIES

Chat rooms, internet games and virtual worlds are often seen as new types of encounter. This applies in everyday life just as in the scientific world. In the World Wide Web some (such as Vilém Flusser) even see an evolutionary advance of humankind. Through global networking a large part of humanity has the possibility to come into contact with almost all other people – with only slight time lag through the information transfer. Are we entering a new phase of evolution, what Teilhard de Chardin called the "Noosphere?"[17] Have we taken an important step closer to the "convergence point" Omega, the last goal of the evolution, the (spiritual) unity of all beings? Some who sing praises of the global network surmise that this hypothesis is the godfather. But the question remains of whether it is truly the spirit that has made advances. One must understand the wires and electromagnetic waves as sensorily perceivable or technically controllable representatives of the spirit. Then, however, we are no longer far away from Hegel's

---

17 cf. Teilhard de Chardin, P. (1969). He divided the developmental stages of evolution as follows: After the geogenesis he took on the biogenesis, followed by the psychogenesis. Birth and development of the spirit characterizes the noogenesis, which began "as the instinct of a living thing saw itself in the mirror for the first time." (ibid., 182)

idea of a "cunning of reason" which makes individuals believe that they act autonomously, while in reality they follow a cosmic law.

If we abstain from these global or cosmic models of thinking and turn towards the virtual realities, then a different perspective results. Often the dealings with people in the virtual worlds (apart from, naturally, their use in science, e.g. in simulations) seems to outsiders as an escape into an ideal world where everything is possible. You pick out your "characters" yourself, acquire or buy features that you would like to have etc. It seems easy to start new friendships, and just as easy to end friendships (in real life this is much more difficult). Even death is not threatening any more. If a figure "dies" or is locked by the providers, it is easily replaced by a new one – unless you are excluded from the community by the people responsible! So-called "avatars,"[18] artificially produced alter egos of real people can outlive their creators and are potentially "immortal" (depending on the technology and the programmers).

Individuality and community seem able to be much more flexibly created in cyberspace than in everyday life. If one looks more carefully, then we find only a reflection of the real world in these virtual worlds. The basic constituents of both worlds are the same. They are the same people who move in the virtual world via the screen in the same way as those who must dispute their everyday life. This awakens the suspicion that the people here, as there, have the same desires, longings and fears. Only the opportunities to handle them are different.

Let's bring the question about the encounter into play. Do encounters take place in the virtual world? At first glance, this is unquestionable. However, if we take Martin Buber's guidelines as a standard, then it is not a matter of a true encounter, as real people don't encounter each other here but rather their (self-constructed) masks or their "pseudo."

However, now the internet offers even more possibilities for communication: Email, Skype, chat rooms etc. Even here, Buber's restriction applies. So, how far do communities in the virtual space reach? Have we found a new form of community?

It would surely be wrong to generally dispute the community character of this new form of human connection. But whether one can describe hundreds or thousands as "friends" simply because they have been entered into a list or declared on a form remains questionable. It is not a true encounter. For here also

---

18 "Avatar" is actually a term from the Hindu religion, which means an enlightened being which has obtained full freedom. An avatar reincarnates itself voluntarily and only in order to help others to find salvation. In Buddhism we find the equivalent in the representation of the bodhisattva.

the mask rules. This can be self-produced or constructed by others as an image that they create from a person and hold to be true, or hold up as true to others.

THE SEARCH FOR IDENTITY

An important part of community is that it allows us to experience ourselves through the others. The answer to our announcement is a decisive moment of self-awareness and our search for identity. We only find this in the mirror of others. The finding of identity is, however, not a one-time event that is then finished once and for all, but rather a process that continues throughout life.[19] Finding implies searching; searching implies the idea of a goal or something being sought. Something that we're searching for is something we don't yet have. So it is – to express it this way – initially a "virtual" size. We are looking for ourselves. We are doing it but we haven't fully grasped this reality. In order to find it we must, so to speak, go beyond ourselves. This sounds like a paradox. But we can't think of it in any other way. When we respond to someone else, truly let them in, then we also exceed the boundaries to our "I." Therefore one could say: We then find our true self.

THE GOAL AS "VIRTUAL" SIZE

Community is something that surrounds the humans in all the areas of their lives. Whether family, school, training, studies, country or religion, no area does without it. But what does a community live from? Initially it is shared interests, common goals, and joint commitments. Much, perhaps most things cannot be managed by *one* person alone. We are dependent on others. This has two sides: It contradicts our egoism and helps us overcome it. We need the others and the others need us. This applies to the richest just as it does for the poorest people in the world, for the most powerful as for the powerless. Anyone who can live outside of the community is either a wild animal or a god, said Aristotle.

Common goals, shared points of reference, this seems to be what is decisive. The higher the goal the stronger the effect, one could conclude. It affects the individual and it affects the community. A pressure can also create community, e.g. a command in war, or in an emergency the attempt to survive.

---

19 Cf. in particular Möller, J. (1979)

A goal is something that one wants to obtain, that one doesn't yet have. So it is – as stated – a virtual size. One could describe a goal as an idea. It is a mental size. If we transfer this to the topic of community then it follows that a community only comes into being through a common approach, a shared goal. In other words: A community lives from a common view or a shared spirit. As this spirit is not something that we can have or hold, the only thing that is left for us is to "believe" in it. This means that we trust in the sense of this common goal, and that the other members of the community are equally convinced of the common goal. Understood and lived this sense, every form of community can help humans to grow beyond themselves and make progress in their humanity. But as the human is a physical and spiritual being, an encounter that integrates the human in his wholeness is still in the highest position and will remain so unless the human succeeds in becoming a pure spirit.

SPACES OF ENCOUNTERS – PUBLIC – FREEDOM

Howard Rheingold, in his publication from 1993[20] who coined the term *virtual community,* understood the virtual community as an extension of the physical community. Via the internet he kept in touch with people who he could also encounter in real life without much effort. If one can take the recent study by Bernadette Kneidinger[21] as representative, then this connection still applies for the majority of those who participate in virtual communities. In the virtual world they see a supplement, an expansion or a deepening of their real-life contacts.

Encounters take place in spaces or at locations. While in the past external spaces were a prerequisite for encounters with other people, today we find virtual spaces for them. There is no major difference between the two as locations of (possible) encounters. What differentiates them, however, is the level of publicness and the external controllability. Even if one can determine for oneself the degree of public-ness of an encounter or a community, then there is still the "big brother" that has an insight into everything. This restricts the freedom of the individuals and the communities, or makes them unintentional participants in a system of commercial or political interests.

---

20 Rheingold, H. (1993)
21 Kneidinger, B. (2010)

DECAY OF COMMUNITY?

Is there a threat of the decline of community with the new media? For the time being, this strikes me due to the fact of what one perceives in public life. But this seems to be one-sided, a view from the external perspective. If the new mediums hold a certain addictive potential then they offer many possibilities for interpreting encounters and community. As well as this, they offer many people the opportunity to approach others, a step that some cannot otherwise take for personal reasons.

A form of this encounter can be friendship. If we ignore the quantifying measurements of friendship, e.g. on Facebook, and understand friendship from the qualitative side as a voluntarily entered community that is based on freedom but that does not remain arbitrarily, then we can also maintain friendships via the internet. However, it would be preferable that the constructors of the virtual spaces for these friendships do not pursue commercial or political interests.

The new mediums cannot create encounters in the sense of Buber. But they can open new ways to true encounters for us, in that they prepare them. We can use them as a substitute and thereby go astray. We can, however, use them wisely if we don't let ourselves be dominated by them, but rather use them consciously as a *means* of communication that are seen to be useful to us as a way to reach other people. Then they can promote community. We must, however, learn to distinguish which different types of community there are. If we can gain this knowledge and learn to act on this knowledge, then the new technologies can even be promoted as an advance with regard to our humanity.

Do we win or lose through the (modern) technological opportunities? Do they support community or interfere with it? One can not resort to a simple answer. In the 21st century we live with diverse points of reference and orientation. The reduction of this complexity to a couple of manageable areas is tempting because it seems to make life simpler. But with this, we are in danger of passing by reality and establishing ourselves in a special world. On the other hand, this can occur just as much in the real world as in cyberspace. Today virtual realities are just as much "reality" as the neighbor with whom we talk about everyday problems. We must try to integrate both. What is decisive in all realities is authenticity. This means that we should try to "mask" ourselves as little as possible. Then communities also offer opportunities for "true" encounters even if quality "holistic" encounters are not achieved. What do we gain through community? We find ourselves in the encounter with others.

ACKNOWLEDGEMENTS

This article has been translated into English by Rhona Voegele and Melanie Restle.

REFERENCES

21st Brockhaus Encyclopedia (2006), fully revised edition, Leipzig/Mannheim: Brockhaus Verlag

Buber, Martin (1973): *Das dialogische Prinzip* (The Dialogue Principle), (therein 5-136: "I and you" [1923]), Heidelberg: Verlag Schneider

Heidegger, Martin (1994): *1 Einblick in das was ist* (Insight into what is) Bremer Vorträge (Bremen lectures) 1949, in: Bremer und Freiburger Vorträge (Bremen and Freiburg Lectures) [= Gesamtausgabe (Complete Edition), vol. 79], Frankfurt a.M.: Verlag Vittorio Klostermann

Höffe, Otfried (1999): *Aristoteles* (Aristotle), 2nd revised edition München: Verlag c.H. Beck

Kneidinger, Bernadette (2010): *Facebook und Co. Eine soziologische Analyse von Interaktionsformen in Online Social Networks* (Facebook and Co. A sociological analysis of forms of interactions in online social networks), Wiesbaden : VS Verlag für Sozialwissenschaften I Springer Fachmedien

Möller, Joseph (1979): *Menschsein: ein Prozeß. Entwurf einer Anthropologie* (Humanity: A process. Design of Anthropology), Düsseldorf: Patmos Verlag

Opielka, Michael (2006): *Gemeinschaft in Gesellschaft. Soziologie nach Hegel und Parsons* (Communities in Society. Sociology according to Hegel and Parsons, 2nd revised edition Wiesbaden: VS Verlag für Sozialwissenschaften I Springer Fachmedien (1st edition 2004)

Rheingold, Howard (1993): *The Virtual Community. Homesteading on the Electronic Frontier*, Addison-Wesley Publishing Company

Spitta, Juliane (2013): *Gemeinschaft jenseits von Identität? Über die paradoxe Renaissance einer politischen Idee* (Community beyond identity? About the paradoxical renaissance of a political idea), Bielefeld: Transcript Verlag

Teilhard de Chardin, Pierre (1969): *Der Mensch im Kosmos* (Le Phénomèn humaine [The Phenomenon of Man], 1947), München, Verlag C.H. Beck

Tönnies, Ferdinand (1972): *Gemeinschaft und Gesellschaft* (Community and Society) [1887], Darmstadt: Wissenschaftliche Buchgesellschaft

Real Virtuality

GERD STERN

"Do I dare disturb the universe," T.S. Eliot inquired in 1917. My wonder is what valence of value to use in describing such a disturbance? If one considers the question of separation, distance, for instance from the position of a still image to a succession of filmic images, or better even -the reverse continuum from filmic to still image, we face apolarity of borderlines involving such basic considerations as real time, somewhat in an apparently frozen format, and for the other case in easily numerical, finitely digital, motion.

The Eliot quote is from Freeman Dyson's *Disturbing The Universe* and as Dyson comments, "it is true that we emerged in the universe by chance, but the idea of chance itself is only a cover for our ignorance. I do not feel like an alien in this universe. The more I examine the universe and study the details of its architecture, the more evidence I find that the universe in some sense must have known that we were coming."[1] A reflection from a somewhat other POV by Albert Einstein reads, "Coincidence is God's way of remaining anonymous."[2]

In Hebrew the term "Pilpul" is derived from the terms to spice or season, metaphorically a process of dialectic disputation and drawing of conclusions. And the prefix "dis" as a language conditioner allows specifically the use of "disturb" as a negation or reversal on the interruption of a settled and peaceful condition which by extension leads me to parallel the still/film demonstration with a parallel exemplar of the present confrontations of our, so called, real remaining real, as the binary nature of augmented reality we term virtual is recognized and remains virtual.

The prefix "vir" pertaining to the constellation Virgo requires the appendage of "tual" in order to attain "the quality of having the attribution of something

---

1   Dyson, F. (1979): 250
2   Einstein cited from www.mybeautifulwords.com

without sharing its physical form." My intention for this writing is in accordance with my reliance on the subject of prophetic technology as principally evidenced by the work of Marshall McLuhan. For those ideas I rely mainly on his last major book, *The Global Village*, a collaboration with Bruce R. Powers, posthumously published in 1989, after McLuhan's death in 1979, since the formulation of ideas in that work are more explicitly pertinent to this anthology than the more popularly quoted 1964 "Understanding Media – The Extensions of Man," which in its original report form to the National Association of Educational Broadcasters was lent to me by the composer John Cage and the potter/poet Mary Caroline Richards and inspired my first multi- media explorations which resulted in our first meeting with McLuhan in 1963 at the University of British Columbia, Vancouver.

Powers prefaced *Global Village* as follows; "Marshall McLuhan and I constructed this book from two points of view: the aesthetic and the technologic..." And the envoy quoted Nathaniel Hawthorne, "...by means of electricity, the world of matter has become a great nerve, vibrating thousands of miles in a breathless point of time. Rather the whole globe is a vast head, a brain, instinct with intelligence! Or shall we say, it is itself a thought, nothing but a thought, and no longer the substance which we deemed it!"[3] Try pairing this to McLuhan's "...the entire world was in the grasp of a vast material shift between the values of linear thinking, of visual, proportional space, and that of the multisensory life, the experience of acoustic space."[4]

McLuhan wrote extensively concerning what he termed the left hemisphere controlling the body's right side and the right hemisphere controlling the left side as in "...another way of saying that visual and acoustic space are always present in any human situation... The latter is the invisible counter environment that forms the background against which the civilization of the written word is seen."[5] Christian von Ehrenfels, the originator of *Gestaltist Structuralism*, clearly showed that configurations (*Gestalten*) exist only because of our tendency to see figure against ground, to prefer geometrically perfect forms against irregular shapes.[6]

And again "For use in the electronic age, a right-hemisphere model of communication is necessary because our culture has nearly completed the pro-

---

3 Nathaniel Hawthorne is cited there from his poem *Thew house of the Seven Gables*, written in 1851, at the very start of US-industrialization.

4 McLuhan, M. (1989): ix

5 McLuhan, M. (1989): 55

6 von Ehrenfels quoted in McLuhan, M. (1989): 55

cess of shifting its cognitive modes from the left to the right hemisphere and because the electronic media themselves are right hemisphere in their patterns and operations."[7]

The seminar I gave at Karlsruhe University of Arts and Design in June of 2013, titled "McLuhan Plus" on the subject of prophetic technology began with the biblical Isaiah then skipped to Erasmus of Rotterdam, Rilke's first Duino Elegy and focused more than half our time on McLuhan's predictive insights starting with *Understanding Media's*, "The restructuring of human work and association was shaped by the technique of fragmentation that is the essence of machine technology. It is integral and decentralist in depth, just as the machine was fragmentary, centralist and superficial in its patterning of human relationships... Positively, automation creates roles for people, which is to say depth of involvement in their work and human association that our preceding mechanical technology had destroyed."[8] *The Gutenberg Galaxy*, one of his first published writings witnessed his encyclopedic understandings of the impact and consequences of that time's technology which led to his assumptions and prescience concerning the digital present. Our in the seminar ended with 21st writers on media Hansen and Fuller and ended with the digital dilemma lamentations of *Present Shock* by Douglas Rushkoff.[9]

In September of this year, 2013, Jenna Wortham wrote in the New York Times about "Life as Instant Replay, Over and Over Again"[10] – the replay Web, in many ways, exists because information is coursing through sites like Facebook and Twitter with knock-you-down force. But no single event can emerge from that stream of information unless it is amplified by the replay of voices. Amplification is one of the few ways we can sieve through the gushing stream for bits of conversational gold. "Real time is yesterday's experience," said Alex Chung.[11] It's just that critical mass and amplification or repetition become much more valuable for helping ideas or pieces of information gain momentum and become common cultural reference points.

During the early nineteen hundred sixties when USCO, The Company of Us was formed, I wrote the mantra, Take the NO out of NOW, then take the OW out of NOW, Then take the THEN out of NOW. That mantra in the form of dif-

---

7 McLuhan, M. (1964): 23

8 McLuhan, M. (1964): 23

9 Rushkoff, Douglas (2013)

10 Wortham, Jenna, *Life As Instant Replay, Over and Over Again*, New York Times, BITS, Business Day Sept. 22, 2013: 4

11 Chung, Alex of Giphy, in: New York Times, BITS, Business Day Sept. 22, 2013: 4

fraction gratings, magnets, posters, sand blasted glass, songs has been circulating repetitioning, reverbing for these past decades. Although my impression was that this mantra's meaning was self evident I've often had to explain, you need to remove the negative, the pain and in English the past and future out of the present, to whomever indicated that they were mystified by these lines.

More recently a series of my video poems are titled *Prefixables*,[12] and in earlier paragraphs the reader has encountered mention of both "dis" and "vir". We're all familiar with the wiseass phrase, "ontology recapitulates phylogeny" as if the potentialities of existence, being, were subject to philosophical manipulations. Taking note of the pregnant prefixes "per" as in personal and "co" as in communal we add the suffix "ity," from the Latin "itas," to virtual, denoting quality or condition, an instance or degree of, that affords quantification, measurement, to our evident difficulties in determining the distancing effect of separating our overstandings of reality versus virtuality.

USCO, *The Company of Us* was our solution to the question of how to identify ourselves as an early nineteen sixties collaborative membered, at first by Michael Callahan, "Electro," Stephen Durkee "Weirdo" with wife Barbara and Gerd Stern, "Beardo," with wife Judi, living variously in the San Francisco Bay Area, mostly at our hundred year old church building in Rockland County, N.Y and at our Maverick Road cottage in Woodstock, Ulster County, N.Y. and growing by numbers with art and tech world participants in our multi-media performances, exhibitions and activist efforts, not just in collaborations but also of an inner group living as a commune with involved outside friends, contributors and supporters.

A certain kind of withdrawal from the "per" idea of the artist as a special person with a recognized signature and status toward the "co" of communal participations came through my friend Grace Clement's recommendation of the writings of art historian and metaphysician Ananda K. Coomeraswamy. He wrote at length about the roles of artists in traditional societies, stressing in the collection "Every Man An Artist" and other of his works such artists acceptance in their times as ordinary persons without special status. The quality of relative equality and no need for individual leadership appealed to us and for quite a few years all the work accomplished by the up to fifteen or more individuals who contributed ideas, techniques, labor, hardware and software was credited as USCO instead of by our personal names.

---

12 Stern, Gerd: *Prefixables*. A series of poems available as Video DVDs.

In 1960 I left my barge on the waterfront in Sausalito, California and drove back east, living in Rockland County, N.Y. across the road from "The Land," an intentional community which included Paul Williams and family, M.C. Richards, John Cage and many others, some of whom I had met during my short 1950's stay at the avant garde Black Mountain College in North Carolina. The community was a center of cultural radicalism with constant visitations by leading figures in civil rights, activism, protest, anarchism, involved in the support of political action, contemporary visual arts, and music in *The Living Theatre*. It was while living there that my written poetry slowly expanded into visual collage poems as well as electro/mechanical poem sculptures which Paul Williams, architect and designer helped me build in his shop. And it was there I met painter Steve Durkee, who introduced me to his NYC gallery owner Allen Stone, where I had my first exhibition of art in 1962. That opened on the day of a vast newspaper strike in New York City and my then companion Judi Wilson and I left for my barge in Sausalito in her VW bug.

Figure 1. Early virtualized realities at the dawn of digitalization.[13]

---

13 Section from *The Verbal American Landscape*. Photograph U. Gehmann, with permission of Gerd Stern.

Through Steve and Judi and the "Land" folk I'd become friendly with the then names of the art world including Robert Indiana, whose word paintings were influential particularly in combination with my McLuhan report readings. During that cross country hegira and our immersion in highway iconography, I sketched an octagonal image which on arrival I made into a bright traffic yellow seven foot diameter cut-out incorporating the words Merge, Yield, Go, On, Enter With Caution, Do Not Cross Line, Turn Ahead, titled *CONTACT IS THE ONLY LOVE* which I shlepped around to my art loving friends and their gallery contacts until one such suggested I see George Culler, then director of San Francisco's MOMA who was so friendly and appreciative that he promised me an exhibition, sent and pay for the shipping of the work from the Stone gallery, vestended to me the use of the museum's tax exemption for any donations toward the construction of *Contact* which involved fluorescent, neon and incandescent lighting, eight speakers and a loop tape drive for sound, plus motors and a heavy masonite covered plyboard exterior, constructed with the help and in the shop of Roger Sommers on the slopes of Marin County's Mount Tamalpais.

From McLuhan's ideas regarding the importance of the effect to content relationship I ideated a multi leveled media performance work which grew like Topsy as the possibilities exfoliated. One early element was a three screen slide show, *The Verbal American Landscape* shot by Ivan Majdrakoff and Stewart Brand of single street words, accompanied by an early version of our audio collage, *Billie Master*.

We needed various forms of collaboration, technical and logistic. Through fellow poet Michael McClure I was introduced to Morton Subotnick, Ramon Sender and Pauline Oliveros of the S.F. Tape Music Center and when I told them what I wanted to achieve they suggested their youthful technical director, Michael Callahan, with whom I quickly bonded as a most perceptive and capable associate. Since now, some sixty years later, he and I are still working together successfully, they were obviously correct in their recommendation.

My artist friends Bob Rheem and Liam O'Gallagher suggested that their friend Judith McBean was interested in assisting in the arts and she wound up organizing the borrowing of the necessary equipment including telephones connecting four sociologists to sixteen celebrities including the city's mayor, Allen Ginsberg and columnist Herb Caen in four plastic gazebos, closed circuit television cameras and monitors et al., as well she organized those participants, our promotion and publicity and made sure that we filled the seats. A second proof of collaborative practice is that Judith McBean and I are still involved working together in mutual arts activities, after that *?Who R U & What's Happening?* in San Francisco.[14]

"Contact Is The only Love" was the star of my SF MOMA exhibition and later as part of USCO, traveled to museums in the United States and elsewhere, inter alias to *Kunst, Licht, Kunst* at the Abbemusum of Eindhoven Holland.[15] Parts of it can be viewed on VIMEO.[16] With my long term painter friend Ivan Majdrakoff and Michael we made a first 16mm film titled by the highway sign "Y" with dozens of fast cuts of such signs, the episodic center line rushing by and close ups of nude female intimacy moving along to sounds of trucks trafficking and orgasmic breathing. After meeting McLuhan and performing the second version of *?WHO R U?* at UBC, Vancouver, Judi and I took off back across the country showing early multi media wherever we knew anyone and when *Y's* nude footage hit the screen at the university in Salt Lake City the head of the art department pulled the plug and advised us to get out of town before the police were alerted. When we arrived at the church in Garnerville with tales of our media adventures the Durkees both wanted to participate and when I explained about Michael's technical proficiency, Steve suggested we ask him to join us and after several telephone conversations, he did and after that the many stories have become USCO history.

Among the first persons to favor our increasingly multi channeled sound and visual channeled shows titled *Hubbub*, after a quote of Martin Luther's regarding chaos, suggested by professorial Paul Lee who sponsored us first at Brandeis and then at MIT, was Jonas Mekas, the still present foremost entrepreneurial advocate of avant garde cinema, and. organizing the first *Expanded Cinema Festival*.

Through John Brockman, we competed to create the first big multi-media discotheque *The World* in the hangar Lindbergh had taken off from on Roosevelt Field, Long Island. *The World* was featured on the cover of LIFE Magazine.[17] Brockman and I became consultant on the BBS film featuring The Monkees "Head" which I named. The bold psychedelic poster on mirrored mylar USCO produced is in the collection of NYC's MOMA. John and I also proposed and produced the New York State Council on the Arts, Intermedia "68" during which

---

14 *?WHO R U & What's Happening?*: Multi-Media Performances, San Francisco Museum of Art Nov. 12 & 14 1963.

15 *Kunst, Licht, Kunst* - Exhibition, Stedelijk van Abbemuseum Eindhoven, Sept 25 – December 4, 1966

16 *Contact Is The Only Love*: online VIMEO, or at www.intermediafoundation.org

17 LIFE Magazine May 27th, 1966: cover, and p. 72

USCO's "Fanflashtic" strobe environment toured. John Brockman founded "The Reality Club" of which I was an early member. The motto, printed on our T shirts was, "To arrive at the edge of the world's knowledge, seek out the most complex and sophisticated minds, put them in a room together and have them ask each other the questions they are asking themselves..."

One became a member only by talking to the club about some new work, not yet published and the members came from all fields, among them Ellen Burstyn, Murray Gell-Mann, Richard, Baker Roshi, Ken Kesey, Elaine Pagels, Stephen Jay Gould, Benoit Mandelbrot, Betty Friedan. We usually met in New York City but the one exception was in San Francisco after Rollo May spoke, I read my long poem, *Poemthink*, written for the occasion. Poemthink is about not writing down the poem, but simply thinking the poem. After my reading Heinz von Foerster spoke saing "This is exactly what our young scientists need to know and practice and I would like to publish it in our Cybernetic Journal" Which he did in 1985, paged right after his address to a conference of librarians titled, *To Know and To Let Know –An Applied Theory of Knowledge*. One statement of his therein was "I will touch upon potentials and limits of the new technology which could become subservient to your needs instead of you becoming the servants of that technology."[18]

Figure 2. The Whole World as a formatted series of fragmented formats[19]

---

18 von Foerster, H. (1985): 1
19 Photo (U. Gehmann) from *The World*; with permission of Gerd Stern. The phrase "Why haven't we seen a photograph of the whole earth yet" was by Stewart Brand who worked with us at USCO and who was responsible for *The Whole Earth* catalogue.

At present we are eating dinner, at Sonoma's Timber Cove Inn, while looking out at the moonlit Pacific surf, washing a rocky coast, with an iconic ninety-three foot Bufano tribute to peace obelisk, *Expanding Universe* within our gaze – while I am wondering whether the pulsing LED in a frosted glass cylinder on our table is a virtual flame. That question was also posed to me by a New York Times review of the film *Gravity* proposing that "Life in space is impossible...the standard is not realism but coherence."[20] Or Henry Waxman's 1926 statement "a portrait portrays a possibility, a still depicts a world."[21] Our very title *Real Virtuality* is the proof of the put-on cliche that "seeing is believing." and cannot even be said to contradict, "faith moves mountains." For "gemuetlichkeit" or comfort I resort to Margaret Morse's *VIRTUALITIES – Television, Media Art and Cyberculture* in which she writes, "Cyberculture is personal rather than impersonal, irrational rather than rational, perceptually elaborated rather than abstract.... While objects and images can be virtual, the virtual relationships that people in physical reality have with machines and images of various types are the primary focus of this book."[22] And toward the end of that volume she adds, "If empathy is the capacity to visualize and experience the world from the position of the other, to walk in another's shoes...then the distinguishing characteristic of a virtual environment – that you as a visitor experience an artificial world from inside – can function quite literally as an invitation to empathize, to see a world from another position, and with other eyes..."[23] And, finally, although a virtual environment is an invention and a simulation that is prepared in advance, we cannot fully anticipate what it means to experience that realm until we are "inside."

The separation, those distances between for instance, wherever and the "inside," subject and object are solely measurable in terms of the supposed relationships balancing true realisms with established coherence. Agreement, in such a process of faith, was the basis which established our communal brand of collaboration during the vital working years of The Company of Us, USCO and remains a bonding issue of overstandings which inhabit the spirit of "We Are All One" as a continuum.

---

20 Scott, A.O.: *Gravity* (*Between Earth & Heaven*): Critics' Pick Film Revew, New York Times Oct. 3, 2013: p. C3

21 Henry Waxman was a famous Hollywood portrait-photographer.

22 Morse, M. (1998): 6

23 Morse, M. (1998): 210

As McLuhan predicted, "Communication media of the future will accentuate the extensions of our nervous systems, which can be disembodied and made totally collective."[24]

We, the cultural we, have taken, lived and jumped through times inculcated with the moral suasions of Wiener's Cybernetics and Marshall McLuhan's piety at a short airport meeting after my complaining about too little time, he replied by putting one arm over the other and telling me, "You never know what you get in the We, crossing," as we catapulted into our present situation replete with email, social media and other forms of effective information possibly defined as overload. So what, for instance, became of our public awareness of effect, before considerations of content, as we past then performed, manifested, marched, loved and altered our consciousness, embracing visions cataclysmic and ecstatic, seeking to be freed of constraint and punishments. That included entire crews of like thinkers and doers, crossing generations, races, genders and economic boundaries. Gehmann, in his journal essay *Formats*, supposes "the proverbial whole world turned into a content-generating artefact of living and meaning altogether, Expressed in the terms of computer language, it became our immersive environment. The only world we can conceive really, and truly, as world."[25]

There's plenty of recent dissent to cite as if it were by a reflection or even a consequence of our "We Are All One"ness. According to the Kurtz's of Electronic Civil Disobedience, "Any work which can create the conditions for people to engage in the transgressive act of rejecting a totalizing and closed rational order and to open themselves up to social interaction beyond the principle of habituation, of exchange, and of instrumentalty within an environment of uncertainty, is one which is truly resistant and truly transgressive, since participants can revel in a moment of autonomy." And Paul Virillio points out, "Television exposes the world to the accident. I believe that McLuhan was wrong wrong in his idyllic view of television. What is accidental is reality Virtuality will destroy reality. Cyberculture is an accident of the real. Virtuality is the accident of reality itself."[26]

In *Here is Berlin* by JM Stim it reads, "Berlin no longer forces people to do anything. The city contents itself with a complementary role, serving as a clearing house, a facilitator. What that's led to is thousands of parallel worlds scat-

---

24 McLuhan, M. (1964): 112

25 Gehmann, U. (2012): 31

26 Paul Virilio on "Cyberwar, God & Television", interview 1994.

tered across the entire city (which) has today become one of the last bastions of unfettered individual freedom."[27]

As a collagist I have drawn from a compendium of resources, so it will not be a surprise if I now close with another point of view regarding what's real by Constantin Stanislavsky's "It is necessary to picture not life itself as it takes place in reality, but as we vaguely feel it in our dreams, our visions, our moments of spiritual uplift."[28]

REFERENCES

Dyson, Freeman (1979): *Disturbing The Universe*, New York: Basic Books

Gehmann, Ulrich (2012): "Formats", Vol. 4, *Journal of New Frontiers in Spatial Concepts*: 13-33

McLuhan, Marshal (1964): *Understanding Media – The Extensions of Man*, New York: Mentor Books

McLuhan, Marshal (1989): *The Global Village*, New York: Oxford University Press

Morse, Margaret (1998): *Virtualities*, Bloomington: Indiana Uuniversity Press

Rushkoff, Douglas (2013): *Present Shock*, New York etc.: Current

von Foerster, Heinz (1985): *Cybernetic Journal*, Volume 1, No.1

---

27 Stim, J. M. (2011): *Here Is Berlin*, facebook.com: 13

28 Constantin Stanislavsky, quoted in *Experimental Theatre*, Avon 1970

The Ambiguous Construction
of Place and Space

KATERINA DIAMANTAKI

> It is hard and difficult to conceive of what
> place is.
> ARISTOTLE

INTRODUCTION

Modern culture is a technological culture, making even the most mundane activities all but unimaginable without the use of, and increasing reliance on, the
technological infrastructures of our lives. Firmly embedded in a culture of
connectivity and technologization, our contemporary world is one where the
powerful structures of the Web and social networking are gradually penetrat-
ing the core of our daily routines and practices.

As the current network of networks becomes literally interwoven into the
continuum of our daily lives, the mediatization effects that begun with so-
called "mainstream" mass media today seem to reach a new climax, introducing an entirely new ontological relation between humans and technology. Media increasingly become not media we live *with* but media we *live in*, an "invisible" environment in which we find ourselves increasingly enmeshed, the
very fabric of our daily lives. Sonesson called this situation one of the "complete multimediation of the lifeworld,"[1] while Deuze asserts that "we can only
imagine" but no longer "experience" "a life outside of media."[2] Friesen and
Hug go even further to postulate that media become epistemology – the
grounds for knowledge and knowing itself – or what they call "the mediatic a

---

1   Sonesson, M. (1997)
2   Deuze, M. (2012): x

priori," the contention that media play an important role in defining the epistemological preconditions or characteristics of cognition, such as the perception of time, space, and the shaping of attention and communication.[3] Mediatization has become a fact of our ontological being-in-the world and a ground for lived experience as such.

In this regime, media can no longer be viewed as mere content transporters; they become powerful mediators critically relevant to cultural and societal change. This is another of way of stating that for mediatization to be relevant today it has to be focused and interpreted in relation to other meta-processes like individualization, mobilization, spatiality or virtualization, that describe the contemporary Zeitgeist.[4] First and foremost, mediatization has affected the very processes of how people interact and communicate in society. Winfried Schulz (2004)[5] identifies four kinds of processes whereby the media change human communication and interaction. First, they *extend* human communication abilities in both time and space, by enabling remotely located people to communicate in non-physical contexts; second, the media *substitute* social activities that previously took place face-to-face. For example, for many, internet banking has replaced the physical meeting between banks and their clients. Third, media instigate an *amalgamation* of activities; face-to-face communication combines with mediated communication, and media infiltrate into everyday life. Finally, actors in many different sectors have to adapt their behavior to *accommodate* the media's valuations, formats and routines. For example, politicians learn to express themselves in 'sound-bites' in inpromptu exchanges with reporters.

This essay builds on these perspectives and explores the transformed media landscape and how it impacts on the way we conceptualize and experience *place* and *community*, two of the most fundamental elements of our human condition. Questions to ask include: Does digitilization change what counts as place and how much place matters? How is space experienced today, via the new anytime-anyplace, always-on digital media that have permeated all aspects of our lives? And what do these changes mean for how our social identities and our social worlds are constructed?

---

3   Friesen, N., and Hug, T. (2009)

4   Schulz, W. (2004) and Krotz, F. (2007) have being suggesting, among others, that the phenomenon of "mediatization" must be articulated in connection with broader cultural and social shifts in various realms of social life.

5   Schulz, W. (2004): 88-90

TECHNOLOGY, SPACE AND PLACE

Space, and consequently all that space encloses, are central to our human condition and a precondition of human relationality. Space is both that which brings us together and that which sets us apart from each other. It is thus crucial to how relationships emerge and evolve. Different spatial patterns impact differently on how people communicate with each other, what kind of associations they pursue and what linkages they form. In this sense, what seems to matter most for the human condition is not our relationship directly with spaces, but our *relationships with others* in and through space. This human-centered understanding is the background against which one can explore technology's structuring impact on both place and community.

It could be said that place and technologies are entangled in a reciprocal relationship of mutual influence: on the one hand, media are the product of structural reconfigurations in spatial relations, but, at the same time, they construct space by producing new, historically-specific tropes of accessing, engaging with and experiencing the elements – tangible and intangible, human and non-human – of the social world. As Curry has noted, "in a particular era one cannot really make sense of those technologies without having an understanding of the ways in which space and place are conceptualized, just as one cannot understand those conceptualizations without having an understanding of the available technologies."[6]

In fact, epochal shifts can be seen as co-evolving with changes in the technological media for information-sharing and communicating. In the largely "unmediated" or "premediated" *oral* societies, storytelling in face-to face interaction contexts (e.g. epic poetry, myths, condensed wisdom, proverbs, narration of past events) was the main mode of social communication, and this was accompanied by a *local sense of place* and specifically-framed time-periods. Places were understood to be synonymous with small-scale bounded territoritorial communities, grounded in history, ancestry and a rather homogeneous common culture. The transition from orality to literacy, initiated by the *invention of writing* (script), generated an *extended* but *still localized* conception of space, broadening the spatial span of communication and its viability in time. The *emergence of print media* further expanded the notion of place, giving rise to both local and extended national spaces, and contributing to the formation of nation-states, which though not necessarily corresponding to some national territory (as in the case of the Jewish nation) were nevertheless

---

6   Curry, M. (2002): 502

places of strong cultural consciousness, resting on processes of identification and imaginary construction.[7] Later, in the first half of the 20th century, the *invention of broadcasting* and cinematic media led to a radical stretch of spatiality, by making the content of communications available and accessible to everyone around the globe, thus fundamentally challenging perceptions of farness and spatial barriers. By connecting places that were physically remote through a hyperlocal visibility, electronic media, and television in particular, allowed viewers to be simultaneously in *two places* and *two times, at once*; on the one hand, rooted in the spatial-temporal context of media reception (e.g. the house, the cinema room) and at the same time transferred to the site of a media-represented reality, generating what Scannell described as "the magical liveness of a here-and-there, now-and-then"[8] and giving rise to a global, non-localized perception of space and time. By their sheer overreaching presence as the most quotidian public site for cultural production, and uniquely positioned to do so due to their pervasiveness and their capacity to offer spectatorial experiences, electronic media also produced an array of figurative "places," giving rise even to the phenomenon of 'intimacy-at-a-distance' and "despatialized communality" that is characteristic of mediated fan communities and neo-tribal groups formed around cultural symbols and common interests.[9] Besides allowing the generation of new symbolic "places," electronic media have also been playing an important role in shaping citizen's bonds with the places of the "real," historical world, whether these are cities, regions or nations. Through selecting what is to be seen and remembered, the mass media have been working aside other institutions, like schools, churches or governments, in disseminating the narratives, symbols, representations and all the cultural proto-material around which places like nations are constructed.

---

7   In his celebrated book titled "Imagined Communities" (1983) Benedict Anderson argued that the expansion of people's access to vernacular script languages, the dissemination of print literature in the form of books and the overall technical development of print led to the rise of nationalism in 18th and 19th century Europe and to the creation of a new type of political communities, the socially-constructed "imagined communities" that differed from the actual communities in that they were not based on everyday face-to-face interaction between its members, but instead on how its members formed a mental image of their affinity and their belonging to a common national community.

8   Scannell, P. (1996): 172

9   Thompson, J. (1995): 224

In the current, post-broadcast, digital era successive waves of media change and technological development have been once more altering the human perception and experience of space- time and related concepts of "place" and "community." Digital media not only shrink space-time distances to the point of rendering them irrelevant as coordinates of interaction; they also open up possibilities for connectedness and interaction in "places" that might have no reference whatsoever to any pre-existing social reality. Digital technologies embody the paradox of a parallel de-spatialization and re-spatialization of social and communicative processes.

It must be noted, parenthetically, that despite technology's decisive impact on issues of space-time and place-community, many accounts of modernity did not factor in their analyses the force of technological change, even as they had devoted their intellectual energy on emphasizing the gradual erosion of place and community under the forces of modernization. While sociologists for example explained how meanings of time and space were central to the cultural change from agricultural to industrial societies, not much credit was given to the structuring power of technology on forms of social interaction. Most accounts of modernization in classic sociology focused on factors like urbanization, division of labor, or political and bureaucratic change – with the exception of Georg Simmel and his perceptive insights on how modernization affects the very processes of social interaction by ushering in a post-traditional order were people are increasingly connected through multiple, non-homogeneous and physically extended "web of affiliations."[10] It was later on, in the mid to late 20th century, with the writings of the Medium Theory school of the pre-digital era,[11] that realization grew of media technologies' capacity to cause social change, both in terms of newly emerging social structures and in terms of how people relate in interpersonal and public contexts.

However, in today's late modern post-print and post-broadcast digital era, the reciprocal relation between technology and place has become more pronounced and acute, and consequently more difficult to ignore or disregard. Following a century of technological developments, personal and collective places are increasingly being produced in conditions of high technological mediatization. Major contemporary social changes, such as the emergence of a

---

10 Simmel, G. 1922 [1955]

11 Harold Innis (1950), Walter Ong (1982), Marshall McLuhan (1962, 1964, 1967) and Joshua Meyrowitz (1985) are considered to be the main proponents of Medium Theory.

networked structure of social organization[12] and mobile society[13] give shape to new forms of sociality as well as calling into question the meanings of space and place, proximity and distance, home and away, private and public. Our whole way of *thinking* about space has been challenged throughout the history of modernity, and the development of cyberspace and globe-spanning diffuse networks of information and communication is just the latest challenge. What is then so novel about the current historical moment? How does digitalization and always-on connectivity change how places are constructed, experienced and conceptualized?

The gradual dispersal, decentering and multiplication of social places brought about by previous waves of mediatization seem today to be radically accelerated. The continuous presence of the network – both in its human-centered sociological meaning and in terms of its technological apparatus – substantially changes the definition of what counts as place and community. In fact, it could be argued that as a result of their inherent properties of interactivity, flexibility and multimodality and their interference in how the social rituals of interaction, information-sharing, exchange, cooperation and identity are performed today, digital media are more *actively* involved in *constituting* self-contained media-driven and media-dependent places. Our networked reality, therefore, requires a new understanding of place where human practices and technics are completely intertwined. It is safe to say as we stand firmly on the 21st century that our places have become essentially mediated, either partially or entirely. Hence the term "media places" or "mediated places" that encapsulates the debate on how place are constructed through mediation.

Of course, we do still lead our lives in offline, geographically-bounded and historical places, whether it is our hometowns, our holiday destinations, our workplaces, our educational institutions or the third places where we socialize informally. Major urban places support dense webs of face-to-face "co-presence" that cannot and will not be simply mediated by telecommunications.[14] Nevertheless, these places are increasingly technologized, as digital tools and platforms are increasingly put to use in helping these places or institutions improve their functionalities and enhance their internal and external communications. Schools, universities, banks, hospitals, theatres, libraries, museums and galleries, manufacturing firms and service providers increasingly become embodied through their presence in both material spaces and electronic spaces.

---

12 Castells, M. (1996)

13 Urry, J. (2000)

14 Boden, D. and Molotch, H. (1994)

Furthermore, these places are inhabited and experienced by individuals who have an increasing, even symbiotic, reliance on them, having adopted digital media as a staple of their daily lives. That integrated matrix of networks of networks and systems of systems, that is cyberspace, is immaterial and placeless in the sense of not having a territorial configuration related to its nodes, it has however literally penetrated the material infrastructures of the world. William Mitchell explains how digital technologies have infiltrated contemporary urbanism and how material spaces are now being infused with cyberspace "entry points" of all kinds and how the power to function economically and link socially increasingly relies on constructed, place-based, material spaces intimately woven into complex telematics infrastructures linking them to other places and spaces. "Today's institutions," argues Mitchell, "are supported not only by buildings but by telecommunications and computer software."[15]

Most importantly, though, the internet has generating its own internal spatial logics by redefining two fundemental spatial concepts: *distance* and *presence*. The advent of a new interactional time, instantaneous time, annihilates the perceived and actual distance between places and lifts all time-barriers in information exchange and communication. Messages, texts, images, ideas, now travel in nanoseconds from one place to the other on a global scale, establishing new regimes for fundamental spatial concepts of near and far, presence and absence, here and there. Heidegger's predictive observation that "the abolition of every possibility of remoteness"[16] would be achieved by television seems to have been materalized with increased vitality in the contemporary digital condition. The fact that online communication is increasingly being measured not as a metric distance but as a time-distance inevitably leads to the relativization of space and locality as a precondition for communication.[17] Space and time are irreversibly dissociated and social relations, previously dominated by the "situated visibility of co-presence"[18] and what Riva calls the "expression of the proto-self"[19] as the body's orientation in the here-and-now, can now be formed between distant others, without the need of a face-to-face interaction.

These changes concomitantly introduce new ways of being "present" and "being there" and new ways of managing both distance and presence from the

---

15 Mitchell, W. (1996): 126

16 Heidegger, M. (1971): 167

17 Urry, J. (2000): 126

18 Thompson, J. (2005): 35

19 Riva, G. et al. (2004): 405

part of the user. The active social subjects must combine in their online strategies a new economy of presence, one that is no longer related to one's position in and movement through space, but is primarily contingent upon how individual users manage proximity and distance in terms of time and attention, meaningful and relevant messaging and discursive online practices. On the Internet, presence is presence-in-time rather than presence-in-space and is achieved through acts of speech and rhetorical self-presentation: Online we are present to other through our messages, texts, comments, posts, tweets, photos and videos – in a new context where what Gofman calls the "the shared vocabularies of the body's idiom"[20] a central element in how one present oneself in public space, loses its relevancy altogether, giving way to a new ontology where – to use another of Goffman's frames –the "communicable" supplants the "expressible,"[21] a situation that leads people to evaluate others based on their ideas and texts and not on their physical features. Interestingly, though, this proximity through speech may create a more personal relation because it revives the feelings of unity and because it requires intellectually and/or emotionally significant content that binds people together.

By enacting new ways of presence, interaction and narrative, digital media technologies also create the conditions so that meaningful interactions, even places and communities, emerge online. The Internet, the first medium in history to enable not only interaction with the content but also most importantly many-to-many conversations between people and groups scattered all over the planet, is today positioned not as a mediating channel, but as a self-sustaining ecosystem of social and personal places, of varying degrees of emplacement, authenticity and realness. This capacity can be seen as signaling an expansion of humans' place-making capacities, although such a claim crucially necessitates that we make clear what particular definitions of "place" are adopted.

ONLINE COMMUNITIES AS PLACES

Its unsettled intellectual history notwithstanding, community remains a "persistent" concept and a metaphor that still captures both the popular and academic imaginaire. In the first scholarly accounts of Internet culture, starting around the mid 1990s, "virtual communities" constituted one of the most conspicuous topics

---

20 Goffman, E. (1963): 35
21 Goffman, E. (1971): 5

of study, with the main debate revolving around their contested "realness" and authenticity. While the vision of virtual communitarianism as an alternative and valid form of human association had reverberated since the internet's early countercultural days, many thinkers would uphold the view that "virtual communities" is a contradiction in terms, an oxymoron that can only be accepted as a metaphor, or even a cultural pathology that obliterates the very possibility of genuine social relations. The overarching question that many belabored was if *"we can we have community without place."* Their lack of physicality and materiality, thus of real place-quality, was taken to be the most problematic feature – hence the recurring juxtaposition between offline communities that were real and online communities that were virtual. Place-related themes taken to be dominant tropes in late modern societies, such as the "emptying out of space" or "phantasmagoric space,"[22] "placelecess of place,"[23] cities "without a place"[24] and "non-places"[25] were assumed anew in much of internet culture scolarship. Online groupings were likewise described as non-places themselves, "pseudo-communities,"[26] and ethically dangerous hyperrealities that displace organic social realities by allowing people to "offer one another stylized versions of themselves for amorous or convivial entertainment" rather than allowing the fullness and complexity of their real identities to be engaged.[27]

However, seen from another perspective, virtual communities were interpreted not as space-dissolving but as space-making phenomena – symptomatic of (late) modernity's dialectical potential to both disembed and re-embed social relations in space and time, to dislocate or outright evacuate traditional spaces and at the same time substitute them with novel and more self-reflective spaces for practice, belonging and imagining.[28] Gradually, accounts that saw the internet as inherently de-realizing and de-spatializing appeared to be incapable of accounting for the multiple and diverse groupings that would spring up in the digital networks and through which a sense of mediated to-

---

22 Giddens, A. (1990):19

23 Relph, E. (1976)

24 Sorkin, M. (1992): xi

25 Auge, M. (1995)

26 Beniger, J. (1987): 353

27 Borgmann, A. (1992): 92

28 The thesis of "reflexive modernization" put forward by Beck, Giddens and Lash (1994) has been emphasizing that much of modernity's dynamism stems from this dual movement towards the disembedding and re-embedding of social relations in space and time.

getherness was experienced in a non-material, non-reified social space. Moreover, such accounts were contradicted by a plethora of empirical findings that pointed to the existence of "real" online communities, meaning online groupings that exhibited the characteristics of genuine places and were governed by a web of norms for "embodied" social action.

The result was a gradual theoretical agreement that a complete antithesis between the online-as-virtual and the offline-as-real could no longer hold sway. As the internet was becoming a communicative membrane enwrapping our entire lifeworld, the definition of reality through media started fusing with the social definition of reality and it became increasingly difficult to distinguish between mediated and non-mediated activities as two distinctly different realms. Following from this, the virtuality vs. reality theme was starting to be understood in non-essentialist terms; the virtual is no longer to be understood as the opposite of the real, but as a part of the real, as a *potentiality* that has not yet been actualized in real-life terms. Likewise, there was a gradual overall acceptance of the "interpretative flexibility of technology"[29] leaving space to a range of different uses and designs or appropriations to which existing technology can be used. In other words, the "realness" of a technologically-mediated group is not dependent on the medium's inherent features (e.g. its lack of physical copresence or reduced non-verbal cues), but is instead conditional upon human intentionality and actions, and other contextual factors that account for the differences observed between diverse online groups. That said, accepting the potential realness of virtual places requires a clear definition and clarification of what real community is and how it can be differentiated from other mediated formations that do not merit the community characterization. Otherwise stated, if we take online communities to be *new kinds of places*, we then have to ask about the irreducible features that any definition of place should have and how they are transformed through digitalization.

Operationalizing and defining "community" has never been an easy task, and it becomes even more difficult when the prefix of "virtual" or "digital" is added to it. What cannot be disputed is that community is one of the most idealized forms of social life. Community is also one of the "strongest" manifestations of place. When we talk about Community-as-Place we imply that community may only emerge concomitantly with a Sense of Place. In other words, online groups have to produce some kind of sense of place if they are to be considered real online communities, establishing what philosopher Pierre

---

29 Pinch, T., and Bijker, W. (1992)

Levy would describe as the reality of the virtual (rather than the virtuality of the real).[30]

Human geographer John Agnew provides us with a useful distinction between the three requirements that need to be met for a space to become a place: location, locale and a sense of place.[31] *Location* answers to the question of "where" a place is located; it denotes the "there" of a place and the objective point that it occupies in the expanses of space. *Locale* refers to the setting of interaction, which is the visible and perceptible environment and its particular shape, structure and architecture, including its material infrastructure. In the case of an online community, its *location* is the particular website indicated by its web address, the point that it occupies as a node in the vast online realm. Its *locale* is demarcated by the interface and its design features, corresponding to a more or less bounded structure, visible on the scene and delineated by the edges of the screen as its inherent boundaries. An online locale's materiality would include the required hardware (the PC, the laptop, the tablet, the mobile), but primarily the software with all its substantive elements (menus, threads, rooms, comment areas, user profiles) which, while immaterial, works as the substructure that gives life to the hardware, and can thus be also considered part of the material culture.

The importance of an online location and locale is that they provide the scene for interaction, the setting that is necessary for communication to unfold in a shared common space. Additionally, the way a locale is structured in terms of design and architecture, is not without significance, neither is it random. Harrison and Dourish are right in stating that "the structure of the space around us moulds and guides our actions and interactions."[32] Structures and architectures have an orienting function and impact on how communication and sociability processes will be experienced. However, an online locale provides only the necessary but not the sufficient conditions for a community to materialize online. Communities, like places, are locations where we *do* something meaningful, rather than just places where something *is*. What online spaces also need if they are to evolve into communities and real human places is what Agnew calls "a sense of place" to denote the personal and emotional attachment people have to a particular place and the symbolic, cultural and experiential significance of that place to the individuals who inhabit it.

---

30 Levy, P. (1998)

31 Agnew, J. (2002)

32 Harrison, S.and Dourish, P. (1996): 67

In this sense, the notion of place goes beyond physical matter and transcends material, physical, tangible qualities such as size, surface, proportions, and structural features, which are more akin to the concept of Space than Place. Space acts as physical support for humans, but as long as there are no human actions upon or interactions within that environment, it is doomed to remain empty of meaning or significance. Raw space is trasformed into a place able to fulfil basic human needs through the enactment of a wealth of experiences and interactions, qualities that may be intangible yet are crucial for creating valued and unique impressions of experience. In Yi-Fu Tuan's words, place is "an organized world of meaning" that emerges out of human interpretation and valuation of space: "What begins as undifferentiated space becomes place as we get to know it better and endow it with value."[33] Places are subjectively valued to the extent that they may also function as bases for personal identity (who I am), they may end up defining identity as well as difference (who the others are not).[34] This incorporation of the place into one's core identity will usually result in that person feeling "responsible" and "accountable" for that place, longing for its maintenance and well-being and fearing its loss or damage, as a damage of place would result in the damage of the person's self-identity.

Although described as a primarily subjective feeling, "sense of place" is in fact a concept that connotes a set of intersubjective and collective features of the anthropological place.[35] Places and communities are "practiced," sustained by regular interactions, narratives exchanged, meanings shared and collective actions performed by those who inhabit them. It is in fact those practic-

---

33 Tuan, J. F. (1977): 6. The concept of a "sense of place" is also a key concept in Yi-Fu Tuan's humanist geography. In eloquently arguing about the significance of places as entities which above all incarnate the experience and aspirations of people, Tuan conceptualized "sense of place" as a qualitative experiential and emotional element distinct from other concepts like space or location.

34 For instance, see Jorgensen, B., and Stedman, R. (2001); Altman, I. and Low, S. (1992); Korpela, K. (1989).

35 Such terms as experiential perspective (Tuan, 1977), localised experience (Bachelard, 1958) or anthropological space (Merleau-Ponty, 1945) have been proposed at different times, and within the two disciplines of Humanistic Geography and Phenomenology to express the same concept of space and place as a complex locus of interaction, and not just as a shell or the mere background for human activities.

es that turn places into "dwellings"[36] and endow locations with a unique and distinctive culture, what Norberg-Schulz called a place's "genius loci,"[37] to distinguish between Space that is characterless and abstract and Place that is always idiosyncratic, specific and particularistic and therefore always in plural (places).

It would therefore be a mistake to equate the site or technological web-space of an online group with community itself, in the same manner that it would be erroneous to equate the buildings or roads of neighborhood with the human community that may be nurtured within it, a university building with its academic community or a house with a home and the bonds between the members of the family that resides in it. Communities, whether offline, online or mixed, cannot be held together by the mere existence of a shared space, although this is an absolutely necessary condition, a *sine qua non*, for interaction. Communities presuppose the cultural thickening that is provided by a certain binding definition of the situation, specific shared practices, as well as the development of interpersonal linkages, emotive relations and a "We" consciousness that reflects the community's particularity. Locations that lack these place-making qualities are indifferent containers of space, and as Casey writes they can even be utterly "inimical."[38] Likewise, online spaces that do not manage to engage people and fill up with meaningful relations cannot be considered to be anything more than an "empty space," a "pure" technology.

To date, computer networks have generated such online communities, frequented, "inhabited" and experienced like physical places. While initial skepticism ruled out the possibility of a real community emerging in the online world, we now have sufficient empirical, mostly ethnographic, evidence to prove that robust communities (having the strong place qualities that we outlined above) may emerge online. Those virtual places may be lacking physical places' emplacement and cultural fixity, yet they create an inverted hollow that is able to contain place. In effect, it is this "social place element" that makes many online groups attractive and significant for their online inhabitants. As Urry suggests: "The most successful virtual environments will be those that reproduce in the best way the types of dwellingness of the pre-virtual environment, especially where there already exists a strong sense of locality or

---

36 To dwell is a Heideggerian concept that has been picked by various theorists, such as Malpas, Norberg-Schulz and Urry among others. Briefly explained, Heidegger described to "dwell" as the process of making a place a home (1971).

37 Norberg-Schulz, C. (1980)

38 Casey, A. (1987): 190

communality."[39] It is also what makes the broader phenomenon of online community sociologically interesting and contested. Places, online or offline, are not an independent variable; they are constitutive elements of social reality by virtue of being meaningful sites of human activity that help stabilise human goods such as social integration, a sense of belonging, purposes that give meaning to life and a sense of Self.[40]

SOCIAL NETWORKING AS PERSONALIZED PLACES

In the so-called Second Internet Era, marked by the advent of Web 2.0 services, there has been a conceptual displacement from "community" to "networks" as the central form of organizing social interaction online. Social Networking Sites (SNSs) like Facebook, LinkedIn or Twitter to name the most popular, are positioned today as the primary environments for mediated sociability and group-formation. However, despite the predominance of the networking gestalt, the metaphor of "community" continues to resonate powerfully. As Parks notes, today's social networks "are direct heirs to the community metaphor [...] popularized nearly 20 years ago."[41] Furthermore, "the internal logic of social network sites often valorizes communal language and imagery as well."[42]

However, it is argued here that despite their appeal to community, SNSs in their current form cannot easily nurture genuine online communities, primarily because they lack many of the qualities of the "real" virtual communities as described above. Social networks are diffuse, ego-centered and essentially personalized networks; they may contain ritualized practices of information-sharing and communicative exchanges, they may even create in individual users a sense of place and attachment, however they are short of the publicness and collectivity that are essential elements of real places or communities (both offline and online). Networking does not equal placeness or community since the latter presuppose the existence of a public quality that is not the norm in contemporary social networks.

A public space is by definition a place that is accessible and visible to all, a common place where members meet to interact, shape common understand-

39 Urry, J. (2000): 72
40 Williams, D. R., Patterson, M. E., and Roggenbuck, J. W. (1992): 29-46.
41 Parks, M. (2010): 104
42 Parks, M. (2010): 106

ings and and where conflicts and differences are balanced. Structured as ego-centered networks, SNSs are sites where each user exercises their powers of strategic selectivity in a radically privatized manner: the individual user alone decides what profile to build, what "friends" to include, what interactions to be exposed to and what aspects of personal identity to disclose to distant others. These decisions and the ensuing interactions are not visible to all, to any single common group of people, and each user sees one's own personalized set of interactions which are never identical to those of other users, even to one's own "friends." In social networks, where no two people have exactly the same network of human connections, the public space of interaction is in fact the personal profile itself, privately constructed, strategiacally presented, often in dramatized and blatantly narcissistic mannerisms. This lack of a "public quality" in SNSs does not create conditions that are favorable to the project of community. As Gotved writes: "The visible shared space benefits the individual's sense of community – the visibility of others and the visibility of oneself interacting in the space are crucial factors in online community life [...]. However, the lack of a meeting place makes the group harder to grasp, and it may take more time to establish a sense of commonness."[43] Communicating in social networks is more akin to speaking to an audience and/or showcasing the Self, rather than engaging in sustained interactions with many others or producing collective goods. Parks is right in suggesting that while SNSs provide "affordances of membership, expression and connection" that may facilitate or "call forth" the constitutive elements of community, they very rarely achieve community status and the "higher-order characteristic of community."[44]

Functioning as web technologies to customize and memorialize the Self, SNSs are therefore better seen as "personal places" or a set of practices to *personalize* the space of networks, rather than communal places of shared meanings and sustained interaction. They may be platforms for socialization and interpersonal interaction, but they fall short of being real online communities. Their sociological value of social networks, like facebook or twitter, lies in that they provide new channels where people can fulfill their long-standing desire to want to "personalize" and own spaces so that these spaces eventually signal out something that is representative of one's identity.[45] Even a quick observation of facebook pages reveals that most of the content circulated in them is of the "personal type:" autobiographical, self-referential, often trivial and

---

43 Gotved, S. (2002): 408-409
44 Gotved, S. (2002): 109 and 116
45 Lemley, M. (2003): 521-542

banal information, that incrementally constructs the user's profile and online identity, even one's trajectory in life, albeit in a fundamentally fragmented way. In fact, what the rather fluid nature of SNSs can generate at best is some kind of "ambient awareness,"[46] like being physically near someone and picking up on his mood through the little things he does – body language, sighs, stray comments – out of the corner of your eye. As Soojung-Kim Pang writes: "Each little update – each individual bit of social information – is insignificant on its own, even supremely mundane. But taken together, over time, the little snippets coalesce into a surprisingly sophisticated portrait of your friends' and family members' lives, like thousands of dots making a pointillist painting."[47]

Social networking's paradoxical nature is already evident: these narratives of the Self, while undoubtedly self-referential and ego-centered, are continually shared with others and continually paralleled with the narratives of others, through the sharing of comments, stories, images, events, tags, likes and dislikes. What was formerly private and disclosed only to a limited number of relatives, friends and intimates (from the interiors of our houses, to our pets, family moments and bedtime muses) is now being inserted in a "semi-private, semi-public" space, visible to an increasing numbers of "friends" and "friends of friends" many of which may have never met in real life. Therefore, social networks become textual-audio-visual records of both the "personal" and the "networked, relational self," the outcome of internet's inherent paradox of providing tools that simultaneously support individualization and connectivity with others. In attempting to balance between individualism and collectivity, privateness and publicness, SNSs are ambiguous in nature and complicate how online spaces can be perceived in these social environments. They are iconic of a shift towards a new "personal communication society" taken to be a key trope of late modernity and evidenced by several key areas of social change, including the symbolic meaning of technology, the personalization of public spaces, new forms of coordination and networking, and mobile youth culture.[48] Last, in generating practices that are simultaneously private and public, but none of these in an unambiguous way, SNSs are rechanneling the two innate and contradicting longings of human nature: on the one hand, our longing towards placeless, embededness and rootedness, and on the other hand, the longing for departure, for leaving place behind, for unrestrained individuality, what Rapport and Dawson eloquently described as a situation where we as

---

46 Reichelt, L. (2007)
47 Soojung-Kim Pang in Thompson, C. (2008).
48 Campbell, S. W. and Park, Y. J. (2008)

humans "desire the freedom of space but always remain attached to the need of place."[49]

HYBRID AND MOBILE SPATIALITIES

The Internet and the concept of the cyberspace unquestionably opened our consciousness towards the possibility of a "space of flows" defined not by movements through pathways demarcated in territorial space, but as a discontinous connection between immaterial and distributed nodes. The Internet also created a new type of social spaces that are completely disconnected from physical spaces, as well as a new type of distributed community shaped by the interactions and experiences of distance others. Mobile technology may be seen as culminating this process by embedding the "space of flows" in the very structure of the city and turning cities into networks. In another sense, mobile interfaces seem to reverse the process by turning Internet into a mobile experience and embedding it in public spaces, thus opening the possibility for the creation of privatized spaces inside public spaces. Location-awareness, the additional technological affordance of being able to locate a person (and his device) in space, alters not only how space is perceived but how people interact under these new conditions and through these new mobile interfaces.

As result of successive technological innovations in wireless technology, location-awareness and mobile telephony over the last years, our conceptions of the internet and social networking in relation to space and place are undergoing some considerable changes. The mobile phone has not only become a fixture of modern culture, but it has recently evolved from being a medium for dyadic oral or text-based communication into being a veritable communicational hub; a multi-tasking microcomputer via which we can invariably make phone calls, text messages, search for all kinds of information, consume cultural products and network with others on the internet's various social media platforms. This evolution of mobile technology has introduced us to an age often described as one of "intermediality,"[50] whereby the choice of what medium to use is detached from the location of stationary media and begins to follow the user across all contexts of daily life, given the integration of practically all known media (phone, internet, video, film, music, press, etc) on a single, mobile interface.

---

49 Rapport, N., and Dawson, A (1998): 33
50 For instances, see Jensen, K. B. (2008) and Helles, R. (2013)

At the same time, the internet is becoming the very fabric of our daily lives, *always there*, permanently accessible on a 24/7 basis, embedded in our homes, in our workplaces, and since its integration on our web-enabled mobile phones, even *on our bodies*. In the post-desktop paradigm the internet is freed from the restricting fixity of a big desktop screen; it becomes ubiquitous and pervasive, increasingly spread out into the physical environment and continuous with life itself. By facilitate anytime-all the time, anyplace-all places connectivity, our miniaturized mobile devices become *transparent* in the sense that they recede into the background and their presence becomes increasingly invisible. The ease of google searching while on the move, the perpetual give-and-take of text messages and emails, tweets and facebook comments or photos, means that the technologies we now live with (or live in) become always and permanently present, oscillating between the periphery to the center of our attention. "Without the traditional distinction between physical and digital spaces, a hybrid space occurs when one no longer needs to go out of physical space to get in touch with digital environments. Therefore, the borders between digital and physical spaces, which were apparently clear with the fixed Internet, become blurred and no longer clearly distinguishable."[51]

To add to these, we witness today an unstoppable trend towards location-awarenessand an increasing reliance on different types of location-based, mostly GPS-based, services to geotag and navigate urban space, (think of Google maps, mobile local search, location-enabled social networking such as in Foursquare and Facebook Places, locative games, augmented reality browsing, etc.) The result is that urban spaces are increasingly being populated today by system or user-generated spatial annotations and informations (often called the geoweb), trasposed on physical urban spaces in the form of layers of geocoded data. In this way, what was previously digital-only is now merged with the physical, as locative technologies capture data from the physical environment and add them to the digital network.

Therefore, location-awareness inserts into the online environment the notion of navigation through physical space. It altogether changes the structure of the internet itself as it exists and develops in the urban environment, while the online experience assumes dimensions that are directly dependent on geographical parameters. As Gordon and Souza e Silva write: "new technologies are making us aware of locations, and making locations aware of us" and call this new type of spatiality "net locality."[52] Graham and Zook also make an in-

51 De Souza e Silva, A. (2006): 264
52 Gordon, E., and Souza e Silva, A. (2011)

teresting observation when they explain that the multiplication of spatial annotations has also precipitated as a consequence the emergence of processes of
stratification of space that has rendered certain places – and some aspects of
those places – visible while others have been left obscured.[53]

As an upshot of these new modalities, the very nature of physical space
undergoes a silent yet fundamental change. For one, physical space has been
loosing its one-dimensional nature as it is being traversed by digital technologies used in public space as points of direct entry to the online world of digital
representations. Additionally, the urban environment takes a new unpredictable form not so much in terms of its purely spatial aspect that is visible and
perceived by the senses, but also in terms of how users themselves conceive
and experience that space. Location-awareness technology, for example, allows users to develop a peculiar relation with the internet as much as with the
physical space. When an online application can locate one's geographical position, a sense of navigation in place is automatically added onto the online experience. In such an environment the user may experience the internet as a real
and manageable object of the environment, rather than a restricted two-
dimensional space on the screen of a computer.

Based on these observations, many new media theorists have talked about
the emergence of a new spatiality whereby space is being conceived as a unified space that has a physical as well as a digital/virtual dimension. In fact, the
much-discussed opposition between the virtual and the real, the digital and the
physical, the online and the offline becomes so radically redefined that it loses
its relevancy. These dualisms can no longer be a useful analytical tool to understand the latest technologically-induced changes in space. New concepts are
needed to describe the new spatialities which are forming in shape. The concepts of "hybrid spaces," "augmented space" and "mixed reality" have been
devised to describe this ontological shift in urban spatiality.

In effect, hybrid spaces emerge when the user no longer needs to "dis-
connect." This perpetual, round-the-clock connectivity blurs the boundaries
between the two levels of reality, while the human mind gradually adapts to a
new spatial consciousness that is engendered through this new hybrid reality.
Hybrid reality is the amalgamation of sociospatial relations and activities that
are produced and reproduced simultaneously in the physical and in the digital
world, in a continuous seamless exchange of mixed realities that result in the

---

53 Graham, M., and Zook, M. (2011): 115-132

production of an "augmented space."[54] Rather than being placeless, these mobile communication flows produce *a doubling of place*[55] in providing the contemporary experience of being at once at two distinct, yet increasingly interconnected, spaces. According to Katherine Hayles space is becoming enfolded, "so that there is no longer a homogeneous context for a given spatial area, but rather pockets of different contexts in it."[56] Concomitantly, all contemporary places could be said to have a *synthetic* character today, marked by the interlocking of direct and mediated experiences. To be true, the production of places today is as much the work of individuals as the work of the media that increasingly appear to be powerful "actants" and agents together with humans in the constitution of realities. The end result is that "all reality becomes mixed reality."[57]

These changes in urban spatiality and human connectivity clearly signal a fundamental change in the ontological relationship between Humans and Technology. The very registering of place is no longer "human only," but techno-human, the result of the "encounter" of human practice with the technology that mediates it. With technologies literally pervading the environing world of self, others and things, the intermediation of humans and machines becomes a permanent feature of the human condition. Ubiquitous computing carried on us as we move not only through urban but also in rural spaces, tourist places, travel spaces, makes users' navigation through different realms of reality an almost unnoticeable, seamless experience. This is why we are more likely to feel the absence of these possibilities than their presence (e.g. the panic of having misplaced our mobile phones or having left our tablets run out of battery). Being deprived of our mobile devices feels like falling automatically into a state of exclusion from our connected realities and the "continual conversations"[58] to which we increasingly participate in the different social

---

54 The concept of Augmented Reality was first used by Lev Manovich in 2002 to describe the physical space which is overlaid with data and digital information: images, graphics and mixed forms. The use of the "augmentation" concept reveals its underlying assumption concerning the almost perfect blending between the two realms of reality: not only do digital and analog places not overlap or conflict, rather they merge in ways that enhance and empower each other.

55 Moores, S. (2003)

56 Hayles, K. in de Souza e Silva, A. (2006): 269

57 Hansen, M. (2006): 6

58 Rice, R., and Hagen, I. (2007)

networks of the web, a metaphorical amputation of our normally digitally-augmented physical bodies and minds.

Digitilization is no longer an option, but the very infrastructure and context of all our social activities, the communication membrane that wraps around all that we humans do in our daily lives. Not only are digital technologies increasingly layered upon physical areas and surfaces, they are also permeating the ultimate physicality, our own bodies. They become veritable extensions of our bodies and minds, "technologies of embodiment," a concept coined by philosopher Don Idhe[59] used to describe technologies through which the environment is perceived and acted upon. Their characteristic is that they are no longer an object that is encountered in the world, but an indispensable mediator in humans' encounters with the world of humans, things and information. They "withdraw" and serve as (partially) transparent means through which the world is encountered, thus engendering a partial symbiosis of oneself and it. If we cast our vision into the not altogether distant or fantastical future, we can anticipate individuals engaging with the world through devices (e.g., Google Glass) that will both augment the physical world by layering it with information and generate a near continuous audio-visual record of our experience. This might be the starting point for a new understanding of Human-Technology relationships. As technologies become increasingly transparent and visible only through their absence, reality becomes inseparable from its digital representations, fostering the illusion of an entirely "unmediated" and "augmented" life.

A NOTE ON RISKS AND DANGERS

The vision of augmented and ubiquitous socio-technological spaces can be seen as reflecting processes of respatialization or at least the expansion of interaction into new mixed spatialities. It has often been interpreted as a fulfillment of the human desire for liberation from spatial and time-barriers, as well as an acclamation of the human need for connectivity and unobstructed access to people, ideas, information, opportunities. However, this is a vision that also harbors great risks and potential losses that may ultimately neutralize all assumed benefits of technologization.

---

59 According to Ihde, *Embodiment Relations* are characterized by a "partial symbiosis" of a person and a technology during which the technology in use is "embodied" and becomes "perceptually transparent". Idhe, D. (1990): 99.

First of all, we suggest that in heralding the coming of new enhanced or augmented era we must never loose sight of the fact that the digital media we use to access vital information, confirm ourselves and communicate with others, are commercially-driven services that represent a burgeoning segment of contemporary consumer culture. Anne Galloway, taking the stage to dispel digital utopianism, points out: "Certainly, by claiming an *immanent* future, researchers are able to align themselves with existing, and present-focussed, commercial markets, research agendas and funding opportunities."[60] She also sites on her blog the comment of one of her blog's visitors: "For all the talk about "user-centered design," most design work is actually "profit-centric" at its core." Being aware of the commercially-driven nature of our contemporary engagement with technologies, will help us maintain a critical composure and remain skeptical, as we should, towards all alleged "enhancements," "augmentations" and "creative opportunities" that tend to monopolistically occupy debates concerning new media.

The proliferation of such technologies also raises the dystopian issue of "control," "loss of privacy" or "continuous surveillance." While users may become more liberated in terms of their ability to access information and communicate with others in non-restraining personal and public, offline and online spaces, at the same time they are subject to processes of systematic profiling and monitoring of their movements in real space, but also of the users with whom they communicate, the kind of activities they partake in, even the content of their online and mobile exchanges. Indeed, our habits of social networking, google searching and location-detecting are silently contributing to an incredible and unprecedented amount of accumulated data (Big Data) that can be used not only for profit-making – as in the already widespread practice of internet advertising and online marketing based on user profiles – but potentially also for the statistical enclosure and control of human behavior by economic and political forces. As Katz notes, the fact that one's totality of life can be digitally recorded and archived, inevitably "raises the perennial question of whether these technologies will fundamentally alter the practice of freedom and the level of anonymity that is the bedrock of contemporary sociopolitical life in democratic nations."[61]

Another risk inherent in hyperconnectivity is that the same technology that can be used to facilitate sociality may also be used to avoid it in urban public spaces. Sherry Turkle is convinced of this negative unintended conse-

---

60 Galloway, A. (2008): 165
61 Katz, J. (2007): 392.

quence of our growing emotional and narcissistic dependence on networking, when she writes of our continously plugged selves, the "tethered selves" that are becoming increasingly individualized solipsistic selves.[62] The colonization of public spaces by egocentered subjectivized connections might lead not to more "presence" but instead to "a new absence," the absence of the direct contact with the others in flesh, and concomitantly the absence of the communal. The Self moves around public spaces but is essentially absent from others, engrossed in digital media worlds, constantly transported in the virtual ether. The imagery of a coffee shop where many people coexist in the same place yet each one is absorbed in one's mobile device is an iconic image of the contemporary age. These practices may end up becoming the norm of public space behavior, privileging fragmented interactions with the distant interactants we encounter online rather than real communication with our co-located others. What this situation might eventually amount to is "a psychological emptying out of public space: bodies remain, but personalities are engaged elsewhere."[63]

Another unintended loss of pervasive digitalization may result from the very seamlessness of the digital experience. The continuous movement from place to place within the holistic hybrid space of a real virtuality might actually lead to the blurring of those places, creating in individuals a state of confusion whereby they loose track of places' particularities and all they are left with is a disorienting and ungratifying a sense of moving through an abstract homogeneous space.

CONCLUSION

In today's media-saturated culture, networked systems of information and communication remediate the practices and the perceptions relevant to space, place and community. By highlighting a number of cultural shifts in how place and community are practiced today, this paper attempted to offer a perspective on how space, place and human community are experienced today via the new digital media that increasingly mediate our contemporary reality. While every epoch brings new meanings of space, place and community, the current shift into a networked or informational society affords a radical reconceptualization of many of the fundamental notions related to our human condition. Even if media and communication technologies are not taken to have a radically deterministic

---

62 Turkle, S. (2008)
63 Katz, J. (2007): 390

role in the structuring of place as such, they nevertheless remain crucial constituents of the character of late modern spatiality, transforming the spatial underpinnings of social life.

This essay has argued that media technologies are contributing to the spatially-textured experience of everyday life via two fundamental changes: first, by the generation of new places for connectivity and community within the online world (albeit in varying degrees of "placeness" and quality of space), what we can call "mediated places." Secondly, public spaces, both private and public, are being rearticulated as "media/technologized spaces" that are increasingly connected, portable, hybrid and also invisible in nature. Human places do not have to be composed in physical space only anymore. Some social spaces today exist in physical space, some in virtual space with no identifiable location in physical space (*virtual space*), and some in a mixture of physical and virtual spaces. This trend of virtualization does not by definition make some places more real than others, neither does it make "place" redundant as a key social and mental framework. Instead, place today matters as much as it has always been.

Onlineness and ubiquitous communication have eventually resulted in a dynamic circular-dialectical relationship between the external and the internal, the visible and the hidden, the outside and the inside, the objective and the subjective, the collective and the individual, the textual and the corporeal, as well as the local and the globally distributed. These Cartesian opposites have now become so thoroughly integrated on the level of experience that one can only distinguish between them analytically. The boundaries between the offline-as-real and the online-as-virtual have become so opaque that the very understanding of social space and experience on the basis of such a distinction has a decreasing sociological significance. As the category of the "virtual" looses its sovereignty we become more able to grasp both the constructed or "fictional" character of the virtual as well as the reality of the virtual.

That said, we need to be equally wary of the dangers of adopting simplistic or mythological concepts of space and place and new media affordances. While some formations may be construed as real places, others cannot meet up to this characterization and are nothing more but invocations of place, lacking the qualitative ingredients that should be identified with notions of place and community. Sociality in digital habitats is characterized by indeterminacy and ambivalence. Digital culture allows for the exercise of these ambiguities but our technological present is beset with more ambiguities than ever. Most crucially, in announcing the coming of an enhanced, augmented future, we should be aware of the long-term impact that unintended consequences of technologization – ranging from the de-naturalization of space to the loss of privacy and the commercialization of connectivity – may have not only on the authenticity of the places where our lives transpire, but also on the very autonomy of human condition.

REFERENCES

Agnew, John (2002): *Place and Politics in Modern Italy*, Chicago: University of Chicago Press.

Altman, Irwin, and Low, Setha (1992): *Place Attachment*, New York: Plenum

Anderson, Benedict (1983): *Imagined Communities. Reflections on the Origin and Spread of Nationalism*. London: Verso

Augé, Marc (1995): *Non-places: Introduction to an anthropology of supermodernity*. London: Verso.

Bachelard, Gaston (1958): *The Poetics of Space*. Boston, MA: Beacon Press; First Edition edition (1994)

Beck, Ulrich, Giddens, Antony, and Lash, Scott (1994): *Reflexive Modernization. Politics, Tradition and Aesthetics in the Modern Social Order*. Cambridge: Polity Press

Beniger, James (1987): "The Personalization of Mass Media and the Growth of Pseudo-Community", *Communication Research*. Volume, 14 (3), 352-371

Boden, Deirde, and Molotch, Harvey (1994): "The compulsion of proximity", in: Friedland, Roger and Boden, Deirde (eds) (1994): *Now/here: space, time and modernity*. Berkeley, CA: University of California Press, 257-286

Borgmann, Albert, (1992): *Crossing the Postmodern Divide*, Chicago: University of Chicago Press

Campbell, Scott, and Park, Yong Jin (2008): "Social Implications of Mobile Telephony: The Rise of Personal Communication Society", *Sociology Compass*, 2/2: 371–387

Casey, Edward (1997): *The Fate of Place*, Berkeley, California: University of California Press

Castells, Manuel (1996): *The rise of the network society*, Oxford: Blackwell Publishers

Curry, Michael (2002):"Discursive Displacement and the Seminal Ambiguity of Space and Place", in: Lievrouw, Leah, and Livingstone, Sonia, eds. (2002) *The Handbook of New Media: Social Shaping and Consequences of ICTs*. London: Sage Publications, 502-517

De Souza e Silva, Adrianna (2007): "Interfaces of Hybrid Spaces", in Kavoori, Anandam, and Arceneaux, Noah, eds. (2007): *The Cell Phone Reader*. New York: Peter Lang, 19-43

De Souza e Silva, Adrianna (2006): "From Cyber to Hybrid: Mobile Technologies as Interfaces of Hybrid Spaces", *Space and Culture*, 9: 261-278

Deuze, Mark (2012): *Media Life*. Cambidge: Polity Books

Dourish, Paul, and Harrison, Steve (1996). "Re-place-ing space: the roles of place and space in collaborative systems", in *Proceedings of the 1996. ACM Conference on Computer-Supported Cooperative Work*, Boston, 1996

Friesen, Norm, and Hug, Theo (2009): "The Mediatic Turn: Exploring Concepts for Media Pedagogy", in: Lundby, Knut, ed. (2009): *Mediatization: Concept, Changes, Consequences*. Frankfurt: Lang, 63-83.

Galloway, Anne (2008): *A Brief History* of the Future of *Urban Computing* and Locative Media Ph.D.Thesis in Sociology and Anthropology at Carleton University in Ottawa, Canada.

Giddens, Anthony (1990): *The Consequences of Modernity*. Oxford: Polity Press.

Goffman, Erving (1963): *Stigma: Notes on the Management of Spoiled Identity*. Englewood Cliffs, New Jersey: Prentice-Hall.

Goffman, Erving (1971): *Relations in Public. Microstudies of the Public Order*, New York: Harper and Raw Publishers, 1972

Gordon, Eric, and de Souza e Silva, Adrianna (2011): *Net Locality*. Chichester, UK: Wiley-Blackwell

Gotved, Stine (2006): "Time and space in cyber social reality", *New Media and Society*, (2006) 8(3):467-486

Graham, Mark, and Zook, Matthew (2011): "Visualizing global cyberscapes: Mapping user-generated placemarks." *Journal of Urban Technology*, 18(1): 115-132

Hansen, Mark (2006): *Bodies in Code: Interfaces with Digital Media* . New York: Routledge.

Heidegger, Martin (1971): "Building, Dwelling, Thinking", in Heidegger, Martin (1971): *Poetry, Language, Thought*. trans. Albert Hofstadter, New York: Harper Perennial Modern Classics, 2013, pp. 141-161

Heidegger, Martin (1971): *"The Thing"*, in Heidegger, Martin (1971): *Poetry, Language, Thought*. trans. Albert Hofstadter, New York: Harper Perennial Modern Classics, 2013, pp 161-185

Helles, Rasmus (2013): "Mobile media and intermediality", *Mobile Media & Communication*, 1 (1): 14-19

Idhe, Don (1990): *Technology and the Lifeworld: From Garden to Earth.* Indiana: Indiana University Press (Indiana Series in the Philosophy of Technology)

Innis, Harold (1950): *Empire and Communications.* Oxford: Clarendon Press

Jensen, Klaus Bruhn (2008): "Intermediality", in Donsbach, Wolfang, ed.: *International Encyclopedia of Communication.* Malden, MA: Blackwell Science, 2385-2387

Jorgensen, Bradley, and Stedman, Richard (2001): "Sense of place as an attitude: Lakeshore owners' attitudes toward their properties". *Journal of Environmental Psychology,* 21: 233-248

Katz, James (2007): "Mobile media and communication", *Communication Monographs,* London: Routledge, 74 (3): 389-94

Korpela, Kalevi (1989): "Place-identity as a product of environmental self-regulation", *Journal of Environmental Psychology,* 9: 241-256

Krotz, Friedrich (2007): "The meta-process of 'mediatization' as a conceptual frame", *Global Media and Communication* 3(3): 256-260

Lemley, M. A. (2003): "Place and cyberspace". *California Law Review* 91(2), 521-542

Lévy, Pierre (1998): *Becoming Virtual: Reality in the Digital Age.* New York: Plenum Trade

Malpas, John (1999): *Place and Experience: A Philosophical Topography,* Cambridge: Cambridge University Press

Manovic, Lev (2002): "The Poetics of Augmented Space", *Visual Communication,* 219-240, 2006.

McLuhan, Marshall (1967): *The Medium is the Message: An Inventory of Effects* (1st edition). New York: Random House

McLuhan, Marshall (1964): *Understanding Media: The Extensions of Man* (1st ed). New York: McGraw Hill

McLuhan, Marshall (1962): *The Gutenberg Galaxy: The Making of Typographic Man* (1st ed), Toronto: University of Toronto Press

Merleau-Ponty, Maurice (1945): The Phenomenology of Perception (translation in Greek)

Meyrowitz, Joshua (1985): *No Sense of Place: The Impact of Electronic Media in Social Behaviour.* New York: Oxford University Press

Mitchell, William (1996): *City of Bits: Space, Place and the Infobahn.* Cambridge MA: The MIT Press.

Moores, Shaun (2003): "Media, Flows and Places", *Media@LSE Electronic Working Papers Series. No.6, Programme in Media and Communications,* London School of Economics and Political Science.

Norberg-Schulz, Christian (1980): *Genius Loci. Towards a Phenomenology of Architecture*, New York: Rizzoli Publications

Ong, Walter (1982): *Orality and Literacy: The Technologizing of the Word* (2nd ed.), New York: Routledge

Parks, Malcolm (2010): "Social Network Sites as Virtual Communities", in Papacharissi, Zizzi, ed. (2010): *Networked Self: Identity, Community, and Culture on Social Networking Sites*, New York and London: Routledge

Pinch, Trevor, and Bijker, Wiebe (1992): "The social construction of facts and artifacts: or how the sociology of science and the sociology of technology might benefit each other", in Bijker, Wiebe, and Law, John, eds. (1992): *Shaping Technology/Building Society*, Cambridge, MA: MIT Press

Rapport, Nigel, and Dawson, Andrew (1998): *Migrants of Identity. Perceptions of Home in a World of Movement.* Oxford and New York: Berg

Reichelt, Leisa (2007): "Disambiguity". Leisa Reichelt's Professional Blog. Published March 1, 2007 http://www.disambiguity.com/ambient-intimacy/

Relph, Edward (1976): *Place and Placelessness.* London: Pion

Rice, Ronald, and Hagen, Ingunn (2007): "Social Connectivity, Multitasking, and Social Control: U.S./Norwegian College Students Use of Internet and Mobile Phones". *Paper presented at the annual meeting of the International Communication Association, TBA, San Francisco, CA*, 2007

Riva, Guiseppe, Waterworth, John, and Waterworth, Eva (2004). "The Layers of Presence: A Bio-cultural Approach to Understanding Presence in Natural and Mediated Environments", *Cyberpsychology and Behavior*, Vol. 7 (4), 405-420

Scannell, Paddy (1996): *Radio, Television and Modern Life*: A Phenomenological Approach. Oxford: Blackwell

Schulz, Winfried (2004): "Reconstructing Mediatization as an Analytical Concept", *European Journal of Communication* 19 (1): 87-100

Simmel, Georg (1922): *Conflict and the Web of Group Affiliations*, translated and edited by Kurt Wolff, Glencoe, IL: Free Press, 1955

Sonesson, M. (1997): "The multimediation of the lifeworld", in Nöth, Winfried, ed.: *Semiotics of the Media.* Berlin and New York, Mouton de Gruyter, 61-78

Sorkin, Michael (1992): *Variations on a Theme Park: The New American City and the End of Public Space.* New York: Hill and Wang

Thompson, Clive (2008): *Brave New World of Digital Intimacy*, New York Times. Published 7. Sept. 2008. http://www.nytimes.com/2008/09/07/magzine/07awareness-t.html

Thompson, John (2005): "The New Visibility", *Theory, Culture and Society*, 22-31

Thompson, John (1995): *The Media and Modernity*. Cambridge: Polity Press

Tuan, Yi Fu (1977): *Space and Place: The Perspective of Experience*. Minneapolis, MN: University of Minnesota Press.

Turkle, Sherry (2008): "Always-On/Always-On-You: The Tethered Self", in Katz, James, ed. (2008): *The Handbook of Mobile Communication Technologies*. Cambidge: MIT Press, 121:139

Urry, John (2000): *Sociology beyond societies*. London: Routledge

Williams, Daniel, Patterson, Michael, and Roggenbuck, Joseph (1992): "Beyond the commodity metaphor: Examining emotional and symbolic attachment to place", *Leisure Sciences* 14, 1: 29-46

The Destruction of Space by Augmentation

Martin Reiche

> [...] it exists, and it does not contain any organic society.[1]

If we talk about virtual spaces and virtuality in general, one term that usually comes up is *augmentation* – the fusion of the real space with a virtual space making it a hybrid one. Augmenation, as used in the term *augmented reality*, is not a new concept. Originally, augmentation stems from the Latin word *augmentum*, the growing or adding of something, derived from the word *augmentare*, to add in order to enrich something to become more than the something itself.[2] This process of enriching is an active one in a sense that the process of augmentation is believed to make the something in question "better" by endorsing additional qualities.[3] Augmentation aims to transform a real world entity into something more, something more than it actually is, by adding something different (but nevertheless something that is logically connected to the entity).

This article will deal with the idea of augmentation itself, not with the idea of augmentation as used in *augmented reality*, which can be defined as alteration of perception of reality by computer-generated sensory input.[4] Our idea of augmentation is a more general one and stems from the original meaning of the term augmentation as introduced above, which means that the sensory input does not necessarily have to be computer-generated, nor does it have to be digital. This definition is rather vague and applies to every kind of virtual element that adds information to an element of the real space. Therefore, augmented reality devices

---

1   Augé, M. (1995): 111-112.
2   Heinichen, F. A. (1903).
3   Reiche, M., and Gehmann, U. (2012).
4   This is a common definition which is also shared by Milgram, P. et al (1994).

such as head-mounted displays (HMDs) as well as information about specific buildings on virtual maps[5] are both capable of augmenting reality with virtual elements – and this is of course not a comprehensive list. This great variety in different approaches towards how to achieve augmentation of real space makes it difficult to create a consistent anthropology of the augmentation process. In order to better understand the process of augmentation, we have to get back to its etymological origins. Augmenting space, i.e. adding in order to enrich, means that the idea is to make this object more than it already is, more that the "it" just seen by itself. It means that the object gains more qualities, finally transforming the object in question to becoming something new, altering its very identity.[6] Exactly this identity alteration is the core idea of augmentation and should serve as the common ground of any form of augmented reality.

Giving an important example of a piece of software for real space augmentation, the location-based software Foursquare[7] aims at giving its users the ability to check-in at places they like, to explore new places based on their and their friends' preferences and to share their findings to their friends on Foursquare as well as on other social networks. Foursquare therefore can be seen as a social network in itself offering its users the ability to discover places they have not been to before by augmenting it: every discoverable place on earth can be electronically enhanced by a check-in, discussions, suggestions and ratings. The user of the software experiences it as a convenient way to gather information about places in the real world he has not visited so far, getting suggestions for restaurants he has not yet visited and so on. When the software enhances a place with the necessary information to fulfill the goal for its users to explore something new in the real world, the place, as seen through the map of such software, gains a new history, a history consisting of the aforementioned check-ins, ratings, suggestions and discussions, no matter what its original history has been. What counts for the software is that every place on earth can be turned into what they call a "location," an entity on a map with a name, address and a history inside of the virtual world created by the software itself. Each place being converted to an entity also means that its internal software-side representation becomes a general one: For each entity, the data structure is the same[8] meaning that all places are

---

5   An explanation about how maps serve as virtual realities has been outlined in Gehmann, U., and Reiche, M. (2013).

6   Cf. Reiche, M., and Gehmann, U. (2012).

7   www.foursquare.com

8   The data structure might not be completely the same as it can still differ based on different types of entities: clubs, bars, restaurants, sights etc. may need different data

internally handled as if they were the same, except for the part of information that is important for the software to work the way it should: the name of the place and its internal history. Creating augmentations this way is a design choice: collecting, saving and maintaining data about locations is a costly endeavor and in the end the system does not need to care about the specific history and site-specific properties of its "locations" as they do not matter for the function that the software tries to fulfill: offering its users information and suggestions for places they might enjoy visiting, restaurants they might like or clubs that might play the music they appreciate or any other function that the location-based software wants to fulfill. However, this functionalized view of these entities, or locations as the software calls them itself, has consequences on the way how the user perceives the quality of the places that he or she visits: if every entity of the real world, every discoverable part of the physical world is pressed into the same uniform data structure, then ultimately important qualities of the places will get lost. Entities of reality get abstracted in order to make them functional entities of a software system, they get standardized. This in itself is not yet a problem. It starts to become a problem though when the software system becomes a point of reference for its users. With some of these software system becoming the de facto standard for its users to explore places they have not been to (by checking them out in the software before going there, for example), then the software system already is the point of reference for the user.

The understanding of augmented entities in real space from the above paragraph is very close to what Marc Augé refers to as *non-places*, which are "spaces which are not themselves anthropological spaces and which […] do not integrate the earlier places."[9] This is what happens in many reality-augmenting location-based systems: the original history of the place is neglected in order to create a new one that fits the data structure of the software system. This ultimately overrides the original history of the place and enforces a new one, at least through the eyes of the system. Even more, real world entities get "[…] listed, classified, promoted to the status of 'places of memory', and assigned to a circumscribed and specific position."[10] Also, Augé explains the need of non-places to use text to describe the entities in question as a result of the process of stripping off the

structures. However, the most important point is that not every entity has its very own data structure but is generalized to belong to a category which then has a predefined data structure.

9   Augé, M. (1995): 78.
10 Augé, M. (1995): 78.

places original qualities.[11] As the places have lost their qualities, they have to be explained again to the user. Location-based software exaggerate this property: not only the software itself offers information about the location, but every user is able to change, add and comment on the information provided for each location. Together with check-ins and rating capabilities, this forms the new history of the space through the lens of the system. Every other quality of the former place gets neglected; the only thing that counts is the new, artificial history provided by the system. Furthermore, many location-based systems use codifications such as icons and badges to explain properties of the locations. The reasons therefore are obviously that it is easier to distinguish between different categories of locations as well that it makes translations of these properties obsolete if the code can be understood the cultural context of the user. However, this gets very close to the need for "explicit and codified ideograms"[12] that Augé refers to when talking about non-places.[13] These codifications are by themselves abstractions of ideas[14] and therefore fit the context of a space abstraction harmonically.

The mentioned ideograms might even serve new functions in themselves. This is the case in the already mentioned Foursquare software as well as in a lot of other software pieces. *Badges* there are small ideograms that serve as collectibles and are awarded to the user if he behaves the right way,[15] i.e. serves the goal of the software to visit as many places as possible in a short amount of time, many places in a high frequency and so on. If locations in location-based software can already be seen as abstractions of places,[16] than badges can be seen as abstractions of the former, meaning that badges serve as meta-collectibles and by

---

11 Augé, M. (1995): 99.

12 Augé, M. (1995): 96.

13 For Augé, these codified ideograms can be for example traffic signs on highways. In fact, Augé argues that highways are important archetypes of non-places, which also shows that the space-destruction explained in this article is not a completely new phenomenon created by location-based software but rather a general result of augmentation of real space.

14 Cf. Hughes, R. (2011) on the origin of symbols and codes.

15 Collectibles such as badges are used to improve the user's engagement with the software system. They are one application of the idea of *gamification*, i.e. the usage of game mechanics in software systems that are not necessarily games as defined by Deterding, S. et al (2011). Gamification elements that are commonly used in software are leaderboards, experience points, high scores, awards or virtual goods.

16 And they can be seen as abstractions of places as they reduce the place to the physical qualities of its position in space, i.e. the location of the place.

that are abstractions of abstractions of places. Even more, the badges themselves define a space (the space of the sum of all badges that can be collected in the software) without any time or location whatsoever. As the badges serve as an incentive to visit more locations, collecting all badges becomes a goal of the software. Following this goal means that each place the user visits loses its importance as the goal is just to visit as many places as possible. The software thus effectively overrides the space that it utilizes in order to justify its own existence.

However, a location whose history is only defined by the software itself, of course still serves a social function: users get connected not only by visiting the location but also by checking in at this location. Therefore, a group of people that might have never met in person is created: all users who have once been at the location in question and thus are part of the virtually created history of this place. Augé refers to the idea of this ever-growing community of people who may not even know each other as an "experience of perceptual presence" – it seems to the user as if he is connected to all of these people who have once been at this location – the act of the check-in seems to acquire meaning through the artificially constructed social sphere that seemingly belongs to the location. It may be argued that this artificially constructed social sphere can create liberation for the individual: the user does not have to take part in any social activity and is still integrated into this society of the social sphere belonging to the location. The user may feel as part of a society that is not a real society in an anthropological sense. It must be argued that this feeling is intended by the designers of the software as it leads to a positive state of mind through approval and compliance, making him more likely to use the software more often again and/or even pay for it.[17]

Another question that has to be asked is if also the effects on *anthropological* space that we experience right now through location-based software might be intended. We have seen that by transforming places into non-places (locations) by augmenting them, we are destroying essential qualities of the real world for the user who uses the location-based software as a point of reference for his world. This destruction at the same time creates the need for a new world, a virtual one that gives back the lost quality, even if in a different way. Just that now, the virtual world is designed and therefore controlled by the designer of the software, which most likely is an economic institution. The new virtual replica of the destroyed real world can be created to serve the goals of the company that creates it. It is obvious that this might imply the abuse of all information ac-

---

17 A similar effect has been shown for social networks in Gehmann, U., and Reiche, M. (2013).

quired as well as trying to control this new virtual world. It is important to stress that the destruction of space is essential to create a virtual space that can be harvested.[18] At the same time, the new virtual replica of the destroyed real space has to be designed to feel like anthropological space on first view so that users do not refuse it in the first place. Embedding social components (as seen in social networks) can serve as such a feature.

A slightly different way of seeing the idea of augmentation is the way in which fusion of reality and virtuality is done in a genre of games called *augmented reality games*. These games transform digital games into real environments and can usually be played using smartphones so that if you view the world through the camera of the smartphone, it gets enhanced with the virtual features of the game, such as characters, game elements, and so on, which seem to be part of the real world even though only visible through the digital device.[19] This kind of augmentation is a special form of augmented reality as discussed earlier in this anthology,[20] but it is nevertheless important as it has the quality to overcome the problem of world destruction as by the bare fact of being a game, it does not necessarily need to fulfill a function besides its very existence for entertainment reasons at all.[21] From that point of view, one can argue if augmentation of space is only taking the drastic consequences outlined above when the augmentation itself takes place out of functional reasons, i.e. to optimize a function in the real world, like maximizing the return on investment. If that is the case, than de-functionalized augmentations, i.e. augmentations that do not fulfill a function and that are not *intended* to fulfill a function, might be a key to using the potentials of augmentation without touching the anthropological space that the augmentation is embedded into.

---

18 This can be seen analogous to the myth of a second creation in posthuman culture, as Flessner, B. (2000) puts it, that man can overcome his older frame of reference: his anthropological belongings.

19 The first augmented reality games have been created long before the advent of the smartphone using head-mounted displays in outdoor scenarios. A prominent example is explained in more detail by Piekarsky, W., and Thomas, B. (2002).

20 See the article "Mixed Reality" by Panagiotis Ritsos in this anthology.

21 This can be compared to explorative games and de-functionalization phenomena which have been investigated by Gehmann, U., and Reiche, M. (2013a)

REFERENCES

Augé, Marc (1995): *Non-places*, translated by John Howe, London/New York: Verso

Deterding, Sebastian et al. (2011): "Gamification: Toward a Definition", *Mindtrek 2011 Proceedings*, Tampere: ACM Press

Flessner, Bernd, ed. (2000): *Nach dem Menschen* [After Man], Freiburg: Rombach litterae

Gehmann, Ulrich, and Reiche, Martin (2013): "Virtual Urbanity", in: *Proceedings of the Hybrid City II Conference*, Athens

Gehmann, Ulrich, and Reiche, Martin (2013a): "Functionalization and World Conception", in: *Proceedings of the 2013 International Conference on Cyberworlds*, Yokohama

Heinichen, Friedrich Adolph (1903): *Lateinisches Schulwörterbuch* [Latin school dictionary], Teubner

Hughes, Ryan (2011): *CULT-URE*, Fiell

Milgram, Paul, et al. (1994): Augmented Reality: A class of displays on the Reality-Virtuality Continuum, *SPIE*, vol. 2351, Telemanipulator and Telepresence Technologies.

Piekarsky, Wayne, and Thomas, Bruce (2002): "ARQuake: the outdoor augmented reality gaming system", in: *Communications of the ACM*

Reiche, Martin, and Gehmann, Ulrich (2012): "How virtual spaces re-render the perception of reality through playful augmentation", in: *Proceedings of the 2012 International Conference on Cyberworlds*, Darmstadt

Chapter 4. Facets of Acceleration in Hybrid Spaces

Mixed Reality

A paradigm for perceiving synthetic spaces

PANAGIOTIS D. RITSOS

INTRODUCTION

As our life becomes more intertwined with technology our capabilities in interacting and communicating with each other take a new form. In the distant past we relied on posted letters and postcards to contact each other, often requiring a lot of days for the correspondence to reach the intended recipient. Our perception of distance from each other – and therefore our world as space – changed with the introduction of telephony. Communicating with distant relatives was easier, albeit associated with physically being present in front of a telephone and, therefore, still locus dependent. Mobile telephony brought even further immediacy of communication. Space matters even less now. We are either within network coverage – but maybe in the cinema and unavailable – or somewhere with poor reception. From being miles and days apart, we now feel like we are mere seconds apart. Our perception of space changes, as our friends and family seem closer, despite the fact they may be, physically, in a location that a century ago would take us weeks to reach with posted mail.

Nonetheless, it is not only communicating that has, consequently, changed. Entertainment, commerce, education have also changed due to technology. We do not need to travel to our nearest urban center to buy something but we can order it on the Internet. We have access to lots of entertainment programs on the go, on our mobile devices. We can watch our favorite football team while traveling on the train. Education leaves the physical space of schools and universities and becomes available worldwide through massive open online courses (MOOCs) and virtual laboratories.

Overall, science and technology have changed the way that we see ourselves in the world and consequently changed our perception of space. As technology becomes more capable, faster, cheaper and easier to carry or embed in our world, our perception of our physical surroundings, as well as information embedded within, will change even further.

In particular, the introduction of three-dimensional (3D) graphics imagery allows us to employ computers to generate (synthesize) objects as stereo representations, thus appearing much like real objects in our spatial surroundings. The introduction of head-mounted displays (HMDs), which dates back to 1968,[1] adds the capability of seeing such objects from various viewpoints dynamically, with the synthetic representation changing as if the person was looking at a real object.

Technologies, like computer vision, can place (register) these synthetic objects in the real world, among real objects[2] while haptic and tactile interfaces allow us to feel them.[3] We are gradually moving into a world that increasingly combines real and computer generated objects and resources. Into a reality that brings the real and computer generated together – *a mixed reality*.

The Mixed Reality (MR) paradigm proposes to superimpose, with intent to enhance, our real surroundings with computer-generated objects and information. From the standpoint of vision, MR systems enable the user to see the real physical environment and any digital objects, simultaneously, implying the use of some form of transparent display system. To ensure that real and digital appear as a unified space, there is need for spatial registration of any computer-generated objects to real objects. However, MR may extend beyond the sense of vision, to the extent that digital information can be 'accessed', i.e., perceived, through other senses. Evidently, MR is by its nature an inter-disciplinary field, encompassing notions of computer engineering, computer vision, human factors, computer graphics, information visualization, mobile and wearable computing, context awareness, affective computing, networking as well as display and sensory technologies.

In the context of this work the author treats the notions of *Augmented Reality* (AR) and *Augmented Virtuality* (AV) as subsets of MR, as discussed in the section "Defining Mixed Reality," where academic definitions are revisited. Likewise, pure *Virtual Reality* (VR) and real life are the extremes beyond MR

---

1   Sutherland, I. E. (1968)

2   Kato, H., and Billinghurst, M. (1999)

3   Srinivasan, M. A., and Basdogan, C. (1997)

and in principle do not involve any degree of synthesis between the real and virtual.

On the contrary MR and its subsets AR and AV do involve this synthesis in varying degrees and hence offer a hybrid view of space. Throughout this investigation, we focus mainly on MR and AR as these are the paradigms that have received most attention in research and in commercial solutions. Furthermore, in the author's opinion, these paradigms will fundamentally change our perception of space in the not so distant future, in a way captured most expressively in Vernon Vinge's *Synthetic Serendipity,*[4] a futuristic tale that describes a space pervaded with computer-generated objects, seamlessly integrated to the real world.

This article does not serve as an overview of the current state of art in the field of MR, despite describing many prominent research efforts. It does, however, aim to describe how the perception of, and interaction with, our surrounding physical space can be enhanced through the use of computer-generated objects. It also attempts to look into the future, beyond the synthesis of real and computer-generated objects in our physical environment, presenting how the informational space around us has shaped and will continue to shape through immersive technologies. Last but not least, it highlights the relation of MR to other research fields in the area of *human computer interaction* (HCI).

DEFINING MIXED REALITY

When we refer to immersive environments, in relation to computer science and in particular HCI, probably one the most encountered term is Virtual Reality. Implementation examples of such immersive environments date back to the early 1960s, with *Sensorama*, a mechanical multimodal immersive 3D movie booth, dubbed *"experience theatre"* by its developer, Morton L. Heilig. However, the term 'Virtual Reality' is often credited to being popularised by Jason Lanier, chief executive officer of VPL Research, which focused on commercializing early VR technologies. An even earlier mention of virtual reality can be found in the work of the French playwright, poet and theatre director, Antonin Artaud *"The Theatre and Its Double,"* where theatre is called as *"la réalite virtuelle"* – a reality both illusory and fictional. Notice, the *"theatricality"* element in both Heilig's and Artaud's interpretations of VR. It also noteworthy, that the

4   Vinge, V. (2004)

contributions of Ivan Sutherland and his first head-mounted display (HMD)[5] Douglas Engelbart with his pioneering work on user interaction[6] and Myron Krueger with his work on immersive video projections[7] have been instrumental on how VR took shape.

In the scholarly world, VR is usually defined with some reference to a particular hardware system, such a computer capable of rendering 3D graphics in real time, motion-sensing data gloves for interaction and a head-mounted stereoscopic display for visual output. Steuer[8] provides an overview of such definitions and in an attempt to separate VR from a specific hardware infrastructure he defines it as *"a real or simulated environment in which a perceiver experiences telepresence,"* where telepresence is defined as *"the experience of presence in an environment by means of a communication medium"* and presence is defined as *"the sense of being in an environment."* Despite the fact that Steuer's definition appears independent of hardware it does imply the use of a communication medium and, thus, distinguishes VR from merely experiencing our immediate surroundings in a natural, non-technology dependent manner.

Despite its initial popularity, VR never actually delivered the services and the commercialization of the high level of immersion it promised. For many people VR came to its demise, sometime in the beginning of the 90s, with the paradigm finding shelter in research laboratories. However, that preserved the concept of immersive technologies and lead to the introduction of new, more complex concepts, with varying integration with the real world.

In 1994 Milgram and Kishino[9] defined Mixed Reality (MR) as the part of a virtuality continuum (Figure 1), extending between the completely real and completely virtual but not including these extremes. The definition is primarily focused on the visual aspect of reconstructing and synthesizing our surroundings with computer generated objects, in different proportions. The one end of the continuum defines environments that consist of real objects, i.e. *"those that have an actual objective existence,"* and can be viewed through a display, say a video feed of a real room. The other end consists of environments built entirely out of computer-generated object, i.e. *"those that exist in essence or effect but not formally or actually,"* such as a virtual simulation environment – or in other world

5   Sutherland, I. E. (1968)
6   Englebart, D. C. (1962)
7   Krueger, M. W. (1993)
8   Steuer, M. W. (1992)
9   Milgram, P., and Kishino, F. (1994)

VR. A Mixed Reality environment is, therefore, one where real and computer-generated objects can be viewed as coexisting.

Milgram and Kishino's definition is heavily influenced by developments in the area of Virtual Reality (VR), when mobile computing was at its infancy. It is nonetheless indicative of how we perceive the environment and therefore our surrounding space – predominantly with our vision. This emphasis on the visual representation has influenced research to a great extent, with various efforts focusing in realistic representation, computer-vision spatial registration and the development of display technologies.

Nonetheless, despite the all-inclusive nature of this definition, when it comes to degrees of synthesis of computer-generated and real objects in our environment, the term MR has not being as popular as its subset, Augmented Reality (AR). The term, coined by Caudell and Mizell,[10] two years before Milgram's and Kishino's definition, was used to describe an experimental system, employing a see-thru HMD (referred to as heads-up display) used in aircraft maintenance by Boing. The most widely mentioned definition of AR was provided three years later, by Azuma,[11] by which an AR system *combines real and virtual, is interactive in real time* and *is spatially registered.*

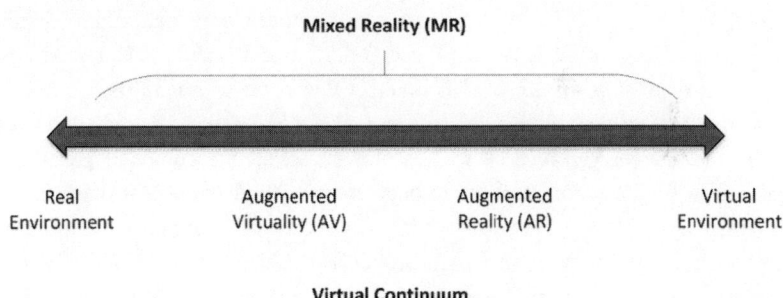

Figure 1. Simplified representation of the "reality - virtuality continuum".[12]

Azuma's definition is predominantly focusing on vision, much like Milgram's and Kishino's, and, consequently, a subset of the latter. Of particular interest is the emphasis on the interactive nature of the environment and on spatial registration, a notion that has direct implications on how space, positioning and orienta-

---

10 Caudell, T. P., and Mizell, D. W. (1992)

11 Azuma, R. (1997)

12 Milgram, P., and Kishino, F. (1994)

tion is fundamental for AR systems. By requiring the objects to be spatially registered AR systems can combine real and computer generated images, viewed through a display in our immediate vicinity. This consequently implies the use of transparent, see-through display technologies.

Mackay[13] offers an alternative to the aforementioned definitions, focusing on User Experience (UX) and describing the notion of augmenting the environment through interactive, networked objects – effectively moving away from the vision-focusing definitions of the past. Mackay highlights three strategies for creating AR applications: a) *Augmented the user*, usually using wearable or handheld devices that provide information about the user's surroundings, b) *Augment the physical objects*, through computational power, sensors, input and output embedded in physical objects, and c) *Augmented the environment surrounding the user and object* by using independent devices to capture Information from the user's surrounding environment, regarding his interactions with objects and presenting it on the latter – neither the user nor the object are affected directly.

Despite the fact that Mackay's definition does include concepts of AR as defined by Azuma, it moves towards a different notion of our surroundings, where interactive, networked objects enhance UX. As noted by Barba et al.[14] this definition approaches Weiser's[15] notion of Ubiquitous Computing, often regarded as the antithesis of VR. As per Weser's definition Ubiquitous Computing is *"a new way of thinking about computers in the world, one that takes into account the natural human environment and allows the computers themselves to vanish into the background"* – we are not immersed in a computer generated space, as in VR, but computers are embedded everywhere in our real space.

Interestingly, the other subset of the MR continuum, Augmented Virtuality (AV) has not been as popular as AR, probably because there are limited opportunities to enhance a virtual environment with real information. An example would be using a video feed of a real street, superimposed on the windows of a virtual room, in order to increase the realism of the surroundings (Figure 2). Virtual world designers use this technique to enhance the realism of their creations, in order to increase the sense of immersion of participants.

---

13 Mackay, W. (1998)

14 Barba, E., MacIntyre, B., and Mynatt, E. D. (2012)

15 Weiser, M. (1991)

Extending Physical Space with Synthetic Objects

AR has received much more attention than its superset paradigm, MR, with most important examples of what can be achieved focusing on vision. There are various reasons for this; first and foremost, is the intrinsic importance of vision in the perception of space. We predominantly rely on seeing objects around us, although hearing and touching can be equally important in various cases, such as in darkness, or for visually impaired users. Vision, also, allows us to perceive space of much higher volume than any other sense.

Figure 2. Combining a webcam feed from Times Square, NY adds an element of realism in the Project IVY – Interpreting in Virtual Reality – Visitors Centre, built using the Second Life virtual world.[16]

In particular binocular vision allows us to appreciate depth, i.e. the ability to distinguish relative distance of, and physical displacement between, objects. This process is called stereopsis, from *stereo* – meaning solid – and the Greek term *opsis* (ὄψις) – meaning appearance. It is possible to appreciate depth using one eye through monocular cues such as relative size, interposition etc., however

---

16 Ritsos, P. D. et al. (2013). Image courtesy of the author.

acute stereoscopic depth discrimination is attributed to binocular vision. Inevitably, our ability to perceive space, real or synthetic, is very much based on vision.

Furthermore, during the last couple of decades there has been a lot of progress in display, tracking and sensing mechanisms and algorithms. Thirdly, various specialized devices, such as HMDs or data gloves, have emerged and, although originally built for VR, have found their way into AR prototypes. However, AR should not be limited to vision, but should augment other senses, like hearing or touching, as mentioned. For instance, localized sound, heard through headphones can offer additional information on space.

One of the early efforts to offer an overview of AR research is by Azuma[17] and despite being written almost 15 years before this work, presents technologies, concepts and challenges that still exist, today. A comprehensive and insightful way to explore the characteristics of an AR/MR system is to follow Azuma's definition and classify characteristics and features under the headings of vision, registration and interaction.

Vision

AR systems typically use optical or video technologies to add computer generated or remove (hide) real objects from the composite view (figure 3). Optical devices usually employ an arrangement of mirrors to synthesize the real and computer generated views. Video-based technologies use a combination of camera tracking and post-processing of video feed for the synthesis.[18] For optical systems the most important limitation is the reduced amount of light, compared to natural vision, reaching the user's eyes. In video-based systems delays introduced from the tracking and processing subsystems, results in visual discrepancies, particularly during movement and may adversely affect registration, i.e. the placement of objects, discussed below. Both systems suffer from limited resolution, optical issues like unsuitable inter-ocular distance, poor contrast under sunlight, and focus mismatch, as well as poor ergonomics, in case of heavy and cumbersome systems. Displays can be either head mounted (HMDs)[19] monitor-based,[20] projection-based[21] or as in recent years, hand-held.[22]

17 Azuma, R. (1997).

18 Azuma, R., and Bishop, G. (1994)

19 Feiner, S. et al. (1997)

20 Coles, T. R. et al. (2011)

21 Bau, O., and Poupyrev, I. (2012)

22 Schmalstieg, D., and Wagner, D. (2007)

In addition to problems introduced from the aforementioned technologies, there are other perceptual issues that must be dealt with, inherit to the notion of superimposing graphics on our natural view of the real world. Some of these are occlusion, i.e. the determination of which objects are visible or not from certain viewpoints, reflections and material display properties, particularly for fluids or mirror-like surfaces and color resolution. A comprehensive classification of perceptual issues can be found in Kruijiff et al.[23]

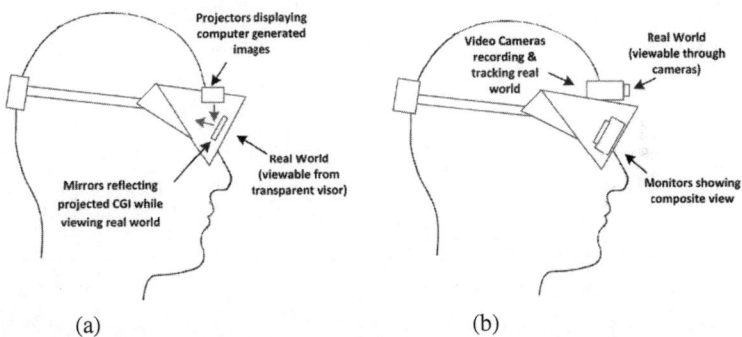

(a)   (b)

Figure 3. Optical (a) and video (b) see-through HMDs are often used to display computer generated imagery, superimposed on the natural surroundings. In both cases the user sees a composite view of the world. Most HMDs are also equipped with some form of inertial tracking to determine orientation of gaze.

What is also interesting to note is that, despite the fact that HMDs have been left aside since the beginning of the millennium, with the attention of researchers focusing on displays in handled devices, they seem to return to life after recent media attention on Google Glass a context-aware HMD developed by Google.[24] Notwithstanding all the problems inherit in HMDs, they are one of the most popular output mechanisms in the history of the field, due to the unique feature of presenting computer graphics imagery simultaneously to the real view, while the user has his or her hands free. Whether these HMDs remain cumbersome and heavy or, in the future, become as unobtrusive as contact lenses[25] it may only be a matter of time.

23 Kruijff, E., Swan, J. E., and Feiner, S. (2010).

24 http://www.google.com/glass/start/

25 Parviz, B. A. (2009)

Registration

The process of superimposing computer-generated objects spatially, with accuracy and stability, is called registration and is an inherit feature in MR/AR systems. Registration is the basic problem of most AR/MR systems as objects need to be seamlessly aligned to the real world to give the illusion of the co-existence of virtual and real space and objects. In some cases like medical AR/MR the accuracy requirements are very stringent.[26] In other cases, like for instance archaeological reconstruction less accuracy – say 20cm – may be acceptable, for instance in order to go through virtual doorways.[27] At the moment, registration errors are one of the most important problems inhibiting MR/AR systems, with the most accurate implementations being scenario specific. Registration errors can be attributed to a number of factors, such as delays introduced by the tracking processing systems, inherit inaccuracies of the tracking sensors/algorithms, optical distortions, calibration errors etc.

Computer vision methods on the other hand can be fairly accurate but usually require the presence of a marker[28] or pre-existing knowledge of the tracked objects for model-based tracking.[29] Nonetheless, recent advances in computer vision allowed researchers to develop various tracking and detection techniques, like Simultaneous Localization and Mapping (SLAM), where the 3D position and orientation of an entity and the 3D structure of the surrounding environment are determined in real-time[30,31] without prior knowledge of the world.

A lot of work has been done on registration mechanisms for AR/MR, ranging from sensor-based solutions, like GPS[32] to vision-based systems. In the latter category, one of the most important contributions is that of the *AR-Toolkit,*[27] which uses a camera to track 2D barcode-like markers, identifying position and orientation in space. A particularly interesting method is to use more than one tracking system in conjunction[33] to compensate forn the deficiencies of each other; an approach referred to as 'sensor fusion' or 'hybrid tracking'. Moving one

26 Livingston, M. A., and Ai, Z. (2008)

27 Ritsos, P. D. et al. (2003)

28 Kato, H., and Billinghurst, M. (1999)

29 Comport, A. I., Marchand, E., and Chaumette, F. (2003).

30 Davison, A. J. et al. (2007)

31 Neubert, J., Pretlove, J., and Drummond, T. (2007)

32 Thomas, B. et al. (1998)

33 You, S., Neumann, U., and Azuma, R. (1999)

step further is the notion of ubiquitous tracking[34] where networks of sensors can be widespread to the environment, making AR/MR systems more pervasive, very much along the aforementioned definition of Mackay.[35]

Interaction

Equally important as visual depiction and registration is the capability to interact with the computer generated objects. That can be done either indirectly, for example by changing the view showing though an HMD according to the user's position, orientation of gaze etc., or directly through dedicated interfaces. As demonstrated, indirect interaction is mostly related to registration and vision. Direct interaction often requires special components and can be treated as a discreet module system. Examples of interaction mechanisms for AR/MR are tangible or tactile/haptic interfaces.

The concept of tangible user interfaces (TUIs)[36] has led to the concept of tangible AR[37] used in the *VOMAR* application where a real paddle, markers and camera-based tracking are used to move virtual objects in synthetic space. More recent efforts, like *REVEL[38]* make use of electro-vibration to create an electrical field around the users' fingers, to induce the feeling of touch, when in contact with objects in the synthetic space. Haptics and tactile interfaces have been used extensively in medical AR.[39] The concept involves using haptic devices, where mechanical actuators mediate the feeling of touch. An example application is a simulator teaching surgeons the technique of needle insertion for interventional radiology[40] whilst viewing a composite view of the surgeon's hands, holding the intervention device and looking at the computer-generated view of a virtual patient. Haptic behavior can also be pre-fabricated and added on computer-generated objects,[41] thus enhancing existing implementations.

Recent advances in depth cameras, such as Microsoft's *Kinect[42]* and *Primesense[43]* offer an alternative way of interaction with virtual objects. Depth

34 Zhou, F., Duh, H. B. L., and Billinghurst, M. (2008)
35 Mackay, W. (1998)
36 Ishii, H., and Ullmer, B. (1997)
37 Kato, H. et al. (2000)
38 Bau, O., and Poupyrev, I. (2012)
39 Coles, T. R., Meglan, D., and John, N. (2011)
40 Coles,T. R. et al. (2011)
41 Panëels, S. A. et al. (2013)
42 http://www.xbox.com/kinect

cameras provide precise per-pixel range data, essentially measuring the distance between a point and the surrounding objects in space, in real-time. This way such systems can track gestures which can be used to manipulate computer-generated objects; for instance when projected on tabletops.[44] Other systems like *HoloDesk* employ depth-cameras along with see-through HMDs to allow direct, dexterous freeform interactions with synthetic objects.[45]

One fundamental element of our real-world interaction is the presence of other people. It is important for a new synthetic environment to accommodate the presence of other users, allowing us to interact and if possible – in essence to the MR/AR intent – augment any interaction and enhance the opportunities for collaboration. The *Studierstube*[46] framework was developed towards that goal, allowing multiple users to view a synthetic world from individual viewpoints – thus providing the sense of co-presence and enabling users to interact in the synthetic space. Other collaborative AR systems include *MapLens,*[47] an application enhancing paper-based city maps and *Raptor*, a prototyping tool for creating collaborative AR games.[48] The notion of collaboration and the multi-user nature that MR/AR entails are also discussed earlier in this article.

PERSONAL SPACE –
WEARABLE COMPUTING & MIXED REALITY

One aspect of AR/MR research that always intrigued researchers is mobility. Some of the early efforts to implement mobile AR systems, were wearable (body-worn) computers using hardware borrowed from VR, like HMDs, Datagloves and miniaturized processing units, often encountered in industrial engineering and embedded systems. Although early efforts were built around laptops (see Figure 4) developments in miniaturization has allowed researchers to construct lighter and less cumbersome wearable apparatuses that would be powerful enough to render the graphics required for AR systems. An array of modalities was used for location and orientation awareness, like gyroscopes, accelerometers, GPS etc.

---

43 http://www.primesense.com/

44 Benko, H., Jota, R., and Wilson, A. (2012)

45 Hilliges, O. et al. (2012)

46 Schmalstieg, D. et al. (2002)

47 Morrison, A. et al. (2011)

48 Wolfe, C. et al. (2010)

As defined by Steve Mann, a pioneer of the field, wearable computing is *"the study or practice of inventing, designing, building or using miniature, body-worn computational and sensory devices. Wearable computers may be worn under, over, or in clothing, or may also be themselves clothes."*[49] Ideally, wearable computers are: a) portable and controllable while operational, b) not physically tethered and allow hands-free use, thus unrestrictive yet controllable, c) attentive to the environment through context awareness sensors, d) smart enough to not monopolize the wearer's attention when needed, e) always constantly on, f) can be used to communicate with others and g) are inextricably intertwined with their user.[50] The ultimate goal of wearable computers is personal empowerment, i.e. the ability to provide to the user a personalized and owned information space, operated and controlled by the user, constantly. Going beyond desktop computers, who empower the user in a specific location, or portable computers, who provide some increase in personal empowerment yet are mere desktop clones, wearables augment the human body's sensory and cognitive abilities. Consequently, wearable computers allow a unique perspective in our perception of informational space by assisting both in external stimuli reception as well as in the cognitive analysis of said stimuli, through its enrichment and correlation with context specific information.

Due to these characteristics, wearable computing has been instrumental in AR research progress. A number of prototypes have appeared since almost 15 years ago with notable examples the *Touring Machine* from Columbia University[51] (see Figure 4a) and the *Tin Lizzy* systems from MIT[52] used in the *Remembrance Agent.*[53] The Touring Machine was one of the pioneering wearable AR systems, presenting in-situ campus information, employing a 3D graphics accelerated computer backpack, a see-through HMD with gaze orientation tracker, GPS system, wireless connectivity and a stylus-operated tablet input interface. The Remembrance Agent was a plug-in for the Emacs text editor that provided textual information on what the user was reading or writing, i.e. a tool for associative memory.

Other wearable AR systems included the Tinmith series of systems from University of South Australia[54] (Figure 4b) and Romulus from the University of

---

49 Mann, S. (2013)

50 Mann, S. (1998)

51 Feiner, S. et al. (1997)

52 Starner, T., Mann, S., and Rhodes, B. (1997)

53 Rhodes, B., and Starner, T. (1996)

54 Thomas, B. et al. (1998)

Essex, UK[55] (see Figure 4c). The Tinmith systems evolved from 1998 throughout to 2006 and used similar configurations for the wearable unit but most notably a vision-tracked, glove-type input interface and dedicated software for in-situ 3D modelling. Romulus was built using small-factor, low-power consumer electronics boards, GPS and see-through HMD with orientation tracker and presented an AR view of a 3D architectural reconstruction of an archaeological temple, in situ.

| (a) | (b) | (c) |

Figure 4. Examples of wearable computers used in AR projects and demonstrations: a) the Touring Machine,[56] b) Tinmith Metro variants,[57] c) Romulus Wearable[58]

MR IN THE ERA OF SMARTPHONES AND UBIQUITOUS CONNECTIVITY

Despite the fact that wearable computers have been the focus of mobile AR research for quite a few years the emergence of smartphones and tablets has given researchers the opportunity to work on a more socially acceptable platform. Smartphones encompass most of the sensory modalities used in wearables (GPS, magnetic compasses etc.) and are increasingly more powerful in terms of processing power. More importantly, consumer electronics evolved towards a different direction than what was foreseen two decades ago. Instead of HMDs,

---

55 Ritsos, P. D. (2006)

56 Copyright 1997, S. Feiner, B., MacIntyre, T., Hollerer, and Webster, A., Columbia University (image courtesy of S. Feiner).

57 Copyright 1999-2006, W. Piekarski, University of South Australia (images courtesy of W. Piekarsky).

58 Copyright 2004-2006, P. Ritsos, University of Essex. Image courtesy of the author.

datagloves and millions of computers embedded in our surroundings, most of the processing power now resides in smartphones and its connection to the cloud, where data can now be stored and fetched from at will. As argued by Barba et al.[59] this deviation from original predictions can be attributed to the inflated expectations, even nowadays, of what past and current 3D immersive technology can offer, as well as the simple fact that the latter may not fit our current way of living. Arguably, popularity of smartphones and cloud-based services can be attributed to the user's needs and expectations as much as on technological progress.

Smartphones and tablets have attracted the attention of MR/AR researchers long before becoming popular as a consumer device. In 2003 Wanger and Smalstieg[60] presented the first stand-alone AR system on a personal digital assistant, using a ported version of *ARToolkit*. The latter evolved to *ARToolkitPlus,*[61] which was used in other efforts and, subsequently, ported in other mobile OSs like Symbian.[62] A year later Möhring, et al.[63] presented the first see-through AR system on a consumer mobile phone with optical tracking of markers. In more recent efforts Chun and Höllerer[64] used the *ARToolkitPlus* to add gesture input to a mobile AR application in real time, whereas MacIntryre et al. presented a standards-based AR browser for mobiles, named *Argon.*[65] The third generation of the aforementioned *Studierstube* framework was also developed for mobile phones.[66] On the contrary, MR-flavored efforts focused less on vision, both for input and output. Some examples include the *Can You See Me Now?,*[67] *PAC-Lan*[68] and *Capture the flag*[69] games (discussed earlier).

Smartphone technology eventually became mature enough that many commercial MR/AR applications started to emerge and gain popularity. Prominent examples include the popular AR browsers from Layar[70] and Wikitude,[71]

---

59 Barba, E., MacIntyre, B., and Mynatt, E.D. (2012)

60 Wagner, D., and Schmalstieg, D. (2003)

61 Wagner, D., and Schmalstieg, D. (2007)

62 Henrysson, A., Billinghurst, M., and Ollila, M. (2005)

63 Mohring, M., Lessig, C., and Bimber, O. (2004)

64 Chun, W. H., and Höllerer, T. (2013)

65 MacIntyre, B. et al. (2011)

66 Wagner, D., and Schmalstieg, D. (2009)

67 Benford, S. et al. (2006)

68 Rashid, O. et al. (2006)

69 Cheok, A. D. et al. (2006)

70 https://www.layar.com/

the Metaio[72] eco-system of AR tools and the Junaio AR browser. Arguably, any application that uses the GPS and compass modalities to present location-specific graphical or textual information could be treated as belonging in the MR spectrum. Ever since the beginning of this decade, the number of applications marketed under the AR – mainly – or MR concept has been increasing constantly, sometimes with debatable conformity to the scholarly definitions.

It is important to pause at this point and review the emergence progress of MR/AR. In the beginning we had definitions and systems putting emphasis on enhancing space visually, in order to create a new composite world. Hardware systems where mostly wearable apparatuses, borrowing interfaces from VR and integrating location and orientation awareness systems often resulted in heavy and cumbersome systems. However, at some point researchers began to focus on handheld devices, starting with PDAs and cell-phones and eventually smartphones, which encompassed most of the required modalities, modulo HMDs.

In addition, modern smartphones, coupled with cloud-based services form a very unique ecosystem, with enormous technical and social implications. A smartphone, on top of calling and texting, allows its owners to access their e-mail, surf the web, listen to music, connect and update their social networks, play games, access their bank account and make payments 'on-the-go'. Functionality that a couple that a decade ago would, in the best-case scenario, required a small laptop can now fit in the palm of our hand and can remain always connected and powered-on for days. In addition, the development of applications designed for smartphones nowadays form a large portion of the industry, whereas the appearance of flagship smartphone models bedazzles the press and results in surges of purchasing frenzy from gadgetry enthusiasts. Even ownership of specific smartphones is perceived to define, to some extent, social stature much like an expensive cars or expensive clothing do.

Consequently, the notion of MR must be updated and readjusted to this technological and social paradigm shift. The author believes this is done in a most comprehensive way by Barba et al.[73] who take these considerations into account and propose a new approach in MR, adapting original definitions in the following way: *vision* becomes *perception*, *space* becomes *place* and *technologies* become *capabilities*. More specifically, despite the fact that MR/AR traditionally focus on *vision*, space *perception* with MR tools may involve all aspects

71 http://www.wikitude.com/

72 http://www.metaio.com/

73 Barba, E., MacIntyre, B., and Mynatt, E. D. (2012)

of human cognition, particularly in the smartphone ecosystem. For instance, using a smartphone MR application to find a close-by venue to listen to live music in a city[74] may be a combination of music interests, determining cost of a live gig, reading reviews for a particular venue, as well as proximity to one's location – i.e. making a selection based on information beyond what a mere, localized in space, graphical annotation on the user's view can provide. It is evident that the information presented needs to abide to the characteristics and idiosyncrasies of the composite space and provide *contextual* information. Moreover, it can be argued that other senses contribute to our perception of space. Localized stereo sound aids in the perception of space, orientation and the presence of others in space; a fact that gamers often use in multiplayer-games. Touch and gestures, as discussed, can also help in environment perception. Evidently, MR should offer a more holistic cognitive experience and engage all senses.

Accessing cloud services using smartphones and tablets is nowadays something common. Many of us read our emails on our handheld devices on the train to work, or store files in services like Dropbox or Google Drive, to share them with others. We are accustomed to accessing personal and meaningful information, anytime, anywhere. However, despite the fact that we do not need to be in a particular location to access all that information, we do expect the information to be present in that particular – though artificial and not physical – *place*. While in the past users had to be in front of their screen, something not necessary anymore, it is the information that needs to be available and contextualized, as aforementioned, in relation to our place and requirements.

Finally, even though MR/AR applications are a quite popular notion in the smartphone ecosystem, often with questionable efficiency, we have been fast approaching technical limitations, particularly in terms of accuracy of tracking and ease of interacting. There are countless MR/AR applications available that are variations of the same thing; tracking a marker and placing a 3D model on top. Current smartphone technology may be a step forward to the past but there is only so much to do with current technology, as registration is still a considerable challenge. It is therefore apparent that future generations of the smartphone ecosystem will need to encompass novel technologies, like sensor fusion and accurate camera-tracking, enhancing the *capabilities* of devices and applications.

---

74 An example of this is the *All About Music* layer for the Layar browser, created by the author and A. Gougoulis in 2011, showing music venues and studios in Athens, Greece.

MIXED REALITY AND GAMING

Another dimension of MR that is worthwhile of consideration is the concept of the alternate realities of pervasive games, such as massively multiplayer online role playing games (MMORPGs). These games take place in computer-generated worlds with multiple zones, much like real continents and countries, competing factions and social elements like trading, socializing, team-based questing etc. From a vision point of view such games, usually, belong in the 'virtual' end of the MR continuum as they appear discrete and without any element of real and virtual space synthesis.

However, going beyond vision, the characteristics that make such MMORPG games quite intriguing from an MR perspective is their collaborative and persistent nature. The element of collaboration occurs due to the existence of a large number of users working together for a common goal – usually in the form of an adventure or a battle. The multiplayer aspect enhances the sense of immersion of participants, as real users are much more lifelike in their behavior than any artificial intelligence (AI) of non-player characters (NPCs) in a stand-alone game. The persistence element, itself, exists due to the fact that game worlds are always available and continue to exist and evolve, even after a user logs off, due to the actions of other users.[75] In that regard, they are a reality, taking place in parallel with our real life.

Researchers like Taylor[76] and Lehdonvirta[77] argue that the dichotomous approach of "real world vs virtual world" is outdated as the participants themselves interact beyond the boundaries of the game itself. Often, players from the same team, called guilds or clans in game jargon,[78] hold real life meetings or participate in web forums and discussions, sometimes conversing about subjects unrelated to the game itself. In a similar manner, families and friends often participate in such virtual worlds with such relations having direct implication in the social behavior of the players in game.[79] Players often apply to join other guilds following a screening process, using parsed in-game logs that show their performance and in-game character CVs that show their experience in past content and previous guilds they have been in. In many respects this process resembles very much the job hunt of real life.

---

75 Yee, N. (2006)

76 Taylor, T. (2006)

77 Lehdonvirta, V. (2010)

78 Ang, C. S., Zaphiris, P., and Mahmood, S. (2007)

79 Williams, D. et al. (2006)

Another aspect of MMORPGs that enhances the feeling of a life-like parallel world is the in-game economy and the trading that supports it is. For instance, in *World of Warcraft*, by Blizzard Entertainment, players use an in-game auction house and virtual money to sell and buy in-game items – gear, weapons, materials etc. – that support aspects of the game play, i.e. questing or crafting. This trading takes place in real time and auctioned items can be managed either in-game or by means of a smartphone application. Websites that aggregate information on running and historical prices or currently traded items are also being used to monitor trading in real-time, while offline from the game. Consequently, many gamers think of auctioned items in similar terms as they do real, physical objects posted, say, on Ebay or indeed their financial portfolio. In some MMORPGs, like the aforementioned *World of Warcraft* or *Star Wars: The Old Republic* from BioWare, players can purchase in-game items for real money. Real-life items like game deck cards are often associated with in-game rewards that in some cases are traded or sold for virtual money.

Consequently, the notion of space associated with a virtual world becomes an extension of one's physical space, not so much as a specific locale but an environment associated with memories, events, friendship, aspirations and disappointments. Players perceive this parallel world as part of their real lives, where they socialize, compete, make friendships, trade goods and face common, albeit virtual, dangers. Even when not immersed in that computer-generated space, they are aware it evolves, of the existence of other players, of events that take place in it. This synthesis of real and virtual life and space can be treated as a different flavor of mixed reality. A mixed reality where the synthesis is conceptual, event-based yet not, strictly, visual.

The synergy of MR and gaming has been researched, mostly through the use of smartphones. Most of the efforts concentrate on the networking, context awareness, and collaboration and interaction aspects. Examples include *Can you see me now?*,[80] a game where players in a virtual model of a city are being chased by real runners in the actual city, *Pirates*,[81] a naval board game mapping physical locations to in-game ones and *Capture-the-Flag*[82] implementing a typical flag capture game in MR. Beyond smartphones, wearable computers have been used to explore gaming in the AR paradigm, in efforts such as ARQuake,[83]

---

80 Benford, S. et al. (2006)

81 Björk, S. et al. (2001)

82 Cheok, A. D. et al. (2006)

83 Piekarky,W., and Thomas, B. H. (2000)

a single-player AR port of Quake and the multiplayer, Mindwarping[84] and Human Pacman.[85] Obviously, wearable AR research predates efforts using smartphones, as wearable computers where the first platform to have the graphics power required for the vision-based AR. On the contrary, MR efforts using smartphones treat the vision aspect in somewhat a secondary level, using 2D representations or simple 3D. However, most efforts do exploit the camera for computer vision and GPS/accelerometer modalities for location awareness.

Most research efforts of MR-games are nonetheless deployed in a fairly small scale and do not truly investigate the implications of having a massive user pool. However, a recent effort that does is *Ingress*, an MMO playable in MR, developed by Google's Niantic Labs.[86] Ingress, officially launched on November 16, 2012, operational only on Android devices and in August 2013 was reported to have 500,000 players globally,[87] in closed beta. The game is essentially a sci-fi battle for resources where two factions try to locate and claim ownership of virtual portals to another dimension. Such portals are usually created on top of real landmarks or monuments, creating a web of points of interest, superimposed on the real world and viewable through an Android smartphone. Controlling such portals requires for the players to be physically present in close proximity to the landmark and use their – GPS-equipped and wirelessly tethered – mobile phone to attack the virtual defenses on the opposing faction.

Games like Ingress push the envelope, when it comes to mixing real and computer generated objects within the persistent nature of more traditional MMOs, resulting in a more holistic flavor of MR. Players can now literally see another dimension in the form of a synthetic layer, covering their surroundings. In that respect the player's perception of space changes, as a beautiful historical landmark in the center of the city is also a powerful portal, attacked by the opposing faction. Moreover, switching off the phone does not destroy completely the sense of immersion. As the user walks away from the landmark he is fully aware that his opponents, possibly standing nearby in the real world, may contest that portal, in the parallel world.

Ingress is also the setting of one of the most intriguing examples of the crossover between real and mixed realities. That is the in-game ceasefire between factions, following the death of Sean Collier after the Boston Bombing in

84 Starner, T. et al. (2000)

85 Cheok, A. D. et al. (2004)

86 Hodson, H. (2012)

87 Dalenberg, A. (2013)

2013, and the creation of an in-game memorial.[88] A tragic real-life event, very much associated with a particular location and space, has been the seed for an in-game, virtual event with strong symbolism. As is reported by Scott the whole idea was quite controversial as some players, in favor of this action, felt it is an important symbolism, whereas others, wanting the game-world to be a mere break from real life, opposed. Perhaps, the attitudes of the players are more important themselves than the in-game event – the mosaic of behaviors and feelings that may exist in game can indeed be comparable to complexity and variety as real life. For some a virtual space is an extension of their real world. For others it is a way to escape.

CONCLUSION

The field of Human Computer Interaction has changed significantly over the last couple of decades. In particular, the paradigm of Mixed Reality, explicitly defined in the '90s, has promised a novel way of perceiving space, merging real with computer-generated objects and information in a seamlessly aligned way. Different variations of the same notion can be found in Augmented Reality and Augmented Virtuality, with different proportions of real and synthetic information.

Almost two decades of research have resulted in a vast array of systems and applications, ranging from mobile, wearable systems for architectural reconstruction, to static medical AR for simulation and training. MR has eventually found its way in the smartphone ecosystem, one of the most popular processing platforms nowadays, with varying levels of success in terms of adoption and popularity. Yet the challenges of registration in space, realistic graphical representation and visual integration, natural interaction and content provisioning in context-dependent and meaningful ways are ever-present, irrespectively of the underlying platform. Although MR and more specifically AR have been very popular in the media, most current implementations do not push the envelope with regard to those challenges. We are still years away from delivering the seamless and consistent integration of real and computer-generated space that were originally envisioned.

Nonetheless, there is great expectation that MR will eventually become a mainstream consumer technology and it will change, fundamentally, the way we interact with our surroundings. After all MR and related technologies are much

---

88 Kirsner, S. (Wolfe 2010) (2013)

more accessible now. We are immersed in networked communities – social networks, online gaming – much more than in the past. We are accustomed to accessing contextualized information from almost anywhere. Graphics become more and more realistic, even on handheld devices. Processing power increases while device size and power consumption reduces.

It is an exciting time for anyone involved in MR research and development – researchers, programmers, interface designers, entrepreneurs. As technology becomes more and more ingrained in our everyday life, our perception of, and interaction with, our surroundings will change. Whether we embed computers in our environment, wear them on our bodies, or both, we are gradually being immersed in a space where information surrounds us. What has and will continue to change is how we interact with it, gradually employing all our senses, towards the point where real and computer generated will seamlessly merge to a new, synthetic, yet very much existing, reality.

REFERENCES

Ang, Chee Siang, Zaphiris, Panayiotis, and Mahmood, Shumaila (2007): "A model of cognitive loads in massively multiplayer online role playing games." *Interacting with Computers* 19, no. 2: 167-179

Azuma, Ronald T. (1997): "A Survey of Augmented Reality." *Presence: Teleoperators and Virtual Environments* 6, no. 4: 355-385

Azuma, Ronald T., and Bishop, Gary (1994): "Improving static and dynamic registration in an optical see-through HMD." *Proceedings of the 21st annual conference on Computer graphics and interactive techniques - SIGGRAPH '94.* ACM: 197-204

Barba, Evan, and MacIntyre, Blair (2011): "A scale model of mixed reality." *In Proceedings of the 8th ACM conference on Creativity and cognition (C&C '11).* New York, USA: ACM: 117-126.

Barba, Evan, MacIntyre, Blair, and Mynatt, Elizabeth D. (2012): "Here We Are! Where Are We? Locating Mixed Reality in The Age of the Smartphone." *In Proceedings of the IEEE* (IEEE) 100: 929-936

Bau, Olivier, and Poupyrev, Ivan (2012): "REVEL: tactile feedback technology for augmented reality." *ACM Transactions on Graphics (TOG) - SIGGRAPH 2012 Conference* (ACM) 31, no. 4: 89-100

Benford, Steve, et al. (2006): "Can you see me now?" *Transactions in Computer Humans Interaction* (ACM) 13, no. 1: 100-133

Benko, Hrvoije, Jota, Ricardo, and Wilson, Andrew (2012) "Miragetable: freehand interaction on a projected augmented reality tabletop." *In Proceedings of the SIGCHI conference on human factors in computing systems.* ACM: 199-208

Billinghurst, Mark, and Kato, Hirokazu (1999): "Collaborative mixed reality." *In Proceedings of International Symposium on Mixed Reality.* Yokohama, Japan. 261-284

Björk, Staffan, Falk, Jennica, Hansson, Rebecca, and Ljungstrand, Peter (2001): "Pirates! Using the Physical World as a Game Board." *Human-Computer Interaction - INTERACT '01* (IOS Press): 423-430

Caudell, Thomas P, and Mizell, David W. (1992): "Augmented Reality: An Application of Heads-Up Display Technology to Manual Manufacturing Processes." *Proceedings of the Twenty-Fifth Hawaii International Conference on System Sciences,.* IEEE: 659-669

Cheok, Adrian David, Sreekumar, Anuroop, Lei, Cao, and Thang, Le Nam (2006): "Capture the flag: mixed-reality social gaming with smart phones." *Pervasive Computing* (IEEE) 5, no. 2: 62-69

Cheok, Adrian David, et al. (2004): "Human Pacman: a mobile, wide-area entertainment system based on physical, social, and ubiquitous computing." *Personal and Ubiquitous Computing* 8, no. 2: 71-81

Chun, Wendy H., and Höllerer, Tobias (2013): "Real-time hand interaction for augmented reality on mobile phones." *In Proceedings of the 2013 international conference on Intelligent user interfaces.* ACM: 307-314

Coles, Timothy R., Meglan, Dwight, and John, Nigel W. (2011): "The Role of Haptics in Medical Training Simulators A Survey of the State of the Art." *Transactions on Haptics* (IEEE) 4, no. 1: 51-66

Coles, Timothy R., John, Nigel W., Gould, Derek A., and Caldwell, Darwin G. (2011) "Integrating Haptics with Augmented Reality in a Femoral Palpation and Needle Insertion Training Simulation." *IEEE Transactions on Haptics* (IEEE) 4, no. 3: 199-209

Comport, Andrew I, Marchand, Eric, and Chaumette, Francois (2003): "A real-time tracker for markerless augmented reality." *International Symposium on Mixed and Augmented Reality, ISMAR'03 (2003).* IEEE: 36-45.

Dalenberg, Alex (2013): *Ingress, Google's underground game, is being played all around you.* 24 May 2013. http://upstart.bizjournals.com/news/technology/2013/05/24/ingress-the-game-taking-over-the-world.html?page=all (accessed August 16, 2013).

Davison, Andrew J., Reid, Ian D., Molton, Nicholas D., and Stasse, Oliver (2007): "MonoSLAM: Real-Time Single Camera SLAM," *IEEE*

Transactions on Pattern Analysis and Machine Intelligence 29, no. 6: 1052-1067

Englebart, Douglas C. (1962): "Augmenting human intellect: a conceptual framework." *PACKER, Randall and JORDAN, Ken. Multimedia. From Wagner to Virtual Reality. New York: WW Norton & Company*: 64-90

Feiner, Steven, MacIntyre, Blair, Hollerer, Tobias, and Webster, Anthony (1997): "A touring machine: Prototyping 3D mobile augmented reality systems for exploring the urban environment." *1st International Symposium on Wearable Computers*: 74-81

Flintham, Martin, et al. (2003): "Where on-line meets on the streets: experiences with mobile mixed reality games." *In Proceedings of the SIGCHI Conference on Human Factors in Computing Systems (CHI '03)*. New York, USA: ACM: 569-576

Gregory, R. L. "Seeing in depth." *Nature* 207, no. 4992 (1965): 116-117

Henrysson, Anders, Billinghurst, Mark, and Ollila, Mark (2005): "Face to face collaborative AR on mobile phones." *In Proceedings of the 4th IEEE and ACM International Symposium on Mixed and Augmented Reality*. IEEE: 80-89

Hilliges, Otmar, Kim, David, Izadi, Shahram, Weiss, Malte, and Wilson, Andrew (2012): "HoloDesk: direct 3d interactions with a situated see-through display." *In Proceedings of the 2012 ACM annual conference on Human Factors in Computing Systems*. ACM: 2421-2430

Hodson, Hal (2012): "Google's Ingress game is a gold mine for augmented reality." *New Scientist* 216, no. 2893: 19

Ishii, Hiroshi, and Ullmer, Brygg (1997): "Tangible bits: towards seamless interfaces between people, bits and atoms." *In Proceedings of the ACM SIGCHI Conference on Human factors in computing systems (CHI '97)*. ACM: 234-241

Kato, Hirokazu, and Billinghurst, Mark (1999): "Marker tracking and HMD calibration for a video-based augmented reality conferencing system." *In Proceedings of 2nd IEEE and ACM International Workshop on Augmented Reality, 1999. (IWAR '99)*. San Francisco: IEEE: 85-94

Kato, Hirokazu, Billinghurst, Mark, Poupyrev, Ivan, Imamoto, Kenji, and Tachibana, Keihachiro (2000): "Virtual object manipulation on a table-top AR environment." *In Proceedings of the IEEE and ACM International Symposium on Augmented Reality (ISAR)*. IEEE: 111-119

Krueger, Myron W. (1993): "Environmental technology: making the real world virtual." (ACM) 36, no. 7: 36-37

Kruijff, Ernst, Swan, J. E., and Feiner, Steven (2010): "Perceptual issues in augmented reality revisited." *9th IEEE International Symposium on Mixed and Augmented Reality (ISMAR)*, IEEE: 3-12

Lang, Tobias, MacIntyre, Blair, and Zugazza, Iker Jamardo (2008): "Massively Multiplayer Online Worlds as a Platform for Augmented Reality Experiences." *In Proceedings of Virtual Reality Conference, VR '08*. IEEE: 67-70

Lehdonvirta, Vili (2010): "Virtual Worlds Don't Exist: Questioning the Dichotomous Approach in MMO Studies." *Game Studies* 10, no. 1

Livingston, Mark A., and Ai, Zhuming (2008): "The effect of registration error on tracking distant augmented objects." *In Proceedings of the 7th IEEE/ACM International Symposium on Mixed and Augmented Reality*. IEEE: 77-86

MacIntyre, Blair, Hill, Alex, Rouzati, Hafez, Gandy, Maribeth, and Davidson, Braian 0. (2011): "The Argon AR Web Browser and standards-based AR application environment." *In Proceedings of the 10th IEEE International Symposium on Mixed and Augmented Reality (ISMAR), 2011*. IEEE, 2011: 65-74

Mackay, Wendy (1998): "Augmented Reality: Linking real and virtual worlds: A new paradimg for interacting with computers." ACM: 13-21

Mann, Steve (2013): "Wearable Computing." *The Encyclopedia of Human-Computer Interaction, 2nd Ed.. Aarhus, Denmark: The Interaction Design Foundation*. Edited by M. Soegaard and R. F. Dam, http://www.interaction-design.org/encyclopedia/wearable_computing.html

Mann, Steve (1998): "Wearable computing as means for personal empowerment." *Proceedings of the First International Conference on Wearable Computing (ICWC)*. IEEE Computer Society Press, Keynote

Milgram, Paul, and Kishino, Fumio (1994): "A taxonomy of mixed reality visual displays." *IECE Transactions on Information and Systems* 77, no. 12: 1321-1329

Mohring, Mathias, Lessig, Christian, and Bimber, Oliver (2004): "Video see-through AR on consumer cell-phones." *Mixed and Augmented Reality, 2004. ISMAR 2004. Third IEEE and ACM International Symposium on*. ACM: 252-253

Morrison, Ann et al. (2011) "Collaborative use of mobile augmented reality with paper maps." *Computers & Graphics* 35, no. 4: 789-799

Neubert, Jeremiah, Pretlove, John, and Drummond, Tom (2007): "Semi-Autonomous Generation of Appearance-based Edge Models from Image Sequences." *6th IEEE and ACM International Symposium on Mixed and Augmented Reality, ISMAR 2007*. IEEE: 79-89

Panëels, Sabrina A., Ritsos, Panagiotis D., Rodgers, Peter J., and Roberts, Jonathan C. (2013): "Prototyping 3D haptic data visualizations." *Computers & Graphics* 37, no. 3: 179-192

Parviz, Babak A. (2009): "Augmented reality in a contact lens." *IEEE Spectrum* (IEEE) 9 : 1-4

Piekarky, Wayne, and Thomas, Bruce (2000): "ARQuake: the outdoor augmented reality first person application." *In Proceedings of Wearable Computers, The Fourth International Symposium on.* IEEE: 139-146

Rashid, Omer, Bamford, Will, Coulton, Paul, Edwards, Reuben, and Scheible, Jurgen (2006): "PAC-LAN: mixed-reality gaming with RFID-enabled mobile phones." *Computers in Entertainment (CIE)* 4, no. 4: 4

Rhodes, Bradley, and Starner, Thad (1996): "Remembrance agent: A con-tiniously running automated information retreival system." *The Proceedings of The First International Conference on The Practical Application Of Intelligent Agents and Multi Agent Technology:* 487-495

Ritsos, Panagiotis D. (2006): *Architectures for Untethered Augmented Reality Using Wearable Computers.* Colchester: University of Essex.

Ritsos, Panagiotis D., Johnston, David J., Clark, Christine, and Clark, Adrian F. (2003): "Engineering an augmented reality tour guide." *Eurowearable, 2003. IEE.* IEE: 119-124

Ritsos, Panagiotis D., Gittins, Robert, Braun, Sabine, Slater, Catherine, and Roberts, Jonathan C. (2013): "Training Interpreters Using Virtual Worlds." *LNCS Transactions on Computational Science XVIII* (Springer) 7848: 21-40

Schmalstieg, Dieter, and Wagner, Daniel (2007): "Experiences with Handheld Augmented Reality." *6th IEEE and ACM International Symposium on Mixed and Augmented Reality, ISMAR'07.* IEEE: 3-18

Schmalstieg, Dieter, et al. (2002) "The Studierstube Augmented Reality Project." *Presence: Teleoperators and Virtual Environments* 11, no. 1: 33-54

Scott, Kirsner (2013): "In Google's Ingress augmented reality game, a ceasefire at MIT and a memorial to slain officer Sean Collier." *Boston.com.* 24 April 2013. http://www.boston.com/business/technology/innoeco/2013/04/in_goog les_ingress_augmented_r.html

Srinivasan, Mandayam A., and Basdogan, Cagatay (1997): "Haptics in virtual environments: Taxonomy, research status, and challenges." *Computers & Graphics* (Elsevier) 21, no. 4: 393-404

Starner, Thad, Leibe, Bastian, Singletary, Brad, and Pair, Jarrell (2000): "MIND-WARPING: towards creating a compelling collaborative augmented reality game." *In Proceedings of the 5th international conference on Intelligent user interfaces (IUI '00).* ACM: 256-259

Starner, Thad, Mann, Steve, and Rhodes, Bradley (1997): *The MIT wearable computing web page,* http://www.media.mit.edu/wearables/lizzy/lizzy/

Steuer, Jonathan (1992): "Defining Virtual Reality: Dimensions Determining Telepresence." *Journal of Communication* (Blackwell Publishing Ltd) 42, no. 4: 73-93

Sutherland, Ivan E. (1968): "A head-mounted three dimensional display." *In Proceedings of the Joint Computer Conference - Part I.* ACM: 757-764

Taylor, Tina L. (2006): *Play between worlds: Exploring online game culture.* Cambridge, MA: MIT Press

Thomas, Bruce, Demczuk, Victor, Piekarski, Wayne, Hepworth, David, and Gunther, Bernard (1998): "A wearable computer system with augmented reality to support terrestrial navigation," *2nd International Symposium on Wearable Computers.* IEEE: 168-171

Vinge, Vernon (2004): "Synthetic Serendipity." *IEEE Spectrum* 41, no. 7: 35

Vinge, Vernor (2006): *Rainbows End.* Tor Books

Wagner, Daniel, and Schmalstieg, Dieter (2007): "ARToolKitPlus for Pose Tracking on Mobile Devices." *In Proceedings of 12th Computer Vision Winter Workshop (CVWW'07)*: 139-146

Wagner, Daniel, and Schmalstieg, Dieter (2003): "First steps towards handheld augmented reality." *In proceedings of the 7th IEEE International Symposium on Wearable Computers:* 127-135

Wagner, Daniel, and Schmalstieg, Dieter (2009): "Making Augmented Reality Practical on Mobile Phones, Part 1." *IEEE Computer Graphics and Applications*: 12-15

Weiser, Mark (1991): "The computer for the 21st century." *Scientific American* 265, no. 3: 94-104

Williams, Dimitri, Duchenaut, Nicolas, Xiong, Li, Zhang, Yuanyuan, Yee, Nick, and Nickel, Eric (2006): "From Tree House to Barracks; The Social Life of Guilds in World of Warcraft." *Games and Culture* (Sage Publications) 1: 338-361

Wolfe, Christopher, Smith, J. David, Phillips, W. Greg, and Graham, T.C. Nicholas (2010): "Fiia: A model-based approach to engineering collaborative augmented reality." In *In The Engineering of Mixed Reality Systems*, 293-312. London: Springer

Yee, Nick (2006): "The Demographics, Motivations and Derived Experiences of Users of Massively-Multiuser Online Graphical Environments." *PRESENCE: Teleoperators and Virtual Environments* 15: 309-329

You, Suya, Neumann, Ulich, and Azuma, Ronald T. (1999): "Hybrid inertial and vision tracking for augmented reality registration." *Proceedings of IEEE Virtual Reality, 1999*. IEEE: 260-267

Zhou, Feng, Duh, Henry Been-Lim, and Billinghurst, Mark (2008): "Trends in augmented reality tracking, interaction and display: A review of ten years of ISMAR." *7th IEEE/ACM International Symposium on Mixed and Augmented Reality, ISMAR 2008*. IEEE: 193-202

Using Spatial Cognition to Improve Knowledge Construction

CARL SMITH AND PIERRE-FRANÇOIS GERARD

Our current methods for storing and organizing information for knowledge formation are inefficient. We have terabytes of information stored in 'files' but the accessibility to this information is diminishing with the addition of each new file. In parallel, the widespread use of video games, mobile devices and location-based media is rapidly immersing us in a hybrid reality which is expanding the practice of spatial cognition within these virtual and physical architectural environments. The hypothesis is that we can overcome our apparent cognitive limits by combining ancient pedagogies, modern technologies and architectural codes to support the new learning needs that appear as a consequence and response to our immersion within these hybrid environments.

INTRODUCTION

Beyond the function of the organization of things, architecture has always played an important role by its way of influencing our relation to the environment. It has established a whole sign system symbolizing social, religious and cultural relationships of a given era, allowing us to orientate ourselves within the context of a life in perpetual movement. At a time when almost 90% of human populations live in towns, architecture plays a massive role within this "spatio-cognitive" system of visualization that we argue can be enhanced by ICT developments that are leading to a hybrid reality. Our definition of hybrid reality being one in which the virtual and physical dimensions of reality are increasingly merging and taking form as smart cities, augmented realities, virtual realities, amongst other types.

The main focus of this chapter is to understand how architecture can adapt to the demands of this hybrid reality and continue to be a means of producing this spatio-cognitive enhancement, in short, to act as a tool to organize and engineer knowledge. The research questions we address relate to how we can use our experience with the spatial environment from the point of view of architecture to construct a metaphoric system for learning in hybrid environments.

Cognitive science cannot give us a full theoretical framework about what can be deduced from spatial cognition in hybrid environments until it takes into consideration the missing part, that is to say, the new forms of human-computer interaction in hybrid spaces in which we are immersed. In this sense, there is a need to develop a theoretical-practical framework for a more inclusive science of spatial cognition that can be useful not only for abstract thought but also for the inscription of the virtual in the physical environment that constitutes our hybrid condition.

The use of physical or virtual architectural structures for cognitive enhancement has been practiced for centuries. One example is the ancient art of the 'method of loci'[1] that can give us some hints on the potential of interlacing ICT, physical environments and architectural codes to offer possible frameworks for making sense of hybrid environments. Firstly, we will investigate these previous architectural methods and codes to uncover what makes architecture meaningful. Secondly, we will attempt to extract some architectural codes that can be used with the application of new ICT technologies. Finally, as the process of knowledge construction is limited by today's user interface designs, information displays and content design, we will go through a few practical case-studies to show how this is being improved with an increasing focus on hybrid reality.

THE CONCEPT OF SPACE IN ARCHITECTURE

Our goal here is neither to build an architectural theory, as many authors have tried without successfully finding a unified one, nor to reduce architecture to mere spatial experimentation. We will instead attempt to unveil the codes that are specific to architectural space, as well as the methods used by architects to

---

1   Loci, from Latin, is place or location. The Method of Loci is also known as memory palace. It is a method of memory based on visualization to improve memory, organize and retrieve information.

design meaningful spaces. From there we will have a better idea on how to use architecture to enhance knowledge construction via hybrid environments.

In Western culture, we had to wait until the emergence of Einstein's theory of relativity, in order to scientifically reach the conclusion that *"Time and space are inextricably connected through the speed of light within a quadric-dimensional space-time (Plank). Space is generally considered as infinite."* This definition lacks clarity from an architectural point of view because it refers to a dimension of reality beyond our tridimensional experience of reality to which Newtonian laws apply. Let's grasp this from a more philosophical point of view. The encyclopedia reminds us that, *"to Democritus, space is an empty receptacle; to Aristotle, it is the boundary surrounding total beings; to Leibniz, space is not something that exists of its own, but rather a representation of the order reigning amongst co-existing units."*[2] E. Kant leads us to the next important step, since to him space and time are a priori conditions of perception, given before we can even experiment with them. Thus, he defines space as a *"system of laws governing the juxtaposition of things related to figures, sizes and distances, allowing us to perceive them."* By studying the above definitions, we understand that it is a person (Aristotle's "total being," Leibniz's "units," while Kant speaks of perceptions) who perceives space and represents it through different elements ("figures, sizes and distances").

Different fields of study give us different definitions for space. Euclidian geometry describes a very different space than non-Euclidian geometry does. Indeed, a curved space is very much different than an n-dimensional space. Topology is another very interesting way of describing our environment. Therefore, this very much polysemic concept of space can be used to describe a variety of concepts. Each field of research, each art, each culture, each individual determines his own space. The perception of space is a function of the human body. Space is the result of the representation that an individual or a group of individuals have created. As the concept of space is tied to conventions and codes that allow a group of people – who possess the decoding key – to inhabit the same shared space, our goal is to unveil these codes.

Now that we have attempted to approach the concept of space we will concentrate on exploring architectural space, its perceptual properties and its meaningful codes. In order to comprehend architecture's impact on knowledge construction, we must first understand how we perceive architecture.

As a starting point we will use the comparison suggested by Jean Piaget, between the ontogenesis of logical structures in children and the genesis of

---

2   Encyclopaedia Universalis

mathematical concepts. Following those observations we will define the processes by which we create representations of our environment from an early age. Through this evolution appeared five fractal stages that help us to comprehend our surroundings. We will use this fractal approach – each stage of resolution includes the previous ones, the part is contained within the whole and the whole within the part. The five stages include: from form to object, internal space and perceptions, organization of spaces, external space and urban space.

The concept of space is not innate. To tackle the idea of space, we must first incorporate the *concept of form*. This concept requires the range of understanding of a variety of characteristics. During this learning process, we are going through different stages, each depending on the level of structure of the perceived form. Indeed, Jean Piaget,[3] who initiated the study of the ontogenesis of logical structures in children, observed that, since our infancy, we learn to distinguish between forms according to three types of thresholds that we incorporate one after the other, in the following order: typological, geometric and finally metric structures.[4]

The evolution of those thresholds depends primarily on our senses and on our proprioceptive system (movement), without which we would not be able to have all the experiences that make us comprehend the world. Furthermore, it is through analogies and comparisons that we enrich our mental library of information, which in return allows us to gradually grasp the relations between the forms that surround us. Objects, as distinct entities, proceed from the relationships between these forms. Consequently, this first stage of learning formed through topology offers us an important key in order to perceive and comprehend space.

The perception of *internal space* constitutes a second-level of understanding when discovering our environment. Historically, it is only since the 19th century that the treatises on architecture start referring to "space" in a direct manner. August Schmarsow, historian, wrote, insisting on the priority of space in architecture: *"Man first perceives the space surrounding him, not the physical objects bearing symbolic meaning."*[5]

He insists on the fact that one positions himself primarily in relation to a context, an envelope or topological structure, before shifting his attention to the abstract meaning of the objects that this space might contain. Caution must be taken, so as not to confuse the symbolic meaning of objects (paintwork,

---

3   Piaget, J. (1926)

4   Raynaud, D. (1998)

5   Meiss, P. (1990)

sculpture...) with their formal structure. This remark is especially important today, in a time when we are surrounded with an overwhelming amount of information outside of any space of orientation. Also this topological approach acquires new practical applications with the use of modelling 3D software. This kind of software proposes, through the use of mathematical algorithms, an intuitive way of manipulating surfaces and volumes leading us to discover new worlds of shapes, like children do, according to the formal level of topological structures.

Back to our exploration of space, later on during the 20th century, Bruno Zevi,[6] an important architecture theoretician, defined architecture as "*the art of space.*" It is true that one of the first properties of architecture is "*to operate on space,*" but this doesn't mean that we should reduce architecture to a "*spatial experience.*" Besides the three dimensions forming the space of a building, there are a number of other elements that give a building its architectural character. In fact, humans conceive a global idea of space, in connection with the subjective filtering of their perceptions, experiences, language and culture. However, it is possible to isolate a certain number of perceptions from internal space. We can perceive elements, such as depth, density, degree of openness, shadow and light, as well as different types of dividers (floor, wall, ceiling), are an integral part of the architectural language.

There are two indexes of perception of depth: the effect of perspective, especially the *texture gradient* and the *superposition of foregrounds*. An object hiding another object is generally placed in front of the hidden one. Obviously, if foregrounds are placed in shorter distances or if we have a transparency effect, the effect of depth will be minimized.

According to its *density*, space will not have the same resonance. A space filled with mouldings and columns will have more human-scale connotations. A cavity, empty, sparse and undivided space will bring the universe into our minds in a greater degree.

Different devices have the potential of increasing or decreasing the degree of *openness*. By rendering it more implicit through the creation of openings or columns, the sensation of openness will be increased, the space will seem more extroverted. Furthermore, the evolution of industrial era materials has allowed the development of open spaces, especially with Mies van der Rohe's "free plan", to the point of raising it to one of the key points of modern architecture. It transformed the concept of inside – outside.

Architectural space exists, from a visual point of view, thanks to the

---

6   Zevi, B. (1959)

illumination of objects and surfaces. Architectural composition may be considered as *"the art of arranging and mixing in the correct proportions light sources within space."*[7]

If we go beyond geometrical spatial description, we will observe that the *floor*, the *walls* and the *ceiling* have each a meaning of their own. To begin with, they induce the two axes, the horizontal and the vertical, which do not possess the same force. "Ascending", "descending", "being high" are actions (see above figures) more meaningful than just looking to the left or to the right. To put it briefly, the floor has a pragmatic meaning, due to gravity. It supports life and objects. The walls, and every vertical structure, are there in order to carry the ceiling, as well as to guide our movements, to contain our activities, our objects and tools, to welcome us and to help us pass from one place to another. Their mouldings, their texture and their capacity to host messages play a primary role in determining a place's character and ambience. As for the ceiling, which, besides its protective role, acts as an antithesis to and an accomplice of the floor, it can take on more metaphysical meanings. Remote as it is, and very often untouchable, it is a favorite place for the expression of dreams, ideals and the sacred.

The third stage considers the *organization of spaces* according to their articulation and to their geometry. This fundamental organization of architecture has to be part of the design process from the early stage. It is when we start to move from one room to another, that the internal space start to get organized (*"Without internal space there is no architecture"*[8]), to articulate itself within our representations. Different activities take place in different spaces. Spatial juxtapositions and interpenetrations influence the type of spatial relations and their degree of autonomy. The general geometry of planes, sections and volumes allows us to understand how rooms are connected, how the building is functioning, hence how to navigate in it.

The fourth stage of resolution helps to comprehend the meanings behind architectural form. The *external form* of a building gives rise to and is generated by a certain symbolism. In order to better grasp the origin of architectural forms (the envelope), we studied two different approaches. The first one is "architecturology," presented by Philippe Boudon,[9] with a focus on the question of scale. The other one is the "anthropology of representations"[10] explained by

---

7   Meiss, P. (1990)

8   Zevi, B. (1959)

9   Boudon, Ph. (1992)

10 Raynaud, D. (1990)

Dominique Raynaud whose main focus is on myths and symbols. At the intersection of these two sciences of "architecturology" and "anthropology of representation," Raynaud suggests that symbolic and mythological factors are at the origin of architectural forms. In order to establish the relation between architectural form and the symbolic form, his research is based on the study of the semantic similarities (isomorphism) among these representations. These similarities would be possible through the use of "schemes," a concept borrowed from Kant, who defines it as the function or the association between two images, one of architectural form and the other of symbolical form. A modern analogy of this phenomenon is the mapping technique used to apply texture on 3d models in video games. He then seeks to mark out a certain number of conditions for isomorphism by insisting on the following essential fact: *"It is architecture that serves as a model for symbol."*[11] Indeed, if the vault represents, almost universally, the sky, one should keep in mind that the idea of a celestial "vault" originated from the architectural model and that this holds even for nations that are not familiar with its use. (Certain tribes designate the sky as the *"cosmic tent"*). In the previous analogy we would have a night sky photograph mapped on a curvy surface above our head. As Raynaud stipulates: *"Rationality is in the heart of imaginative processes."*[12]

One of the concepts developed by Raynaud is *"morphism."* The concept of morphism is borrowed from the mathematic field where it refers to the mapping of one preserve structure of a domain to another. Morphisms distribute symbolic images according to a typology consisting of six items: the cosmos, the plant world, the animal world, man, his technical environment and his abstract ideas. The architectural imaginary complies mainly with the category of *cosmomorphism* (sky and night, stars, sun, moon, air, fire and smoke, rainbow, mountain, river, waves), then comes anthropomorphism (phallus, vertebral column, skull, eye, vulva, heart, navel, uterus, skin, hair) and technomorphism (ladder, échelle, arrow and spear, wheel, door, pillar, sabre, tent, hut, helmet, basket). Other kinds of morphisms such as phytomorhism, zoomorphism or idiomorphism are much less represented categories. This cosmomorphism has been developed over thousands of years within the hermeticism tradition. During the Renaissance, Giordano Bruno, a fervent representant of this Western esoteric tradition, applied this knowledge into the Art of Memory[13] which we will discuss later in the article.

---

11 Raynaud, D. (1990)

12 Raynaud, D. (1990)

13 Yates, F. (1966)

The fifth stage proposes to contextualize all the previous stages across the *urban phenomenon*, the ultimate sharing space. Following our journey, we move outside the space of the building. Streets, squares, canals are those subtracted spaces that make the city. In order to orientate ourselves, we recall all we already know, within our memory, with the goal of comparing it to what we will discover. Hence, by way of analogy, we will manage new information according to our representation of the world and we will construct a cognitive map of the place discovered that will help us to orientate ourselves and navigate through the city.

To sum up, the five stages suggest a global view of the role of architecture as a *"human product that should bring order to and improve our relations to the environment."*[14] The discovery of our environment gives us the opportunity to understand how we learn about space. A fractal approach has allowed us to break down this journey into five stages of resolution. The last stage introduces us to many concepts like memory, cognitive mapping, orientation and navigation. Those notions have been studied thoroughly by cognitive psychologists over the last couple of decades. It will be interesting to understand how Piaget's theory, mainly based on observations, has been updated by neuroscientists and cognitivists later in the chapter.

THE DAMAGE CAUSED BY (THE DOMINANCE OF) LINEAR PERSPECTIVE

The evolution of our architectural understanding and therefore our potential for knowledge construction is dictated by spatial conventions that have been built into our cultural constructs since the Renaissance. Panofsky in his book *'Perspective as a Symbolic Form'*[15] established a parallel between the history of spatial representation and the evolution of abstract thought.

Linear perspective is a way of representing space yet it remains a code, one amongst many, with no pre-eminent claim to representing reality better or more accurately than others. It is an ideal of space and of vision itself. The selections of images and modes of presentation are inherently related to aesthetic and technological conventions established within the culture of the creator (whether or not the creator is consciously aware of these conventions).

---

15 Norberg-Schulz, Cr. (1974)

15 Panofsky, E. (1924)

»Different perceptions of space are born and die like societies themselves; they live, they have a history. Before the scientific revolution the world was more like a garment men wore about them than a stage on which they moved. In such a world the convention of perspective was unnecessary. It was as if the observers were themselves in the picture.«[16]

One point perspective is based on a particular act of looking where the spectator's relation to the painting determines how the pictorial space is developed. The observer is built into the act of looking. The eye now adjusts so readily to the effects of linear perspective that it is considered to be an innate process. We are all so familiar with the narrow field-of-view of photographs (that are constructed using linear perspective) that we think they are natural.

Crucially the viewer had to become familiar with and learn about perspectival images before they could seem natural; seeing is not automatically given to the sighted. Much of what we are tempted to call "objective seeing" originates in the activity of the seeing subject. Linear perspective cuts out a vast amount of what is involved in the act of looking. The space is created as an object rather than through the act of seeing. Previously it was as if the observers were themselves in the picture. Now it is given autonomous existence and does not need the viewer to produce it.

»As important as the development of perspective was for picture making and information design, it is doubtless even more important to general thought, because the premises on which it is based are implicit in every statement made with its aid.«[17]

The convention of linear perspective is important to the theme of this article because of its limited capacity to organize the representation of reality around a single point of view. As a result any form of abstract reasoning which is developed through the use of media tools and media content that are constructed using this convention can be augmented with other more 'realistic' forms of spatial construction. For instance parallel projection has been identified as a potentially more suitable way to symbolize the vision and knowledge of a collective. This is due to the fact that in the case of parallel projection the projection rays are parallel to each other, instead of originating from a single point of view.

»Vision and optical experts have noted that linear perspective is not a good approximation to so-called natural or real visual perspective [...] Curvilinear perspective has a strong foundation in reality as the human visual field has a natural curvilinear shape [...] It has

---

16 Barfield, O. (1965)

17 Manovich, Lev. (1993)

been claimed for example that the Ancient Greeks made the Parthenon columns bow outwards to account for — and correct — the curvilinear shape of the human visual field. Also painters like Leonardo Da Vinci and Turner added curvilinear effects into their depictions to more closely mimic reality as seen by the human eye.«[18]

FROM SPATIAL COGNITION TO MEMORY

Now that we have a practical understanding of how we perceive and decode our architectural surroundings we need to explore how those perceptions are processed and memorized by the brain. Some background in cognitive psychology will give us an update on Piaget's theory and provide us with some insights on the nature of memory and spatial cognition.

An inspiring study by McNamara, *"Human Spatial Memory and Navigation"*[19] gives us a good starting point in this field. Firstly the comparison between Piaget's five stages described above and the "types of spatial knowledge" described by McNamara et al. gives us an update to our understanding of human spatial cognition. They describe four stages which are "Objects Identity," "Route Knowledge," "Environmental Shape" and "Survey Knowledge" which have direct parallels with Piaget's stages. Secondly, the nature of spatial knowledge is described as fragmented, distorted, hierarchical and orientation dependent. Those descriptions give us relevant cues on the kind of space we should design to enhance the construction of spatial memory.

But most importantly, the scope of their study corresponds very much to ours as it focuses on how spatial memories are acquired from direct experience such as vision and motion. Other types of spatial memory such as those obtained from language or maps have been studied by cognitive psychologists. But those ask for more abstraction and less direct interaction from the user's point of view. Our interests lie more with the direct experience that can be enhanced by technologies and interaction. The abstraction will come in a second stage with the principle of visualization and representation which we will discuss later in the chapter.

An important issue is why do we memorize space in the first place? It is a question of survival. It is deeply anchored in our brain, in our hypothalamus, to remember where to find food and water and where to find our family members. Following memory theories, we can say that memorizing space happens

---

18 Radley, A. (2013)

19 McNamara, T. P., Sluzenski, J., and Rump, B. (2008)

effortlessly as an automatic process.[20] Moreover, those memories are encoded at a deep level in our *Long Term Memory* (LTM).[21] We don't have to explicitly memorize the space we are moving in to remember it. Because we are using all our senses, we perceive forms, objects, features and internal space vividly. Those multi sensorial perceptions make it more memorable implicitly. It makes us construct an implicit spatial knowledge recorded straight in our LTM. This type of memory is of particular interest to our study. Studies in psychology have already demonstrated that human LTM is essentially infinite.[22] Wouldn't it make more sense to use it more actively?

The last theory we will focus on is related to the principle of *association*. Paivio's *Dual – Coding Theory* (DCT)[23] explains how to encode, store and then retrieve information in association with our LTM. According to DCT, cognition involves the activity of two distinct subsystems, a verbal system specialized for dealing directly with language and a nonverbal (imagery) system specialized for dealing with non-linguistic objects and events. By using our knowledge and imagination, by being aware of our surrounding and the architecture, we are already building our own library of verbal and nonverbal assets effortlessly every day. The Art of Memory will give us some clues to understand how to use those assets stored in our LTM such as places including streets, buildings and rooms, or things like objects, animals, people, etc, and their actions, or words and their meaning.

Cognitive psychologists and neuroscientists have carried out all sorts of cognitive studies and experiments. Although the laboratory set up is not ideal, they give us incredible insights on how the brain works and how we make sense of and interact with our environment. In addition, the widespread use of video games, mobile devices and location-based media is rapidly immersing us in a hybrid reality which is expanding the practice of spatial cognition within these virtual and physical architectural environments. Motion sensors and natural interfaces are becoming the norm to interact with those worlds. Although the majority of these games are still entertainment, the potential for knowledge construction is huge.

Cognitive science provides us with a considerable number of pointers towards our research questions and objectives however their inputs often remain highly abstract. As a result we shall employ a more pragmatic approach in our

20 Hasher, L., and Zacks, R. T. (1979)

21 Atkinson, R. C., and Shiffrin, R. M. (1968)

22 Eysenck, M. (2001)

23 Paivio, A. (2006)

attempt to understand how we can use spatial cognition and architectural language to improve knowledge construction through the use of hybrid reality tools.

AUGMENTED ARCHITECTURE
FOR KNOWLEDGE CONSTRUCTION

With that in mind and before going into more practical studies a little exploration of the past will bring us some very interesting insights about ancient memory techniques. Those techniques can then help inform the design and use of modern technological knowledge devices. An investigation about this method and how it can be actualized is part of the core research questions of this chapter.

The Art of Memory (AoM) is a collection of mnemonic techniques. It remains the main method to remember information from the classical period of Simonides of Ceos in Ancient Greece to the renaissance era of hermeticism with Giordano Bruno. These techniques were almost universally practised by the thinkers of the ancient world who believed that mnemonic training was essential to the cultivation of creativity. Creativity was an act of synthesis that could only occur within the mind of a trained mnemonist. Appropriately, in Greek mythology, Mnemosyne, the goddess of memory, was the mother of the muses[24]. It was common for orators to memorise their speeches or any other items by imagining a journey (perhaps from their doorstep to the fora) and mentally tracing their steps to recall each articles or paragraphs associated to an image, they would have place along. Those techniques can be synthesized with the three pillars of memory: Imagination, Association and Location. Imagination and Association gives memory (IAM). Location gives the flow.[25]

Memory techniques were then adopted by early Christian monks. They became the principal method by which Monks would meditate upon the bible after committing it to memory. Safe within the curriculums and cloistered walls of Christian monasteries, the art of memory made it through to the later Middle Ages. By The Renaissance, mnemonic training was taught to almost all students, alongside grammar, rhetoric and logic. Even the invention of the Gutenberg printing press and the relative availability of books had little effect on the status of a trained memory; books were considered aids to recall rather than a

---

24 Kilov, D. (2012)
25 Buzan, T. (2010)

replacement for a well-stocked mind. The Renaissance did however give rise to a technological trend that would eventually contribute to the decline of the AoM. As far back as 1550, Italian thinker Giulio Camillo published a book outlining plans for construction of what he called a memory theatre. Only a few years after Camillo published his plans, the AoM became the target of religious persecutions that signalled its decline and eventual removal from education systems. In 1584 in England, the Puritans launched a fervent campaign against the AoM because of its frequent use of sexual, violent and absurd thoughts. Memory in education eventually turned a full 180 degrees. Mnemonic practice, which depended on the creative and mindful painting of mental pictures, was replaced with rote learning and repetition. Memorization went from being an intrinsically rewarding activity to being a task that elicited boredom at best, and reluctance at worst.[26]

It wasn't until historian Frances Yates published "The Art of Memory"[27] in 1966 that those techniques once again caught the public imagination. Today, although those mnemonic techniques are mainly used by memory athletes, numbers of authors like Tony Buzan and Joshua Foer[28] made them available to everyone.

How does this method of remembering work? It has always been quite an elaborate practice with different sets of rules for places, things and words. The first step consists in memorizing an architectural structure such as a palace, a temple or any kind of building, by going through its corridors and rooms in order to know it thoroughly. Then, after having integrated this spatial organization internally, the user will place, in the correct sequence, the images he will have constructed for visualizing the things s/he wants to recall. The last step is about associating words with those images to allow more depth to the memory/ knowledge construction. This method is context dependent and uses the principle of association outlined earlier in the DCT. What makes it interesting in the case of our project is that the user doesn't have to be in the environment physically, he just has to visualize it in his mind's eye.

»The problem of seeing and retaining complex information is older than print. [...] The principle ancient mnemonic device was called 'The Method of Loci' and places its emphasis on memorability (via intelligibility and transparency) through visual structures such as concept maps. It is very much concerned with the *acquisition of new knowledge*. It plays upon methods that we use informally, and it is a tradition that survives today. [...]

---

26 Kilov, D. (2012)

27 Yates, F. (1966)

28 Foer, J. (2008)

Visualization was in itself an important method of theory building. It may have been more important than text.«[29]

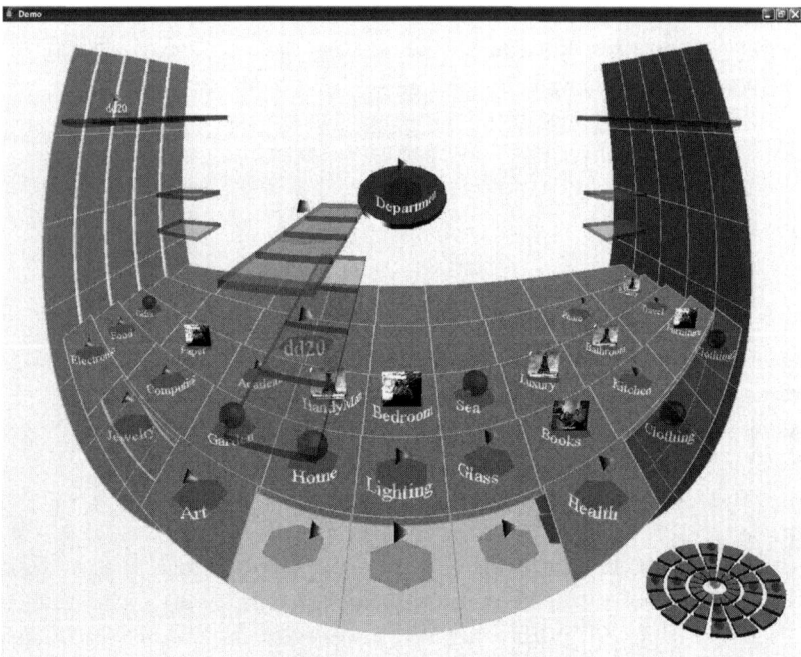

Figure 1. A modern 'method of loci' interface called Spectasia[30]

The method of loci stipulates that we use our mind to "locate within space" certain information. Ask yourself where you have tucked away such-and-such book and you will intuitively understand the recall process: "...on the desk shelf, upper left...." etc. Evidently, each of us has his/her own ideas for the arrangement and organization of things; we visualize the world according to our individual experiences; each one constructs his/her own *"mental space."* The question therefore is to discover if there aren't any independent structures, any symbolical universal codes, allowing us to work at this level of exchange between the external (our environment) and the internal (the way we visualize the world)? Could these codes offer us the means to organize our perceptions, to

29 Wong, J., and Storkerson, P. (1997)

30 https://sites.google.com/site/alanradley3/software-images

memorize them (in the form of cognitive representations), and ultimately, to have access to any particular piece of information at a given time?

The way information is spatially represented directly impacts on our cognition.

»In the everyday world, humans organise and manipulate objects in space to facilitate thinking. We are constantly organising and reorganising space to enhance performance.«[31]

Unfortunately, our current methods for storing and organizing information for knowledge formation are inefficient. We have terabytes of information stored in 'files' but the accessibility to this information is diminishing with the addition of each new file. The main tool we use to find information is a word based search engine.

»Why bother investing in one's memory in an age of externalized memories? How we perceive the world and how we act in it are products of how and what we remember [...] No lasting joke, invention, insight, or work of art was ever produced by an external memory. Not yet at least. Our ability to make connections between previously unconnected notions, to create new ideas, to share in a common culture: All these essentially human acts depend on memory [...] Now more than ever, as the role of memory in our culture erodes at a faster pace than ever before, we need to cultivate our ability to remember. Our memories make us who we are. They are the seat of our values and source of our character.«[32]

If architecture were intended solely at protecting us from our natural environment, it would not have developed all the styles and all the effects that we know and understand through experience. Some caves, huts or stone houses would have sufficed. One of architecture's main roles is to mark the socio-cultural behaviors of each era. Buildings, their ornaments and their architectural styles, organize our lives by announcing identity, signaling scale and even influencing how we think. Landmarks are there to guide us through the city. Architecture has evolved into a language with its own grammar and codes. We argue that this grammar and these codes can be used as engines of association to power up the distribution and manipulation of what we know, what we learn, how we make sense of it and create new ideas in an architectural environment.

The application of meaning on space is a native concern for architecture.[33] As a result if it is possible to 'physicalize' the process of knowledge construction

31 Kirsh, D. (1995)
32 Foer, J. (2011)
33 Smith, C. (2012)

using architecture then the resulting web of relationships between the physical, digital and conceptual aspects should increase the potential for making the process of cognition more transparent.

Between those two poles of architecture and ICT, the method of loci gives us some hints on the potential of interlacing them together.

ENGINEERING KNOWLEDGE CONSTRUCTION

Our challenge is to establish a dynamic equilibrium between technology and human nature within the very heart of this hybrid world. Marcos Novak[34] has an interesting point of view on the matter.

»To the extent that this development [i.e., the creation of cyberspace] inverts the present relationship of human to information, placing human within the information space, it is an architectural problem; but beyond this, cyberspace has an architectural structure of its own and, furthermore, it can contain architecture. To repeat: cyberspace is architecture; cyberspace has an architectural structure; and cyberspace contains architecture.«

According to Manovich,[35] the 1990s were all about the virtual where we became fascinated by the new virtual spaces made possible by computer technologies but we soon discovered that these new spaces left physical space useless. Dreyfus[36] agrees, claiming that in cyberspace, without our embodied ability to grasp meaning, relevance slips through our non-existent fingers. If Maher[37] is correct in her research that fluidity of thinking can be shown to relate to fluidity of physical movement then we must use methodologies and techniques that take advantage of our embodied ability to generate meaning.

A good example of this lies in the difference between regularly using GPS to find your way around a real city vs playing a 3D game which simulates a real 3D city like the ones in the computer game series *Grand Theft Auto*. Arguably depending on GPS for navigation has the potential for diminishing our memory and spatial cognition as we rely on GPS as a surrogate memory whereas playing a simulation of a 3D game which simulates a real 3D city has been shown to actually enhance your memory and cognition of the real city. A striking example

---

34 Novak, M. (2001)
35 Manovich, L. (2006)
36 Dreyfus, H. (2008)
37 Gero, J., and Maher, M. (1993)

of this was when someone was able to catch a thief during a long chase around the city streets of Venice even without having physically been there before. His only experience of the city was via frequently playing a 3D game where Venice was simulated to a high degree.

Similarly the author's experience of working in the field of architectural reconstruction (mainly working with ancient buildings) meant many large buildings were 3D modeled in tremendous detail. Interestingly, even after many years these models are available as 'cognitive structures' to the author due to the fact that every detail of the models can be remembered in his mind's eye. One hypothesis for this longevity in the memory is because they were virtually and physically built and not just navigated through.

Arguably it is not the tool (for instance GPS) that is the problem but the way we use it. Google street maps help me to see where I have to go before I go which in turn helps me to recognize the place once I am there. So here I definitely use the power of spatial memory to anticipate what will happen in the physical world. So it is more about educating people to use their minds and tools properly.

The problem is that thanks to the ever present 'Google search' we no longer need to internalize (deep learn) anything as almost all knowledge is stored in one warehouse with no features with which we can use to locate it.

A contemporary example of the use of the method of loci in a cognitive context is that of *Body Mnemonics*.[38] Body Mnemonics is a concept and an application that aims to reduce the attentional load of mobile interfaces. *"The problem is the fact that portable devices are often used in situations where the user is simultaneously engaged in other cognitive tasks. Consequently, it is desirable to reduce the attentional requirements of the interface."[39]* The fundamental concept behind Body Mnemonics is that information can very successfully be accessed and stored in the space defined by the user's body image. The cultural construct through which we view our bodies can be used as an aid to the storage and subsequent recall of information *"the body space is a very individual culturally defined construct, and thus can provide a highly personalised and meaningful interface."[40]*

The creation of hybrid worlds has become increasingly possible, even necessary, suggesting and informing a way of navigating through a universe of

---

38 Ängeslevä, J. et al. (2003)

39 Ängeslevä, J. and al. (2003)

40 Ängeslevä, J. and al. (2003)

information. However it has been argued that VR computer scientists and engineers should have sought advice from the vision experts...

»The VR system designers forgot that it is distance itself which constitutes a scene and which provides room for the user to contemplate the whole. It is critically important to be able to achieve a reasonable amount of distance from which to survey a scene efficiently in an overall sense, and this is a context related rule of human perception. Thus if we are to be able to build an efficient 3D user interface, we need to ensure sufficient distance is achievable.«[41]

So tentatively we can argue that a key rule of building cognitive architecture is that of an adjustable viewing distance onto the content.

Hybrid reality tools are now shaping our experience of a new blended digital/analogue space. These tools include gesture interaction, field of view technologies, wearable, smart things, cloud computing, and ambient computing. The possibilities of these hybrid reality tools are creating new mechanisms and design languages that are radically evolving the interface between man and his environment. We will concentrate on two of these developments which we refer to as 'post digital design' and 'context engineering.'[42]

POST-DIGITAL DESIGN

Post-digital design (PDD) attempts to manipulate these hybrid reality tools to humanize knowledge technology via social and cultural applications. Hybrid reality is fundamentally changing the way we interact with space, allowing us to access new ways of seeing and knowing.

According to Cheok[43] advances in mobile technology are moving us from an era of 'information communication' to 'experience communication'. This provides us with a new era in architectural understanding and can be summarized here by Uricchio:[44] *"We continue to have access to the city's materialities, but how can we recover its experiential contingencies and the ephemeral views? How might we give voice to its pluriform significance? How can we activate, articulate and put into play these assignments of meaning?"* As

41 Radley, A. (2013)

42 Smith, C. (2013).

43 Cheok A.D. (2012). Viewed 2013/10/25 http://adriancheok.info/category-speech/icalt 2012-keynote-talk-multi-modal-sensory-human

44 Uricchio, W. (2012): 45-49

Miller[45] states *"One's destination should never be a place but a new way of seeing things."*

Well-designed PDD techniques and tools should enable the creation of situations and concepts that could not have been realized before by uniting the strengths, features and possibilities of both the physical and the virtual space.

»In order for any kind of information to be presented to us in a way which is not fragmented or disruptive of our current activities, for it to become a part of our cognitive space, and be remembered and integrated with the flow of our mental activities, we need to be able to map, directly or by analogy, some of the real world architecture back into the computer display.«[46]

The New Aesthetic[47] is a term used to refer to the eruption of the digital within physical space, the increasing appearance of the visual language of the motifs of digital technology in the physical world. With hybrid reality the emphasis is firmly on bi-directional knowledge construction which creates a requirement for an increase in spatial literacy.

Post Digital Design is centered on the navigational shift that results when the world itself becomes the interface and is concerned with generating experiences which need to be co-created in order to exist.

CONTEXT ENGINEERING

Context engineering is a spatial experience design technique that can be employed for exploring perceptual analysis. *Field of view* (FOV) technologies such as the FlyVIZ headset (figure 2) augments the sense of sight by giving the user 360-degree vision. The 360 view is compressed to fit into the human field of view. According to initial reports it takes 15 min for the brain to adjust and then this *new way of seeing* is 'accepted as normal.'[48] The use cases for such a new form of context engineering are still emerging but *the ability within one field of view, to be both in the world and to see yourself in it, the power of looking through, and occupying, your own field of vision*[49] is becoming a tool for (co-)creating an entirely new form of architectural experience.

---

45 Miller, H. (1957)

46 Sparacino, Fl. et al. (1997): 8-13.

47 'The New Aesthetic'. http://new-aesthetic.tumblr.com/

48 Ardouin, J. and al. (2012).

49 Webb, M. (2009)

Figure 2. FlyVIZ headset

Another example of context engineering is being developed in Japan by Professor Michitaka Hirose with a project called 'diet goggles'[50] (figure 3). The goggles are designed to trick dieters into eating less by digitally enlarging food whilst they are actually eating it. This example highlights the extent to which context engineering can be used to subvert our perception of the physical world. The context becomes available for the subject to 'get to everything, add to everything, keep track of everything, and tie everything together.'[51]

A further example of context engineering is ClayVision[52] which re-engineers the design conventions of *mobile augmented reality* (MAR). ClayVision uses computer vision and image processing techniques to dynamically transform the appearance of building structures in real time. The digital data is not overlaid in the usual "bubble metaphor" of traditional MAR but actually becomes "fused together with the urban environment." This is achieved through the use of two techniques referred to as "default texture" and "diminished background." This project is an example of computer vision based localization for mobile devices which does not require the use of markers. The basic idea of their localization technique is simple: each frame of the real-time

50 Hirose, Michitaka. (2012). *Future Of WEIGHT LOSS Diet Goggles Exposed.*

51 Horn, R. (1989).

52 Takeuchi, Y., and Perlin, K. (2012)

video feed is compared to a collection of photos, shot from the same location using the same device beforehand.[53]

Figure 3. Professor Michitaka Hirose – diet goggles.

The individual 'coding' spaces of a knowledge landscape should inherently provide the ability to interactively re-program associations for alternative juxtapositions and points of view. One method of achieving this in terms of a navigational methodology is to use context engineering to create a *macroscope*. The macroscope effectively provides the overview and the local point of view (POV) of the object under investigation simultaneously. This is designed to enable learners to look across data sets and turn every 'object of study' into a file. These files can be subsequently mined to rapidly reframe interpretation and understanding. An example of this is a map of Manhattan named 'Here & There' (figure 4) which places the viewer simultaneously above the city and in it and allows the observer to plot a path between the overview and the local POV.

Macroscopic navigation and the subsequent opportunities for visualization can promote the formation of patterns, processes, and systems. This can help create a richer, more contextualized experience that extends working memory and amplifies cognition allowing many insights to be grasped, at the same time and often for the first time.

---

53 Takeuchi, Y., and Perlin, K. (2012)

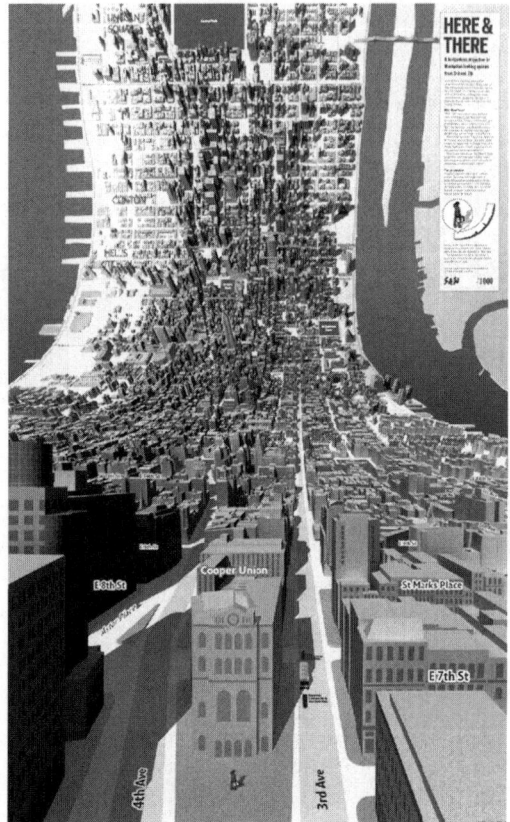

Figure 4. "Here & There."

In contrast to the microscope, which was turned on tiny bits of matter, de Rosnay claimed that the macroscope would be an important tool of action for focusing on ourselves; *"The macroscope is unlike other tools [...] It is a symbolic instrument made of a number of methods and techniques borrowed from very different disciplines [...] It is not used to make things larger or smaller but to observe what is at once too great, too slow, and too complex for our eyes."*[54] As John Thackera[55] states a macroscope is something that helps us see what the aggregation of many small actions looks like when added together.

Sula[56] suggests that the macroscope affords a wide and unpredictable range

---

54 De Rosnay, J. (1979)

55 Thackara, J. (2005)

56 Morrow, D., and Sula, Ch. (2009)

of applications across disciplines, including opportunities for understanding the ways in which ideas and knowledge are produced and exchanged within creative spaces.

According to Gattis, to be useful for abstract cognition (knowledge construction), spatial transformations must be adapted to contexts other than those in which they were acquired. He also raises the issue of whether this process of 'context engineering' is automatic or not which in turn appears to be dependent on whether the spatial organization is available in the environment or must be (re)constructed.[57]

CONCLUSION

In this article three concepts have been introduced: the concept of space in architecture as an interface between humans and their environment; the representation of space and his transmission that depends mainly on the medium used to communicate; the concept of spatial cognition in relation with long term memory and the power of associative processes inherent of the mind. We looked to the past to explore the most popular technique ever used to enhanced human memory over the centuries, the method of loci. Then we mentioned new research emerging from the post digital design and context engineering trends.

Spatial design can foster knowledge construction and this knowledge can be used to improve the design space. By unveiling the codes that are specific to the construction of virtual and physical architectural space we are better prepared at dealing with the design of hybrid environments. In contrast, a deep understanding of the way humans processed information and construct knowledge will help us to design more efficient tools that will enhanced the way we learn.

As these technologies and techniques become more and more spatial in their design and implementation, the role of the post digital shifts from composing for screen based interaction to engineering co-created experiences via actual structures and forms which often require the activation of full embodiment. This research is concerned with mixing analogue and digital material in post digital 'context engines' in order to understand the navigational shift that results when the world itself becomes the interface. A deeper re-examination of spatial literacy is required to provide these new designs with a real improvement on knowledge construction.

---

57 Gattis, M. (2001)

REFERENCES

Ängeslevä, Jussi, Oakley, Ian, Hughes, Stephen, and O'Modhrain, Sile (2003): 'Body Mnemonics Portable Device Interaction Design Concept', in *Proceedings of UIST*, 3:2–5. http://www.somodhrain.net/palpable/UIST2003 Final.pdf.

Ardouin, Jérôme, Lécuyer, Anatole, Marchal, Maud, Riant, Clément, and Marchand, Eric (2012): 'FlyVIZ: a Novel Display Device to Provide Humans with 360° Vision by Coupling Catadioptric Camera with Hmd', in *Proceedings of the 18th ACM Symposium on Virtual Reality Software and Technology*, 41–44. http://dl.acm.org/citation.cfm?id=2407344.

Atkinson, Richard C., and Shiffrin, Richard M. (1968): "Chapter: Human memory: A proposed system and its control processes.", in: Spence, K.W.; Spence, J.T. The psychology of learning and motivation (Volume 2). New York: Academic Press.

Barfield, Owen (1965): *Unancestral voice*, Connecticut: University Press.

Boudon, Philippe (1992): *Introduction à l'architecturologie*, Paris: Dunod.

Buzan, Tony (2010): *The Memory Book*, Pearson

Cheok, Adrian (2013): "ICALT2012 Keynote Talk", *Adrian Cheok*. Accessed 14 October 2013. http://adriancheok.info/category-speech/icalt2012-keynote-talk-multi-modal-sensory-human. 2012

Dreyfus, Hubert L. (2008): *On the Internet*, London: Taylor & Francis US.

Eysenck, Michael W. (2001): *Principles of Cognitive Psychology*, London: Taylor & Francis, Psychology Press.

Foer, Joshua (2011): *Moonwalking with Einstein: The Art and Science of Remembering Everything*. London: Penguin.

Fosnot, Catherine Twomey (2005): *Constructivism: Theory, Perspectives, and Practice*, New York: Teachers College Press.

Hirose, Michitaka (2012): *Future Of WEIGHT LOSS Diet Goggles Exposed*, http://www.youtube.com/watch?v=spk-2EuZ3hk&feature=youtube_gdata_player.

Gattis, Merideth (2001): "Space as a basis for abstract thought.", *Spatial Schemas and Abstract Thought*, Denver: Bradford Books.

Gero, John S., and Maher, Mary L. (1993): *Modeling Creativity and Knowledge-based Creative Design*, Mahwah, New Jersey, L. Erlbaum.

Hasher, Lynn, and Zacks, Rose T. (1979): "Automatic and Effortful Processes in Memory." *Journal of Experimental Psychology* General, no. 108, pp. 356-388.

Waltham (1989) cited in p.259, Horn, Robert E. (1989): *Mapping Hypertext: The Analysis, Organization, and Display of Knowledge for the Next Generation of On-Line Text and Graphics*. Lexington Institute.

Kilov, Daniel (2012): "The Rise and Fall of Remembering", Issue 398, Australian Mensa magazine, *TableAus*.

Kirsh, David (1995): "The Intelligent Use of Space". *Artificial Intelligence* 73, no. 1-2 (février): 31-68. doi:10.1016/0004-3702(94)00017-U.

Knauff, Markus (2013): *Space to Reason: A Spatial Theory of Human Thought*. MIT Press.

Manovich, Lev (2006): "The Poetics of Augmented Space", *Visual Communication* 5, no. 2 (1 June): 219-240. doi:10.1177/1470357206065527.

Manovich, Lev (1993): "The Engineering of Vision from Constructivism to Computers.", PhD diss., University of Rochester.

Matussek, Peter (2001): 'The Renaissance of the Theatre of Memory'. *Janus* 8: 4–8.

McNamara, T. P., Sluzenski, J., and Rump, B. (2008): "2.11 - Human Spatial Memory and Navigation", in: *Learning and Memory: A Comprehensive Reference*, edited by John H. Byrne, 157-178. Oxford: Academic Press. http://www.sciencedirect.com/science/article/pii/B9780123705099001765.

Meiss, Pierre von (1990): *Elements of Architecture: From Form to Place*. London; New York, NY: Van Nostrand Reinhold.

Miller, Henry (1957): *Big Sur and the Oranges of Hieronymus Bosch*. New York: New Directions.

Morrow, David R., and Sula, Chris A. (2009): "Naturalized Metaphilosophy", *Synthese* 182, no. 2 (29 September): 297-313. doi:10.1007/s11229-009-9662-1.

Norberg-Schulz, Christian (1974): *Système logique de l'architecture*, Bruxelles: Editions Mardaga.

Novak, Marcos (1991): "Cyberspace" edited by Michael Benedikt, 225-254, Cambridge, MA, USA: MIT Press. http://dl.acm.org/citation.cfm?id=114772.114788.

Paivio, Allan (2006): *Mind and its evolution; A dual coding theoretical interpretation*, Mahwah, NJ: Lawrence Erlbaum Associate

Panofsky, Erwin (1927): "Die Perspektive als symbolische Form", in: *Vorträge der Bibliothek Warburg*, Leipzig, Berlin, 1924-25.

Piaget, Jean (1926): *La représentation du monde chez l'enfant*, Paris: Presses universitaires de France.

Radley, Alan (2013): "The Lookable User Interface and 3D". http://www.alaipo.com/HCITOCH-2013/workshop_hcitoch_2013_publications.html.

Raynaud, Dominique (1998): *Architectures comparées: essai sur la dynamique des formes*, Marseille: Editions Parenthèses.

deRosnay, Joël (1979): *The Macroscope: a New World Scientific System*, New York: Harper & Row. http://pespmc1.vub.ac.be/macrbook.html.

Sparacino, Flavia, Pentland, Alex, Davenport, Glorianna, Hlavac, Michal, and Obelnicki, Mary (1997): "City of News", *Linz, Austria, Ars Electronica Festival*: 8-13.

Smith, Carl (2012): "Enhancing Spatial Cognition to Improve Pattern Recognition within Mixed Reality Environments". Electronic Visualisation and the Arts 2012. London: British Computer Society.

Smith, Carl (2013): "Experience Communication through Post Digital Design", Electronic Visualisation and the Arts 2013. London: British Computer Society.

Takeuchi, Yuichiro, and Perlin, Ken (2012): "ClayVision: The (elastic) Image of the City", in *Proceedings of the 2012 ACM Annual Conference on Human Factors in Computing Systems*, 2411-2420. http://dl.acm.org/citation.cfm?id=2208404.

Thackara, John (2005): *In the Bubble: Designing in a Complex World*, Cambridge, MA: MIT Press.

"The New Aesthetic". Accessed 18 October 2013. http://new-aesthetic.tumblr.com/?og=1.

Uricchio, William (non-dated) "A Palimpsest of Place and Past: Location-based Digital Technologies and the Performance of Urban Space and Memory", http://www.tandfonline.com/doi/abs/10.1080/13528165.2012.696860#.Um6yaSRQ2i8

Webb, M. (2009): "Maps and Macroscope", in: *Scroll Magazine*, http://berglondon.com/blog/tag/map/.

Wong, Janine, and Storkerson, Peter (1997): "Hypertext and the Art of Memory", in: *Visible Language*. sec. vol 31.

Yates, Frances A. (1966): *The Art Of Memory*, New York: Random House.

Zevi, Bruno (1959): *Apprendre à voir l'architecture*, Paris: Editions de Minuit.

Creating and Retrieving Knowledge in 3D Virtual Worlds

MIKHAIL FOMINYKH

INTRODUCTION

In this article, I discuss the role of 3D space and affordances of 3D Virtual Worlds (VWs) for facilitating collaborative creation and retrieval of knowledge. Knowledge resides in and is accessible from repositories. It may be stored not only in tangible artifacts, such as written instructions and databases, but also in activities, practices, relations between participants, and in their shared experiences. The former type of knowledge is known as explicit and the latter as tacit.[1] In a professional development in a given trade or education, the two types of knowledge are mutually dependent and mutually constituting.[2] Tacit knowledge is usually conveyed to explicit knowledge through narratives in addition to iterative training that create embodied experience through such activities. If knowledge is stored as activities that can be re-experienced, analyzed and reflected upon, it can be used for mastering high-level skills such as pattern recognition. The technology of 3D VWs has potential and, in some cases, affordances for conducting interactive activities that can simulate real-life experience, store, and retrieve them.

This technology has been extensively used for preserving cultural heritage and making the knowledge accessible by implementing virtual museums and reconstructions of artifacts and places.[3] To date, a large number of disciplines have been implemented in 3D VWs in both experimental and everyday teaching na-

---

1   Polanyi, M. (1966)
2   Nonaka, I., and Takeuchi, H. (1995)
3   Styliani, S., Fotis, L., Kostas, K., and Petros, P. (2009)

ture. Around 2009, it was estimated that about 300 higher education institutions had presence in Second Life alone.[4] Still, the full impact of as well as understanding of learning in virtual environments is relatively underdeveloped.[5]

However, studies suggest that 3D visualization can improve learning significantly[6] and assist learners in relating theoretical knowledge to practice.[7] At the same time, a collection of static or even interactive objects and environments do not provide a solid enough representation of community knowledge. Learning communities may carry and communicate part of their knowledge, both tacit and explicit, through collaborative activities, practices, relations, and experiences. Such fluid 'knowledge containers' are difficult to capture and store in traditional repositories, but the knowledge they carry is essential for many high-skill professions. Drawing upon the work in activity theory,[8] activity can be seen as a primary source of knowledge development and distribution. Therefore, visualizing and crystallizing activities are crucial for learning.

In this article, I discuss the process of collaborative construction and other activities in 3D space as means for visualizing knowledge, based on the results of empirical studies. Then, I focus on the possibilities for storing and retrieving traces of these 'crystallized activities' and knowledge they contain. I discuss our earlier explorative experience of crystallizing activities in 3D VWs in different ways, e.g., as traces of activities held in 3D constructions, as 3D constructions themselves, and as 3D virtual recordings. Further, I explore what knowledge can be created conducting activities in 3D virtual space, how it can be stored and retrieved, considering both educational potential of such knowledge and technological challenges and opportunities of this approach.

The goal of this article is to provide a different view on the notion of 'crystallized activity' as a container of knowledge created in a 3D space. In addition, it presents examples and a discussion of the new learning scenarios becoming available using this approach.

---

4   Salmon, G., and Hawkridge, D. (2009)
5   Savin-Baden, M. (2013)
6   Korakakis, G., Boudouvis, A., Palyvos, J., and Pavlatou, E. A. (2012)
7   Behzadan, A. H., and Kamat, V. R. (2013)
8   Leont'ev, A. N. (1981), Engeström, Y. (1999)

BACKGROUND

Overview of 3D virtual worlds

Formal definitions are rare in the area of three-dimensional desktop virtual environments, since it is relatively new and complex.[9] The technology appeared on the interception between virtual reality and networked computers. There exist few terms to call the technology itself. These terms have overlapping meanings and are often used to describe the same phenomenon. Most commonly used terms include collaborative virtual environments (CVEs), Multi-user Virtual Environments (MUVEs), Desktop Virtual Reality (DVR), and Virtual Worlds (VWs). In this work, I will use the term three-dimensional Virtual Worlds (3D VWs), as the platforms I use for case studies chosen this term, stressing their global nature and the type of navigation interface.

Based on several sources, 3D VWs can be defined as three dimensional, multiuser, synchronous, persistent environments, facilitated by networked computers.[10] It should be noted that three-dimensional interface is a relatively recent feature that has been applied to the VWs which existed long before it.[11] The technology discussed in this article should also be distinguished from highly immersive environments such as head-mounted displays[12] and immersive projection technology displays.[13] I consider the 3D VWs designed for (but not limited to) desktop. In such 3D VWs, users are represented by animated avatars and can interact using text-based chat, voice chat, and gestures. In addition, 3D technology allows interaction with various types of objects, including 3D objects and other media, such as text, graphics, sound, and video.

There are many application domains of 3D VWs, and their use has been growing rapidly in the first decade of the 21st century. Although entertainment remains one of the most successful application domains throughout the history of VWs,[14] many platforms are created to be used for 'serious' purposes.[15] Education is often considered to be the main serious use of 3D VWs.[16] However, there

---

9   Bell, M. W. (2008), Schmeil, A., and Eppler, M. J. (2009)

10 Bell (2008), de Freitas, S. (2008b), Schmeil and Eppler (2009)

11 Bartle, R. (2003)

12 Holliman, N. S., Dodgson, N. A., Favalora, G. E., and Pockett, L. (2011)

13 Cruz-Neira, C., Sandin, D. J., DeFanti, T. A., Kenyon, R. V., and Hart, J. C. (1992)

14 Bartle (2003)

15 Wrzesien, M., and Raya, M. A. (2010), de Freitas, S. (2008a), Messinger, P. R., Stroulia, E., and Lyons, K. (2008)

16 de Freitas (2008b)

are many others, such as training, research, commerce, and socialization. Developing quality specialized 3D VWs is expensive, but there are examples in the military and health care training. Examples of medical schools using VWs include virtual lectures, training interaction with patients, managing healthcare facilities, various visualizations, and collaborative tasks.[17] Four major areas of VWs healthcare applications are professional information sharing, clinical simulation, healthcare delivery, and research.[18] Examples of VWs used in military training include Tactical Iraqi and First Person Cultural Trainer.[19] Such environments are typically very expensive to develop, but attempt to create low-cost alternatives are starting to appear.[20] 3D VWs and other virtual reality technologies are becoming increasingly integrated to the military training practice.[21]

Educational use of 3D virtual worlds

3D VWs have long been attracting attention of educators and researchers. This technology provides a unique set of features that can be used for educational purposes, such as low cost and high safety, three-dimensional representation of learners and objects, interaction in simulated contexts with high immersion[22] and a sense of presence.[23]

Possibilities for synchronous communication and interaction allow using 3D VWs by various collaborative learning approaches.[24] In addition, possibilities for simulating environments on demand and for active collaborative work on the content allow applying situated learning[25] and project-based learning[26] approaches.

Constructivist approaches, such as problem-based learning, are also popular among the adopters of 3D VWs.[27] Social constructivism is often applied for

---

17 Hansen, M. M. (2008)

18 Holloway, D. (2012), Foronda, C., Godsall, L., and Trybulski, J. (2013)

19 Johnson, W. L. (2009), Zielke, M. A. (2011), Surface, E. A., Dierdorff, E. C., and Watson, A. M. (2007)

20 Prasolova-Førland, E., Fominykh, M., Darisiro, R., and Mørch, A. I. (2013)

21 Lele, A. (2013)

22 Cram, A., Hedberg, J., and Gosper, M. (2011)

23 Mckerlich, R., Riis, M., Anderson, T., and Eastman, B. (2011), Dede, C. (2009)

24 Lee, M. J. W. (2009)

25 Hayes, E. R. (2006)

26 Jarmon, L., Traphagan, T., and Mayrath, M. (2008)

27 Bignell, S., and Parson, V. (2010)

learning in 3D VWs, as the technology allows learners to construct their understanding collaboratively.[28]

Exploiting advantages of the content manipulation, 3D VWs can be used as cost-effective prototyping platforms to build and evaluate models or realistic simulations of existing or planned spaces.[29] A well-known example is prototyping a hospital Palomar Pomerado Health in Second Life before constructing it.[30] The virtual environment allowed all the stakeholders involved into the construction to explore the building in the way they would do in reality. Using the avatars, they could walk the corridors, offices, and open spaces of the virtual hospital test and experience how it feels. They could also do that collaboratively.

VWs can be well used as information visualization environments, immersing users and providing them with rich sensory experience.[31] In addition, VWs are used for educational simulations[32] and demonstrating complex concepts.[33]

Despite the repeated positive conclusions, researchers often report that their studies have experimental nature. At the same time, many learning approaches are already used in 3D VWs, and even a new phenomenon "Virtual world pedagogy" is being discussed.[34]

Collaborative work with 3D content

One of the major topics discussed in this article is creation of knowledge in 3D VWs by the process of collaborative visualization, an activity that is both a promising learning approach and well supported by the technology.

3D VWs have the possibility for supporting collaborative work with various types of content, as discussed in several studies.[35] Most 3D VWs allow advanced content manipulation, uploading, creating, and sharing 3D objects and

---

28 Molka-Danielsen, J. (2009), Coffman, T., and Klinger, M. B. (2007), Huang, H.-M., Rauch, U., and Liaw, S.-S. (2010)

29 Minocha, S., and Reeves, A. J. (2010)

30 Zensius, N. (2009)

31 Chen, C., and Börner, K. (2005), Bowman, D. A., North, C., Chen, J., Polys, N. F., Pyla, P. S., and Yilmaz, U. (2003)

32 Falconer, L., and Frutos-Perez, M. (2009)

33 Youngblut, C. (1998), Dekker, G. A., Moreland, J., and van der Veen, J. (2011)

34 Dawley, L. (2009)

35 Atkins, C. (2009), Hwang, J., Park, H., Cha, J. and Shin, B. (2008), van Nederveen, S. (2007), Arreguin, C. (2007), Perera, I., Allison, C., Nicoll, J. R., Sturgeon, T., and Miller, A. (2010)

other media, such as text, graphics, sound, and video. In this context, the term 'content' can be understood more widely than media objects. It can be "objects, places, activities" or any valuable information or experience.[36]

Besides the possibilities for active and collaborative manipulation on the content, the technology allows storing, sharing, and exhibiting the content in a community repository as well as live presentation, discussion, and experience. Wide possibilities for conducting meetings, events, and performances extend the use cases for collaborative work on 3D content.[37] 3D VWs support creating and sharing content – the key features of social networking.[38]

Virtual space as an educational environment

The design of educational environments in 3D VWs has long been and remains an important issue recognized by researchers, educators and developers.[39]

Using place metaphors in the design of educational 3D VWs is a common practice.[40] Virtual campus metaphor might be seen as one of the most appropriate for an educational VW. However, there are many other metaphors that are used in different contexts, such as virtual museums, galleries and theatres,[41] virtual laboratories and workshops,[42] virtual libraries,[43] and virtual health-care centers and hospitals.[44]

The choice of the metaphor and its design is usually based on particular learning goals and on the role of the VW. In most cases, the design focuses not only on the appearance of the 3D environment, but on the functionality, tools,

---

36 Bessière, K., Ellis, J. B., and Kellogg, W. A. (2009)

37 Sant, T. (2009)

38 Owen, M. L., Grant, L., Sayers, S., and Facer, K. (2006), Smith, R., Oblinger, D., Johnson, L. F., and Lomas, C. P. (2007).

39 Minocha and Reeves (2010), Dede, C. (1996), Molka-Danielsen, J., Deutschmann, M., and Panichi, L. (2009)

40 Prasolova-Førland, E. (2005), Gu, N., Williams, A., and Gül, L. F. (2007), Li, F., and Maher, M. L. (2000)

41 Sant (2009)

42 Dalgarno, B., Bishop, A. G., Adlong, W., and Bedgood, D. R. (2009)

43 Hill, V., and Lee, H.-J. (2009)

44 Boulos, M. N. K., Hetherington, L., and Wheeler, S. (2007)

and features.[45] Educational environments are often created within bigger virtual worlds using their advantages but also being restricted by their limitations.[46]

Recent research suggests that 3D VWs may provide a strong sense of space, place, and location.[47] In this research, it is held that a 3DVW is a 'new kind of space' sharing with the real world a visual topology that includes ownership and belonging, and is invested by the understanding of the participants as to what is appropriate in the community. Whereas *space* is the opportunity, as provided by the 3D virtual environment, it becomes a *place* of experienced reality when acting.[48] Similarly, the concept of presence in a VW can be seen as spatial immersion that is related to technology and sensory data and as social presence that is related to interaction and cognition.[49] The emerging place is constituted as a social process in the intersection of human behavior, experience, and the materiality of the space available. Social interaction and performance of activities in a virtual space are meaningful experiences that may allow creating a sense of place and create intention to return to the places in a VW.[50] VWs can provide users with location awareness or a sense of where they are both in terms of navigation in space and being in a place.[51] Human memory is closely tied to space that can act as a repository for memories and a trigger that brings them up.[52]

A virtual space becomes a container of artifacts used by the visitors in their activities. This process is contributing to the creation of a place. VWs have higher flexibility in comparison to the real world, allowing a community build, modify, and preserve the space with the possibility accessing them from anywhere at any time. These features of the technology led to the idea of virtual places as crystallization of personal and group memories, constituting the memory of the community.[53]

---

45 Prasolova-Førland (2005)

46 de Freitas (2008b), Hendaoui, A., Limayem, M., and Thompson, C. W. (2008)

47 Boellstorff, T. (2009), Thorpe, S. J. (2011)

48 Harrison, S., and Dourish, P. (1996)

49 Saunders, C., Rutkowski, A. F., Genuchten, M. V., Vogel, D., and Orrego, J. M. (2011)

50 Goel, L., Johnson, N., Junglas, I., and Ives, B. (2013)

51 Benford, S., Bowers, J., Fahlén, L. E., Mariani, J., and Rodden, T. (1994)

52 Yates, F. A. (1966), Huxor, A. (2001)

53 Prasolova-Førland, E. (2004)

Activities in 3D virtual worlds

Activity is very closely related to experience, memory, and knowledge. The possibility for conducting rich interactive collaborative activities makes 3D VWs outstanding. Considering all the technical and other types of the technology limitations, the experience it may provide is closer to the reality than with other types of technologies. Such activity can be thought from the perspective of activity theory, that links the development of knowledge to action and the use of artifacts.[54] It is also related to the notions of community memory, communities of practice[55] and the theory behind organizational memory.[56]

According to Wenger, continuous negotiation of meaning is the core of social learning and involves two processes: participation and reification. Participation is the "complex process that combines doing, talking, thinking, feeling, and belonging." Reification is the "process of giving form to our experience by producing objects that congeal this experience into thingness."[57] The collection of such artifacts comprises the shared repertoire and history of the community. Walsh and Ungson propose that interpretations of the past can be embedded not only in systems and artifacts, but within individuals through the narratives they may convey. Organizational and community memory consists of mental and structural artifacts,[58] but it can also be thought of as processes and representational states.[59] In addition, a community memory consists of histories and trajectories of its members expressed in narratives.

Considering the background presented above, learning process and knowledge creation can be described as activities and characterized by narratives, collaboration, and social constructivism. Narratives are used for the diagnosis of problems and as repositories of existing knowledge both tacit and explicit.[60] They also contain the tacit knowledge of a given domain or a field of practice, and provide a bridge between tacit and explicit knowledge[61]. Through collaborative activities and shared practices, knowledge may be created and distributed among the participants. The process of socialization may give the learn-

---

54 Leont'ev (1981), Engeström (1999)

55 Wenger, E. (1998)

56 Ackerman, M. S., and Halverson, C. (1998)

57 Wenger (1998)

58 Walsh, J. P., and Ungson, G. R. (1991)

59 Ackerman and Halverson (1998)

60 Polanyi (1966)

61 Linde, C. (2001)

ers access to the episteme or underlying game of a discipline, the most difficult knowledge to access.[62]

Capturing activities in 3D virtual worlds

3D VWs allow conducting various activities, and capturing such activities is a complex task from the technological point of view, as part of the information is usually lost. The most common methods for that include capturing activities in VWs as screen shots, keeping chat logs, social tagging, and keeping track of people met and virtual places visited.[63] Activities in 3D VWs are also often recorded as 'flat' 2D video. This method usually provides a better overview of the activity, but still it eliminates many advantages of the technology, such as immersion, possibility for collaborative work or for further developing the 'crystallized activities', except for commenting and annotating them. This approach is used in Machinima – collaborative film making using screen capture in 3D VW and games.[64]

The need for recording activities in 3D environments keeping the immersive context was acknowledged as early as in the late 90s, e.g. by developers of CAVE and MASSIVE systems. MASSIVE-3 supported a mechanism that allowed "real-time virtual environments to be linked to recordings of prior virtual environments so that the two appear to be overlaid."[65] CAVE Research Network soft system had an application which supported recording of an avatar's gestures and audio together with a surrounding space.[66] Another example is the system called Asynchronous Virtual Classroom that allowed watching a video image of a lecture and to control it, while software agents were playing some of the displayed participants and created a presence effect.[67] Later, Networked Virtual Environment Collaboration Trans-Oceanic Research project developed three approaches to support annotations for asynchronous collaboration in virtual reality,

---

62 Entwistle, N. (2005)
63 Neustaedter, C., and Fedorovskaya, E. (2009)
64 Barwell, G., Moore, C., and Walker, R. (2011)
65 Greenhalgh, C., Flintham, M., Purbrick, J., and Benford, S. (2002)
66 Leigh, J., Ali, M. D., Bailey, S., Banerjee, A., Banerjee, P., Curry, K., Curtis, J., Dech, F., Dodds, B., Foster, I., Fraser, S., Ganeshan, K., Glen, D., Grossman, R., Heil, Y., Hicks, J., Hudson, A. D., Imai, T., Khan, M. A., Kapoor, A., Kenyon, R. V., Park, K., Parod, B., Rajlich, P. J., Rasmussen, M., Rawlings, M., Robertson, D., Thongrong, S., Stein, R. J., Tuecke, S., Wallach, H., Wong, H. Y., and Wheless, G. (1999)
67 Matsuura, K., Ogata, H., and Yano, Y. (1999)

including a tool that allows attaching 3D virtual reality recordings to objects, an email system for virtual reality, and a streaming recorder to record all transactions that occur in a collaborative session.[68] More recently, an Event Recorder feature was implemented (however, not developed further) within the Project Wonderland.[69] It implements recording and playback of the 'events' caused by activities of users or agents in such a way that during playback a user is able to view the activities that those events caused.

All mentioned projects were contributing towards developing technological solutions for capturing and retrieving activities in 3D VWs or other similar environments. However, there is a clear possibility for improvement, as the potential of 3D spaces for community memory repositories was not yet realized.

EDUCATIONAL VISUALIZATIONS IN 3D VIRTUAL WORLDS

We conducted three case studies on using 3D VWs for educational visualizations with colleagues at the Norwegian University of Science and Technology. All three studies were conducted within Cooperation Technology course. The goals of these studies were to explore the educational visualization as a teaching method and to explore the affordances of 3D VWs for capturing learning activities and storing them as part of community memory.

Case studies on educational visualizations in 3D virtual worlds

In this section, I discuss the results of three exploratory case studies conducted within Cooperation Technology undergraduate course in 2009, 2010, and 2011. In all three studies, we used the same environment and gave similar tasks to the students. However, each time we improved both the environment and the learning approach, based on the student feedback. We collected various types of qualitative and quantitative data from the log of the VW and from the student feedback. In addition, we took the anthropological approach, being constantly with the students in the VW, observing the processes of negotiation and construction.

The teaching method we applied[70] is based on *constructionism* – an educational philosophy which implies that learning is more effective through the de-

---

68 Imai, T., Qiu, Z., Behara, S., Tachi, S., Aoyama, T., Johnson, A., and Leigh, J. (2000)

69 Later, Open Wonderland™, http://openwonderland.org/

70 Fominykh, M., and Prasolova-Førland, E. (2012)

sign and building of personally meaningful artifacts than consuming information alone.[71] In this perspective, the knowledge is constructed through an individual cognitive effort that is applied to the creation of a virtual artifact in 3D space or the space itself. Constructionism is related to the *social constructivist* approach, which proposes that learners co-construct their understanding together with their peers.[72] Knowledge and meaning in this perspective are collaboratively constructed through social processes and activities, based on previous experiences. The participants were trying to construct a common understanding to materialize it in the form of 3D space. In other words, they had a certain meaningful 'place' in mind and tried to construct a 'space' that can accommodate it.

In addition, we applied role playing which is a widely used and effective learning and teaching method. It implies an active behavior in accordance with a specific role.[73] We considered a student group a subject within a learning community. The results of activities performed by students are seen as artifacts and reification of experience[74] that is shared with other community members, e.g. future generations of students. In the following, I present the details of the studies in more detail.

In the 2009 study, six groups (3-4 students in each) were asked to build a visualization representing one of the research areas or a course taught at the university in the period of six weeks. The students were asked to consider how their constructions could be used in educational activities on the virtual campus and for promotion of the university. The resultant constructions were presented to the international audience at a joint session (Figure 1). The visitors were guided through the building sites and asked to give their comments and feedback to the projects.[75]

71 Bessière, Ellis and Kellogg (2009), Papert, S., and Harel, I. (1991)

72 Vygotsky, L. S. (1978)

73 McSharry, G., and Jones, S. (2000), Craciun, D. (2010)

74 Wenger (1998)

75 Prasolova-Førland, E., Fominykh, M., and Wyeld, T. G. (2010)

Figure 1. Student visualization project Fuel Fighter, 2009

The study in 2010 was conducted with 25 students in seven groups, 2-4 students in each. Each group was asked to build a visualization representing a research project in the period of one month and present it at a joint session by role-playing (Figure 2). The joint session was extended by two virtual seminars on related topics led by invited experts.[76]

In 2011, the study was conducted with 37 students in 10 groups, 3-4 students in each. The students were asked to build an educational module representing a major curriculum topic and present it at a joint session by role-playing. For example, one of the student groups visualized the concept of 'awareness' by constructing two remote laboratories that were full of elements exemplifying the concept. The activity conducted by the students was a role play in which the labs were working on a joint project and an accident occurred in one of them (Figure 3). The second lab could take appropriate actions thanks to awareness mechanisms. Towards the end of the construction process, the groups received evaluations from students invited from the University of Hawaii at Manoa. After the role-playing session, each group evaluated two other constructions.[77]

---

76 Fominykh, M., and Prasolova-Førland, E. (2011)

77 Fominykh, M., Prasolova-Førland, E., and Divitini, M. (2012)

Figure 2. Student visualization project Solar Skin, 2010

Figure 3. Student visualization project Awareness Lab, 2011

Supporting student visualization projects with Virtual Gallery

The Virtual Gallery (VG) was intended to assist constructing, presenting, and storing student 3D visualization projects in a shared repository and designed based on the results of a case study we conducted in 2009.[78] A library of pre-made 3D objects, scripts, and textures could allow concentrating more on the creativity instead of technical details. In addition, student 3D visualizations occupied considerable amount of space in our virtual campus in Second Life and there was a need for better storage solutions.

The VG was implemented, including a realistically reconstructed building (modeled after an existing student activity house on campus), a gallery for storing and presenting 3D constructions, and a library of pre-made 3D objects, scripts, textures, and links to other resources and virtual places (Figure 4).

In two other studies in 2010[79] and 2011[80], we collected student feedback on their experience of using VG and its functions. The students were constructing 3D visualizations which were later stored in the VG.

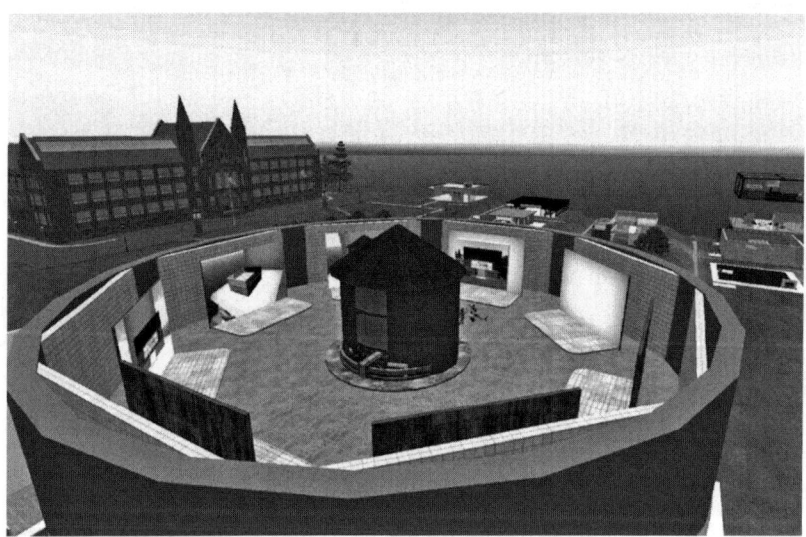

Figure 4. Virtual Gallery

78 Prasolova-Førland, Fominykh and Wyeld (2010)

79 Fominykh and Prasolova-Førland (2011)

80 Fominykh, Prasolova-Førland and Divitini (2012)

Sharing visualization projects across communities in Virtual Research Arena

We studied further the possibilities of 3D VWs for educational visualizations and supporting learning communities that can form around them. We developed a framework, Virtual Research Arena (VRA), for creating awareness about educational and research activities, promoting cross-fertilization between different environments and engaging the public[81] that was later implemented as a prototype in Second Life. We formed a set of requirements for the VRA on three levels.

First, it should support collaborative work on 3D content, i.e. creating it, storing, and presenting. This function was made available through the VG which was integrated into the VRA. Second, it should provide appropriate atmosphere, tools, and facilities for the community activities. VRA should be a place, where students and researchers can visualize ideas and share them. It should accumulate 'reifications' or traces of community activities over time, thus becoming a community repository. Such a repository would be in many ways different from a 'traditional' one due to its fluid and tacit nature, reflecting the nature of the learning communities behind.

VRA functions as a virtual extension of the Norwegian Science Fair festival where research projects are presented to the public in a set of pavilions. A city landmark – King Olav Tower – was reconstructed on the virtual 'central square' that served as a venue for the fair in reality, to create an authentic atmosphere and a meeting place for the local and international online visitors. The virtual science fair exhibited eight research projects and a number of student projects during the live event. Some of the VRA visualizations were later used for holding project meetings and presentations, enriching 3D constructions with activity traces (Figure 5).

While the physical pavilions at the fair were deconstructed at the end of the event after two days, the virtual pavilions and the student constructions with activities traces have been preserved becoming a community repository. The feedback collected in a case study in 2010[82] showed that most of the students and visitors acknowledged the potential of 3D VWs and places like the VRA for supporting social networks and collaboration among various groups of participants as well as the importance of preserving their own constructions as a part of the VRA and the community.

---

81 Fominykh and Prasolova-Førland (2011)

82 Fominykh and Prasolova-Førland (2011)

Figure 5. Virtual Research Arena

VIRTUAL RECORDING IN A 3D VIRTUAL WORLD

Several attempts have been made to capture and activities in 3D space, as discussed earlier in section "Capturing activities in 3D virtual worlds."p In this section, I would like to present a prototype designed on a new platform vAcademia[83] that allows capturing activities in a 3D space, storing them, editing, and retrieving for analysis and secondary recording. vAcademia is a 3D VW that is designed for education. Its most distinctive feature is 3D recording, which allows capturing everything in a given location in the VW in process, including synchronized positions of the objects, appearance and movement of the avatars, media materials displayed, text and voice chat messages.[84] Similar functionalities were realized earlier in few VWs or desktop virtual reality systems. However, 3D recording was never developed into a convenient tool and never adopted for specific use as in vAcademia. In addition, no convenient tools for working with the resultant recordings were developed.

3D recording of classes allows getting a new type of learning content and involving students in new types of activities. A user can attend and work at a recorded class, not just view it as a spectator. In addition, any recorded classes

---

83 http://vacademia.com/

84 Morozov, M., Gerasimov, A., Fominykh, M., and Smorkalov, A. (2013)

can be attended by a group of users. A new group can work within a recorded class and record it again, but with their participation. Thus, there is an opportunity to build up content of recorded classes and layer realities on top of each other.

From the user point of view, 3D recording control is very similar to the regular video player. A 3D recording can be fast-forwarded and rewound, paused, and played again from any point of time. A replayed 3D recording looks exactly like a real class. Of cause, the recorded avatars will always act the way they were recorded. However, it is possible to use all the functionality of the VW inside a recording. Moreover, a replayed 3D recording can be recorded again together with new actions. In such a way, new recordings and new content can be created based on the same original event.

Considering the fact that such features of the vAcademia platform are useful for capturing traces of activities, storing and modifying them, we selected this platform for continuing this line of research.

Training medical personnel in vAcademia

The prototype implements a training environment for medical center managers. It is based on a typical scenario – answering phone calls. The basic training session is intended for a single user (Figure 6). The trainee answers a call from a potential client (pre-recorded voice). Three options written in text are offered by an assisting bot. The trainee reads options and chooses one. If the option is correct, the trainee needs to say it (to continue the phone conversation). If not, the assistant advises to choose another one.

The prototype was evaluated with 44 managers over four months within the medical center it was designed for. The participants had no previous knowledge on the 3D VW technology (including vAcademia), but were provided with written user manuals. The observers recorded the first training attempt of each participant, then 6-8 attempts were allowed to improve the skill (using hints), and finally another control attempt was recorded (without hints). The results were evaluated by the experts. Particular attention was paid the correctness of the phrases, intonations, and the number of mistakes. An attempt was considered passed if a participant makes not more than two mistakes and pronounces all the phrases correctly. The results demonstrate that 20% of the trainees achieved the acceptable result in the first attempt, and 57% did it on the control attempt.

Figure 6. vAcademia training session

Using 3D recording for reflection and deeper learning in vAcademia

Even though the training session was designed for a single user, it can be record-ed, stored, and revisited afterwards. The pauses in the conversation when the trainee is reading answer options are removed, and the recording would appear as a natural conversation. For example, the assistant can help in the first trial, but not in the second one. The resultant 3D recordings can be revisited by the same trainee (see Figure 7) to analyze the performance and note places that can be im-proved or they can be revisited by the trainee and a mentor for more detailed analysis.

Meeting yourself-from-the-past (or even several selves) is an unusual expe-rience. Observing own actions, while acting in the same space and having the same virtual representation, can be a strong trigger for reflection and self-assessment. Such experience goes much further than watching yourself in a vid-eo that captures you from a single point of view and that is separated from the observer. It goes further than just having an avatar in 3D space, as it represents a user in a different, a virtual reality.

An important part of this type of training is the development of profession-al sensitivity of the learners and their understanding of care. This includes high-level skills such as "looking behind the words" of the patients, since patients often are unclear of what their problem is, or do not want to state their problem.[85] The possibilities of practicing a scenario (with some variations) and having multiple reifications of the crystallized actions-in-space can facilitate training of such high-level skills. The notion of care is also complicated since it challenges the learner's preconceptions with the "messy realities of practice."[86] This change in perspective represents a threshold concept – a troublesome knowledge.[87]

Figure 7. Attending a recorded training session in vAcademia

More generally, if using such training sessions regularly, it is possible to build a database of training 3D recordings. This would allow individual workers to track their performance, coming back to their actions-in-space, and the company – to have multiple examples (best and worst cases). It would provide an opportunity to identify what aspects of the learning outcomes are the most difficult to arrive at. This insight could again be fed into a redesign of courses and training programs. 3D recordings can be modified and annotated by experts – inserting additional actions in the same space, for example including theoretical explanations.

---

85 Clouder, L. (2005)

86 Barnitt, R. (1998)

87 Meyer, J. H. F., and Land, R. (2003)

DISCUSSION

Crystallizing activities in 3D VWs can be seen as an affordance of space and time simulated with this technology. It can be done differently from the technological point of view, capturing modified space that contains traces of past activities conducted in the space or capturing action-in-space that contains the space together with the activity that gives meaning it and adding the time dimension. In both cases, virtual space plays the role of a raw material to be modified to contain activities.

The use of 3D VWs as a means for creating and retrieving knowledge may benefit educational process considerably. As demonstrated by the studies presented earlier in this article, this technology provides affordances for conducting complex educational activities, mirroring them from the real life (such as virtual seminars) and enhancing with tasks that are not possible in reality (such as creating visualizations of abstract concepts). These results are confirmed by multiple studies that are summarized in section "Educational use of 3D virtual worlds." However, not much research has been done on trying to capture such educational activities and using them afterwards. The work presented in this article provides an attempt to address this.

Immersion into a well-designed virtual environment in itself may improve understanding of the structure and the complexity of a certain topic, area, or model. However, getting access to activities that are (or were) conducted in such an environment can help grasping the features of the space, improve the sense of place, and simplify the access to the traces of knowledge. This can allow capturing and recovering tacit knowledge, for example as repeated experience or narratives. Narratives prove bridges between tacit and explicit knowledge, while at the same time representing the collective history of a community. The usefulness of narratives increases when they are stored as crystallized activities. Enactment and participation, complemented with narratives, visualize certain aspects of the knowledge of a discipline or a profession, aspects that are more difficult to access through traditional training and learning facilities.

Following the Wenger's social learning process,[88] capturing 'participation' as crystallized activities can be seen as 'reification'. At the same time, if an activity is crystallized in a 3D VW, it contains the traces of the original activity. An activity can be crystallized either as modified space (see examples in section "Educational visualizations in 3D virtual worlds") or as action-in-space (see examples in section "Virtual recording in a 3D virtual world"). Recovering

---

88 Wenger (1998)

knowledge from activities crystallized in any of these ways would allow multiple reifications.

In an earlier work, we refer to this difference in capturing activities as the scale quality from explicit to implicit.[89] This quality describes to what extent a crystallized activity and its components can be experienced in the same way as a live activity.

Crystallizing an activity supplies it with qualities of content (virtual space, objects, and artifacts), making the transformation of some of the tacit knowledge it contains to explicit easier. For example, in educational visualization studies presented earlier in this article, the collaborative activities of negotiating the meaning, discussing ways of visualizing it, trying and failing are crystallized as tangible artifacts – virtual environments with objects and spaces. This allows activities to be operated like any other content, as we did with sharing them at the VRA. However, in order to make the best possible use of crystallized activities, they should be made active again. This challenge can be addressed in different ways, for example technologically by further developing the 3D recording feature. It can also be addressed methodologically by developing approaches for retrieving knowledge from crystallized activities.

Traces of activities can be made active by performing new or same activities in spaces that already contain crystallized activities, for example making a science project visualization 'active' again by performing a role play / seminar in the corresponding construction. 3D recordings are becoming active if someone visits them, but the method for extracting knowledge from them can be improved too.

When thinking of crystallized activities as pieces of content, they can also be seen as elements of knowledge. Crystallized activities may contain both explicit and tacit types of knowledge. Explicit knowledge is usually contained in a particular artifact that is a part of a virtual space, while tacit knowledge can be associated with the whole activity that is crystallized. This means that all the objects of the virtual environment are important to retrieve the tacit knowledge that resides in a crystallized activity.

The qualities of content acquired by the activities when they are crystallized in a 3D VW allow automating the process of knowledge retrieval. A crystallized activity can then be seen as a container of numerous elements (such as avatars, 3D objects, communication streams, and media contents). Automation of the analysis of such data and retrieving valuable information from a crystallized activity is a challenge. The difficulty lies in retrieving the knowledge that

---

89 Fominykh, M., Prasolova-Førland, E., Hokstad, L. M., and Morozov, M. (2014)

resides in activity, but not necessarily in the objects or discrete elements. Automatic analysis of such elements may not reach externalization of tacit knowledge that resides in the crystallized activities, but still provide valuable auxiliary information about the conducted activities (e.g., for assessment, awareness, or recommendations). This task is challenging, as many types of data need to be analyzed and calibrated. For example, a certain activity may contain movements or gestures that matter and another one – phrases and intonations. In the former activity, the data to be analyzed will include distances, angles, and seconds. In the latter – number of words, types of phrases, and intonations.

Activities crystallized as modified space

In the case of activity traces crystallized in modified space, the process of reifications is more implicit and more dependent on the interpretation of those who access them. The educational use of the activities crystallized in this way may vary. For example, a gallery of 3D constructions that represent a topic of topics can be created to contain the meaning invested into them by the authors. A more indicative example is the traces of enactments or role playing captured as decorations, scripts, and artifacts used. Such objects can tell much about the play that was help in the environment or they can be used again for another play or related activity. Another example is a virtual place that holds regular activities, such as seminars, discussions, or training sessions. It may capture the traces of these activities in the design of the space (arrangement of objects and open spaces), artifacts created (minutes of meetings or other results of collaborative work), or scenarios developed over time (scripts or activity/working procedures). Such traces of activities can be used as a history of a learning community or a community memory.

Sharing 3D visualizations in the VRA (presented earlier) received a positive feedback. Most of the groups stressed the importance of studying previous students' constructions to have inspiration. Some of the groups stated also that they get additional motivation from being able to exhibit their construction for other people. Realistic buildings reconstructed in the virtual environment around the student visualization playground were recognized as supporting community and providing a sense of place[90]. Many participating students appreciated the sense of a familiar place that they experience when arriving to and working in the virtual space. At the same time, they wished the constructions of the envi-

---

90 See more about the difference between sense of place and immersion in a virtual space in section "Virtual space as an educational environment"

ronment to be more functional, appreciating the tools and materials available at the VG. Familiar buildings created certain 'focal points' and a sense of place for both local community members and visiting students or researchers at the VRA, which was acknowledged as an important factor for sustaining the learning community.

Many participants have also stressed the importance of preserving their visualizations consequently each year, constituting a history of the learning community. The most popular reason given for this argument was inability to realize the potential of a learning community to the full extent within a short period (one semester). A gallery of crystallized activities provided a bridge between generations of students and constituted a learning community repository.

Activities crystallized as actions-in-space

In the case of activity traces crystallized as action-in-space, the process of reification is more explicit, but allows detailed analysis and reflection. The educational use of such activities is different significantly. From the methodological point of view, two formats can be identified. The first format is visiting a 3D recording, and the second is creating a new 3D recording while conducting activities being inside one.

The first format – visiting a 3D recording is similar to watching a video-recorded lecture or a webinar. However, a 3D recording can be watched being immersed into the virtual space. It can be visited by a group of learners who can actively work inside. All the interaction can be observed in the same way as in the live class. The only limitation is that the recorded avatars and objects cannot respond to the interaction of the live participants.[91]

Re-visiting an activity crystallized as action-in-space (using 3D virtual recording) allows a great range of behaviors and responses. The main advantage of this way of capturing is the possibility to re-enter the activity and observe it from inside or re-experience it. All the actions of the participants (e.g., navigation, conversations, and space modification) and other changes that happen in the environment and influence the participants causing certain reactions (e.g., scenario flow or events) can be analyzed in detail. This method can enhance the students' experience greatly, as they are able to review and improve their skills.

The second format – creating a new 3D recording being inside one – is even more different and promising for education. A group of learners can enhance a 3D-recorded activity by visiting it and recording over again. As a result,

---

91 Morozov, Gerasimov, Fominykh and Smorkalov (2013)

another 3D recording will be created to contain new activities overlaid the ones of the original activity. New actions (e.g., analysis, discussions, questions, and comments) constitute another layer of 3D recording. New media materials and new virtual 3D objects can be used. All new details can be crystallized together with the original ones, in the same virtual space and in the same context.

An additional use case for the second format is editing the original activity. It is possible to fast-forward a 3D recording through the places that should be skipped. Alternatively, the teacher can pause the original 3D recording and add some missing material and objects or discuss a particular part with the students. Some parts of the original 3D recording can be replaced. The new layer of the crystallized activity (that may contain new materials) is synchronized with the original layer. It can be especially useful in the cases when a certain activity has to be repeated frequently. For example, educators can create a template of a class (containing both 3D virtual space and activity), but perform live discussions with each group of students, retrieving some of the knowledge crystallized in the template, and avoiding unnecessary duplication.

CONCLUSIONS

In this article, I discuss the affordances of 3D VWs for capturing and retrieving knowledge as crystallized activities. These affordances open for a wide range of potential usage areas, especially in the area of education, such as in serious games for corporate training, medical and emergency training and even military training, where activity (e.g., role playing) is a central component. 3D VWs can be used not only as virtual spaces for enactment, but also as a place for accessing traces of past activities to be enacted or collaborated into knowledge. Even though, many challenges of this approach were identified in the studies, it is promising and has to be developed further.

REFERENCES

Ackerman, Mark S., and Halverson, Christine (1998): Considering an organization's memory, *ACM Conference on Computer Supported Cooperative Work (CSCW)*, Seattle, WA, USA.

Arreguin, Cathy (2007): *Reports from the Field: Second Life Community Convention 2007 Education Track Summary*, Global Kids, New York, USA.

Atkins, Clare (2009): "Virtual Experience: Observations on Second Life", in: Maryam Purvis and Bastin Savarimuthu, eds. (2009): *Computer-Mediated Social Networking*, Berlin / Heidelberg: Springer: 7-17.

Barnitt, Rosemary (1998): "The Virtuous Therapist", in: Jennifer Creek, ed. (1998): *Occupational Therapy: New Perspectives*, London, UK: Whurr Publishers: 77-98.

Bartle, Richard (2003): *Designing Virtual Worlds*. NJ, USA: New Riders.

Barwell, Graham, Moore, Chris, and Walker, Ruth (2011): "Marking machinima: A case study in assessing student use of a Web 2.0 technology", Vol. 27, *Australasian Journal of Educational Technology*: 765-780.

Behzadan, Amir H., and Kamat, Vineet R. (2013): "Enabling discovery-based learning in construction using telepresent augmented reality", Vol. 33, *Automation in Construction*: 3-10.

Bell, Mark W. (2008): "Toward a Definition of "Virtual Worlds"", Vol. 1, *Journal of Virtual Worlds Research*: 1-5.

Benford, S., Bowers, J., Fahlén, L. E., Mariani, J., and Rodden, T. (1994): "Supporting Cooperative Work in Virtual Environments", Vol. 37, *The Computer Journal*: 653-668.

Bessière, Katherine, Ellis, Jason B., and Kellogg, Wendy A. (2009): Acquiring a professional "second life": problems and prospects for the use of virtual worlds in business, *27th CHI International Conference extended abstracts on Human factors in computing systems*, Boston, MA, USA.

Bignell, Simon, and Parson, Vanessa (2010): *A guide to using problem-based learning in Second Life*, University of Derby, Derby, UK.

Boellstorff, Tom (2009): *Coming of Age in Second Life: An Anthropologist Explores the Virtually Human*. Princeton, NJ: Princeton University Press.

Boulos, Maged N. Kamel, Hetherington, Lee, and Wheeler, Steve (2007): "Second Life: an overview of the potential of 3-D virtual worlds in medical and health education", Vol. 24, *Health Information & Libraries*: 233-245.

Bowman, Doug A., North, Chris, Chen, Jian, Polys, Nicholas F., Pyla, Pardha S., and Yilmaz, Umur (2003): Information-rich virtual environments: theory, tools, and research agenda, *10th symposium on Virtual reality software and technology (VRST)*, October 1-3, Toonaka, Japan.

Chen, Chaomei, and Börner, Katy (2005): "From spatial proximity to semantic coherence: a quantitative approach to the study of group dynamics in collaborative virtual environments", Vol. 14, *Presence: Teleoperators and Virtual Environments (Special Issue on Collaborative Information Visualization Environments)*: 81-103.

Clouder, Lynn (2005): "Caring as a 'threshold concept': Transforming students in higher education into health (care) professionals", Vol. 10, *Teaching in Higher Education*: 505-517.

Coffman, Teresa, and Klinger, Mary Beth (2007): "Utilizing Virtual Worlds in Education: The Implications for Practice", Vol. 2, *International Journal of Human and Social Sciences*: 29-33.

Craciun, Dana (2010): "Role – playing as a Creative Method in Science Education", Vol. 1, *Journal of Science and Arts*: 175-182.

Cram, Andrew, Hedberg, John, and Gosper, Maree (2011): Beyond Immersion – Meaningful Involvement in Virtual Worlds, *2nd Global Conference on Learning and Technology (Global Learn Asia Pacific)*, March 28–April 1, Melbourne, Australia.

Cruz-Neira, Carolina, Sandin, Daniel J., DeFanti, Thomas A., Kenyon, Robert V., and Hart, John C. (1992): "The CAVE: audio visual experience automatic virtual environment", Vol. 35, *Commun. ACM*: 64-72.

Dalgarno, Barney, Bishop, Andrea G., Adlong, William, and Bedgood, Danny R. (2009): "Effectiveness of a Virtual Laboratory as a preparatory resource for Distance Education chemistry students", Vol. 53, *Computers & Education*: 853-865.

Dawley, Lisa (2009): "Social network knowledge construction: emerging virtual world pedagogy", Vol. 17, *On the Horizon*: 109-121.

de Freitas, Sara (2008a): *Emerging trends in serious games and virtual worlds*, Becta, Coventry, UK.

de Freitas, Sara (2008b): *Serious Virtual Worlds report*, Joint Information Systems Committee, Bristol / London, UK.

Dede, Chris (1996): "The evolution of constructivist learning environments: Immersion in distributed, virtual worlds", in: Brent G. Wilson, ed. (1996): *Constructivist Learning Environments: Case Studies in Instructional Design*: Educational Technology Publications: 165-175.

Dede, Chris (2009): "Immersive Interfaces for Engagement and Learning", Vol. 323, *Science*: 66-69.

Dekker, Gerald A., Moreland, John, and van der Veen, Jatila (2011): Developing the Planck Mission Simulation as a Multi-Platform Immersive Application, *3rd World Conference on Innovative Virtual Reality (WINVR)*, June 27–29, Milan, Italy.

Engeström, Yrjö (1999): "Activity theory and individual and social transformation", in: Yrjö Engeström, Reijo Miettinen and Raija-Leena Punamäki, eds. (1999): *Perspectives on Activity Theory*, Cambridge, UK: Cambridge University Press: 19-38.

Entwistle, Noel (2005): "Learning outcomes and ways of thinking across contrasting disciplines and settings in higher education", Vol. 16, *Curriculum Journal*: 67-82.

Falconer, Liz, and Frutos-Perez, Manuel (2009): Online Simulation of Real Life Experiences; the Educational Potential, *21st World Conference on Educational Multimedia, Hypermedia & Telecommunications (Ed-Media)*, June 22–26, Honolulu, Hawaii.

Fominykh, Mikhail, and Prasolova-Førland, Ekaterina (2011): Virtual Research Arena: Presenting Research in 3D Virtual Environments, *2nd Global Conference on Learning and Technology (Global Learn Asia Pacific)*, March 28–April 1, Melbourne, Australia.

Fominykh, Mikhail, and Prasolova-Førland, Ekaterina (2012): "Educational visualizations in 3D collaborative virtual environments: a methodology", Vol. 9, *Interactive Technology and Smart Education*: 33-45.

Fominykh, Mikhail, Prasolova-Førland, Ekaterina, and Divitini, Monica (2012): Learning Computer-Mediated Cooperation in 3D Visualization Projects, *9th International Conference on Cooperative Design, Visualization and Engineering (CDVE)*, September 2–5, Osaka, Japan.

Fominykh, Mikhail, Prasolova-Førland, Ekaterina, Hokstad, Leif Martin, and Morozov, Mikhail (2014): Repositories of Community Memory as Visualized Activities in 3D Virtual Worlds, *47th Hawaii International Conference on System Sciences (HICSS)*, Waikoloa, HI, USA.

Foronda, Cynthia, Godsall, Lyndon, and Trybulski, JoAnn (2013): "Virtual Clinical Simulation: The State of the Science", Vol. 9, *Clinical Simulation in Nursing*: e279-e286.

Goel, Lakshmi, Johnson, Norman, Junglas, Iris, and Ives, Blake (2013): "Predicting users' return to virtual worlds: a social perspective", Vol. 23, *Info. Sys. Jour.*: 35-63.

Greenhalgh, Chris, Flintham, Martin, Purbrick, Jim, and Benford, Steve (2002): Applications of Temporal Links: Recording and Replaying Virtual Environments, *Virtual Reality (VR)*, March 24–28, Orlando, FL, USA.

Gu, Ning, Williams, Anthony, and Gül, Leman Figen (2007): Designing & Learning in 3D Virtual Worlds, *4th International Conference on Cognition and Exploratory Learning in Digital Age (CELDA)*, December 7–9, Algarve, Portugal.

Hansen, Margaret M. (2008): "Versatile, immersive, creative and dynamic virtual 3-D healthcare learning environments: A review of the literature", Vol. 10, *Journal of Medical Internet Research*.

Harrison, Steve, and Dourish, Paul (1996): Re-place-ing space: the roles of place and space in collaborative systems, *ACM conference on Computer supported cooperative work*, Boston, MA.

Hayes, Elisabeth R. (2006): Situated Learning in Virtual Worlds: The Learning Ecology of Second Life, *American Educational Research Association Conference*.

Hendaoui, Adel, Limayem, Moez, and Thompson, Craig W. (2008): "3D Social Virtual Worlds: Research Issues and Challenges", Vol. 12, *IEEE Internet Computing*: 88-92.

Hill, Valerie, and Lee, Hyuk-Jin (2009): "Libraries and immersive learning environments unite in Second Life", Vol. 27, *Library Hi Tech*: 338-356.

Holliman, Nicolas S., Dodgson, Neil A., Favalora, Gregg E., and Pockett, Lachlan (2011): "Three-Dimensional Displays: A Review and Applications Analysis", Vol. 57, *IEEE Transactions on Broadcasting*: 362-371.

Holloway, David (2012): "Virtual worlds and health: healthcare delivery and simulation opportunities", in: N. Zagalo, L. Morgado and A. Boa-Ventura, eds. (2012): *Virtual worlds and metaverse platforms : new communication and identity paradigms*, USA: IGI Global: 251-270.

Huang, Hsiu-Mei, Rauch, Ulrich, and Liaw, Shu-Sheng (2010): "Investigating learners' attitudes toward virtual reality learning environments: Based on a constructivist approach", Vol. 55, *Computers & Education*: 1171-1182.

Huxor, Avon (2001): "The Role of the Personal in Social Workspaces: Reflections on Working in AlphaWorld", in: Elizabeth F. Churchill, David N. Snowdon and Alan J. Munro, eds. (2001): *Collaborative Virtual Environments*: Springer London: 282-296.

Hwang, Jihyun, Park, Hyungsung, Cha, Jiseon, and Shin, Bokjin (2008): Effects of Object Building Activities in Second Life on Players' Spatial Reasoning, *2nd International Conference on Digital Game and Intelligent Toy Enhanced Learning*, November 17–19, Banff, Canada.

Imai, Tomoko, Qiu, Zhongwei, Behara, Sowmitri, Tachi, Susumu, Aoyama, Tomonori, Johnson, Andrew, and Leigh, Jason (2000): Overcoming Time-Zone Differences and Time Management Problems with Tele-Immersion, *10th Annual Internet Society Conference (INET)*, July 18–21, Yokohama, Japan.

Jarmon, Leslie, Traphagan, Tomoko, and Mayrath, Michael (2008): "Understanding project-based learning in Second Life with a pedagogy, training, and assessment trio", Vol. 45, *Educational Media International*: 157-176.

Johnson, W. Lewis (2009): A Simulation-Based Approach to training Operational Cultural Competence, *International Congress on Modelling and Simulation (MODSIM)*.

Korakakis, George, Boudouvis, Andreas, Palyvos, John, and Pavlatou, Evagelia A. (2012): "The impact of 3D visualization types in instructional multimedia applications for teaching science", Vol. 31, *Procedia - Social and Behavioral Sciences*: 145-149.

Lee, Mark J. W. (2009): "How Can 3d Virtual Worlds Be Used To Support Collaborative Learning? An Analysis Of Cases From The Literature", Vol. 5, *Society*: 149-158.

Leigh, Jason, Ali, Mohammed Dastagir, Bailey, Stuart, Banerjee, Andy, Banerjee, Pat, Curry, Kevin, Curtis, Jim, Dech, Fred, Dodds, Brian, Foster, Ian, Fraser, Sarah, Ganeshan, Kartik, Glen, Dennis, Grossman, Robert, Heil, Y, Hicks, John, Hudson, Alan D., Imai, Tomoko, Khan, Mohammed Ali, Kapoor, Abhinav, Kenyon, Robert V., Park, Kyoung, Parod, Bill, Rajlich, Paul J., Rasmussen, Mary, Rawlings, Maggie, Robertson, Danielh., Thongrong, Samroeng, Stein, Robert J., Tuecke, Steve, Wallach, Harlan, Wong, Hong Yee, and Wheless, Glenh. (1999): A Review of Tele-Immersive Applications in the CAVE Research Network, *International conference on Virtual Reality (VR)*, March 13–17, Houston, TX , USA.

Lele, Ajey (2013): "Virtual reality and its military utility", Vol. 4, *Journal of Ambient Intelligence and Humanized Computing*: 17-26.

Leont'ev, Alexei Nikolaevich (1981): *Problems of the development of the mind.* 4 ed. Moscow: Progress.

Li, Fei, and Maher, Mary Lou (2000): Representing Virtual Places - A Design Model for Metaphorical Design, *22nd Annual Conference of the Association for Computer-Aided Design in Architecture (ACADIA)*, October 19–22.

Linde, Charlotte (2001): "Narrative and social tacit knowledge", Vol. 5, *Journal of Knowledge Management*: 160-171.

Matsuura, Kenji, Ogata, Hiroaki, and Yano, Yoneo (1999): Agent-based Asynchronous Virtual Classroom, *7th International Conference on Computers in Education (ICCE)*, Japan.

Mckerlich, Ross, Riis, Marianne, Anderson, Terry, and Eastman, Brad (2011): "Student Perceptions of Teaching Presence, Social Presence, and Cognitive Presence in a Virtual World", Vol. 7, *Journal of Online Learning and Teaching*: 324-336.

McSharry, Gabrielle, and Jones, Sam (2000): "Role-Play in Science Teaching and Learning", Vol. 82, *School Science Review*: 73-82.

Messinger, Paul R, Stroulia, Eleni, and Lyons, Kelly (2008): "A Typology of Virtual Worlds: Historical Overview and Future Directions", Vol. 1, *Journal of Virtual Worlds Research*: 1-18.

Meyer, Jan H. F., and Land, Ray (2003): "Threshold concepts and troublesome knowledge: linkages to ways of thinking and practicing", in: C. Rust, ed. (2003): *Improving Student Learning – Theory and Practice Ten Years On*, Oxford, UK: Oxford Centre for Staff and Learning Development (OCSLD): 412-424.

Minocha, Shailey, and Reeves, Ahmad John (2010): "Design of learning spaces in 3D virtual worlds: an empirical investigation of Second Life", Vol. 35, *Learning, Media and Technology*: 111-137.

Molka-Danielsen, Judith (2009): "The new learning and teaching environment", in: Judith Molka-Danielsen and Mats Deutschmann, eds. (2009): *Learning and Teaching in the Virtual World of Second Life*, Trondheim, Norway: Tapir Academic Press: 13-25.

Molka-Danielsen, Judith, Deutschmann, Mats, and Panichi, Lusia (2009): "Designing Transient Learning Spaces in Second Life - a case study based on the Kamimo experience", Vol. 2, *Designs for Learning*: 22-33.

Morozov, Mikhail, Gerasimov, Alexey, Fominykh, Mikhail, and Smorkalov, Andrey (2013): "Asynchronous Immersive Classes in a 3D Virtual World: Extended Description of vAcademia", in: MarinaL Gavrilova, C. J. Kenneth Tan and Arjan Kuijper, eds. (2013): *Transactions on Computational Science XVIII*: Springer Berlin Heidelberg: 81-100.

Neustaedter, Carman, and Fedorovskaya, Elena (2009): Capturing and sharing memories in a virtual world, *SIGCHI Conference on Human Factors in Computing Systems*, Boston, MA, USA.

Nonaka, Ikujiro, and Takeuchi, Hirotaka (1995): *The Knowledge-Creating Company: How Japanese Companies Create the Dynamics of Innovation*. New York: Oxford University Press.

Owen, Martin L., Grant, Lyndsay, Sayers, Steve, and Facer, Keri (2006): *Social software and learning*, Futurelab, London, UK.

Papert, Seymour, and Harel, Idit (1991): "Situating Constructionism", in: Seymour Papert and Idit Harel, eds. (1991): *Constructionism*, Westport, CT, USA: Ablex Publishing Corporation: 193-206.

Perera, Indika , Allison, Colin, Nicoll, J. Ross, Sturgeon, T., and Miller, Alan (2010): "Managed Learning in 3D Multi User Virtual Environments", Vol. 1, *International Journal of Digital Society*: 256-264.

Polanyi, Michael (1966): *The Tacit Dimension*. Glouchester, MA: Peter Smith.

Prasolova-Førland, Ekaterina (2004): A repository of virtual places as community memory: an experience of use, *SIGGRAPH International Conference on Virtual Reality Continuum and its Applications in Industry*, Singapore.

Prasolova-Førland, Ekaterina (2005): Place Metaphors in Educational CVEs: An Extended Characterization, *4th Conference on Web-based Education (WBE)*, Switzerland.

Prasolova-Førland, Ekaterina, Fominykh, Mikhail, Darisiro, Ramin, and Mørch, Anders I. (2013): Training Cultural Awareness in Military Operations in a Virtual Afghan Village: A Methodology for Scenario Development, *46th Hawaii International Conference on System Sciences (HICSS)*, January 7–10, Wailea, HI, USA.

Prasolova-Førland, Ekaterina, Fominykh, Mikhail, and Wyeld, Theodor G. (2010): Virtual Campus of NTNU as a place for 3D Educational Visualizations, *1st Global Conference on Learning and Technology (Global Learn Asia Pacific)*, May 17–20, Penang, Malaysia.

Salmon, Gilly, and Hawkridge, David (2009): "Editorial: Out of this world", Vol. 40, *British Journal of Educational Technology*: 401-413.

Sant, Toni (2009): "Performance in Second Life: some possibilities for learning and teaching", in: Judith Molka-Danielsen and Mats Deutschmann, eds. (2009): *Learning and Teaching in the Virtual World of Second Life*, Trondheim, Norway: Tapir Academic Press: 145-166.

Saunders, Carol, Rutkowski, Anne F., Genuchten, Michiel Van, Vogel, Doug, and Orrego, Julio Molina (2011): "Virtual space and place: theory and test", Vol. 35, *MIS Quarterly*: 1079-1098.

Savin-Baden, Maggi (2013): "Spaces in between us: a qualitative study into the impact of spatial practice when learning in Second Life", Vol. 11, *London Review of Education*: 59-75.

Schmeil, Andreas, and Eppler, Martin. J. (2009): Formalizing and Promoting Collaboration in 3D Virtual Environments – A Blueprint for the Creation of Group Interaction Patterns, *1st International Conference on Facets of Virtual Environments (FaVE)*, July 27–29, Berlin, Germany.

Smith, Rachel, Oblinger, Diana, Johnson, Laurence F., and Lomas, Cyprien P. (2007): *The Horizon Report*, The New Media Consortium, Austin, TX, USA: The New Media Consortium.

Styliani, Sylaiou, Fotis, Liarokapis, Kostas, Kotsakis, and Petros, Patias (2009): "Virtual museums, a survey and some issues for consideration", Vol. 10, *Journal of Cultural Heritage*: 520-528.

Surface, Eric A., Dierdorff, Erich C., and Watson, Aaron M. (2007): *Special Operations Language Training Software Measurement of Effectiveness Study: Tactical Iraqi Study Final Report*, Special Operations Forces Language Office, Tampa, FL, USA.

Thorpe, Stephen J. (2011): "Sense of Place and Emotional Connections Using Collaborative Storytelling in Second Life", Vol. 1, *International Journal of Information and Education Technology*: 292-297.

van Nederveen, Sander (2007): Collaborative Design in Second Life, *2nd International Conference World of Construction Project Management (WCPM)*, October 24–25, Delft, The Netherlands.

Vygotsky, Lev Semyonovich (1978): *Mind in society: the development of higher psychological processes*. Cambridge, MA, USA: Harvard University Press.

Walsh, James P., and Ungson, Gerardo Rivera (1991): "Organizational Memory", Vol. 16, *The Academy of Management Review*: 57-91.

Wenger, Etienne (1998): *Communities of Practice: Learning, Meaning, and Identity*. New York, NY, USA / Cambridge, UK: Cambridge University Press.

Wrzesien, Maja, and Raya, Mariano Alcañiz (2010): "Learning in serious virtual worlds: Evaluation of learning effectiveness and appeal to students in the E-Junior project", Vol. 55, *Computers & Education*: 178-187.

Yates, Frances A. (1966): *The Art of Memory*. London: Routledge & Kegan Paul.

Youngblut, Christine (1998): *Educational Uses of Virtual Reality Technology*, Institute for Defense Analyses, Alexandria, VA, USA, D-2128.

Zensius, Natalie (2009): "Palomar Pomerado Health uses Second Life to explore the hospital of the future", *Healthcare Design*: 20–20,22,24, http://www.healthcaredesignmagazine.com/article/palomar-pomerado-health-uses-second-life-explore-hospital-future.

Zielke, Marjorie A. (2011): "The First Person Cultural Trainer Whitepaper", http://www.utdallas.edu/~maz031000/res/FPCT_White_Paper.pdf.

Identity in Virtual Worlds

LYZGEO M. KOSHY, KRISTOFFER GETCHELL, MARC CONRAD
AND TIM FRENCH

INTRODUCTION

Certain activities in the virtual world have benefited individuals, schools and organizations with the provision of efficient communication methods reducing the costs encountered through travel expenses and other inaccessible activities in the real world.

The geography and architecture of a virtual world may be defined and programmed by users, thereby allowing its users to actively participate in the shaping of their environment. By removing barriers that exist in the real world, virtual worlds offer the opportunity to enhance the interactions that avatars can have between each other, as well as the interactions they may have with the environment around them. This powerful feature makes possible modes and types of interaction that is never be supported within the real world. This has the ability to create a sense of empowerment amongst users and offers opportunities to effect change in the behaviors seen in real world society.

One important factor affecting the virtual experience is *identity*. In this chapter we consider identity as the collective aspect of the set of characteristics or features by which a thing, be it a person (real world) or avatar (virtual world), is definitively recognizable or known. In both environments, we take a number of attributes or characteristics to be proxies of identity when assessing an identity. These include, but are not limited to, factors such as visual appearance, fingerprints, name, personality and behavior. The relative strength of these attributes varies between the real and online worlds, as does the way in which we approach the task of recognizing and confirming identity. Does the virtual world identity have an impact on the identities in the real world? It is important that we understand if social behaviors in virtual worlds induce the user to behave the same way in the real world. Certain behaviors such as change of persona are induced due to the pressure experienced both in the virtual world and in the real world.

The real world is considered to be a high signaling environment, in which many attributes of identity are transmitted without explicit action on the part of a person: attributes such as facial composition, gender and ethnicity are all relatively difficult to change and are transmitted automatically when people are within visual range. In this way, it is possible for the identity of a person in the real world to be validated without explicit actions being taken by those whose identity is being assessed or indeed by those making the assessment. Contrast this to the online world, which can be considered a low signaling environment. Unlike in the real world, many of the attributes we traditionally deem to be strong proxies for identity either do not exist; for example fingerprints and DNA, or are readily changeable; such as facial composition, gender, age, ethnicity. As such it is not possible for identity to be validated in a passive way as is the case in the real world and so those making the assessments must gauge validity using alternative attributes which are often more subjective and less clearly defined; for example behavior analysis or language use.

Users expose to fewer restrictions in the virtual world in contrast to real world enabling the inhabitants of the virtual world to take full advantage of this privilege. Certain behaviors in the virtual world create a positive and negative impact in the real world. For example, disabilities are less prevalent in the virtual world, which is difficult to accomplish in the real world. This can cause a positive effect on a person with disability in the real world as it may help to boost confidence and self-esteem leading to a better quality of life. The sense of value of life increases through the interaction with other users, which can be difficult at times in the real world.[1]

By understanding the impact that changes to the dynamic of identity on the way in which users interact, we explore the dynamics that are possible when the feedback loops between virtual world and real world are understood and exploited in real world activities. By doing so we explore how the freedoms offered in the virtual world can have an impact on the way in which people interact in their real world lives, and thus we assess the extent to which virtual actions in virtual environments have the ability to impact and shape our real world societies. Our research helped us to understand the impact of anonymity on the users due to the changes in their behavior and self-perception leading to desensitization to violence. Desensitization is the process through which less psychological arousal to

1   Stewart, S., Hansen, T. S., and Carey, T. A. (2010): 254–259

violence in the real world after the exposure of activities in the virtual world.[2] This process is common in users exposed to virtual environments including gaming environments.[3]

Virtual Worlds

Whilst virtual worlds such as Second Life and Open Simulator provide the ability for users to form relationships in much the same way as social networks such as Facebook and Twitter, they differ in the approach adopted, with virtual worlds de-emphasizing the importance of information sharing in preference to focusing primarily on user interactions.[4] Unlike social networks, virtual worlds allow users to present themselves through a 3D representation. By providing a simulated environment within which multiple users can interact with avatars, virtual worlds are often used for social and educational purposes.

Originating from Hindi, avatar means incarnation and conveys the belief that God has the ability to take any form.[5] Virtual environments such as Second Life and Open Simulator offer users the opportunity to customize avatars based on their personal features, personal interests and fantasies, many of which may be difficult to incorporate in the real world. Even though avatars represent the users, they do not necessarily represent the user's true self as portrayed in the real world. Identities in virtual worlds may be fabricated or duplicated varying on the purpose of the users' involvement in the environment. Users of virtual worlds are not obligated to provide accurate personal information. Instead, identities may be created to meet the theme of the community a user is involved with. By extension, the behavior of users within a virtual world can also deviate significantly from the types of behavior they would exhibit in the real world. This trend is the subject of a growing research agenda focusing on the ways in which virtual world behaviors manifest themselves in the real world.

Within a virtual world, each user has their own perspective on the environment, with the underlying world presenting a consistent state to all users. The environment of a virtual world is not fixed and can be modeled and altered by some or all of the users who inhabit it. In addition, each user's avatar can be customized to portray the personality of the owner. As the environment is persistent, any changes to it, or a user's avatar, remain over time and are not reset each time

---

2   Carnagey, N. L., Anderson, C. A., Bushman, B. J. (2007): 489-496

3   Carnagey, N. L., Anderson, C. A., Bushman, B. J. (2007): 496

4   Nagy, P. (2010)

5   Partridge, C. (2005): 148

a user logs in. This allows long-term changes to the environment to be retained in perpetuity. Virtual worlds do not impose many set rules or objectives, which users must follow. Instead, the inhabitants are able to decide what rules and conditions they wish to impose. This makes it possible for virtual worlds to be used to host a variety of different activities including music concerts, games and university lectures. In addition, the underlying world is not limited in size or the number of simultaneous users, with multiple servers used to host different regions of the world. This allows the environment to grow in accordance with demand.

Virtual worlds have no rigidly defined set of goals, but instead aim to enable users to develop their own communities and environments. As such, virtual worlds generally exhibit a number of generic characteristics[6] in order to enable a user centered approach to the development of the environment:

Realism: The environment presented by the virtual world mirrors many aspects of the real world. This ensures familiarity with the environment amongst users, making operation within the virtual world more intuitive.

3D perspectives: Users are provided with a personalized 3D view of the virtual environment.

Avatars: Users experience the virtual environment through their avatar. As the avatar acts as a representation of a given user, it is possible for relationships to be formed between users who may or may not know each other outside of the virtual world environment.

User control: There are no predefined goals or objectives in the virtual environments. The users are fully responsible for developing any rules or objectives as they see fit.

Mutability of environment: Users are empowered to create content and edit areas within the virtual environment. Whilst the virtual environment may provide some initial content, users are not confined to using this and may develop new content based on their own requirements.

---

6   Kalyuga, S. (2007): 19, 387–399

Persistence: The virtual environment persists over a long period, with changes made by one user experienced by all other users within the environment.

Distributed environment: Virtual worlds have no fixed size, with the environment growing and shrinking with demand. In order to facilitate such expansion and contraction, the underlying environment is often distributed over several servers, with each managing a defined area. From a user perspective, this distribution is seamless, with the virtual world client application handling the communication with multiple servers as required.

In addition to these generic properties, virtual world client applications often provide a series of tools which can be used in the virtual environment to allow users to modify the landscape and scenery and construct buildings and areas of shared space such as parks, gardens and neighbourhoods. Many virtual worlds also support access controls, which allow authorized users to define access restrictions on parcels of land, thereby making it possible for private spaces to be developed within the shared environment. In addition virtual world clients also provide tools to allow users to communicate both synchronously and asynchronously through text (and often audio) messages.

In many ways, the environment is very similar to that of the real world, with the laws of physics often emulated to provide an environment representative of the real world. As such, some of the behaviors we are familiar with (such as not being able to walk through walls or objects falling towards earth due to gravity) are mirrored in the virtual environment. There are, however, some notable exceptions which are designed to make movement within the virtual world easier; users are often able to fly or teleport to different places within the environment.

Even though virtual worlds can offer a massive amount of freedom, they do also have various restrictions. Virtual worlds restrict the ability for users to make character judgments, something that is frequently done in the real world through non-verbal communication that occurs during face-to-face interactions. As identity is dynamic in virtual worlds, this problem is further compounded by the relative difficulty associated with reliably attributing reputation to individuals in the virtual world. Only after a long period of interaction between users it is possible for some of these limitations to be overcome, with users able to reliably identify close friends through recognition of common behaviors and methods of communicating.

Virtual worlds are often seen as providing a way of escaping from the real world for users who feel unable or ill equipped to deal with real world situations.[7] This can have an impact on the types of behavior seen in the virtual world, with the extreme cases seeing users attaching disproportionate amounts of weight on negative behaviors within the virtual world. As shown by the Hannah Smith case,[8] when users are overly focused on their actions in the virtual world they can often fail to recognize the consequences of their actions in the real world. When coupled with a user who has a disproportionate focus on the negative aspects of their interactions in the virtual world, the results can be devastating as shown by Ms Smith eventually taking her own life. Whilst the extremity of the Hannah Smith case is rare,[9] more minor cases are routinely reported.

Second Life

Second Life is a popular commercial virtual world in which anyone can sign up for an account and rent land to build upon. Using the Havok physics engine[10] to provide an approximation of the laws of physics in the virtual world, Second Life presents users with a broadly realistic representation of the real world. With an economy that is tied to that of the real world, Second Life is often used for commercial purposes with residents creating, buying and selling goods in order to earn currency in Second Life that can be exchanged for those of the real world.

Managed and hosted by Linden Labs,[11] the virtual world presented by Second Life is broken up into a series of islands, with up to four separate islands hosted by a single server.[12] Using a client-server model, all of the simulation in Second Life is conducted by the hosting servers, with the client application acting as a viewer, which displays the resulting visual scenes. Predominantly open source, the client application has been ported to a variety of platforms including: Windows, Mac OS and Linux. Second Life has been adopted by academia as a tool to support both teaching and research. In addition, many institutions use

7   Zhou, Z., Jin, X.-L., Vogel, D. R., Fang Y., Chen, X. (2011): 264

8   Evans, J. (2013)

9   Evans, J. (2013)

10 *Havok Physics*. [cited April 2009]

11 www.lindenlab.com

12 Antonello, R., et al. (2008)

Second Life as a marketing and recruitment tool, with a number establishing sizeable communities in the virtual world.[13]

Open Simulator

Open Simulator is an open source virtual world, which can be used to create 3D worlds similar to those of Second Life. Using a client-server architecture, which mimics much of the behavior of Second Life and uses the same communication protocols, Open Simulator virtual worlds, can be accessed using the Second Life client application.

As the hosting of Open Simulator is managed directly by individual organizations, it is possible for more control to be exerted over the virtual environment. This makes it possible for entirely private virtual environments to be established by an organization either with or without an economy – something that Second Life cannot support. Furthermore, as Open Simulator provides support for multiple systems to group together into a grid structure, it is also possible for a single virtual environment to span multiple administrative domains, thereby making it possible for multiple organizations to cooperate in establishing a shared virtual world.

As indicated by the already widespread use of virtual worlds within the educational sector, the technology offers real opportunities with regards to the development of alternative approaches to learning which centers on the learner.[14] By providing, the social and collaborative tools required in order to allow physically disparate learners to communicate effectively using technological means, virtual worlds are well placed to support distance and anytime-anywhere learning, thereby empowering the learner by allowing them to decide when and where they wish to learn.

Furthermore, as virtual worlds share many of the expressive properties of 3D game environments they are well placed to provide support for alternative approaches to visualization to be developed, thereby allowing educators to employ new abstractions as a way of depicting complex real world behaviors. With none of the preconceived notions of goals or objectives that games have, virtual worlds are somewhat better suited to educational use, with educators able to spend more time focusing on the development of new and innovative learning materials and not on overcoming the inherent limitations associated with the ideas of goals, objectives and progression that a game may impose.

---

13 Kirriemuir, J. (2008)
14 Perera, I., Allison, C., Miller, A. (2010): 114-120

However, it is not the case that the 3D environments presented by virtual worlds are suitable for all educational activities. As users are often more familiar with 2D presentation, the use of 2D interfaces should not be precluded. As an example, reading text from a Web page is more easily attained than reading a similar piece of text from within Second Life.

Identity

Identity plays a key role in virtual worlds as well as in self-concept.[15] According to Rosenberg,[16] self-concept is the sum of a person's thoughts and feelings. How others know us is through our identity.

Virtual worlds are increasingly used in alternative contexts and are no longer just a platform to connect and socialize for their users. As businesses increasingly make use of virtual worlds and distribute information on them, the role of identity within the virtual world plays an increasingly important role in providing a positive user interaction and experience. In order to understand this role, one needs to understand the definition of identity. At its most basic, the definition of identity can be defined as "a socially distinguishable feature that a person takes a special pride in or views as unchangeable but socially consequential."[17]

Furthermore, within virtual worlds avatars can also be controlled by computer controlled agents, thus further complicating the ability to establish trust. However, as shown by Nagy Peter,[18] when a human controls an avatar in a virtual world, users are more readily able to establish trust. Our work is a replicate of this finding. In the work of Hoyt et al.[19] and Okita et al.,[20] it was found that people's behaviors and physiological responses while interacting with an avatar were similar to those observed when interacting with a person in the real world. Further investigation will help to understand if changing identities affects the way people interact with avatars.

An important factor raised from the experiment is the *anonymity* of users in virtual worlds. Users are keen on not disclosing their real name to keep their identity discreet for privacy reasons. This can have both positive and negative ef-

15 Zhao, S., Grasmuck, S., and Matin, J. (2008): 24

16 Rosenberg, M. (1986)

17 Fearon, J. (1999): 25

18 Nagy, P. (2010)

19 Hoyt, C. L., and Blascovich, J. (2003): 34

20 Okita, S. Y., Bailenson, J. N., and Schwartz, D. L. (2008)

fect when immersed in the virtual world. Whilst being anonymous can help users to be private, it can also create problems between users due to the issue of trust. Findings from the experiment described below show that users struggle to develop any form of trust if the user is anonymous. On the other hand, users question the authenticity of the user's virtual identity.

EXPERIMENT

The experiment was carried out using 16 final year students from the Computer Science department. Some of the participants were experienced users in the virtual world (Open Simulator) whereas the others were amateurs. The experiment involved participants demonstrating the avatar they created for their assignment. Participants were interviewed on the appearance of their avatar. Questions were asked based on their answers and so this was an unstructured interview. An unstructured interview involves asking open-ended questions in order to discover accurate information about the participant's feelings as well as the reasons behind creating the avatar of their choice. This helped to gather a deeper understanding of how identity is being used by virtual world users. This experiment allowed consideration of the participant's emotions. The data collected from the experiment were analysed using grounded theory. For example, participants were asked "Did you intend to portray yourself using the avatar you have created?" or "Do you want to expose your identity in such environments?" If the participant answered "No" to any of these questions, the direction of the interview changed along with the questions asked later on. This helped us to avoid superimposing our views on to the participants while allowing the participants to share their views. It was vital to understand the participant's perception in order to gain representative results. This has helped us to gather a thorough understanding of how users impose their identity on to the avatar.

All the questions asked prompted the users to provide an answer related to identity and avatars.

Results

Majority of the individuals from the male gender preferred to keep their gender the same whereas some prefer to be of the opposite gender. As this experiment was carried using the avatars the students created for their assignment, they were not allowed to amend the name of the avatar. However, some users stated the use of real names is seen as appropriate based on the purpose of the interaction (such as professional services). These users provided less importance on using real names during personal interactions. The main finding of this experiment is that, very few use their own identity in such environments.

An interesting finding from this experiment is that 81.25% of the participants out of the 100% of male gender have used the same gender for their avatars whilst 18.75% of the participants used the opposite gender. When these participants were asked the reasons to their gender preference, they stated that creating an avatar with different identity and features are far more interesting than using the same identity all the time. According to the participants, virtual world is an environment where one is exposed to the choice of having multiple identities. Majority of the participants (81.25%) shared no similar features between the participant and their customized avatar. Some of the participants mentioned that they want to conceal their real identity from other users, which affected their decision of being discreet. More than half of these participants were new to the digital role-play experience as well as the creation of avatars. This had a huge impact on the customization of the avatars, as they were less experienced in implementing certain features.

Impact of online behavior while offline

As mentioned earlier, avatars are controlled by human users in computer-mediated environments such as virtual worlds. Previous research shows that people behave differently when they believe a human user as opposed to a computer controls an avatar.[21] However, recent studies also show that when people interact with avatars, their physiological responses, and behaviors are similar to when they interact with a real person.[22] Most social networks share such characteristics but what makes virtual worlds different amongst social networks such as Facebook and Twitter is that users are able to interact in real time using fully customized avatars. Customizing avatars provide users flexibility with how they present themselves. All these characteristics induce a very strong presence sensation in virtual worlds, hence enabling users to immerse in the environment.[23]

As users are able to customize their avatars according to their preferences, users are able to be anonymous in these environments. Being anonymous affects the users' self-perception, which changes the way all the users behave in virtual

---

21 Nagy, P. (2010)
22 Bailenson, J. N., and Blascovich, J. (2004)
23 Nagy, P. (2010): 169

worlds.[24] The change in self-perception has an impact on desensitization. Virtual worlds provide users interaction using audio and visual features but even with the engagement of these features, anonymity can be maintained through the withholding of personal information such as the user's real name and location. Earlier analysis by researchers and the findings from our experiment massively resonates the effect of anonymous virtual world behaviors while offline. Anecdotal evidences (evidences seen when communicating with users online) as well as scientific evidences[25] show that anonymity plays an important role in how users behave virtually due to how collaborative virtual environments are programmed to filter and alter user behaviors. Such findings show that every virtual incarnation allows the users to create an identity unrelated to their past or any self-commitments. Anonymity is the state of being unknown, which is seen as a normal practice in the virtual worlds. Being anonymous in digital systems allow users to be discreet about their real life identity as well as allow the users with lower status and power to have more say virtually than in face to face communications.[26] Face-to-face, communications or real life situations make people feel more obliged to respect orders that contrasts to virtual world where there are fewer established orders for users to follow. Anonymity can help users to be private but at the same time, it *deindividuates* them. Deindividuation is the loss of self-awareness and individual responsibilities. Tentative evidence[27] shows that users' behavior in a virtual setting through avatars can affect the users' behavior in real life settings. However, this depends on whether the user deindividuated themselves during their presence in a virtual setting. Empirical evidences have found that users conform to group norms when deindividuated and show an independent identity when individuated such as in face-to-face meetings.[28] Research shows that a user in the virtual world deindividuates by inferring their expected behaviors and attitudes onto an avatar.[29] The users expected behaviors and attitudes are based on the appearance of their avatar. This phenomenon is scientifically known as the *Proteus effect*.[30] The Proteus effect is evident in experimental settings within an immersive virtual reality.[31] The study by Yee and

24 Postmes, T., Spears, R., and Lea, M. (2002)

25 Yee, N., Bailenson, J. N., and Ducheneaut, N. (2009): 14

26 Postmes, T., Spears, R., and Lea, M. (2002)

27 Yee, N., Bailenson, J. N., and Ducheneaut, N. (2009): 36

28 Yee, N., Bailenson, J. N., and Ducheneaut, N. (2009): 285-312

29 Yee, N., and Bailenson, J. N. (2007): 33, 271-290

30 Yee, N., and Bailenson, J. N. (2007): 271-290

31 Yee, N., Bailenson, J. N., and Ducheneaut, N. (2009): 285-312

Bailenson shows that the attractiveness and the appearance of avatars have an impact on how users interact. This has also been evident in our experiment described above.

In contrast to the Proteus effect, research shows that most interactions in a collaborative virtual environment can be programmed to strategically filter and alter user behaviors.[32] It is difficult for users to make changes to their physical appearance analogously but digital systems (virtual environments) enable the users to dramatically make changes such as altering their height. Virtual environments provide users with the control over their self-presentation allowing users to alter their behaviors based on their appearance known as the *Transformed Social Interaction* (TSI).[33] Studies in TSI show that changes in the users' appearance or behavior can influence how other users interact with the avatar.[34] However, studies have also shown[35] how these changes affect the users' behavior in real life.

One major benefit of virtual world is that it provides space for the expression of the users' hidden selves as well as the ability to create chosen identities.[36] Creating identities allow users to leverage social support whilst increasing personal performances. This is normally achieved through the customization of avatars to create an attractive avatar. Attractive avatars help to expand the user's social network than those with unattractive avatars. This shows that users of social networks including virtual world base their relationship on the attractiveness of the avatar. The attributes of identity used in this concept is the appearance of the avatar. In real life, more individuals form relationships with attractive people than unattractive people do. It applies to virtual world and social networks where users perceive attractive people to have more positive attributes than the unattractive. These attributes include performance variables such as competence,[37] self-esteem, and confidence. It is believed that behaviors that stem from the Proteus effect are carried on to face-to-face interactions through self-perception. It is vital that positive behavior is portrayed on the users' customized avatars in order to carry on positive behaviors in face-to-face interactions. Having negative behaviors in virtual worlds can contribute to desensitization due to the user exposed to negative behaviors.

---

32 Bailenson, J. N., and Blascovich, J. (2004)

33 Bailenson, J., Beall, A., Loomis, J., Blascovich, J., and Turk, M. (2004): 13

34 Yee, N., Bailenson, J. N., and Ducheneaut, N. (2009) : 285-312

35 Peter, N. (2010)

36 Rosenmann, A., and Safir, M. P. (2006): 51, 71-92

37 Jackson, L. A., Hunter, E., and Hodge, C. N. (1995): 58, 108-122

REFERENCES

Antonello, Rafael, Moreira, Josilene, Fernandes, Stenio, Cunha, Paulo, and Sadok, Djamel (2008): "Traffic Analysis and Synthetic Models of Second Life", *Multimedia Systems Journal*, vol. 15, ACM/Springer

Bailenson, Jeremy N., Beall, Andrew, Loomis, Jack, Blascovich, Jim, and Turk, Matthew (2004): "Transformed social interaction: Decoupling representation from behaviour and form in collaborative virtual environments", *Presence*, vol. 13: 428-441.

Bailenson, Jeremy N., and Blascovich, Jim (2004): "Avatars", in: W.S. Bainbridge (ed.), *Encyclopedia of human-computer interaction*, Great Barrington, MA: Berkshire.

Carnagey, Nicholas L., Anderson, Craig A., and Bushman, Brad J. (2007): "The effect of video game violence on physiological desensitization to real-life violence", *Journal of Experimental Social Psychology*, vol. 43: 489-496

Evans, Julie Lynn (2013): *Hannah Smith has shown us the dangers online*, http://www.telegraph.co.uk/health/children_shealth/10234854/Hannah-Smith-has-shown-us-the-dangers-online.html

Fearon, James D. (1999): *What is Identity (As we now use the word)?* Mimeo, Stanford University

Havok Physics. http://www.havok.com/content/view/17/30/

Hoyt, Crystal L., and Blascovich, Jim (2003): "Transformational and transactional leadership in virtual and physical environments", *Small Group Research*, 34: 678-715

Jackson, Linda A., Hunter, John E., and Hodge, Carol N. (1995): Physical attractiveness and intellectual competence: A meta-analytic review. *Social Psychology Quarterly*, vol. 58: 108-122

Kalyuga, Slava (2007): "Enhancing instructional efficiency of interactive e-learning environments: A cognitive load perspective", *Educational Psychology Review*, vol. 19: 387-399

Kirriemuir, John (2007): *A July 2007 "snapshot" of UK Higher and Further Education Developments in Second Life*, Eduserv Foundation.

Nagy, Péter (2010): "Second Life, Second Choice? The effects of virtual identity on consumer behavior. A conceptual framework", *Proceedings of FIKUSZ '10*: 169

Okita, Sandra Y., Bailenson, Jeremy, and Schwartz, Daniel L. (2008): "The mere belief in social interaction improves learning", *Proceedings of the 8th International Conference for the Learning Sciences*, Mahwah, NJ: Erlbaum

Pan, Zhigeng, Cheok, Adrian D., Yang, Hongwei, and Zhu, Jiejie (2006): "Virtual reality and mixed reality for virtual learning environments", *Computers & Graphics*, vol. 30, 20-28

Partridge, Christopher H. (2005): *Introduction to World Religions*, Fortress: 148

Perera, Indika, Allison, Colin, and Miller, Alan (2010): "A Use Case Analysis for Learning in 3D MUVE:A Model Based on Key e-Learning Activities", *The 5th International Conference on Virtual Learning ICVL*: 114-120

Postmes, Tom, Spears, Russell, and Lea, Martin (2002): "Intergroup differentiation in computer-mediated communication: Effects of depersonalization", in: Rosenberg, M. (1986): *Conceiving the self*. New York: Basic Books

Rosenmann, Amir, and Safir, Marilyn P. (2006): "Forced Online: Push Factors of Internet Sexuality: A Preliminary Study of Online Paraphilic Empowerment", *Journal of Homosexuality*, vol. 51: 71-92

Stewart, Stephanie, Hansen, Terri S., and Carey, Timothy A. (2010): "Opportunities for People with Disabilities in the Virtual World of Second Life", *Rehabilitation Nursing*, vol. 35: 254-259.

Yee, Nick, and Bailenson, Jeremy N. (2007): "The Proteus effect: The effect of transformed self-representation on behaviour", *Human Communication Research, vol. 33*: 271-290

Yee, Nick, Bailenson, Jeremy N., and Ducheneaut, Nicolas (2009): "The Proteus effect: Implications of transformed digital self-representation on online and offline behaviour", *Communication Research*, vol. 36: 285-312

Zhao, Shanyang, Grasmuck, Sherri, and Martin, Jason (2008): "Identity construction on Facebook: Digital empowerment in anchored relationships", *Computers in Human Behavior*, vol. 24: 1816-1836

Zhou, Zhongyun, Jin, Xiao-Ling, Vogel, Douglas R., Fang, Yulin, and Chen, Xiaojian (2011): "Individual motivations and demographic differences in social virtual world uses: An exploratory investigation in Second Life", *International Journal of Information Management*, vol. 31, issue 3: 264

Beyond the Visible Autonomy

ERHAN ÖZE

> We should understand the society of control, in
> contrast, as that society (which develops at the
> far edge of modernity and opens toward the
> postmodern) in which mechanisms of command
> become ever more "democratic," ever more im-
> manent to the social field, distributed throughout
> the brains and bodies of the citizens. The behav-
> iors of social integration and exclusion proper to
> rule are thus increasingly interiorized within the
> subjects themselves.[1]

In light of Michael Hardt and Antonio Negri's description of control and behavior of citizens, *Autonomy* becomes one of the crucial concepts for Internet users
in today's world because it allows each Internet user to create and claim his/her
private virtual space and control over it. However, the main difference between a
spatial and a virtual world is approached depending on how we perceive 'freedom & privacy'[2] in different contexts, and on how we relate our decisions ac-

---

1   Hardt, M., and Negri, A. (2001): 23
2   "The concept of privacy is not a static phenomenon but a developing social construc-
    tion. This always has to be kept in mind when thinking of solutions for privacy related
    problems. Especially if technology is considered as neutral, the effect of technology
    hardening social practices is disregarded. Social imaginations of how to solve a prob-
    lem however are implemented in technologies and thus its functions are constructed
    according to the social views of the designers and engineers. If we consider technolo-
    gy as neutral the inscribed social practice seems given and objective – or even natu-
    ral." Guagnin, D., Hempel, L., and Ilten, C. (2011): 101

cordingly. In spatial contexts, everybody is subject to the laws[3] that are put in use by the ruling powers and written somewhere reachable by citizens. In real life citizens are subject to interpretations of written laws which then regulate their freedom according to the society in which each citizen lives. The same principle applies to the use of Internet. Regardless of a country's ideological system, each one has its own laws or at least it has the sovereign right to have laws about Internet use. However, due to the Internet's networked nature, different nations, irrespective of their ideologies and beliefs, can meet online. This could lead to a neutral, friendly, productive, offensive, and even, aggressive encounter. And, according to international cyber security law, "the general principles of international law [are] applied to cyberspace"[4] when it comes to the cross-national cyber relations or conflicts. As mentioned earlier, each country's society has its own understanding of its own integral laws regarding Internet use, just as each also has different laws and regulations which constitute cybercrimes. Thus, the consequences of cybercrimes differ from law to law, country to country, except where there is a certain regulation on common standards among countries, administered by a greater 'regulator', such as the European Commission, the Arab League, the African Union, The Organisation of Islamic Cooperation, International Telecommunication Authority, Shanghai Cooperation Organization, or the United Nations. Nevertheless, in some countries laws are exercised in a more flexible or stricter way than in others.

Each country has a different perception of the spatial relations of people in public spaces, and sometimes social relations even have an impact on privately used spaces, depending on each society's customs, traditions, prejudices, ideologies, and even the social pressure which points to how people imagine freedom and privacy on the internet space, as well. In principle, this can reflect on the Internet governance, too. Even so, in some countries, due to a State's lack of ability, the control mechanisms are not set clearly concerning Internet use. Therefore, both the Internet and non-virtual spatial relations could become domains hosting 'illegal' activities. In other countries, however, citizens are highly regulated and every piece of data transferred is controlled, and every act monitored by the national security agencies where citizens' freedom and privacy rights over the internet, or in spatial contexts, can become disputed. For a human rights'

---

3 Irrespective of their ideologies, most countries regulate spatial interactions by law. In the case of a country in conflict, in which the United Nations sends its mandates, the UN's rules and regulations are usually intact for the concerned territory. These rules are often negotiated with the internationally recognized side(s) of the conflict.

4 Schmitt, M. N. (2013): 14

record, as well as for the right of 'freedom & privacy', this can be judged problematic, but, on the other hand, this sovereign power's exercise on Internet use may assist on managing cyber security, and this might be an advantage for a state's security. At the same time, this also has an economic impact. The level of impact becomes clear according to the developments of the (internet) economy of each country concerned, in terms of whether it regulates or not the spatial commercial relations through the Internet. Hence, this impact has different consequences for national interests, causing other countries to benefit from it or making them lose their interest in doing business with the country concerned.

So, freedoms and modes of privacy of Internet use can also be affected depending on the particular and different conditions, experiences, and variety of contexts of effective Internet laws in each country, at the same time that they establish spatial social contexts as a result: in some countries, internet cafes become favorable, while in others, Wi-Fi spots. These simple contexts can give an idea of how people establish their perception of available internet infrastructures in which people employ available internet and spatial domains to claim an *autonomous* identity within the spaces that they use and disclose spatial (cultural, political, ideological, etc) relations as part of their everyday life, such as using smart phone applications, like, Facebook to *'check in'* their present location, which reveals information about what they do and with whom and when they do it.[5] In this sense, social networks can be considered as a new domain for Internet users to either forge personae, support their characters, carriers, businesses online, or, to simply use it for practical reasons to reach and communicate with friends and families. In any case, using the domain of Internet does not change the fact that any data transferred in it, can potentially become political or politicized by others, to the extent that they have access to it and know enough about it to make speculations. By the same token, "even-non sensitive data may become sensitive if it is connected with other data available – the possibility of

---

5   Users voluntarily feed in their own personal information to the social networks, such as, Twitter, Facebook, etc. And using this social software aims to make users' personal data publicly visible to others or to a selected audience, as it designates friends, as in LinkedIn or Facebook. However, when it comes to the other personally used applications, such as Skype, E mail providers, browsers, etc, parts of the telecommunication that is carried through the internet, and many other services and software, also obtain users others bits of personal data with their consent however without making it as *'visible'* as Facebook, LinkedIn or Twitter...

connecting huge data sets (data mining) has become very easy through modern information technologies."[6]

As a sociopolitical consequence, mainly in developed and developing countries, exposing complex human spatial relations and making data mining maps that attempt to represent social relations, have rapidly become part of everyday life. This is due to having technology available, to be able to evaluate mass data and also have researchers who are eager to understand more about the transformation of societies by using social media that generate overwhelmingly diverse data. Hence, to be able to make general assumptions about societies and their evolving processes, or problems, or to speculate about future acts has proved to be important. However, "it is clear that naïve or brute-force incorporation of large scale data into simulation models may not lead to the expected results in terms of achieving relevant progress in social science. While it is apparent that the analysis of the data will certainly contribute to understand mechanisms, it is also clear that further input often be needed, in particular input obtained from experiments under controlled parameters or situations. These will shed light on decision-making mechanisms that sometimes can be obscured among the midst of the data."[7]

Moreover, part of the marketing strategies of social networking companies is to make personal data available in order to be commodified by other users. This normalizing and normalized situation enforces financial opportunities and advantages for the national security agencies to figure out networks and communicators of 'crime suspects' easier. Social networks also offer other individuals the opportunity to know a little more about them, other things and happenings, and, instantly, by making an online inquiry either through social sites or over Internet engines, and by matching bits of information, one has a better profile of the aspect concerned. As a result, this has a sociological impact by making people feel more engaged, whether as part of a group which supports their psychology, or, as a safer and more aware community, and even as a more obsessed type, which simply makes them feel different, informed, in control of things, and, perhaps, more alert compared to non-users.

However, social networks can also turn into a threat to the sovereignties of some autocratic-regimes in countries like, Egypt, Syria, Bahrain, Libya, Tunisia and Saudi Arabia. In other countries, these networks have turned into a threat to the ideological structure, as in, North Korea, Iran and China. As for democratic

---

6   Guagnin, D. Hempel, L., and Ilten, C. (2011): 103
7   Bonelli, G. et al. (2012): 342

countries 'opposing' these obsessive regimes, social networks have become a potential tool for the support of opposing groups of people by influencing them peacefully, and helping them overthrow their regimes. In these instances, negative or positive influence on regimes infringe on their sovereignties. Harold Honhgu Koh[8] supports this idea by saying that, "States conducting activities in cyberspace must take into account the sovereignty of other States, including outside the context of armed conflict."[9]

To understand these interventions on countries' sovereignties, it is crucial to first understand how global social networks on the Internet influence citizens of other nations. Because this uncontested "power is now exercised through machines that directly organize the brains (in communication systems, information networks, etc.) and bodies (in welfare systems, monitored activities, etc.) toward a state of autonomous alienation from the sense of life and the desire for creativity."[10]. This is how citizens agree to use these services online at the risk of losing their autonomy and becoming a subject of global trends, which affect everybody. Understanding this further by exploring the etymology of the word *autonomy* is important. The words of 'auto-' and '-nomy' have their origins[11] in Greek. 'Auto' derives from 'autos', which means 'self' and '-nomy' derives from '-nomia', which is related to the notion of *'nomos'[12]*, 'law'. In other words, it relates to the power that the 'law' imposes in order to *"justify the violence."[13]* In this context, the law could be our own rules applied within a boundary, or the law we are supposed to follow, dictated by the regulators of the boundary in which we are supposed to conduct our practices. In either context, how violence is justified becomes the crucial aspect. This is why it is important to understand the word autonomy. Overall, 'auto-nomy' may refer to 'self and law', and it may resemble the notion of *nomos* in 'sovereignty' without indicating the boundaries which also describe the boundless Internet data and network maps, while emphasizing their power as well as weaknesses. Thus, *nomos* is the notion that this paper inquires through the sovereignty or *'visible and invisible autonomy'* that is perceived by users of the Internet while crawling through, forming or reforming their private data and trying to erase the data either on intranets or the Internet.

---

8   He is Legal Advisor in the Department of the State of the USA.

9   Koh, H. H. (2012): Remarks on International Law in Cyberspace: Answer 9.

10 Hardt, M., and Negri, A. (2001): 23

11 New Oxford American Dictionary (2005-2009)

12 Greenberg, N. (2002). Notes on *nomos and physis*

13 Agamben, G. (1998): 24

According to Agamben,[14] *"Nomos is the power that, within the strongest hand, achieves the paradoxical union of these opposites"; "violence and justice."* This paradox also describes what the Internet hosts both for *users' data and for the scripts.* Simply put, in each country, the Internet offers a certain degree of 'freedom & privacy' with certain provided functions, which shape services to access the available or selected data, as well as to be used as access points by users who might be monitored by Internet service providers, hackers or the national agencies, responsible for the national security, and allowed into the service providers' databases. In any case, the data that is available for the Internet is represented to the world as indexes in absence of other data. Quite often, the regulated part of the Internet and its relation to the sovereign states are what ordinary users see as prescribed regulations through which they seek justice, depending on the contract they have with their Internet service provider, and the national or international regulations on privacy, concerning the country in which they live. However, for other users, additional layers of the Internet exist with different data where violence, as well as illegal actions, are legalized by being hidden within the 'dark' or the 'deep' net, not visible to many Only the *autonomous* users, who make their own laws, demand to know and to govern the knowledge accessed through the *dark net.* In other words, the "lawless"[15] part of the Internet where the sovereign powers and their apparatuses are not the 'legal' subjects, or regulators of the power, or contributors of the existing knowledge in the dark net, is regulated by users who introduce new rules through scripts under their own sovereign *non-territories* within their own *'nomos', law.*

Describing the Internet, including the dark net, as non-territory, is important because there is neither a universal law nor defined boundaries of the Internet, which regulates the actions of the users and what is offered within the dark net. One opportunity to control and patrol the *dark net* is to be in control of the gatekeeper software of the *dark net,* such as the *Tor.*[16] On the other hand, concerning when it comes to the ordinary Internet use of Internet, how its users use or and how to secure and maintain the data flow, things become a little more complicated due to having an immense amount of users and a big amount of the data flow in many different data forms. Beyond the Internet's need of vast infrastructures to make things technically available and safe for those who have ac-

---

14 Agamben, G. (1998): 25

15 Lawlessness does not necessarily mean that there is not a system or laws that are intact by its own users. However, the dark net could be considered as the backbone of the Internet databases that governs all.

16 It is a software invented by the Central Intelligence Agency of the US itself.

cess to it, the encryption is the medium that is used by the Internet service providers. The Internet has also started to host its adjacent "critical life-sustaining infrastructures that deliver electricity and water, control air traffic, and support our financial systems all depend on networked information systems."[17] To keep a nation's sensitive infrastructure' data flows safe (banking sectors, telecommunication systems, transportation, remote control systems of industrial plants, data transfers of research centers, communications of private companies, in some cases, military correspondence), there exist various different types and levels of encryptions if the data travels via internet. But if the data travels within a secure intra network, then it usually does so without an encryption. In this respect, Internet encryptions and protected intranets have started hosting control over some sovereign domains in which they become points of interests for counter powers. And the Internet has become a showcase of these intra infrastructure networks' vulnerabilities as belonging to different countries. In this sense, a reliance on the Internet is unavoidable. Therefore, each person, group, business firm, network for the correspondence of the police, military, secret agency, or any similar sort of organization, eventually including, the state and their correspondences with their embassies or their spy agents, could be tapped by other powers which have an interest and capacity to do so. As a result, there is not a singular sovereign power, which could claim sole control over the Internet because there are many networks which could easily remain beyond the reach of a single country unless they have insiders helping them obtain the specific data they need. Countries may build intra Internet systems to control data flow through the Internet, as is the case with Iran or China. Instead of an intranet, data filters are used to block the incoming data to the end users. Opposing this, the United States has imposed a freedom of speech on the Internet, regulating it by way of the laws that are intact. However, the U.S Government's position is close to the Tallinn Manual's Rule 1, which is also close to the obsessive regimes stated above. According to Rule 1, "Sovereignty: A State may exercise control over cyber infrastructure and activities within its sovereign territory." Under its first chapter, it is stated that: "…although no State may claim sovereignty over cyberspace *per se*, States may exercise, sovereign prerogatives over any cyber infrastructure located on their territory, as well as activities associated with that cyber infrastructure."[18] The Tallinn Manual recognizes the fact that there is an extraterritorial side of the cyber infrastructure and it covers the sovereign rights of the governments further on in Rule 1, Chapter 10 by stating: "The fact that cyber infrastructure located in

---

17 Obama, B. (2009): 3
18 Schmitt, M. (2013): 16

a given State's territory is linked to the global telecommunications network cannot be interpreted as a waiver of its sovereign rights over that infrastructure."[19] And these sovereign rights are supposed to be exercised through international laws since "international law principles do apply in cyberspace" in which "cyberspace is not a "law-free" zone where anyone can conduct hostile activities without rules or restraints."[20]

On the contrary, the above stated legal framework that 'regulates' cyberspace, is ruled against all by the secret agencies of those countries, such as the United States, China, the United Kingdom, Canada, Australia, Germany, Russia, Syria, Iran, etc., which could also gather data, evaluate and retaliate against any cyber attack without being visible to others. This non-territory and paradoxical sovereignty is the result of having partial laws from the countries mentioned above, imposing regulations on the Internet, as well as partial laws and sovereign interests that regulate the practices of intelligence agencies and their interferences on each other. Therefore, having NATO's Tallinn Manual on the International Law Applicable to Cyber Warfare or national strategies to regulate[21] cyber warfare, while having ineffective international bodies, such as the United Nations, has created a new frontier for intelligence wars for the benefit of individual hackers, corporations, and nation states, and for their supported businesses. In absence of a universal law, this is how the Internet functions paradoxically, even if it is highly regulated in some parts of the world, or not at all, in others. As a result, each country's laws remain within their own exception or partiality, while the *dark net* remains hidden to most people as a whole, again, within its own exception, being out of law.

Another evident paradox is the case of Edward Snowden. He showed the world that all personal data of almost all users of the Internet could be accessible through their email address(es) by some secret agency, even within their own country. These paradoxes emerge because the notion of sovereign could stand both *"outside and inside the juridical order."* And any juridical power that grants the power to declare *"a state of exception"* in which the sovereignty stands out of law is the key concept that represents the lawless, and at the same

---

19 Schmitt, M. (2013): 17

20 Koh Speech, *supra* note 4, at 2-4, cited in Schmitt (2009): 15

21 It seems like the author is not aware of the existence of other regulatory manuals about cyber warfare by the Chinese, Russian or other governments.

time, lawful power structure of being sovereign. Here, Agamben[22] bases the sovereign concept on Carl Schmitt's idea of the '*state of exception*.' He[23] places emphasis on having the power to suspend the *"validity of the law,"* in which the sovereign places itself outside of the law. This is the context in which the National Security Agency of the US, and many other national secret agencies operate. As a result, the notion of the sovereign is not set up according to the one who makes the law, the juridical order, but rather through the one who is responsible for implementing it, and who makes the decision in the state of exception. In this sense, the power that is gained lawfully from the juridical order by standing outside of the law, establishes the freedom of the secret agencies, thus allowing them to access all private and confidential data both about the state, and its citizens. At the same time, being inside the 'law' where the exception is created, denies the presence of the *dark net* and its access to the data bases where private information of the users are stored. So, the paradox of the sovereignty within the Internet could be represented by the idea that everything is lawful and nothing is outside the law, even if "the law is outside itself." In this sense, the power that can make everything lawful is the sovereign user. However, seeing the limits of the sovereignty happens through understanding the paradox's structure that is embedded in the juridical order and in the ability of the user. To understand this, Agamben[24] employs Schmitt's *"structure of the exception"* in which Schmitt distinguishes the condition of exception as a pure decision that sets up clear distinctions in between conditions. And he describes the exception's ultimate moment when it can create the exception within the law. This is also valid for *the dark net*. The way to create the exception is to create the regular law as if it is something like a general rule, for instance, to regulate the data flow on the Internet that is visible to the users. This is how exception on the Internet is normalized, even if the act seems lawless and chaotic. The use of the Internet is both to embed itself into the law in order to be able to stand outside it, and to normalize its practices across the globe (both in visible and invisible terrains) creating a virtual politics, while affecting a spatial one.

---

22 Agamben, G. (1998): 17
23 Agamben, G. (1998): 17
24 Agamben, G. (1998): 17

VIRTUAL AND SPATIAL PRACTICES

The politics of the scripts[25] could also refer to the unconscious scripts of 'the mind,'[26] which would decide and act in accordance to its algorithmic 'autonomous' codes in combination with the other scripts. Hence, *"what is needed are descriptions of 'power through the algorithm', developed by focusing on those working with and designing the applications and software, by focusing on the applications and software as material entities, or by focusing on those who engage with the software in their everyday lives (or through a combination of these three areas)."*[27]

Although, some web sites such as Last FM[28] or other search engines such as Google, use scripts containing presupposed patterns with pre-emptive measures to collect the users' preferences, which make the script learn through the interactive scenarios from their activities. Google's scripts are not really unconscious, but aware of what personal data they obtain from the users, and which allow these scripts to classify and categorize their clients according to their behaviors, and the choices they make. But these "communications technologies often operate at the level of the 'technological unconscious.'[29] In other words, they operate in unseen and unknown ways."[30] The unseen and unknown, to the ordinary user,

---

25 Depending on which scripts are referred to, the word 'scripts'/codes have multiple meanings within the context of this paper. Simply, software scripts that are used on computers would have different politics than the initial BIOS codes that are running the computer itself. And the software scripts would differ also from the browser scripts, which crawl in the Internet. In this paper, scripts refer more to the Internet based web page scripts, and, the scripts that change the forms of the data, either encrypting them or turning them into a command and then making them travel through the servers. However, the servers, individual computers, as well as other intermediary machines, and tools that make the Internet function, and, the Internet system itself, refer to different codes and spatial relations, in each unique context.

26 The mind refers both to each Internet user that exists around the world, and the dark net which contains both the information and the scripts that allow the whole internet to function.

27 Beer, D. (2009): 999

28 Beer, D. (2009): 997

29 Thrift, N. (2005): Knowing Capitalism. London: SAGE; quoted in: Beer, D. (2009): 988

30 Beer, D. (2009): 995

functions, establish some of the politics of the indexed metadata and related virtual[31] experiences on the Internet for the users. However, adding the interactive manner into the thread of the 'scripted thought' as pieces of code, and expanding the script with gained and interpreted new information might contest the virtual intelligence and the machine's capacity to function. Or, these particular codes make it crawl only among certain preferred servers, among many others available online. In addition, narrowing down the scope of the research sounds contradictory to the nature of a search engine that is designed to index available and searchable data online.[32] Hence, a combination of the coders' preferences and how the script learns through the users' experiences narrows down the results for the users,[33] then forming a way to manage the interests of the users. Nonetheless, how a machine captures the moment through its cognition relies on its scriptural cognitive ability and its scripts' politics, which are written by the coder.

Besides indexing the impact of coders, search engines generate lists, in which each result leads to an interface: a document or a web page. But the script's interface may contain other hidden threats under indexed hyperlinks. Any hyperlink on a web page may represent a hidden script that leads to a malware or to a Trojan, thus building a bridge for a hacker to take control over an individual computer, network, server, system, and other available or vulnerable connected domains.[34] This is not always the doing of an incontestable knowledge of hackers; it might simply be a trap that captures the mistakes of a user, and, without realizing it, they hand over their autonomy to hackers to enjoy the private data and confidential information. Here, the politics of the hyperlink is a crucial subject since it is one of the most basic domains of the Internet, which represents the link between, at least, two defined domains and a command that scripts and computers should follow. At the same time, the potential of hyperlinks to become a camouflage to an invisible script is highly probable, having an open port to a machine to be enslaved by a hacker. Or, in another context, how a virus enslaves a computer in order for a hacker to take over a vulnerable user's control and impair the private, public or confidential data indicates another versatile ability of the script. So, to function as programmed or to be hijacked by another alien user becomes an option for the machine in the *exception* of what hyperlink bridges under the script's command. In this respect, a machine that is

---

31 The notion of 'virtual' does not indicate three-dimensional reality that both games and software, such as AutoCAD, Rhino, Revit and many others generate.

32 Miller, J. (2013)

33 Beer, D. (2009): 997

34 BBC (2013)

established to function autonomously and in relation to various types of networks for the benefit of the user, might become a weapon against its own, while losing its autonomy and diminishing its users' privacy. The machine[35] might also lose its own control, reveal secrets and be misused since it cannot distinguish an enemy from an ally in terms of a signal or a script, unless it is being coded or encrypted in a way that it can trace and defer the enemy action from trespassing into its own territory via its ports, with programs, such as firewall,[36] that define the private (z-)one and filtrate both incoming and outgoing data while warning and allowing the user to regulate the data flow.

Firstly, however, the cognitive scripts' relation has to be established with the parts that the cognitive mind deploys as the hardware to evaluate and capture the spatial moment. In this way, the mechanic and electronic ability of machines to send the signal back to the cognitive 'virtual mind', according to what it 'feels' and how the signal is carried through, is also important. As a matter of algorithmic nature, the data would choose the fastest route to travel, through servers where more space is provided, especially on the Internet. In this sense, politics is embedded both in the travel route of the data, as well as in the fastest Internet service provider of that particular network. And in this context, the political conjecture is created depending on whether an authority tabs into the data flows infrastructure on its route where it is established by the sovereign state itself; by another private subsidiary within and outside its own sovereign borders, or, in international boundaries where the internet infrastructure passes through the sea

---

35 A reconnaissance drone can be described as a flying computer in control of an operator. An example of this is found in the extreme case for hijacking a computer by the US Military stealth drone that Iran downed in 2011 (Press TV, 2013). The most interesting aspect of drones is that they cannot use encoded satellite links, that is why it was easier to interfere with the American drone signal and take it over. Simply stated, having equipment and the infrastructure to send more frequent signals to the drone and at the same time jam the American controllers' signals was the key method to bring down the drone. In this context, a drone can also be perceived as a machine that is hijacked from a military network, not a public one, which is operating beyond the sovereign borders of its own making.

36 According to Wikipedia: "A firewall is a software or hardware-based network security system that controls the incoming and outgoing network traffic by analyzing the data packets and determining whether they should be allowed through or not, based on a rule set. A firewall establishes a barrier between a trusted, secure internal network and another network (e.g., the Internet) that is not assumed to be secure and trusted."

beds. According to documents leaked by Edward Snowden,[37] some prominent examples would be the National Secret Agency of the US, which creates alternative and fast rerouting infrastructures, especially servers with a big storage capacity around the world to obtain substantial information from global networks.[38] This would take advantage of existing infrastructures within their own and other sovereign countries, such as the 'five eyes':[39] Canada, Australia, New Zealand, Great Britain and the US. Therefore, by connecting to the Internet network, even without hosting spy servers that are built by foreign companies within the sovereign states, the countries' internet infrastructure can also be used to spy against its own data in the exception of its own law. Moreover, multiple strategies are usually used to achieve the goals and obtain more data by the intelligence agencies. However, beyond obtaining the targeted data about individuals or firms, the main problem is to sort it out and make use of it. According to more documents leaked by Edward Snowden, "xkeyscore" software is used by NSA to organize mass, or as it is called 'metadata'. This program works with keywords such as: names, surnames, e-mail addresses, telephone numbers and, its intermediary plug-ins., etc., and these are the main search query technique, which asks the supercomputers to create a category to distinguish information and eliminate unnecessary data. To do this, however, these metadata, which have been gathered by intermediary plug-ins, create 'metadata tables' for the NSA system user.[40]

Moreover, the signal carried as encrypted or decrypted data through the Internet infrastructure is as crucial as the scriptural political ability of the cognitive algorithms, plug-ins, which would distinguish and generate the responses of the supercomputer in order to create an overall image about the researched subject or person. Depending on the purposes of spying plug-ins (xkeyscore, prism,[41] etc.) in which some add a new understanding to their virtual perception through regenerative scripts, autonomy over the metadata can be established by recognizing the right decrypted keywords. Spying programs might also be disqualified if the decrypted data is registered with a wrong name or wrong e-mail, unless national security users match the forged user's various descriptions as potential suspects. But within data sorting backdoor programs, like "xkeyscore," the aim

---

37 BBC (2013)
38 Want China Times (2013)
39 Ng, K. (2013)
40 Want China Times (2013)
41 Australian Government (2013), Attorney-General's Department, Schedule for Freedom of Information Request no. 13/132.

is rather straightforward regarding the logistics of the data in order to match the separate information which a targeted person produces, such as, sent and received emails, logins to different sites, telephone and Skype conversations, etc., and which are turned into tables to allow the intelligence analyst to search through the content, at different moments. Depending on the available stored data resources of the NSA, a suspected person's activities could instantly be under online surveillance through the web browsers s/he uses or the "xkeyscore" software, which can also dig up information from almost a decade ago and show previous contacts, calls, and videos of a targeted individual.

Finally, the problem is beyond how the Internet Service Provider companies such as, Yahoo, Google, LinkedIn, Facebook and many others exploit their own customers' data through the scripts that they use to learn the personal preferences of their users. This is only one of many layers of the politics that take place between the registered companies and the sovereign states in which state agencies establish other sort of political relations about how the company should handle its customers' data. The double facade of the companies both confronts and constructs the double faceted relations of the state itself, which invents its own rules. The state as the ruler obliges the company to protect its customers' private data and prohibits its use within privacy rights, at the same time, however, that the same state employs another organ, such as, the intelligence agency to reach into what had been made private by rule. This contradiction emerges from the concept of sovereignty and how power is exercised in order to create the law for the lawless to create its own *nomos*: to *'justify the violence.'*[42]

CONCLUSION

The Internet has, on the one hand, become the new terrain for democratic states to claim sovereignty over. For this purpose, states form laws to exercise power on the rights of people and regulate the data flow that goes through the infrastructure, which exists within their national borders. But due to the nature of the Internet not being bound to a universal law, each state can only weaken their own citizens' rights to access whatever domains in other countries provide or even what is provided from within their own country. In this sense, how a state effectively regulates the information flow could give the impression to its users that things are under control. However, to regulate data within the depth of the

---

42 Agamben, G. (1998): 24

Internet is not that easy since there are other ways to access the immense amount of data through the *dark net,* which also hosts illegal activities influencing the globe. In this respect, the Internet has a paradoxical nature, and what belongs to law and what remains out of the law are both accessible by the users, and inseparable from one another. Similarly, *"The principle according to which sovereignty belongs to law, which today seems inseparable from our conception of democracy and the legal State, does not at all eliminate the paradox of sovereignty; indeed it even brings it to the most extreme point of its development."*[43]

On the other hand, however, the Internet has become a platform to foster 'democracy' around the world where voices can be heard, and a place to struggle against injustice. In the last decade, this democratic process has been taking place, more evidently, through social media; as a result, some regimes came under scrutiny in recent years since their citizens found new ways to inform and create empowered masses, to defend their causes better since they became more visible, through the domains of the Internet, within local contexts, as well as global ones. In the same way, counter groups which are either in a position to rule or manage, also urged the use of similar means to fight back to defend their obtained 'rights' to be visible, in order not to let the internet platform to be claimed by opposing groups. Beyond claiming the available Internet domains, it has also been used for some to identify against whom they have been fighting, by following their virtual traces through IP numbers or simply through their posts on Facebook, Twitter, and many other social media tools. By the same token, rulers could identify their opposing groups' methods of retaliation. This is how the Internet became another terrain for the rulers and ruled to justify both justice and violence. And this fight resembles a dichotomy that started to take place under different names: for example, the 'propaganda' of the Third Reich; the 'public relations' of the US;[44] and, part of the information war along with the real spatial wars which took place on the ground during the First and Second World Wars. After the wars, the world reinvented itself as a polarized virtual space whereby the US, taking the lead in its invention of the Internet, transformed itself into today's monopoly in cyber warfare. To be able to take part in this world affair, other nation states also established similar infrastructures and tried to exercise power on the Internet. To justify their secret activities, they used a similar rhetoric to that of the US, calling it "national security." This has been a way for intelligence agencies to declare their own positions legal and the others'

---

43 Agamben, G. (1998): 24
44 Chomsky, N. (1997): "What Makes Mainstream Media Mainstream": a talk at Z Media Institute, quoted in Bernays, E. (1928)

actions illegal. In both cases, to be able to carry on their causes and activities, the secret agencies of nation states either misinform the crowds or do not inform them at all, creating false impressions about the virtual and spatial world. This is one of the main problems of the sovereign powers and their politics, whereby they establish their sustaining power based on falsehoods, to influence their societies and the world, at large. In the same way, in today's world, words are marketed to mass users in order to mislead them, and this is most visible on the Internet medium to inform, interact and communicate with them. The keywords that communicate with people's mind to affect their opinion are, at the same time, used against them to trace their tendencies while they click various links on ordinary webpages used to obtain data, to work or to send data to others through e-mails, or by other methods. In this context, the information that users produce and provide as the data has become the main aspect of interest to the sovereign powers, especially those powers which desire to obtain the new data of inventions or to trace the activities of both their citizens, and the foreign nationals in the name of "national security."

REFERENCES

Agamben, Giorgio (1995): *Homo Sacer: Il potere sovrano e la nuda vita*. Trans. Heller

Aljazeera News (2013): "Egypt jamming Al Jazeera's satellite signals", http://www.aljazeera.com/video/middleeast/2013/09/201393183256834226.html

Australian Government (2013), Attorney-General's Department, Schedule for Freedom of Information Request no. 13/132. http://www.scribd.com/doc/174279139/Ag-Department-Prism-Foi#download

BBC News (2013): "Edward Snowden documents show NSA broke privacy rules", http://www.bbc.co.uk/news/world-us-canada-23721818 BBC News Technology (2013): "How big a threat is state sponsored computer hacking?", http://www.bbc.co.uk/news/technology-23733397

BBC News (2013): "Iranian government pursuing 'national internet'", http://www.bbc.co.uk/news/world-middle-east-22837506

BBC News (2013): "Scale and significance of NSA snooping claims", http://www.bbc.co.uk/news/world-22860964

BBC News (2013): "Snowden leaks: US and UK 'crack online encryption'", http://www.bbc.co.uk/news/world-us-canada-23981291

BBC News Technology (2013): "The computer hackers and phishing experts 'on our side'", http://www.bbc.co.uk/news/technology-23008088

BBC News UK Politics (2011): "GCHQ to help firms combat cybercrime", http://www.bbc.co.uk/news/uk-politics-15881297Beer, David (2009): "Power through the algorithm? Participatory web cultures and the technological unconscious". *New Media & Society*, Sage Publishing. http://nms.sagepub.com/content/11/6/985

Bernays, Edward (1928): *Propaganda*. http://www.historyisaweapon.com/defcon1/bernprop.html

Betancourt, M. (2013): "Bitcoin", Ctheory, http://www.ctheory.net/articles.aspx?id=724

Bonelli, G., Cioffi-Revilla, C., Conte, R., Gilbert, N., Deffuant, G., Flache, A., Helbing, D., Kertesz, J., Loreto, V., Moat, S., Nadal, J.-P., Nowak, A., Sanchez, A., and San Miguel, M. (2012): "Manifesto of computational social science". *The European Physical Journal Special Topics:* 214, 325-346.

Charter Of The United Nations, Chapter VII: Action With Respect To Threats To The Peace, Breaches Of The Peace, And Acts Of Aggression

Chatfield, Tom, BBC Future (2012): "Cyber warfare: Fear of system failure", http://www.bbc.com/future/story/20120608-system-failure-in-cyber-warfare

Council of Europe (2011): Convention On Cybercrime, CETS No.: 185. http://conventions.coe.int/Treaty/Commun/QueVoulezVous.asp?NT=185&CL=ENG

Dyer, Gwynne, Cyprus Mail (2013): "A system that is too big to monitor properly", http://cyprus-mail.com/2013/08/30/a-system-that-is-too-big-to-monitor-properly/

ECM Plus – The Voice of Content (2013): "Domain name campaigners battle corporate monopoly of gTLDs", http://ecmplus.wordpress.com/2013/02/13/domain-name-campaigners-battle-corporate-monopoly-of-gtlds/

EconomicCrisisReview (2010): "The Century of Self Happiness Machines part 5", http://www.youtube.com/watch?v=M-MksApggT0&list=PLECD73AEED6720B65

Euronews (2013): "Brazil and Mexico call for investigation into US spying claims", http://www.euronews.com/2013/09/03/brazil-and-mexico-call-for-investigation-into-us-spying-claims/

Federation of American Scientist (2012): "Obama Administration Documents on Secrecy Policy, National Insider Threat Policy and Minimum Standards for Executive Branch Insider Threat Programs". http://www.fas.org/sgp/obama/insider.pdf

Gadkari, Pia, BBC News (2013): "US National Security Agency 'is surveillance leviathan'", http://www.bbc.co.uk/news/technology-23669003

GeekBlog.tv (2012): "The Hidden Internet - Exploring The Deep Web", https://www.youtube.com/watch?v=wMgqTWdk3tw&list=PLCYgHhJbKmS zwgiXR0JFt-7P6obNPYzi

Greenberg, Neil (2002): Notes on Deep Ethology: Determinism; *nomos and physis*. https://notes.utk.edu/Bio/greenberg.nsf/0/3dbf9db5e278888385256e7900 0cc792?OpenDocument

Guagnin, Daniel, Hempel, Leon, and Ilten, Carla, eds. (2011): *Towards Responsible Research and Innovation in the Information and Communication Technologies and Security Technologies Fields*, European Commission, European Research Area, Science in Society. Luxemburg: Publication Office of the European Union.

Hardt, Michael, and Negri, Antonio, eds. (2001): *Empire*, Cambridge, Massachusetts & London: Harvard University Press.

Hristova, Stefka (2013): "Digital Animalized Camouflage: A Zone of Biopolitical Indistinction", *Interstitial Journal*. http://interstitialjournal.files. wordpress.com/2013/07/hristova-digitized.pdf

Koh, Harold Hongju (2012): "Remarks on International Law in Cyberspace", USCYBERCOM Inter-Agency Legal Conference, Meade, http://www.state. gov/s/l/releases/remarks/197924.htm.

Miller, Joe, BBC News Technology (2013): "Jonathon Fletcher: forgotten father of the search engine", http://www.bbc.co.uk/news/technology-23945326

Mitchell, Liam (2013): "Because none of us are as cruel as all of us": Anonymity and Subjectivation", Ctheory. http://www.ctheory.net/articles.aspx?id=724

Mix, Derek E. (2011): "The United States and Europe: Current Issues", Congressional Research Service 7-5700. www.fas.org/sgp/crs/row/RS22163.pdf

New Oxford American Dictionary, (2005-2009), Apple Inc.

Ng, Keith (2013): *ich-bin-ein-cyberpunk*, http://publicaddress.net/onpoint/ich-bin-ein-cyberpunk/

NTVMSNBC News (2013): "Bir yılda 5 zettabayt veri depolayacak", http://www.ntvmsnbc.com/id/25449681

NTVMSNBC News (2013): "NSA skandalında Alman damgası", http://www. ntvmsnbc.com/id/25458786

Obama, Barack (2009): "International Strategy for Cyberspace". http://www. whitehouse.gov/sites/default/files/rss_viewer/international_strategy_for_cyb erspace.pdf

Press TV, (2013): "Iran releases decoded footage obtained from captured US drone", http://www.presstv.com/detail/2013/02/07/287743/iran-releases-decoded-video-from-us-drone/

Roazen, D. (1998): *Homo Sacer: Sovereign Power and Bare Life*, Stanford, California: Stanford University Press.

Russia Today (2013): "Australian Government talked PRISM before Snowden revelations", http://rt.com/news/australia-knew-prism-before-879/

Schmitt, Michael N. (2012): "International Law in Cyberspace: The Koh Speech and Tallinn Manual Juxtaposed", Harvard Journal of International Law On-Line: 13-37

Schmitt, Michael N., ed. (2013): *Tallinn Manual on the International Law Applicable To Cyber Warfare*. Prepared by the International Group of Experts at the Invitation of the NATO Cooperative Cyber Defence Center for Excellence, Cambridge: Cambridge University Press.

Taraf 2013): "İstihbaratta sınır yokmuş", http://www.taraf.com.tr/haber/istih baratta-sinir-yokmus.htm

Want China Times (2013): "NSA spy server in Chongqing could be used to bury Bo Xilai: Duowei", http://www.wantchinatimes.com/news-subclass-cnt.aspx ?id=20130808000136&cid=1101

Wakefield, J., BBC News Technology (2013): "Prism: Just how much do the spooks know?", http://www.bbc.co.uk/news/technology-22811580

Wikipedia (2013): "Firewall (computing)", http://en.wikipedia.org/wiki/Fire wall_(computing)

Virilio, Paul (1977): *Speed and Politics; An Essay on Dromology*, (Semiotext(e), Foreign Agents Series), New York: Columbia University Press

Chapter 5. Beyond Acceleration

"Unheimlich": The Uncanny and Narrative Space in Digital Arts

MARTIN RIESER

THE PARADIGM

As computing leaves the desktop and spills out onto the pavements, streets and public spaces of the city, we increasingly find information-processing capacity embedded within, and distributed throughout the material fabric of everyday urban space. Ubiquitous computing evangelists have heralded a coming age of an urban infrastructure, capable of sensing and responding to the events and activities transpiring around them. Imbued with the capacity to remember, correlate and anticipate, this near-future "sentient" city is envisioned as being capable of reflexively monitoring its environment and our behaviors within it – becoming an active agent in the organization of everyday life in urban public space. The reality is somewhat less than ideal with augmented reality merely becoming a flashy and ubiquitous tool for finding restaurants and friends in one's vicinity. However, the use of mobile code-based technologies can give new agency to the public narratives, and create a distinctive meld of embedded history and imagination, which in the projects described in this paper, represents a very different form of 'sentience' one that recognizes the role of the 'unheimlich' in such technologies and exploits it as a narrative strength.

Our mental representations of cities are necessarily complex, and to me it seems problematic for artists to merely map literal representations back onto space using locative technologies, but this appears to have been the predominant practice of many early projects, such as the first Locative Media workshop[1] and Urban Tapestries.[2] Research into spatial representation shows how mental maps create subjective distortion, describing not space, but the objects or nodes in it, and so our inner representations appear to be a direct contradiction to the continuous Euclidian 'space between' of a (Google) map, which is the dominant trope of the age of GPS.[3] Many of my own and the other projects considered here are an attempt to view the city as a series of social markers, landmarks and imagined human presences, rather than as simply abstract representations of space.

In current artistic interventions deploying locative technologies, it seems to me that there exist two distinct domains of practice – one that engages the "digital tame" of social media, online consumer culture and easy post-Situationist urban interventions, and another, which critically interrogates the digital "wild" by considering the liminal: the marginal and the excluded – both in fact and imagination.

While media arts using locative tools have naturally gravitated towards urban environments and have been drawn from either game or Situationist strategies, this paper will develop a theory and practice of situated and embodied arts related to a broader spectrum of ambulant and location-based practice making use of the new digital affordances. This paper will discuss how particular artworks that use technologies such as GPS have transformed landscape from a "picture" to a multi-layered, multi-channel experience, often incorporating multiple-sense modalities and extending beyond the instant into a highly durational, expanded spatio-temporal field. This field may reconnect the human experience of landscape, through the newer opportunities provided by mobile technology, to its very long artistic and cultural traditions. My use of Liminality also refers to the increasingly shaded edge area between virtual and physical experience, as well as the sense of 'otherness' or the uncanny, engendered by technologies of this kind.

---

1 Locative Media Workshop: The international workshop entitled "Locative media" took place from July 2003 at the K 2 Culture and Information Centre on the Baltic Sea http://locative.x-i.net/ (July 2005).

2 UrbanTapestries. http://urbantapestries.net/. Proboscis: Urban Tapestries (2002)

3 Barbara Tversky, Joseph Kim, Andrew Cohen (1999) Mental Models of Spatial Relations and Transformations from Language, Stanford University / Indiana University (http://www.psych.stanford.edu/~bt/space/papers/tverskykimcohen99.doc.pdf.) (1999).

LOCATIVE ART

Karlis Kalnins coined the phrase 'locative media' as the title for a workshop hosted by RIXC, an electronic art and media center in Latvia during 2002. Whilst locative media is closely related to augmented reality (reality overlaid with virtual reality) and to pervasive computing, locative media concentrates on social interaction with a specific place through mobile technology. Hence, many locative media projects have a background in social, critical or personal memory. In this paper I will describe attempts to use location-specific media in narratised contexts, both as a researcher's tool and a way to bring contemporary stories alive for the new technologically driven public.

Much reflection on Locative media art has been premature, for as Drew Hemment observed:

»It is too early to offer a topology of locative media arts, however, or to tie the field down with strict definitions or borders... We have not yet reached the point at which the technology disappears – all too often the tendency is to focus on the technology and tools rather than the art or content.«[4]

The waters have been further muddied by the convenient way in which artist's projects have often aligned with the consumer research interests of the mobile phone companies, where yesterday's locative project becomes tomorrow's "killer app". Mike Liebhold of the Institute for the Future (IFF) regards "geohackers, locative media artists, and psychogeographers" as key players in developing the "geospatial web," in where the web becomes tagged with geospatial information, a development that he sees as having "enormous unharvested business opportunities" and believes that this context-aware computing will emerge as the "third great wave of modern digital technology."[5]

Locative art, by its very nature, trespasses into the realm of Public Art, but by its interaction with the public, transforms our notions of site-specific and ambulant practices, defined over the last few decades by artists such as Richard Long, Robert Smithson, Hamish Fulton, Vito Acconci and Sophie Calle. The history of located and nomadic art is indeed a very long one stretching back to Aboriginal Songlines and spatialized religious rituals. I pose here the question whether, by similarly rooting locative practice in profound cultural and psychological structures, locative work can gain a greater artistic resonance. The explo-

---

4 http://socialinterface.files.wordpress.com/2007/12/locativearts.pdf
5 Tuters, M., and Varnelis, K. (2006)

ration of the syntax of spatial language and its relevance to current practice is the subject of this essay. Respect for place and space has long disappeared from our social uses of location-based technologies and in many instances of locative gaming just use the city as game grid, regardless of spatial specifics and histories, but the resonance of space may still perhaps be reclaimed by artists through the same technologies.

Which brings me to a further question relating to the art practice in this new medium. Much of what is named 'Locative Art' is not really art, but rather games-based work or spatialized documentary or simply advanced toolsets that happen to use this technology. To illuminate further we must ask a central question: what are the pleasures and modes of mobile user experience and how can we distinguish these from other media art forms or genres of work?

This extension of interactive technology from fixed installation to real urban geographies is radically altering the modes of audience participation and reception. When the physical space overlaps the space of diegesis, the emergent space for art and performance appears to open new perceptions of space and place in the audience. We need a redefinition of the concept of physical space (including hybrid environments), since through such technologies a new form of urban space seems to be emerging, which is not primarily visual, but in essence, conceptual.

Understanding emergent forms and visual and auditory artistic strategies of locative and pervasive media, which may enhance interactive narrative in urban and site-specific environments is still a huge challenge; but only through such an understanding of these new and radical forms of experiment, can we attempt to both map changes in sociability and communication patterns and to understand these new forms of collaborative art.

The "Mobile Bristol"[6] project made an attempt to define the pleasures of the medium through a seminar series in 2005, where for example, it was discovered that the accidental overlapping of ambient environmental sound and augmented sound within a locative work created a delicious ambiguity and a sense of extra resonance for an audience, a phenomenon termed "Magic Moments." Now what is needed most is to not only the pleasures of reception and use in this medium, but also to understand the social and physical context of these new artworks. These are increasingly dependent on haptic and spatial senses such as proprioception, which are little understood by artists, but are within the affordances of the emerging technologies.

---

6   A series of locative artwork experiments by Hewlett Packard, Watershed Media Centre and Bristol University 2004-2005

HOSTS AND STARSHED: UNCANNY SPACES

In 2006 I developed Hosts[7] for display in Bath Abbey, in an attempt to create an experimental ubiquitous artwork, sensitive to a specific location, by adapting new technologies to give a fully realized and embodied audio-visual user experience which touched on some universal thematics in art, in both its ancient and modern incarnations and explored the sense of uncanny associated with such technology. The piece was designed as a reflection on human life and death, presence and absence. Vertical screens were placed at strategic points of the space. A visitor triggered the presence of a variety of unfocused and evanescent video characters through the use of positional detection microphones, ultrasound emitting badges or 'Chirpers', and interpretative software. Characters appeared seemingly at random, but then spoke to an individual visitor and accompanied them from screen to screen. These "Hosts" were of a wide range of ages and of different gender, but always appeared singly to the particular participant wearing the unique ultrasound-code.

The "Hosts" could be taken to represent a variety of presences: from the angels of the Jacob's Ladder, sculpted on the building's exterior, to the spirit of people who had inhabited the same spaces, or even be seen as fragments of an individual psyche. The emotional mood was deliberately made variable and the encounters changed depending on a randomized selection sequence for the video sprite characters and sounds. A 3D audio landscape of accapella tonal voices accompanied the visitor between the screens, accessible on wireless headphones, and formed a tangible changing audio landscape dependent on user motion. I worked with singers, musicians and sound designers in Bristol/Bath on this aspect of the piece.

If a visitor stood for more than a few seconds in front of a particular screen, the figure turned in the direction of the viewer and returned the visitor's stare. The video sprite looked the visitor up and down, or turned away in distraction or approached and uttered a series of poetic aphorisms, also seen as animated text on the screen. On a separate screen evanescent figures were continually climbing up and down two ladders, mirroring the motif carved on the Abbey. It was out of this initial project that I developed a series of mobile art experiments to answer some of the research questions emerging in this new field. Simultaneously, I was researching a book on the subject: The Mobile Audience.[8] One of the first tasks

---

7 See http://www.martinrieser.com/Hosts.htm

8 http://www.digicult.it/en/2011/TheMobileAudience.asp

was to gain an overview of the phenomenon of artworks in this domain of embodied experience, an emerging arena for self-performance.

Figure 1. Hosts in Bath Abbey 2006.

Hewlett Packard has coined the term for mobile interaction spaces as "mediascapes"; and this hybrid media space is an in between, threshold place, an amalgam of imagination and the physical. De Certeau understood space as something that is produced through social practices.[9] With new social behaviours, emerge new spatial possibilities, so if Locative Media is to move beyond the production of novel experiences for extremely limited (art) audiences, it has to realize its potential by also addressing cultural, social and political contexts, and its practices need to be evaluated against the larger social framework of urban public space, critically engaging with the social and political realities of contemporary cities.

This project was followed in 2006 by a collaborative commission for the Electric Pavilion event at the Watershed Media Centre by the Ship of Fools[10] artist group, where we constructed an interactive map of Bristol, correlating each

9   Lefebvre, H. (1991)

10   http://www.shipoffools.pwp.blueyonder.co.uk

place with a starry map of the heavens. Stories of the uncanny sent in by the general public, were aligned star by star with real locations in the city. Participants were able to log sites and add rich-media stories of strange or uncanny happenings and encounters found across the city. The spatialized log of the uncanny grew rapidly and was collated through a two stage submission process from online and mobile sources. As the first serious attempt to use mobile media for this purpose, it stands as a unique piece and opened out in graphic form the liminal and uncanny nature of the medium itself and demonstrated how metaphoric mapping could elide the physical and the imagined in a single interface.

THE CITY AS STORY TRAJECTORY

Spatial annotation has emerged in the last few years as a major Internet phenomenon, particularly with the growth of Google Maps and social photo-sharing sites such as Flickr. In spatial annotation projects like Yellow Arrow[11] and Neighbornode[12] and in my own Starshed,[13] for Electric Pavilion (which mapped public stories of the 'uncanny' across a specific city space using early mobile technology) cities were increasingly being treated as surfaces on which individuals could inscribe annotation, and which ultimately became repositories of collective memory. Such story-telling projects allow for new social and cultural readings of space, allowing private narratives to become public and subject to reinterpretation.

The collective project *The Third Woman*[14] is relevant to this mapping of imagined worlds onto the physical city. It was an interactive mobile film, part of the European emobilArt initiative, which combined mobile game and performance based on a contemporary Vienna, revisiting the familiar territory of the post-war *film noir* The Third Man and re-imagined it for the 21st Century. The public participated in a guided performance game in the Viennese *U-Bahn* system, using QR codes as triggers for film-noir fragments and text messages, which moved them through a scenario that varied, depending on location or choice; driven by an intelligent film engine derived from Pia Tikka's Enactive cinema research.[15] The film itself was structured into three parallel dramas,

11 http://yellowarrow.net/index2.php

12 http://www.neighbornode.net/

13 http://www.electricpavilion.org/content/roots/starshed/index.html

14 See: www.thirdwoman.com

15 Tikka, Pia; Enactive Cinema – Simulatorium Eisensteinense, University of Art and Design Helsinki, 2008.

where the same scene was refilmed and made available in three different emotional versions.

Noir proved to be an excellent genre choice for intense and cryptic dramatology well suited to the constrictions of small-screen media, where dramatic lighting and camera angles helped to draw the audience into the distorted Noir universe.

The work toured internationally and was reworked substantially for each succeeding venue. Latterly, The Third Woman film-game explored a theme of pervasive global threats using bio-engineered terrorism in the 21st century. The film was the central element in a more complex interactive event. Using smart phone technology, participants could interact with media by responding to questions derived from ethical, moral, and social perspectives embedded in the content of the film. The use of hybrid or mixed reality tools: mobile media, *animateur* performers and situated artifacts related to the created narrative world distinguished this approach to interactive narrative.

In New York, performers on stage, wore fashion items made of QR images, used their bodies to demonstrate how to scan the codes and link to The Third Woman media. Spilling off stage into the audience, they invited people to play the film-game. Participants playing the game became part of The Third Woman interactive performance and could choose routes through the multi-stranded narrative by selecting subtle statements on their smartphones, related to character behaviors. Their choices could be examined individually or form a 'vote' for the preferred version which would then appear on a larger communal screen.

Figure 2. The Third Woman: Peformance at Galapagos Brooklyn

This experiment in hybrid mobile film and performance broke new ground, particular by envisaging the narrative as a story space which could connect with audiences in a variety of ways both online and through live performance and installation, and offer unique story routes to each individual depending on their interaction and conscious choices. This use of a hybrid narrative helped to bring closer together the diegetic space and the physical location, although in future incarnations the alignment of a meaningful spatial context to content would need to be more carefully considered.

It was invaluable as a crucible for refining hybrid mobile experiences for new audiences, equipped with smartphones, and was instrumental in finding the simplest and most inclusive method for singular and collaborative engagement with mobile-based narratives.

MAPPING AND HISTORY

At first sight it seems contradictory that engaging locative works tend to deal with an historical past rather than the lived present. After all Paul Virilio identified new media as promoting the change from considered diegesis to continuous and automatic present; the user creating the narratives both as subject and object. The visual subject is transferred to a mere technical effect, which forms a sort of 'pan-cinema,'[16] turning our most ordinary acts into movie action.

However where these locative works succeed, they seem to overlap the user's enactment of a continuous present with the user's immediate perception of a contiguous past.

The ever increasing technologizing and enclosure of urban and public spaces is a phenomenon associated with the growth of 'Herzian' Space and what Mark Augé[17] has termed to growth of "no place" (The anonymous motorway or mall). Stephen Graham points to how: "places [are] becoming increasingly constructed through consumer decisions which, in turn, are influenced through the... surveillance, and sorting, of cities."[18]

Such cities, increasingly "sorted" through the software and networking, point up a related political question about the embedding of previous relations of power, class and ownership in the new infrastructures and whether this perpetu-

---

16 Virilio, P. (1989).

17 Augé, Marc, Non-Places: Introduction to an anthropology of supermodernity, Verso, 1995

18 Graham, S. (2004).

ates ancient divisions or raises further questions related to the potential for community and individual empowerment.

A project of mine used the city as both metaphor and as a multi-layered repository of meaning, Riverains[19] was developed for the B'tween festival in Manchester and was predicated on the idea of underground presences derived from the city's past, which lingered in the underground spaces riddling our cities. These presences could both be detected and unlocked by the public, using mobile devices in the manner of a water douser. It was planned to later add user contributions in the form of avatars to create an ever-growing layer-cake of histories and narratives. It was further developed for the Illumini Festival in Shoreditch, where multiple histories were placed along Shoreditch High Street and Old Street.

Both Manchester and London have rich underground worlds of hidden or "lost" rivers, nuclear fallout facilities and command centres and Second World War bunkers, in addition to Victorian sewers and underground railway systems. They also have an archaeology going back through medieval to Roman times. The Riverains were drawn from this rich history of poverty, industrial revolution, immigration, political protest, commerce and innovation, gang warfare and crime. The project is planned to map video and photo-stories across central areas of other cities.

Riverains was run in Pilot form at the Illumini Festival in September 2010 tracing a portion of Old Street and Shoreditch High Street. Secret Subterranean London was the third Illumini event, curated by Jane Webb, and located in the basement of Shoreditch Town Hall.

Riverains at Illumini was designed to comprise four elements, offering interaction to users with varying levels of technical requirement (users are expected to provide their own mobile phone). The work built on the Riverains development for Manchester's B'tween festival, extending it through collaboration with artists Ximena Alarcon and Kasia Molga, with technical development by Sean Clark and Phil Sparks (Empedia by Cuttlefish Multimedia) and Gareth Howell (using Layar). Two 'guided walks' followed in which participants were supported in using the QR code reader version, and Layar[20] (for those with suitable phones), as they followed the trail along Old Street and Shoreditch High Street. Those without appropriate phones were able to share the experience using

---

19 See http://empedia.info/maps/20?resource=resource%2F557

20 Layar was the first augmented reality app launched for the iPhone and Android platforms

spare iPhones during the walks. Riverains was aimed at the broad spectrum Illumini audience.

The video pieces by Alarcon and myself were either triggered by photographing QR codes distributed on stickers along the route, carrying visual clues as to locations associated with the video content.

As it was, the rich history of Shoreditch was explored with pieces on early Shakespeare, using imagined voices of characters or actors from the plays Henry IV and Romeo and Juliet; verbatim readings from the coroner's report of the "Ripper" murder of Mary Kelly: held in the Town Hall site of the exhibition, with interjections by the Ripper's imagined persona; immigrant voices from Jewish, Huguenot and contemporary narratives were available, as were reflections on the Plague in London, creating dramatized monologues based on Daniel Defoe's Journal of the Plague Year. Suffragette histories became audio-visual sound-image montages echoing their dire treatment in Holloway Prison. Finally there were reflections on the early history of underground rivers that criss-cross the area and notionally held the uncanny historical presences, which were the Riverains.

Riverains, by imagining history as the province of the dead, brought back through augmented reality and intense fictional first-person witness of their former detailed experience, the uncanny nature of the technology was used to create in the user a sense of an immediate co-present, lying just behind the bland map on their mobile screens.

AUGMENTED REALITY AS MYTHOLOGY

Secret Garden was an attempt to recreate a contemporary version of the Eden myth in the midst of an urban environment. It is also one of the first located mobile digital operas. A collaborative work between Andrew Hugill (composer) and myself, it will be available in two versions – a physical installation and as a virtual mobile experience linked to selected site locations. In its installation aspect, it had eleven iPad viewports distributed around the circumference of a circle. Peering into one of the viewports triggered a view of an idyllic three-dimensional scene in the 'Secret Garden' and told part of the mythical story of the Fall, through words, music and actions. This same content will also be made available using Augmented Reality software to any visitor with a smartphone.

The Fall story is common to many of the world's religions, including Judaism, Christianity and Islam. The structure of Secret Garden is loosely modeled on the ten paths of the Sephirot in the Jewish telling of the story, which is itself also a symbol of the Tree of Life and the oldest extant version. Two contemporary human figures enact the story of the Fall, combining sung poetry and video vignettes within 3D generated environments, each scene distributed to a different one of the eleven viewports. The viewer's presence triggers both music and action.

The texts comprise original poems that tell this classic story in a timeless and relevant way, examining choices in a fallen world. The musical composition is adaptive and features vocal settings and digitally treated percussion. The virtual scenography consists of 3D designs based on an idealized garden space, inspired by the 19th century Mezzotints for Milton's *Paradise Lost* by John Martin. Viewing the eleven viewports gradually assembles the elements of a story in the user's mind. However, it is not necessary to see the viewports in any particular order, and a partial viewing will also provide a complete experience in itself.

The installation is a unique virtual reality amalgam of poetry, music, and 3D panoramic images. It plays with sound narrative and myth, transposed into a modern context, using technology both in production and delivery in a synthesized and holistic capacity. Audience movement from viewport to viewport triggers vocal settings of authored verse. An especially designed circular exhibition installation was created. Containing iPad computers and earphones, which can be sited in any gallery. By using 11 small screens, an audience viewed in true 3D vision, with the parallax shift tied to head movements. The software detected user movements and adjusted the scene's parallax in real-time. Viewers were not required to wear any other special headgear or glasses: they simply needed to touch the iPads to trigger the scene.

The musical composition involved highly complex counterpoint, since at any one moment there is a possibility of up to twenty-two vocal lines unfolding from any point around the installation. In other words, this is 'adaptive' music, a term derived from computer game composition. The music is harmonically restricted to a hexatonic gamut. The vocal lines illustrate the words, with gong/crotale strokes acting as punctuation. The composition uses the number symbology that lies behind the Ten-branched Sephirot as an organizing principle.

By aligning locative technologies with the oldest of mythologies, we were building on the notion of the technology offering not simply a portal into the past, but one into the deeper layers of collective cultural myths, revivified for a contemporary audience through the uncanny of motion captured avatars. By using the strange sense of 'otherworldness' of traditional games engines combined with motion-captured smooth avatar movement in the animation, a contradictory experience helped to uneasily position the audience in a physically real sound space and a virtual space quite unlike anything experienced in the real world. The reaction to the realistic movement of the avatars was ambiguous for most audiences, with elements of the 'uncanny valley'[21] phenomenon actually increasing the sense of mythic space. The spatialized sound was very successful in its creation of a sense of a co-present other world in parallel to the audience's present reality.

Figure 3. Scene from Secret Garden[22]

CONCLUSION

The advent of mobile technologies has placed powerful computers in the pockets of more people than have ever possessed a desktop PC. It has created new affordances for artists out in real space, dissolving the traditional gallery walls and has allowed new audiences to relate to the spaces of their urban worlds by turning them both into places and spaces of liminal possibility, where inner and outer spaces, histories and narratives can be interlocked and explored. It has allowed the user the privilege of co-authorship via social media and other two-way interventions. I hope through my examination of a broad range of projects the common thematics have been illuminated. That mobile and digital media can create a

---

21 "Uncanny Valley" refers to the dislocative sense of near-realism in CGI experienced
   by audiences when people are represented

22 Copyright 2012 Martin Rieser

portal to a space where social, physical and virtual worlds can collide and cross-fertilize; enriching our experience of the city as a space of possibility by augmenting our sense of the present and past. It could be said that we are looking at the very beginning of a new art form, one that happily exists in both the hybrid world of the new "Hertzian" spaces and in the imagination of the new audiences addressing both the heimlich of place and the 'unheimlich' of digital space.

REFERENCES

Augé, Marc (1995): *Non-Places: Introduction to anthropology of supermodernity*, Verso

Graham, S. (2004): "The Software-Sorted City: Rethinking the 'Digital Divide'", in Graham, S., ed. (1979): *The Cybercities Reader, and London: Routledge*: 324-331.

Lefebvre, Henri (Trans 1991): *The Production of Space*, Blackwell, UK

De Certeau, Michel (1984) *The Practice of everyday life*, University of California USA

Tuters, Marc, and Varnelis, Kazys (August 2006) *Beyond Locative Media*, Leonardo, vol. 39, no. 4, Massachusetts Institute of Technology: 357-363

Tversky, Barbara, Joseph Kim, Cohen, Andrew (1999): *Mental Models of Spatial Relations and Transformations from Language*, Stanford University/ Indiana University

Virilio, Paul (1989): *War and Cinema; The Logistics of Perception*. Trans. Patrick Miller. London: Verso

Against the Self-Evident

A thorough indefiniteness, a defined obscurity[1]

MICHAEL JOHANSSON AND KRISTOFFER ÅBERG

Creating a world and communicating it among others is not easy. The task is very complex and demanding and the risk of being disappointed by what you achieve is evident.[2]

Where there is architecture there is nothing else. And this "Nothing else" is spreading. The buildings, the laid out streets and marked out parking spaces are not just taking place, they take over the place.

As we, in Walter Benjamin's words, usually experience architecture in a distracted way at that, the result is a universe which in its persistent presence excludes, even precludes, all kinds of *other* things. A kind of everyday totalitarianism, whose frontier towards the potential is not a ban, but a persevering negligence. The frontier towards what's difficult to imagine is drawn as narrow as *what's self-evident* being the only conceivable thing. I am driving down this street, parking in this space and entering this building, not because I wish to, but because obviously there are no other alternatives than not doing this. If nothing else, then a conspiracy of the safe and snug against... well, against what? Maybe the never realized. Even frustration and expectation are channeled into ever-narrowing and ever more directed furrows. I want/don't want (to do) this, turns into a choice between total acceptance of the given and militant extremism against it. What this given is or could be must not be a question of doubt. The Utopia is forfeit, whether it is unthinkable for historical reasons, or because it is realized in history.

---

1 Söderberg, N. (2003)
2 Johansson, M. (2010)

But what if what's difficult and potential is in a tight spot, how manage (one's) resistance then?

In the present situation, the *flat nay* no longer seems to be the most rewarding method. More rewarding, or at least more fun, seems to us a subversive touch based on undermining the (already) known, rather than on trespassing and "novelty." This undermining can be performed in many ways, and this is not the place to enter deeply in every possibility at hand (deconstruction, actualization, ostraniene, modality etc), but briefly to suggest that what they all have in common is the performing of their critical operations *within* the given, rather than beyond this. Undermining, loosening, breaking up that whose rock solidity lies in the self-evident. A method whose applicability in no way is confined to resolute, practical problems, but which can well be used theoretically, poetically, hypochondriacally, hallucinary, phantasmatically.

A "wild thinking" aiming to undermine the present and prevalent must nevertheless have a starting point, and a location in which to perform its laboratory work. Such a location was placed unintentionally on the map of the possible in the mid-seventies when Swedish Public Broadcasting, educating their listeners how to manage the new stereo technique, were establishing that:

> my voice will now be coming from the right
> my voice will now be coming from the left
> my voice will now be coming in between the loudspeakers
> my voice will now be coming from an indefinite location in the room.

This indefinite location in the room is something completely different than the outside location of the natural sciences, the point from which reality is measured and translated into objectivity. [This point too has proven itself absurd (even if strikingly efficient). Gödel, Heisenberg, Bohr etc.] Then instead an indefiniteness within the room, and a voice imperatively calling forth its own elusive presence. Within the room but not clearly where, in many ways resembles the location of the potential in the prevalent, given. A floating possibility hidden in the persistent present. Our voice is now supposed to come from an indefinite location within the room.

This location is The City of Abadyl.

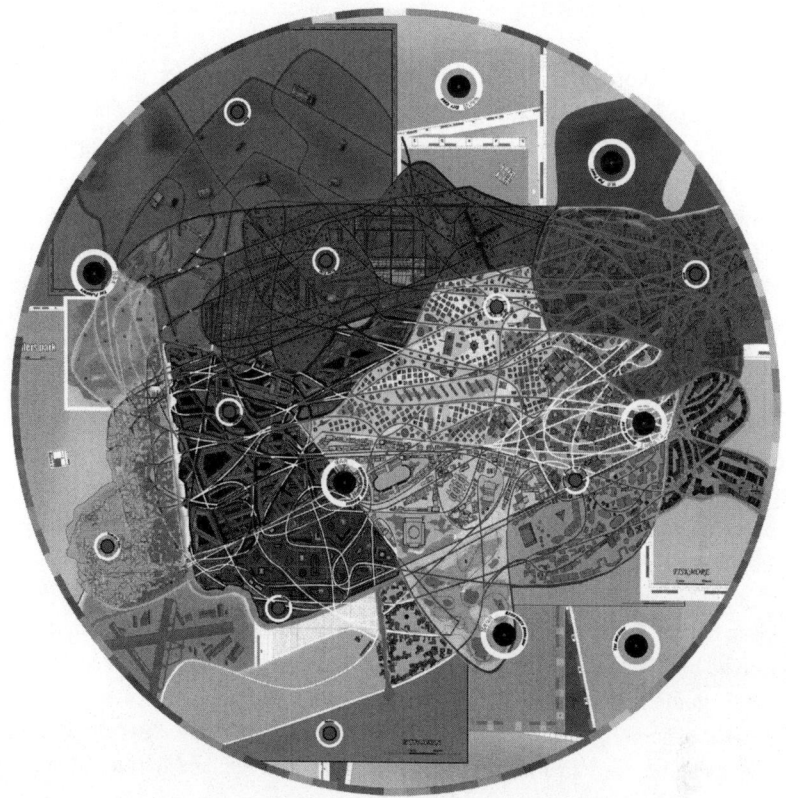

Figure 1. A map of the city of Abadyl 1999-2013 Mobela-C version

Abadyl has been described and written about in several articles and papers before.[3] So to put this chapter in context it is necessary to unfold the general ideas behind it before we can put forward and discuss some of our worldmaking and design fiction tactics. In short the city of Abadyl attempts to understand and redefine our world in a situation where information is lacking. This lack of information is used as a resource. By providing ambiguous fragments as a starting point, it serves as a vital part in the creation of a space where we can be in a constant dialogue with a large database of material that is interlinked through the architecture of a city, regardless of its incompatibilities. This establishes a setting

---

3 Johansson, M. (2013), Johansson, M. (2012), Johansson, M. (2011), Johansson, M. (2010), Johansson, M. (2010), Lund, J. (2008), Johansson, M., and Linde, P. (2004)

similar to fragmented storytelling, often used in computer games such as *Bioshock*.

Abadyl is a proposed city, an urban fantasy, a set of codes and models, a library of artifacts and prototypes, and foremost, it is its co-creators. Since its inception in 1999 it has grown into a large database of materials interlinked through the shape of a city. Our approach is to create an environment which facilitates artistic work practice in complex production environments such as those of digital media, supporting invited artists, researchers, companies, and students. Establish a ready-made, fictitious gravity that others can easily transfer their knowledge and experiences into.

So how do we go about exploring this complex digital space? We could for example let people walk the streets of Abadyl, in a game engine, but we have so far chosen another direction. We have used the framework (figure 2) of Abadyl to stage different events in the form of written scenarios that provide detailed and specific background material. Through the work of writing the scenarios we have learned how to transfer methods from creative writing and other ways of worldmaking into our own work practice in the fields of art and design. In Postscript to the Name of the Rose, Umberto Eco writes about using a generative logic that both limits and expands creativity.[4] The fundamental parameters of this logic guide what can and cannot be included in a fictional but plausible universe. Our concern is not so much with a consistent, watertight universe, but rather what can be generated from limited predetermined real and fictitious parameters. In the city of Abadyl the fixed parameters are seven, 16 and 100.

The seven scale system that we introduced to handle the event space of the city described the different levels on which objects and events can occur.

1. Environment
2. Building
3. Room
4. Furniture
5. Tool
6. Interface
7. Idea

Sixteen locations from different parts of the world constituted the starting point, and were initially held apart. But later they were merged into a connected city.

---

4   Eco, U. (1984)

As joining infrastructure the series of sixteen Formula One tracks was chosen, piled on top of each other into a joint figure hence aiming to expose architecture and cityscape to extreme strain (= life, unpredictability) The formula one tracks became our point of departure, shaping an interesting ornamentation of roads just waiting to be driven on. The city then divides into sixteen parts with the idea to host their own separate ideology, architecture, fashion, sports etc.

One hundred objects were chosen to represent the city or the world, which matched Peter Greenaway's[5] idea of an encyclopedic approach in his project 100 objects to represent the world. In the various quarters of the city 100 objects would be found, each devised in a way that constituted an elegant description and manifesting the aspects of their very own district. These objects are helping us shape the differences on a broader range of levels in every part of the city and serve as a series of obstacles for the explorations. The purpose is to interfere with both the already built objects and the activities that are going to occur here later on. In this way we happened to examine our original objects once again, when we were depicting them in every detail. A very thorough investigation of aspects of each of the 100 objects to create conditions for deconstruction, attaching possible narratives to them and force out every meaning by depicting/modelling – to sort of philosophize from the street level and up.

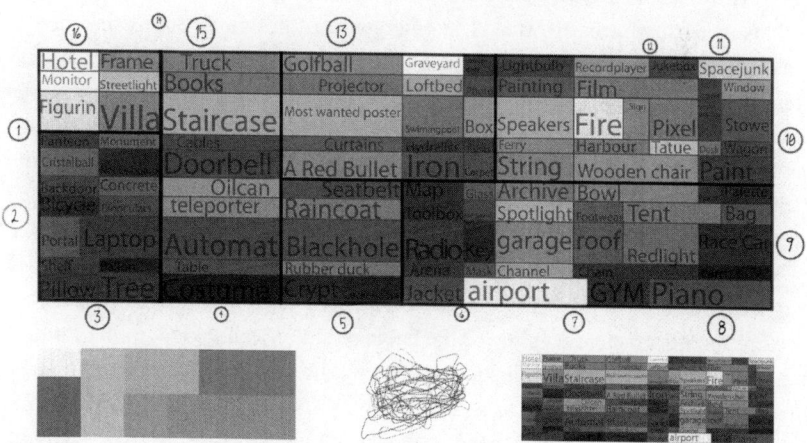

Figure 2. The 7, 16 and 100 framework

5   Greenaway, P. (1993)

Worldmaking in the Unknown Unknown

In 2011 I started a collaboration around design fiction with Science Fiction Designer Kristoffer Åberg. We tried to map out models and methods from our past experience to help us reach the fold of the known and into unknown territory, not only as a theory but as a design practice in different media, materials and formats. The point of departure was the exploration of The City of Abadyl and Kristoffer Åbergs project Life Forms; these have been journeys through parallel planes, one journey being the narratives playing out in the designed worlds themselves. The other journey consists of our own stories as artists and designers, narrating the design process and its inherent learning experiences.

It is interesting to address design fiction as the notion of the "conflation of design, science fiction, and science fact"[6] as a space of tension and entanglement between what is and what could be. In design fiction we have the space to apply design to science fiction, or science fiction to design. For example, methods like scenario planning used by futurologists have been borrowed by science fiction writers to extrapolate from the present into the future. Industrial designers working in the Detroit automotive industry have not seldom ended up designing spaceships for Hollywood, while researchers in aerospace technologies or ubiquitous computing have also consulted for science fiction movie productions. And there is a long history of science fiction influencing innovations, attitudes and values in our own, real worlds. The emergence of design fiction is one sign of this interplay being acknowledged and appreciated as having a potential for experience design in general. One question is how to actually work in practice in this space of tension and entanglement between science fact and science fiction, and especially how to encourage the use of science fiction in design, away from derivative, predictable output and towards speculation and tinkering based on the opportunities afforded by the unknown.

As artists and designers in particular we have the culture and nurturing to explore, create, and tell stories about possible worlds. Design has its roots in the application of artistic discipline to the engineering of technology, in the form of pattern making for mass production, and as styling for product marketing. Later, design has come into its own as a creative discipline and an origin of innovations rather than something only slapped onto existing ones. Design is one activity of creating the future, not solving old problems as much as inventing new opportunities, still with strong ties to empirical science and engineering but also with the story telling of branding and marketing. At the same time, industries and design

---

6   Bleecker, J. (2009)

have evolved from producing products, to services, and recently to experiences, expressing basic human tenets to create and tell stories. This of course is at the core of fiction, helping us make sense of what it means to be human, how to plan and live our lives, and to find some purpose behind our journey. Science fiction expands on this in a speculative and perhaps ultimate manner, leaving our known world to verge into the fringes of the unknown and beyond.

THE HERO'S JOURNEY

"It has always been the prime function of mythology and rite to supply the symbols that carry the human spirit forward, in counteraction to those constant human fantasies that tend to tie it back."[7]

The Hero's Journey outlined by Joseph Campbell is a narrative structure based on the similarities of heroic myths across cultures.[8] In this narrative, an archetypal hero is separated from his Ordinary World, being pulled and pushed over the threshold into the Special World of adventure, where tests of initiation await for him to overcome. After winning a decisive victory, the hero returns home to teach the lessons he has learned through his trials. The hero is transformed through his adventure, the acts and stages of the journey being a metaphor for how we go through the stages of our human lives. We have a need to experience stories for just that reason, for what stories can teach us about life, and the Hero's Journey serves as a structure for that storytelling.[9] In science fiction its use is apparent in the movies The Matrix and Star Wars: Episode IV – A New Hope, as well as in the novel Ender's Game.

We too use the Hero's Journey to inspire narrative structure when designing the experiences of our design fictions. In addition, the Hero's Journey is useful on the meta-level of the design fiction process, where we ourselves are heroes gravitating from the known into the unknown, and back again. The Hero's Journey ends with the hero returning to the Ordinary World, bringing some lesson or treasure from the Special World. This is analogous to a design process resulting both in some knowledge acquired during the process, and some artifact storing parts of that knowledge.[10] The design process can thus be viewed as a process of knowledge acquisition or learning from that which was previously

---

7   Campbell, J. (2008)
8   Campbell, J. (2008)
9   Vogler, C. (2007)
10 Armour, P. (2000)

unknown. The knowledge acquired pertains not only to the particular domain of the artifact, but to the design process itself. That is, we acquire knowledge on how to evolve both artifact and design process.[11]

TERRA INCOGNITA

If the Hero's Journey provides a narrative structure for the design fiction process, an epistemological model of the universe provides the map (Figure 4). Such a map represents the world of physical bodies and energy, the world of mental states and processes, and the world of the products of the human mind.[12] The narrative structure of the Hero's Journey is analogous to conventional design processes consisting of stages in linear succession.[13] The spatial metaphor of the map conveys additional qualities of the design process, such as non-linear movement through a complex design space, including exploration and iteration.

For any one hero exploring a world, some parts of this map will be well known; some will be unexplored and unknown. A low-resolution, non-exhaustive representation contains the following four areas and how they develop over a 100 year timespan.

Known Known – knowledge that can be retrieved from memory, or skills that can be exercised, through conscious volition. Effortful mental activities "with the subjective experience of agency, choice and concentration."[14] Reflection-in-action, that is, thinking about what you are doing.[15] Consciousness, mindfulness.

Known Unknown – basic ignorance. Having a question but not the answer.

Unknown Known – knowledge that cannot easily be retrieved from memory. Automatic and quick mental activities, "with little or no effort, and no sense of voluntary control."[16] The tacit knowledge and skills of experience that cannot be expressed in language.[17] Inconvenient or resisted psychological powers, "the

---

11 Imai, M. (1997)

12 Popper, K. (1978)

13 Jones, J. C. (1992)

14 Kahneman, D. (2011)

15 Schön, D. (1983)

16 Kahneman, D. (2011)

17 Schön, D. (1983)

whole realm of the desired and feared adventure of the discovery of the self."[18]
The unconscious.

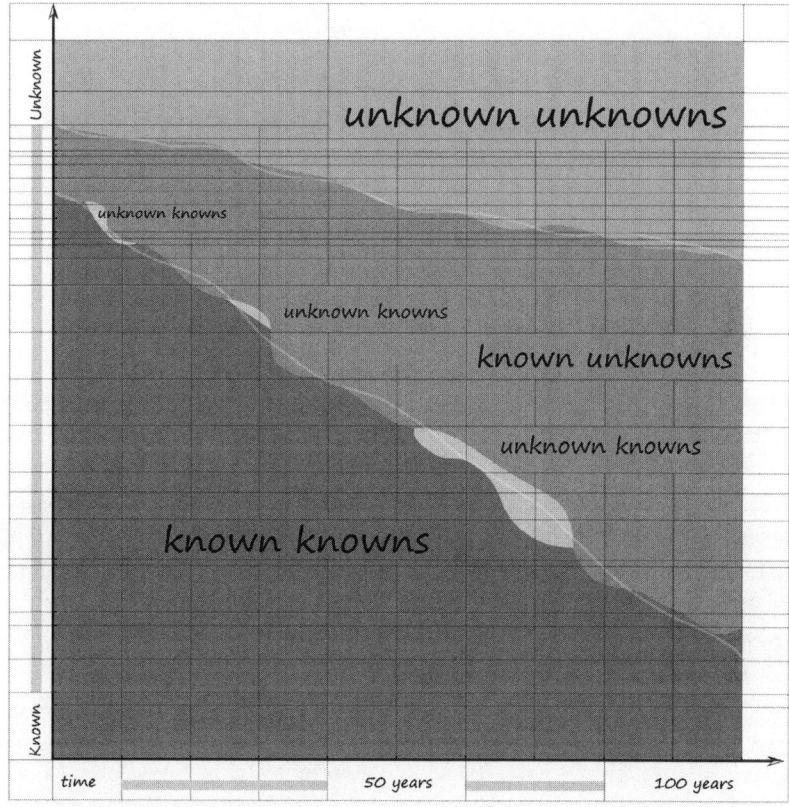

Figure 3. Epistemological model of the universe.[19]

Unknown Unknown – unexpected, surprise discoveries. A region of supernatural wonder.[20] Black Swans, that is, highly improbable, extreme-impact events.[21] Per definition, non-awareness of ignorance.

---

18 Campbell, J. (2008)
19 Copyright Michael Johansson and Kristoffer Åberg, progression over time borrowed från Stross, C. (2013)
20 Campbell, J. (2008)
21 Taleb, N. N. (2010)

Armed with his current knowledge, the hero then ventures into the quadrants of regions the unknown, with the potential for discovery, and self-discovery.

DESIGN FICTION METHOD

»Devotees of the humanities expect to be surprised. An arresting metaphor or poetic image, an unpredicted twist of the plot, a novel style of music, painting, or dance...all these unexpected things amaze and delight us. Scientists, too, appreciate the shock of a new idea – the double helix, the jumping gene, or the benzene-ring. Indeed, unpredictability is often said to be the essence of creativity. But unpredictability is not enough. At the heart of creativity lie constraints: the very opposite of creativity. Constraints and unpredictability, familiarity and surprise, are somehow combined in original thinking.«[22]

For surprising discoveries and creative, original ideas, the design fiction process combines existing knowledge with the capture of new knowledge. Assuming the role of the hero, we are torn between the Call of Adventure from the Special World, and Refusing the Call for fear of the unknown (Vogler 2007). To escape the gravitational pull of the Ordinary World, the hero may need some advice or guidance before venturing to the edge of knowledge, and Crossing the First Threshold into the unknown. A Mentor prepares the hero, in our case with design fiction methods tangled from science, design, and science fiction origins:

»To justify calling an idea creative, then, one must specify the particular set of generative principles – what one might call the conceptual space – with respect to which is impossible.«[23]

»Divergence refers to the act of extending the boundary of a design situation so as to have a large enough, and fruitful enough, search space in which to seek a solution.«[24]

»Design fiction, like science fiction, speculates, reflects and extrapolates, looking at today from the side, or sideways and forming a critical, introspective perspective that can project into new (future) forms.«[25]

---

22 Margaret Boden, Creativity and Unpredictability
23 Boden, M. (1995)
24 Jones, J. C. (1992)
25 Bleecker, J. (2009)

Taking the cue from Bleecker, we entangle rather than outline some design fiction methods as follows, focusing on the Hero's Journey up until after Crossing the Threshold into the unknown (Figure 5). Our approach is informal, and we allow ourselves to be speculative and transformational with regard to the design fiction process itself and the sources that inspire it.

Reflect – Think quietly and calmly, considering some subject matter, idea, or purpose. Express thoughts and opinions resulting from this reflection. Reflect on features, criteria for making judgments, procedures, problem framing, implicit understandings; invite confusion, and use the confusion as a way to think differently.[26] Reflect on the "conceptual space," that is, established styles of thinking defining the range of possibilities; what are the features and structure of this space?[27]

Extrapolate – Project, extend, and expand your knowledge to arrive at conjectural knowledge of an unknown area. Draw deductions or conclusions by reflecting on these tendencies. Extrapolate changes, paradigm shifts, hypotheses, emerging phenomena in society, psychology, science; hypothesize about the not yet known, the theoretically possible, the impossible; invert, exaggerate, and distort; tell yourself "If this goes on..."[28] Relate the unknown and unfamiliar to the known; use analogies and references; recombine extrapolations in innovative ways.[29] Use one or more from the range of scenario planning methods.[30]

Speculate – Be curious, or doubtful. Make assumptions based on premises, ideas, metaphors, insufficient evidence. Post-rationalize the possibility of something imagined. Ask "What if...?"[31] Invoke and provoke change; explore paradoxes; critique the present; prototype, continuously re-evaluating aspects explored, and re-purposing the exploration; communicate intents; suggest effects, potential consequences; connect disparate ideas and intentions.[32]

---

26 Schön, D. (1983)

27 Boden, M. (1995)

28 Samuelson, D. N. (1993)

29 Runberger, J. (2012)

30 Lindgren, M., and Bandhold, H. (2003), Ogilvy, J. A. (2011)

31 Samuelson, D. N. (1993)

32 Runberger, J. (2012)

Transform – Decide what to emphasize and what to overlook. Fix boundaries, identify critical variables, recognize constraints, take opportunities, make judgments; split the whole into parts, and change the parts.[33] Reconsider knowledge taken for granted, conduct thought experiments that invoke paradigm shifts.[34] Drop, or negate a constraint; explore and transform your own cognitive style; put flaws, accidents, and serendipity to use.[35] Transfer principles from other fields.[36]

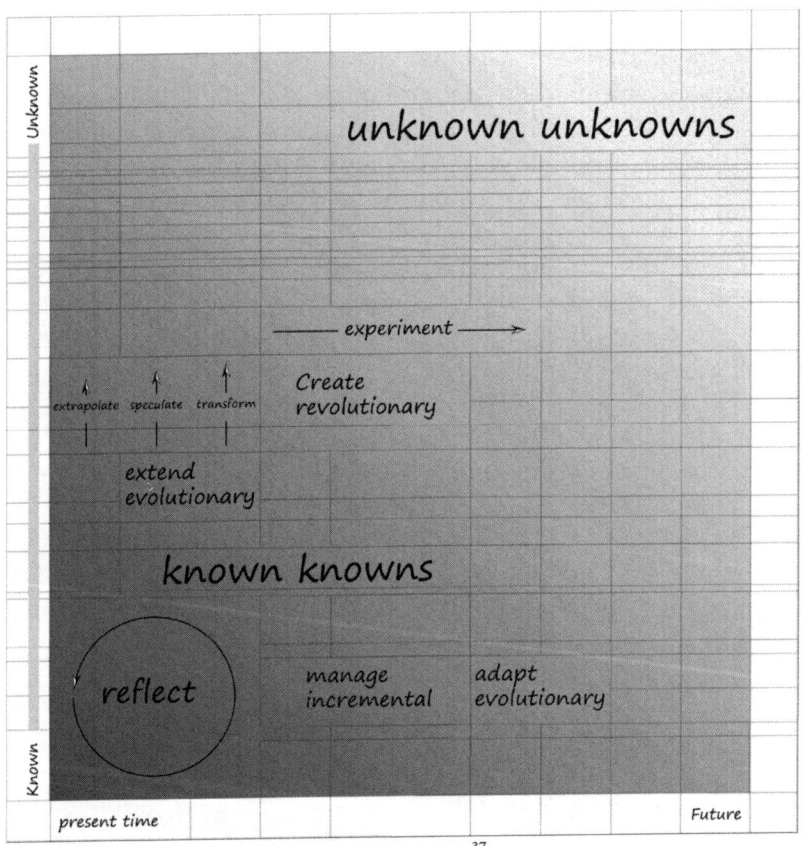

Figure 4. Epistemological model, with method.[37]

33 Jones, J. C. (1992)

34 Samuelson, D. N. (1993)

35 Boden, M. (1995)

36 Runberger, J. (2012)

37 Michael Johansson and Kristoffer Åberg overlaying with Rodriguez, D. and Jacoby, R. Ways to Grow matrix [Brown, T. (2009)]

These are but a selection of possible methods for design fiction; others include sketching[38] and prototyping.[39] To keep true to the spirit of design fiction as a space of entanglement and tension between disciplines, we do not wish to turn the acts of reflection, extrapolation, speculation and transformation into formal methods. Rather, they are modes or meta-methods for design, containers for diverse but related repertoires and concepts which in our future work we intend to evolve further. In the meantime, we see some emerging themes synthesizing the Hero's Journey, the epistemological map, and these modes or meta-methods, which we interpret through the lenses of Mentors from diverse disciplines.

WORLDS ARE AS MUCH MADE AS FOUND

Through these lenses we created perspectives and angles to establish fictional and detailed environments for our worldmaking experiments, where we have played around with both real and fictitious assumptions. Using the Hero's Journey as a narrative structure for our design fictions, we created scenarios, plotting a series of dilemmas that are applicable in relation to what it means to be human, how to plan and live our lives, and to find some purpose behind our journey across different contexts and situations, both future and present. We have also concluded a series of creative methods that can govern shared and inter-disciplinary explorations and sometimes the creation of prototypes and artifacts. Work that always has its implications similar to those described by Poggenpohl and Sato:[40]

»The search for common ground involves resolving problems of terminology, expectation, and process. This is a collaborative act of communication in which competing disciplinary discourses are examined, symbolic values are shared, and a hybrid process that appreciates multiple ways of examining a problem or question is employed; the participants need a willingness to embrace new knowledge and perspective, and resulting new meanings.«

---

38 Buxton, B. (2007)
39 Johnson, B. A. (2011)
40 Poggenpohl, S., and Sato, K. (2009)

POINT OF DEPARTURE

This first part of our journey has now come to an end and we can conclude our efforts and put forward some useful insights. Our own experience and critique of the mundane nature of much contemporary design method based on the known is by no means novel or original in itself, echoing thinkers like Michael Sorkin in his book Local Code (1993).[41] Sorkin's Local code has a lot in common with practicing design fiction since it attempts to imagine a new city via a building code, a regulatory prescription for an urban fantasy:

»The theoretical resources informing social and cultural analysis for more than three decades have been exhausted, and alternative interpretive strategies have yet to be defined. Innovative perspectives once bristling with new insight by now have been repeated and routinized until they yield arguments that are utterly predictable and familiar.«

DIRECTIONS PLEASE

The field of *mediology*, due to Regis Debray, is of particular interest to design fiction practice, drawing a distinct relationship between technological development and cultural transmission – "the culture happens as design does."[42] Mediology proposes three historical ages of transmission technologies:[43]

the *logosphere* (the age of writing, theology, the kingdom, and faith),
the *graphosphere* (the age of print, political ideologies, nations, and laws),
the *videosphere* (audio/video broadcasting, models, individuals, and opinions).

These established directions set us out to capture the action of ideas in the future, and to seek the material forms and the effects of the cultural structuring of a technical innovation, and in the opposite direction, in the technical bases of a social or cultural development. By drawing upon the timeline across the logosphere, graphosphere, videosphere, and beyond, we try to extrapolate and transform on that idea of progression, in different timelines and timeframes, establish-

---

41 Sorkin, M. (1993)

42 Bleecker, J. (2009)

43 Debray, C. (1995)

ing possible connections and disruptions between future technologies, their cultures of use, and how new ideologies may shape and change the future in different ways.

HELPERS – MEET TWIST AND TURN

After Crossing the Threshold into the Special World, the hero faces a series of tests and enemies, but also allies in the form of various helpers, in addition to any aid received by the Mentor. In speculating about design fiction methods, we introduce the idioms of twists and turns of fate, which refers to unanticipated changes in a sequence of events, never knowing what lies ahead.

The twists are the scenarios, whose role in design has been that of writing narrative descriptions of use. Other cultural domains have generated more speculative methods for collaboration and narratives. Originating from the idea of autonomous writing, the surrealists borrowed methods from academic disciplines such as sociology, anthropology, and psychology to elaborate methods in the form of games, for exploring the mechanism of imagination and intensifying collaborative experience. This applies to many aspects of artistic and design work. Changing a constraint might be at the core of creative thinking.[44] The scenarios act very much as constraints, but also as initial generators in a chain of associative artistic work in producing artifacts.

The turns are the modes or meta-methods, like reflection, extrapolation, speculation, and transformation, working within the scenarios or on the scenarios themselves. In these method examples we find agreement with Boden that creativity cannot only and simply be reduced to novel combinations of old ideas. Indeed, many creative methods can be reduced on some quantitative level, being akin to mathematical or logical operations where a set of elements are disrupted by putting them into new combinations or other relationships. For example, Tschumi outlines a framework for multiple combinations and substitutions that exist simultaneously, including the following three concepts:[45]

Cross-programming – the use of a space not as intended.
Trans-programming – the combination of disparate programs.
Dis-programming – disparate programs that contaminate each other. These operations offer possibilities of combinations and permutation of existing programs as well new programs.

---

44 Boden, M. (1997)
45 Tschuni, B. (1991)

But in addition to such methods or programs, we utilize context in the form of scenarios, knowledge of the domain, specific materials and artifacts and knowledge of worldmaking. Co-creators together in these settings give rise to emergent properties of creativity that cannot be explained only through "random word association," "every new idea is a combination of two old ideas," or "think the opposite."

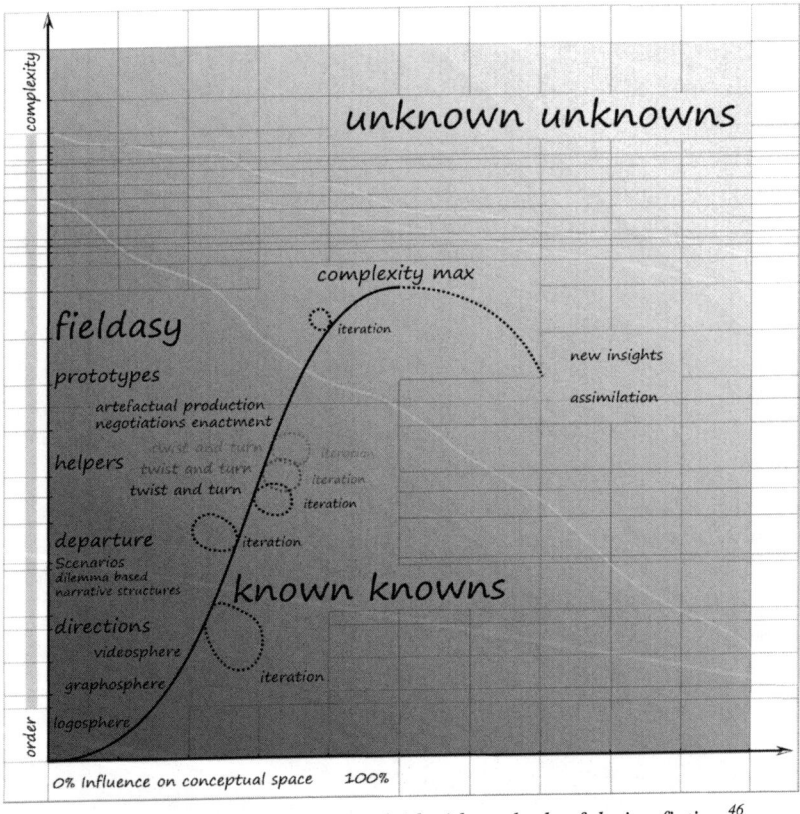

Figure 5. Fieldasy workprocess – overlaid with methods of design fiction.[46]

LET'S GET PHYSICAL

Through the years we have worked with artefacts as one surface of communicating and testing our ideas and concepts that are generative rather that produced. Generative in the sense that they have no original nor final form. They are sprung out of a chain of association through our work process and methods that generates new forms, which in its turn recombines into new stories. The friction created by letting artifacts evolve in specific materials and media specified in the scenarios is there to help the co-creator capture interesting and comprehensive perspectives, that through artifact creation incorporate surprising visual and technical proposals. Working with artifacts as a source of communication lets co-creators explore this area by complex connections through iterating between artistic intentions/screenwriting, digitally generated expressions, physical objects and script/code writing. The key here for the co-creator is the ability to work in ambiguity – to explore different possibilities without jumping too early to conclusions. This negative capability as Keats defines it, "is when man is capable of being in uncertainties, mysteries and doubts without any irritable reaching after fact and reason." The artifacts also act as generators while they generate new and unforeseen processes, which extend into new and likewise unforeseen contexts. Where the co-creators disseminate their knowledge into the artefact, also extracting something which can inform their own future practice.

AN INVITATION TO DANCE

To realize design fiction and turn it into a practice Fieldasy[47] as a method started to evolve in 2003-2004, first presented as an exhibition in Malmoe, Sweden at the Gallery Skanes Konst, later as a research paper for the Pixel Raiders conference at Sheffield-Hallam University in 2004. With Fieldasy we tried to unify different methods into one creative process that attempts to understand and redefine our world in a situation where information is lacking (Figure 6). This lack of information is used as a resource, for example by providing ambiguous fragments as a starting point, removing constraints on the imagination. It was designed with respect to staging a conflict that has a mind triggering influence on the co-creator with a set of problems that only can be captured in a given material. Fieldasy was a process for engaging multiple perspectives in the creation of a world, and

---

47 Johansson, M., and Linde, P. (2004)

the mapping of its virtual space, by extracting artifacts and stories through the developed scenarios, partitur and game-boards.

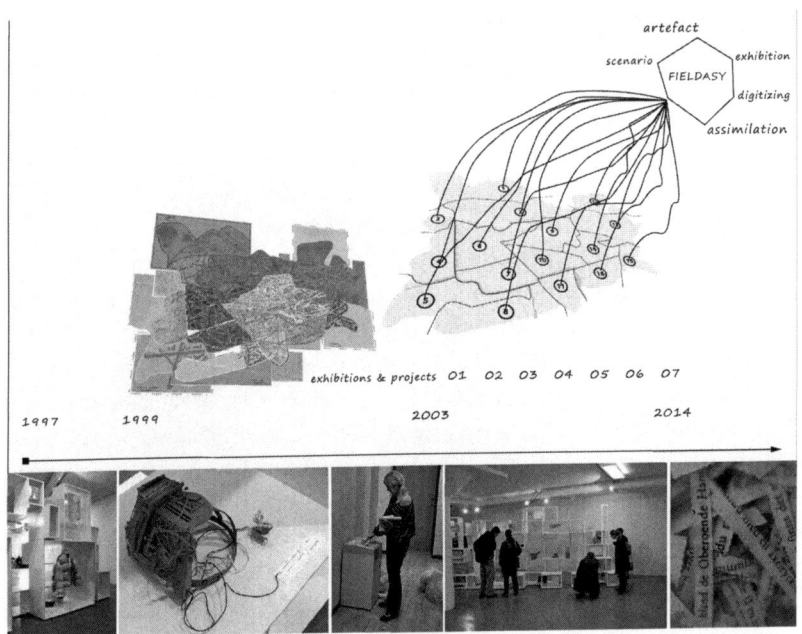

Figure 6. Fieldasy work process with project snapshots.[48]

Fieldasy itself refers to the methods of field working and imagination by using physical objects. The objects constitute a shared ground for collaborative creativity, serve as nodes in a complex narrative and as a basis for worldmaking.[49] Fieldasy plays as a vital part in the creation of a space where we could be in a constant dialogue with a large database of material that is interlinked through the architecture of a city, regardless of its incompatibilities. The method establish a multidisciplinary common ground for an art practice, interaction design and technology development, through an investigation of philosophy and criticism in a dynamic material. This method is an open-ended way of working where the original scenarios originate, at beforehand unknown artifacts. Scenarios relation to the overall project is loosely defined as to allow the creation of artworks, that though enriching the database, still are autonomous from the mother project in the sense that they can be exhibited by themselves. They also act as generators

---

48 Copyright Michael Johansson
49 Goodman, N. (1978)

while they generate new and unforeseen processes which extend into new and likewise unforeseen contexts. Our scenarios are handed over to the invited temporary citizens and co-creators of Abadyl. They can then act in relation to the scenario, in and by themselves chosen tools and materials, that in the end helps them produce an artifact. Hopefully the co-creators themselves import qualities into the world, which do not and cannot stem from the City of Abadyl itself. As one participating artist expressed it:

»Imagination was tickled by the knowledge of being part of a networked mapping I didn't know in detail. The scenario got me going, but I felt no repressing obligation towards it and also felt more liberated than in the situations of my own work where I'm the responsible and potential object for critique.«

Our scenarios try to bring field studies and fantasy together, to slowly create a discrete dynamic tension and/or displacement between person, objects, time, places and events that are not usually – if ever – associated into new and surprising conjunctions. In Abadyl, the openness towards what happens in-between the design cycles is important. We do not formulate any detailed specification or goal for the concept beforehand, apart from some dramatic or situated qualities that indirectly plot the creation of the artifact. Here we work closely with the co-creators going from scenario to concept and further on building different prototypes, later finalizing the artifact. Sometimes we use the prototypes a bit differently, where the shortcomings and quirks of the prototypes themselves can be used as major features and qualities. So when we try to follow the co-creators' intention or concept, we are open for that the prototypes themselves can produce qualities not known beforehand. By continuously evaluating information together with experience, and going from total disarray to a strategy that can be expressed, the co-creators will gradually build up knowledge on how to proceed through their concept development and prototyping, making the final artifact incorporating the findings as it develops. However, the concept first has to reach a certain state of complexity, a complexity max,[50] to ensure thorough exploration and original artifacts. Therefore a production environment is a crucial part to facilitate this kind of work. Since the artifacts consist of both artistic and technological proposals, we do not want them to end up to do art well and computing more dubiously, or do computing well but the art questionable.[51] We have recognized the persuasive act of negotiating a communicative contract with co-

---

50 Hoberg, C. (2006)
51 Bardzell, J. (2009)

creators when proposing scenarios and models of possible worlds. Co-creators accept or refuse this contract based on whether they believe the proposed world to be plausible or not. Our aim is for them to accept the world as a setting where it is safe to play and take risks, exploring the unknown using a range of design fiction methods that are either transferred from other fields or of our own devising, outlined in this chapter and in our own art and design practice. By constantly being able to also change and manipulate our underlying model, game the rules of play, we can better define our final and intended outcome itself. This flux should be seen as a possibility because if some of the parameters are changed so it will not be backward compatible there is an opportunity to run some scenarios of the former projects again and find out new things in relation to both that scenario, project and Abadyl itself.

To be able to both set up and play with the rules at the same time adds an additional level of design thinking. Similar to the parametric and procedural playfulness described in Pamphlet Architecture 27:

»A complex global pattern arises as a result of many individual entities acting independently of one another, and according to a very simple set of local rules. Changes the underlying model of the world, and add new objects and methods without having to completely rewrite the code. Be able to run multiple scenarios, based on different assumptions and focusing different aspects of the underlying simulation.«[52]

To conclude this section about Fieldasy; the co-creators of the city of Abadyl disseminate their knowledge into the platform, but they also extract something which can inform their own future practice. Each component introduced in Fieldasy has the ability to play with and displace the co-creators models of the world in different ways. For us this has been an important experience learning how to design and stage both the details and the whole of the world that the co-creators are going to populate. This is a process similar to fragmented storytelling, often used in games where the player must find fragments during the progression and piece them together. By continuously introducing dilemmas (twists) and turns (creative operations) in this context, Fieldasy serves as an intriguing source that through the narrative it is and based on the artifacts it creates, it generates ideas and concepts not known before, which could guide and help us rethink our assumptions about the future.

---

52 Aranda, B., and Lasch, C. (2009)

FUTURE WORK

The City of Abadyl continues to be an environment to facilitate artistic work practice, and the Life Forms project is still ongoing. We will continue this work in practice and in theory and encourage the readers of this book to continue to evolve and use these methods for design fiction. Building further on the thoughts of mapping the emotions of the creative process onto the Hero's Journey, appreciating the emotional states attached to stages in the design fiction process, or areas of the epistemological model. Taking inspiration from applying narrative structures like the Hero's Journey to games, re-interpreting the design fiction process as a collaborative game of creation with the epistemological map as a game board permitting certain moves. Combining emotional and game elements, emphasizing the different archetypes prevalent in the Hero's Journey like Hero, Mentor, and Helper – that is, appreciating the enactment of different roles particular to stages in the process or regions in the model. Here we intend to play with different roles in the creative process, alienation and verfremdung, as well as the roleplaying inherent in improvisational theatre. We will also evolve particular methods consolidating the elements of the narrative structure of the Hero's Journey and the epistemological model, the roles of the co-creators, the scenarios expressing human dilemmas, and the various modes or meta-methods.

REFERENCES

2K Games (2007): http://bioshock.wikia.com/wiki/BioShock

Altshuller, Genrich (1998): *40 Principles: TRIZ Keys to Technical Innovation*, Worcester, MA: Technical Innovation Center.

Aranda, Benjamin, and Lasch, Chris (2005): *Pamphlet Architecture 27*, Tooling Princeton Architectural Press

Armour, Philip G. (2000): "The Case for a New Business Model: Is software a product or a medium?" *Communications of the ACM*, Vol. 43, Issue 8.

Bardzell, Jeffrey (2009): "Interaction Criticism and Aesthetics". Proceedings of CHI'09: World Conference on Human Factors in Computing Systems. ACM: New York.

Benyus, Janine M. (2002): *Biomimicry: Innovation Inspired by Nature*. New York: William Morrow.

Bleecker, Julian (2009): *Design Fiction: A Short Essay on Design, Science, Fact and Fiction*. Available from: http://drbfw5wfjlxon.cloudfront.net/writing/DesignFiction_WebEdition.pdf

Boden, Margaret A. (1995): "Creativity and Unpredictability". *SEHR* Vol. 4 Issue 2.

Boden, Margaret A. (1997): *The Creative Mind: Myths and Mechanism.* London: Weidenfeld & Nicholson.

Brockman, John (2006): *What We Believe but Cannot Prove: Today's Leading Thinkers on Science in the Age of Certainty.* New York: Harper Perennial.

Brockman, John (2007): *What Is Your Dangerous Idea?: Today's Leading Thinkers on the Unthinkable.* New York: Harper Perennial.

Buxton, Bill (2007): *Sketching User Experiences.* Waltham, MA: Morgan Kaufmann.

Campbell, Joseph (2008): *The Hero With a Thousand Faces.* Novato, CA: New World Library.

Clark, Arthur C. (2004): *Natural-Born Cyborgs: Minds, Technologies, and the Future of Human Intelligence.* New York: Oxford University Press.

Debray, Régis (1995): *Revolution in the Revolution.* Wired Magazine 3.01.

Eco, Umberto (1984): *Postscript to the Name of the Rose.* UK: Harcourt.

Goodman, Nelson (1978): *Ways of Worldmaking.* Indianapolis, IN: Hackett Publishing.

Hoberg, Chister (2006): *Komplexitetsmax.* Stockholm, Sweden: Dialoger Förlag.

Imai, Masaaki (1997*): Gemba Kaizen: A Commonsense, Low-Cost Approach to Management.* Columbus, OH: McGraw-Hill.

Johansson, Michael (2010): "The City of Abadyl". In: Mura, G., ed. *Metaplasticity in Virtual Worlds: Aesthetics and Semantics Concepts.* Milano, Italy: IGI Global.

Johansson, Michael and Linde, Per (2004): *Fieldasy.* Pixel Raiders. Sheffield, UK.

Johansson, Michael (2010): *Metaplasticity: The city of Abadyl.* IGI Global, Pennsylvania, US

Johansson, Michael (2011): *Abadyl of tunes, research paper and exhibition,* Ambience 11 Borås university, SWE

Johansson, Michael (2012): "Abadyl of tunes", Cyberworlds 2012, Darmstadt, DE

Johansson, Michael (2013): "Bring the noise", *International Journal of Art, Culture and Design Technologies (IJACDT),* IGI Global, Pennsylvania, US

Johnson, Brian D. (2011): *Science Fiction Prototyping: Designing the Future with Science Fiction.* UK: Morgan & Claypool.

Johnstone, Keith (1999): *Impro for Storytellers.* London: Routledge.

Jones, John C (1992): *Design Methods.* Hoboken, NJ: Wiley.

Kahneman, Daniel (2011): *Thinking, Fast and Slow*. New York: Farrar, Straus and Giroux.

Lindgren, Mats, and Bandhold, Hans (2003): *Scenario Planning: The Link Between Future and Strategy*. Basingstoke, UK: Palgrave McMillan.

Lund, Jette (2008): *Journey to Abadyl*. BoD – Books on Demand, GmbH, DE

Ogilvy, James A. (2011): *Facing the Fold: Essays on scenario planning*. Axminster, UK: Triarchy Press.

Poggenpohl, Sharon, and Sato, Keiichi (2009): *Design Integration*. Intellect: Bristol

Popper, Karl (1978): *Three Worlds. The Tanner Lecture on Human Values*, April 7, 1978. University of Michigan.

Renander, Bengt (2003): *Himmel-Helvete tur och retur. En bok om kreativitetens känslor* ("Heaven-Hell, there and back. A book about the emotions of creativity"). Stockholm, Sweden: Kreativitetsutveckling.

Runberger, Jonas (2012): *Architectural Prototypes II: Reformations, Speculations and Strategies in the Digital Design Field*. Thesis (PhD). Stockholm, Sweden: Royal Institute of Technology.

Samuelson, David N. (1993): "Modes of Extrapolation: The Formulas of Hard SF". *Science Fiction Studies* Vol. 20.

Schön, Donald A. (1983): *The Reflective Practitioner: How Professionals Think in Action*. London: Temple Smith.

Sorkin, Michael (1993): *Local Code*. New York: Princeton Architectural Press.

Stross, Charles (2013): http://www.antipope.org/charlie/blog-static/2012/01/world-building-404-the-unknown.html [Accessed October 2013]

Söderberg, Niklas (2003): *Excerpts from Fieldasy catalouge*, Galleri skanes konst 2003, Malmoe, SWE

Taleb, Nassim N. (2010): *The Black Swan: The Impact of the Highly Improbable*. London: Penguin.

Tschumi, Bernhard (1991): *Architecture and disjunction*. Cambridge, MA: MIT Press.

Vogler, Christoffer (2007): *The Writer's Journey: Mythic Structure for Writers*. Studio City, CA: Michael Wiese Productions.

Explorable Spaces

A Conclusion

MARTIN REICHE AND ULRICH GEHMANN

To conclude this anthology on reality and virtuality, we want to focus on a concept that has already been briefly touched in Martin Reiche's article "The Destruction of Space by Augmentation" in this anthology: the idea is to search for a possible solution to the problem of functionalization of the real world. And there are solutions, especially if you look at the sector of entertainment media, and there, specifically at games.

Games have the great potential in not having to follow rules as we know them from physical systems. Although common definitions, as probably the most important one by Johan Huizinga state that *play* is "a free activity standing quite consciously outside 'ordinary' life as being 'not serious' but at the same time absorbing the player intensely and utterly. It is an activity connected with no material interest, and no profit can be gained by it. It proceeds within its own proper boundaries of time and space according to fixed rules and in an orderly manner,"[1] we see that these definitions apply for a lot of different sorts of play and as a manifestation of play, of course also for games. Eric Berne collected some behavioral patterns of human beings and referred to them as games, rightly as they share game-like elements, even if not complying with Huizinga's definition.[2] The variety of games is big, and games have the important ability to create something called a 'magic circle', a virtual space where the game itself temporarily becomes the point of reference for the human being, even though (or may-

---

1 Huizinga, J. (edition of 1955).
2 Berne, E. (1967) explains how some human interaction patterns share game-like qualities, and thus qualify as games, especially as regards to those dealing with courtship, relationships, media and self-definition.

be even because) the person knows that he is playing a game.[3] It is obvious to call these spaces that games provide *virtual spaces*, as they are not real, but share an essence of reality – and consequentially, one of the first things that comes to mind when talking about virtual worlds are games or game-like virtual realities, prominent examples thereof being the first-person shooter Counter Strike or the virtual world Second Life. While the latter one is usually not directly referred to as a game, the first one definitely is – and it is a game that was highly popular and subject to a lot of discussions about the ethics of gaming[4] and the potential of computer games to influence the development of adolescents. Especially the question of the influence of games on psychical development makes obvious that games are considered highly influential from the fact of this 'magic circle,' throwing the player into the scene, merging the player with his avatar. The game thus interferes with the mental construction of reality in the player's head, or as Chris Crawford puts it: "Simulation is not a mechanical exercise nor is it a means of bottling truth inside a computer – it is a way to bounce our ideas and values against reality and see how they bounce back."[5]

What computer games are capable of though is that they can serve as functional and non-functional worlds at the same time. While many games have objectives that the player follows or has to follow (such as to kill enemies, capture flags, and so on), some have not, and for some games there might be objectives but it is not crucial to follow them. In the latter case this freedom to choose between following the functional part of the game or to wander around and do what the player likes has especially been an important factor in the game design of the Grand Theft Auto series.[6]

Lately, a new form of digital games has evolved that solely deals with the idea of the non-functional part of games. As a new phenomenon, these games have become called *explorative games*. These games usually lack objectives and almost exclusively focus on the exploration of the surroundings and the narrative. They ground their existence on the 'function' of the freedom to explore – the player is brought into the world to explore and to gaze.[7]

---

3 Cf. Interview with Dan Pinchbeck below.

4 A detailed analysis on this subject is way beyond this article. For more information, refer to Sicart, M. (2009).

5 Crawford, C. (2003).

6 http://www.rockstargames.com/grandtheftauto/

7 Cf. Gehmann, U., and Reiche, M. (2013).

One of these explorative games is a 2012 published work named *Dear Esther*, a ghost story, in which you as the player try to uncover the mystery of the island where the game takes place. You solve the mystery step by step by wandering around and enjoying the beauty of the scenery. The story unfolds as your understanding of the virtual world you as the player are thrown into unfolds. The game creates an own universe, without any functionality, only driven by the player's urge to solve the mystery – to explore the world in its totality.

As the Creative Director of the game, Dan Pinchbeck, puts it, "explorative games are commonly defined by what is not in them," they are defined by how they differ from other games, that is that they lack goals and mechanics. He states that what makes them, or games in general, so interesting as virtual worlds is that they are a way to safely explore a world while the player still knows that it is a game he is dealing with; even if the environment that is depicted is immersive it still stays a "vastly simplified" one, an abstracted one "enriched with codified behavior." And this is what makes it clear for the player to distinguish between the virtual world of the game and the real. At the same time explorative games are using "the most powerful tool: the player's own imagination" – the game becomes more than it is as the player is using his imagination to enhance his game experience: while the player is playing it, he starts to project his own narrative onto the game. In Dear Esther, this projection takes place while the player explores the island which is merely a metaphor for the psychological story that is to discover in the game. The game plays with uncertainty, which gives the user the freedom to fill the gaps of the unfolding story with his own imaginary parts and thus enrich his experience. For Pinchbeck, "virtual worlds manipulate people's perception," and they do so by narration, which is what he does in Dear Esther: "only the most powerful parts of the game" are used in that game, everything else is stripped off. What remains is a strong narrative that provides a "first-hand unmediated story" that feeds the "story-driven animal" human being, embedded into what obviously looks and feels like a game without claiming this term itself.[8]

Even though, in these games function still remains. That is because they are computer games and computers work imperatively, executing lines of code one after the other, on the level of the game the experience is non-functional. You as a player are free to explore the world and the narrative in front of you and you

---

8   Personal communication with Dan Pinchbeck, Creative Director at *The Chinese Room*, on November 5th 2013.

are not bound to *function*, not bound to *perform* – you are simply there, as part of the magic circle of this virtual world.

Figure 1. Screenshot taken from the game Dear Esther.[9]

But the need to free oneself from the constructed worlds of rational functionality and its resulting competitive performance is not confined to contemporaneous times. Like so many perspectives treated in this anthology, these attempts to be freed from the urge to function and to perform (all the time) had their historical forerunners, too. In a way, all these attempts, historical and contemporaneous ones alike, can be interpreted as a kind of counter-movement to the increasing functionalization and abstraction of space – an abstraction needed to optimize performance – which took place since the 17th century onwards, and which culminated in the era we commonly label as "modernity" with its mythos of *form follows function*. It is as if human beings were in need of some counterforce to this crushing dominance of the functional, and the abstracted spaces resulting out of it. This holds true in particular for forerunners of those "explorative" games mentioned, namely in case of virtual worlds designed to meet the requirements for exploration. We can take the English Park or Landscape Garden as an example, serving for explorative issues (see the Introduction), where the visitor – in contemporary terms, the *user* of the park in question – had to perform a "guided tour" given by the parkways in order to see selected, carefully arranged aspects of a constructed nature that was presented as a piece of art; but inside the mesh of parkways, had nevertheless the freedom to choose his or her own individual

---

9   Courtesy of *The Chinese Room*. www.dear-esther.com

route.[10] The resemblance of such arrangements to those of recent games is remarkable, in several respects.

First, we are confronted with a "naturally looking" environment (no matter if landscape or cityscape) but which, in being a piece of art, an *artificial* entity in literal terms, is architecture, and not a "naturally," means historically grown environment. If architecture can be understood in a comprehensive manner as the art of designing and building structures which embody declared spaces "[...] manipulated through human intention beyond that which is previously defined,"[11] then all these explorative, naturally looking worlds are architecture: are constructions, and out of this alone, functional. What is a contradiction to the wish to escape the functional, but a contradiction unavoidable since it stays embedded in the principle of architectural construction. Like their functional counterparts from which they promise relief, those 'natural' virtual worlds are *programmatic spaces* serving certain purposes (e.g., the one of free exploration) and hence, have to obey to strictly since *technically* designed functionalities. Being programmatic is a peculiar form of declaration, and thus, of space. And the contradiction becomes obvious: in order to free myself from functions, I have to rely on functions, technically prescribed ways of how I can free myself. The nowadays *technogene space*, mentioned several times in this anthology, seems inescapable.

Second (and related), if we understand architecture in its comprehensive terms, both the need to construct functionalities and to escape from them seems to be a deeply inherited trait of our occidental culture, at least from its modern age onwards. Next to the urge for a real escape, it seems to be a kind of mythological contradiction: on one hand, world shall be dominated through function (following the occidental mind-over-matter myth), and on the other, we cannot stand this. Seen in such a respect, the architecture of the virtual worlds illuminated in the anthology, being programmatic spaces, is "[...] inevitably an expression of its culture: [...] a result of what is important, and not important to its makers."[12] The mythic longing to dominate the world, also in constructing "ideal" virtual worlds for counter-balancing the effects of that longing, generated another one: the strive for the magic ruse to ban the Being; which is another intention than the one at the beginning of a modern age – on the historical outskirts of which we live – presented in the tale of Pico della Mirandola to come. In this tale, man is posed in the middle of the world to freely wander around, to explore

---

10 Cf. Hunt, J. D. (1993).

11 Two definitions of architecture combined from Dunham, D. (2012): 142

12 Dunham, D. (2012): 140.

it,[13] not to dominate it via reconstruction. Not to speak of worlds man should create by his own account, in parallel to the one yet existing, or even to create mixed worlds, in overcoming an existing cosmic order.

Third, right from their start in a modern age, those virtual worlds were concentrating upon the individual; not only on individual use, but moreover, on a strictly individual perspective. The Central Perspective of the Renaissance already concentrated upon *one* standpoint where from all the world has to be examined, a standpoint of the respective individual.[14] And at the same time, the respective individual perspective has an all-encompassing claim, at least in case of virtual worlds.

Figure 2. Virtual world, from a central perspective.[15]

What we see here is a complete world, but nevertheless from an individual perspective; when looking at the above image of a world as it should be, it is easy to see that any other standpoint would lead to a different prospect. This combination of an all-encompassing claim and self-centeredness is remarkable, and characteristic for our cultural sphere (so the thesis). At the doorway to modernity, it led to the explorable spaces of an English Landscape Garden, and later on, in its further unfolding, to the explorable spaces of today. And still later on, namely quite recently, we are in a process to extend such self-centeredness to the "given" world in its total, through creating hybrids of what really existed so far in physical space with individual additions of a virtual nature; with the aim of generating individual realities of a new kind. Thus, the matter of perspective became

13 della Mirandola, G. P. (1965): 4f

14 To this, and to its implication for a modernity to come, see Damisch, H. (2010): 25-41.

15 Fra Carnevale, prospect of an ideal city. Ca. 1480, Walters Art Museum, Baltimore. Wikimedia Commons, http://en.wikipedia.org7wiki/File:Fra_Carnevale_-_The Ideal City_-_Walters_37677.jpg

a matter of the real, and we will realize what will happen with such a point of view.

Concluding this anthology, we have seen how world got virtualized and by which means this virtualization has changed the physical substrate of the very world we live in. All of this is grounded in myths about how our world works, how it should look like, how we should behave, or how our culture should work. Mixed together to form a self-sustainable system, this anthology wanted to outline this development from its very beginnings into modernity: we have created worlds based on models of the world, and based on that, we have created models again, closing the circle and leading to the world as we know it today. Consequently we have tried to get rid of these parts of the world that do not fit into our models, we have started to neglect our anthropological nature by creating completely functionalized non-places lacking any anthropological character. And at the same time, we have just started to understand what has happened to us. And as regards spatial exploration, what began with the English Landscape Garden was continued *en masse* with the 19th century-*flaneur*, wandering through the newly created spaces of industrialization and consumption, spaces which already resembled the fragmented and essentially illusionist spatiality of passages, world exhibitions and other collectivist dream spaces, to refer to Walter Benjamin. The essential experience of the flaneur, he says, is colportage, virtuality, and self-centeredness: everything what could potentially happen (or has happened) inside a space can be experienced simultaneously, by the flaneur. And the true method to present things to us, he continues, is to imagine them in our space, not us in their space. It is not us giving in to them, they step into our lives.[16]

What he said about the flaneur can be extended into our recent domains of hybrid spaces, and explorability: assisted with technical means we never had before, we are enabled to create spaces which never existed before. If one refrains from their inherent basic problem addressed above – that a dense network of technical functions is to be used, to escape functionality – there remains the hope to regain a world of the not only functional. Because the virtualization, the creation of controllable, model-based worlds that only share aspects of reality, has also shown us how to get out of this development of ongoing virtualization and functionalization. Digital games and art has created solutions by providing outsider positions to the mainstream developments we have faced and are still facing right now. These outsider positions enable us to see the world we live in from a different angle, to freely associate to our anthropological nature again and

---

16 Cf. Benjamin, W. (1983), vol. 1: 524ff. And 527, to colportage and virtuality; and 273, to the flaneur's spatiality.

to give us back the choice whether to follow the mainstream development or to claim back this aspect of life that we have given to our surroundings.

Figure 3. Screenshot taken from the game Proteus.[17]

Or as Pico della Mirandola has put it,

»In conformity with thy free judgment, in whose hands I have placed thee, thou art confined by no bounds; and thou wilt fix limits of nature for thyself.«[18]

REFERENCES

Benjamin, Walter (ed. of 1983): *Das Passagenwerk*, vol. 2, Frankfurt/M.: Suhrkamp

Berne, Eric (1967): *Games people play*, New York: Grove Press

Crawford, Chris (2003): *Subjectivity and Simulation*, Washington, DC, http://www.seriousgames.org/images/Seriousgamescrawfordfinal.pdf

Damisch, Hubert (2010): *Der Ursprung der Perspektive* [the origin of perspective], Zurich: diaphanes

Dunham, Donald (2012): "Architecture *Without* Nature?", in: Giesecke, Annette, and Jacobs, Naomi, eds. (2012): *Earth Perfect? Nature, Utopia, and the Garden*, London: Black Dog Publishing: 136-155

---

17 Courtesy of Ed Key and David Kanaga. www.visitproteus.com
18 della Mirandola, G. P. (1965): 5

Gehmann, Ulrich, and Reiche, Martin (2013): „Functionalization and World Conception", in: *Proceedings of the 2013 International Conference on Cyberworlds*, Yokohama

Huizinga, Johan (edition of 1955): *Homo ludens*, English translation, Boston: Beacon Press

Hunt, John Dixon (1993): "Ut Pictura Poiesis: der Garten und das Pittoreske in England (1710-1750)", in: Mosser, Monique, and Teyssot, George, eds. (1993): *Die Gartenkunst des Abendlandes* [occidental garden art], Stuttgart: dva: 227-237

della Mirandola, Giovanni Pico (1965): *On the dignity of man*, translated by C. G. Wallis, Hackett Publishing

Sicart, Miguel (2009): *The Ethics of Computer Games*, Boston: MIT Press

List of Contributors

Kristoffer Åberg is a Science Fiction Designer creating strategies and concepts for the everyday experiences, interactions, and artefacts of 21st and 22nd century popular culture. He lives in Lund, Sweden.

David Bell is a member of the faculty of the School of Architecture at Rensselaer Polytechnic Institute in Troy, NY. He has written numerous essays on various aspects of architectural history and theory. He is the author of the recently published *Bernini & Borromini: Theater & Heresy* and two other books to be published later in 2013, *Jefferson's University as American Dream* and *Adolf Loos & the Irritation of Modernity*.

Irus Braverman is Professor of Law and Adjunct Professor of Geography at SUNY Buffalo, where she teaches Criminal Procedure, Law and Nature, and topics related to legal geography. Her main interests lie in the interdisciplinary study of law, geography, and anthropology. Writing within this nexus, Braverman has conducted ethnographic research of illegal houses, trees, checkpoints, public toilets, and zoos. Born in Jerusalem, Braverman served as a public state prosecutor and as an environmental lawyer, both in Israel. She acquired her doctoral degree in law (SJD) from the University of Toronto. During this time, she was an Associate with the Humanities Center at Harvard University, a Visiting Fellow with the Human Rights Program at Harvard University Law School, a Junior Fellow with the Center of Criminology at the University of Toronto, and a Visiting Fellow with the Geography Department at the Hebrew University of Jerusalem. In 2013-14, Braverman is a Ryskamp fellow of the American Council for Learned Societies (ACLS) as well as an Atkinson Center for a Sustainable Future fellow at Cornell University's Society for the Humanities.

Marc Conrad, PhD, is Principal Lecturer in the Faculty of Creative Arts, Technology and Science at the University of Bedfordshire in the United Kingdom. Already as an undergraduate Mathematics student in Germany he worked on various software projects that aim to make algebraic problems accessible to computers. He received his PhD in Mathematics in 1998 from the Universität des Saarlandes, Germany, on units in cyclotomic number fields; since then he has published in a variety of areas such as algebraic number theory, modeling, project management, social media and music. Dr Marc Conrad is a member of the British Computer Society, the Institute for Mathematics and its Application and the Croatian Mathematical Society.

Martin Cremers holds a Bachelor degree in Philosophy and Sociology at KIT, Germany. Studies of European Culture and History of Ideas (EUKLID) at KIT. Dedicated to modern myths and the production of electronic music. He currently lives near Frankfurt am Main, Germany, working in the publishing sector.

Katerina Diamantaki holds a PhD in Communication and Media Studies from the National Kapodistrian University of Athens and is currently employed as Assistant Professor of Communication and Chair of the Department of Communication at the Athens Campus of the University of Indianapolis. She has also been a long-time researcher at the Laboratory of New Technology in Communication, Education and Media at the Department of Communication and Media of the University of Athens, where she has participated in various research projects relevant to the personalization of the Internet, social interaction through location-based media and the integration of hybrid technologies into urban environments. Her main are of expertise and ensuing publications fall within the subfield of the "sociology of new media," focusing on the impact digital technologies have on communication, information-sharing, community building, memory, space, audiences and conceptions of the self.

Tim French, PhD, is an internationally renowned scholar in the fields of Organisational Semiotics, Software Engineering and Semiotic Engineering. He has most recently taken a pro-active active role in advancing pedagogic HE provision with respect to Cyber-crime and Security and has active on-going research interests centred upon E-Trust within heterogeneous settings. He is a Fellow of the British Computer Society (FBCS), a Fellow of the HE Academy (FHEA) and a Fellow of the College of Teachers (FCollP). He holds a PhD from Reading University School of Systems Engineering, an MA from Nottingham University, an Open University degree and has wide experience both in academia and in knowledge transfer to local industry/wide experience in a variety of settings. Tim has acted as external PhD examiner at Kings College London and at several other UK universities in cognate disciplines that relate to "applied" Informatics. These have included de Montfort, Software Engineering Institute and at Middlesex, User Experience Centre. He is currently supervising a number of PhD students, and is a visiting Research Fellow (DoS, PhD) at the London College of Commerce. He has over 80+ academic publications and is a former HEIF Industry Fellow. He has a specialist interest in cross-national, trans-national Software Engineering and related pedagogy. He is actively persuing Computer music (performance, generative grammars, analytic studies) in his "spare" time.

Mikhail Fominykh, PhD, has graduated from the Computer Science department at Mari State Technical University in Yoshkar-Ola, Russia in 2006. He started as a PhD-candidate at the Program for Learning with ICT at the Norwegian University of Science and Technology in Trondheim, Norway in 2007. He completed the doctoral thesis under the title "Collaborative Work on 3D Educational Content" in 2012. He has been participating in several national and international research projects in the area of technology-enhanced learning, three of which are EU funded. In 2013, he holds a postdoctoral researcher position at the Norwegian University of Science and Technology, assists on Cooperation Technology course and works on research projects.

Ulrich Gehmann, Dipl Biol. et lic. oec. HSG et MA History, studied Biology, Business Administration, and history. Humanist education. He worked in industry and international consulting, the latter covered enterprise reorganisation and institutional cooperations, many of them funded by international donor agencies (IMF, Worldbank, etc), in former GUS, Central Asia, Levante. Director in charge for management consulting in Bucharest, Romania. Lecturer at Wuppertal University, Germany, for business administration. Founder of the research group formatting of social spaces, and of the journal *New Frontiers in Spatial Concepts*, University of Karlsruhe (KIT), Germany. Publications on occidental mythology and its impact on recent sociocultural reality, spatial issues, and virtual worlds, inter alias at Oxford Univ. Press. Museum projects. Lecturer at Karlshochschule International University, (cultural issues of organizations); partner in a German consulting firm active in the EU-Commission, founding member of the Subformat Research Group.

Pierre-Francois Gerard is currently a PhD Student in the Computing Department at Goldsmith College, University of London. His main research area is the use of space to enhance learning. His background is in Architecture (Graduated in Brussels) and 3D visualisation. During 10 years of professional practice with architects and designers both in Brussels and London, Pierre-François realized the potential of 3D visualisation techniques as a creative force not only in the design process but mainly as a communication tool. He graduated in Information and Communication Technology (MA France). Through this very interdisciplinary lens, his research interests include spatial cognition, long-term memory, 3D learning environments, human computer interaction and game design.

Chris Gerbing, PhD, graduated from the University of Karlsruhe with an M.A. in art history with minors in history of architecture and recent and modern history. She completed her studies in Basle/Switzerland and Strasbourg/France, and worked in France and the USA. For seven years, she chaired a working group tasked with event management. Additionally, she curated exhibitions and taught at university. In 2008, she received her PhD from TU Berlin. Among others, she works as a free lancer with the ZKM | Center for Art and Media Karlsruhe and teaches at the Universities of Karlsruhe, Stuttgart, and the University of Applied Arts Karlsruhe (HfG). Her special interest focuses on border areas of art history. Her publications cover a wide range, including corporate art, the changes occurring in urban areas due to alterations in the understanding of town planning nowadays, and churches in post-war Germany, lastly "Leuchtende Steine in Beton. Die Matthäuskirche Pforzheim (1951-53) von Egon Eiermann: ihre Vorbilder, ihre Vorbildfunktion."

Kristoffer Getchell, PhD, is the Infrastructure Manager for the Department of Computer Science and Technology at the University of Bedfordshire. Kris completed both his PhD and undergraduate studies at the University of St Andrews where he worked with Dr Alan Miller, Dr Colin Allison and Dr Rebecca Sweetman on a variety of topics including virtual worlds, networking, data visualisation, technologically enhanced learning and usability. His research interests lie in the areas of virtual worlds (particularly systems aspects), network traffic measurement and the use of technology to enhance learning. More recently Kris has focused on the ways in which virtual environments can influence user behaviour in both the real and virtual worlds. He has worked in a variety of roles in the academic and commercial sectors and has actively collaborated with researchers in other disciplines at other institutions both within and outwith the UK. Kris is a member of the British Computer Society.

Michael Johansson is a Senior Lecturer/Artist/Researcher at Kristianstad University, Sweden, where he teaches Digital Media and Design. In his work he establish an virtual and fictious environment which can facilitate artistic work practice in a complex production environment such as the one of digital media, supported by invited artists, researchers and students. That creates gravity around a single project (the city of Abadyl) that other easily can transfer their knowledge into without having to provide all of its content from start. Today the city of Abadyl has involved the works of over 120 people, it has been exhibited internationally and been part of several external research projects in areas of smart textile, computer science, interaction design, cultural studies, theatre production and film.

Steffen Krämer, Prof. Dr. phil., art historian. Study of art history, archaeology, philosophy and prehistory at the Universities in Frankfurt/M., Heidelberg and Munich. Academic teaching at the Universities in Munich, Karlsruhe, Trier and Salzburg and at the University of Arts and Design in Karlsruhe. Head of the Winckelmann Academy of Art History in Munich. Numerous publications to architecture, architectural theory and urbanism from the Middle Ages to the present.

Lyzgeo M. Koshy obtained a degree in Software Engineering from the University of Bedfordshire in 2011. On the successful completion of her undergraduate degree, Lyzgeo committed herself to the completion of PhD in Computer Science funded by the University of Bedfordshire. Lyzgeo is investigating how identity implies trust in distributed software systems under the supervision of Dr Marc Conrad and Dr Tim French at the University of Bedfordshire. Lyzgeo's research will deepen her knowledge of human behaviours on social networks and virtual environments leading to the understanding of how identity and trust are related on such platforms. In addition to her research activities, Lyzgeo is passionately engaged in providing teaching support to the Computer Science students of the University of Bedfordshire.

Randolph Langenbach received a Master's of Architecture from Harvard University, and a Diploma in Conservation Studies from the Institute of Advanced Architectural Studies in York, England. He first became known for his groundbreaking work on the Amoskeag Mills in Manchester N.H. resulted in a series of exhibitions and the book, *Amoskeag, Life and Work in an American Factory City*, co-authored with Tamara Hareven. Subsequently, he produced the exhibition and co-authored the book *Satanic Mills*, for SAVE Britain's Heritage, and also received an Indo-American Exchange Fellowship to document textile mills in India. He then taught building conservation as Assistant Professor of Architecture at the University of California, Berkeley, where he became involved with research on earthquakes and masonry buildings. He later served as a Senior Analyst at the Federal Emergency Management Agency (FEMA) and has also served as a consultant to UNESCO for which he authored the book *Don't Tear It Down! Preserving the Earthquake Resistant Vernacular Architecture of Kashmir*. After the 2010 earthquake that devastated Haiti, he served as team leader and co-author of the book *Preserving Haiti's Gingerbread Houses*, published by the World Monuments Fund. In 2003, he was awarded the National Endowment for the Arts Rome Prize Fellowship at the American Academy in Rome, during which he began the *Piranesi Project* that has now become a movie called *Rome Was! A Piranesian Vision*.

Manfred Negele studied Catholic Theology and Philosophy at the universities of Augsburg and Munich. Specializing in GWF Hegel he got his PhD at the university of Augsburg in 1990. He taught as an assistant professor in fundamental theology and he finished his postdoctoral qualification in 2001 with his habilitation treatise on Plotin and the transcendental philosophy. From the winter term of 2005 up to the winter of 2008/09 he was senior professor of philosophy at the Catholic faculty of the University of Augsburg. Teaching philosophy and ecumenical theology temporarily at Augsburg, Benediktbeuren, Eichstätt and Graz he expanded his working field and has taught fundamental ethics in Augburg since the winter term of 2010.

Erhan Öze is building his academic carrier on theory of the spatial politics. His research focuses on theory of spatial politics of conflict zones where notions of sovereignty and biopolitics are under question. Except participating and organising international workshops and field trips, Öze's architectural-artistic interventions have been exhibited at various occasions in Halle, Istanbul, London and Nicosia. Recently, he was invited as guest critic and as a jury to the Critical Spatial Practices Section of SAC at Stadelschule where he also lectured about his research. Currently, he continues pursuing his PhD at Lancaster University, Department of Sociology in England.

Martin Reiche is an audiovisual installation and game artist and computer science scholar living and working in Berlin, Germany. He is co-founder of the *Laboratory for the Analysis of Social Networks (LASN)* at Karlsruhe University of Arts and Design, co-founder of the *Subformat Research Group* with research on theory of space and spatial digitalization phenomena and is regularly presenting on professional computer science and digital art and gaming conferences.

Martin Rieser has worked in the field of interactive arts for many years. He is research Professor in the Institute of Creative Technologies in The Faculty of Art Design and Humanities at De Montfort. His art practice in internet art and interactive narrative installations has been seen around the world including Cannes; Holland, Paris; Vienna, Thessaloniki, London, Germany, Milan and Melbourne, Australia. He has published numerous essays and books on digital art including New Screen Media: Cinema/Art/Narrative (BFI/ZKM, 2002), and has recently edited The Mobile Audience, a book on mobile and locative technology and art from Rodopi. Curation of international exhibitions in electronic art, including *The Electronic Eye* at Watershed 1986, the first International survey exhibition of Digital Printmaking: *The Electronic Print*, Arnolfini in Bristol 1989. *Arcade 2-* 1997, *Arcade 3* 2000, He helped to make a successful lottery bid to fund a national digital arts initiative *Imag@nation* subsequently transformed into *DA2*: a major arts initiative promoting digital art practice nationally, and internationally. More recently he co-curated the *Inside Out* exhibit of rapid prototyped miniature sculptures made as an artists' exchange between Australia and the UK, in Sydney Australia and across the UK. He has also acted as consultant to bodies such as Cardiff Bay Arts Trust, the Photographer's Gallery London, Arkive in Bristol, The Soros Media Institute in Prague and UIAH in Helsinki.

Panagiotis D. Ritsos, PhD, is a postdoctoral researcher at Bangor University, UK. His research interests revolve around Human Computer Interaction and include Mixed Reality, Wearable & Ubiquitous Computing, Haptics, Visualization and User Experience. He has an MEng (2000) and a PhD (2006) in Electronic Systems Engineering, from University of Essex, UK. His doctoral research investigated Augmented Reality using Wearable Computers. Between 2007 and 2011 he worked as a software developer on Operations Support Systems. He joined Bangor University, UK in 2011, working as a postdoctoral researcher, investigating the use of virtual environments in interpreter-mediated communication and training. He is also working on Haptic Data Visualisation and the use of haptics in rehabilitation. He is an active member of the AR Standards community, investigating standardisation for open and interoperable Augmented Reality.

Carl H. Smith is Director of the Learning Technology Research Institute (LTRI) at London Metropolitan University. He is an academic expert, researcher and developer with a long-standing focus on pervasive learning technologies, hybrid reality and digital/mobile learning. His background is in Computer Science and Architecture. He specialises in using various visualization techniques to produce augmented spaces for the generation and transformation of learning. His other research interests include visual and spatial literacy, pattern recognition, intermediality, visualisation as interface, and open source learning. The LTRI conducts research into the application of information and communication technologies to augment, support and transform learning.

Gerd Stern is a poet and visual artist born 1928 in Saarbrücken, who emigrated to the U.S. in 1936. Several volumes of his poems have been published as well as an oral history. He was a founder of the 1960's communal collaborative USCO with performances and exhibitions shown in the United States and globally such as "Summer of Love" at the Tate Liverpool, in Frankfurt, Vienna, and New York's Whitney Museum and "Traces of the Sacred" at the Centre Georges Pompidou. He met editor Ulrich Gehmann while giving a seminar on prophetic technology at Karlsruhe University of Arts and Design in 2013.

Sabine Wilke is professor of German. She is also associated with and teaches in the European Studies Program, and the doctoral Theory and Criticism program. Her research and teaching interests include modern German literature and culture, intellectual history and theory, and cultural and visual studies. She has written books and articles on body constructions in modern German literature and culture, German unification, the history of German film and theater, contemporary German authors and filmmakers including Christa Wolf, Heiner Müller, Botho Strauss, Ingeborg Bachmann, Elfriede Jelinek, Monika Treut, and others. Most recently, Wilke was involved in a larger project about German colonialism and postcoloniality and the question of comparative colonialisms. With assistance from the Alexander von Humboldt Foundation Wilke is now directing a transatlantic research network on the environmental humanities and is working on a new project on environmental criticism, in praticular the overlapping concerns of postcolonialism and ecocriticism.